THE
TIGER

THE RISE AND FALL OF TAMMANY HALL

THE
TIGER

THE RISE AND FALL OF TAMMANY HALL

OLIVER E. ALLEN

Addison-Wesley Publishing Company
*Reading, Massachusetts   Menlo Park, California   New York
Don Mills, Ontario   Wokingham, England   Amsterdam   Bonn
Sydney   Singapore   Tokyo   Madrid   San Juan
Paris   Seoul   Milan   Mexico City   Taipei*

Library of Congress Cataloging-in-Publication Data

Allen, Oliver E.
    The tiger : the rise and fall of Tammany Hall / Oliver E. Allen.
        p.   cm.
    Includes bibliographical references (p.) and index.
    ISBN 0-201-62463-X
    1. Tammany Hall—History.   2. New York (N.Y.)—Politics and
government.   3. Political corruption—New York (N.Y.)—History.
I. Title.
JK2319.N56A698   1993
324.2747′1′06—dc20   93-11435
                                                              CIP

Jacket design by Catherine Neal
Text design by Ruth Kolbert
Set in 11/13-point Electra by Weimer Graphics, Inc.

1 2 3 4 5 6 7 8 9-MA-96959493
First printing, September 1993

CONTENTS

⌐| PREFACE |⌐

NEW YORKERS MAY HAVE THOUGHT THEY WERE used to reports of the evil machinations of Tammany Hall, the city's powerful Democratic political machine, but the story on the front page of the *New York World* on the morning of April 4, 1900, astonished them. The price of block ice—a humble but essential item in city life—was doubling from 30 cents to 60 cents. And Tammany, it appeared, was behind the increase.

The price jump was announced by the American Ice Company, a recently formed concern that had acquired great power in the city. American Ice not only owned most of the ice-making plants in the city but controlled all access to the city-owned piers where ice was unloaded, thereby barring competitors from doing any business in New York. Quite simply, American had a monopoly. From now on, if you did not get ice from American, you could not get any at all.

But American Ice had not achieved its monopoly unassisted. High-ranking members of Tammany Hall (which currently controlled the city government) had reportedly lent considerable support. In fact, the top Tammany leaders—so the *World* charged—were part owners of American and so stood to reap large profits from the company's increased revenues.

To understand the public outcry over the price hike, it is necessary to recall the importance of ice in the lives of everyday people a century ago. Electrical refrigeration was not yet invented. To preserve

food and other perishables—medicines, for example—block ice had
no substitute. It was not a luxury: Every household in the city had to
have ice and would need it even more in the summer months, which
were fast approaching. If ice was not available or affordable, disease
would spread. Children especially would suffer. The higher cost of
ice might not bother the well-to-do, but to vast numbers of New
York's poor living in crowded, squalid tenements on the Lower East
Side (and who up to now had usually voted the straight Tammany
ticket), the increase would be punishing. For may of them, the extra
30 cents would mean the difference between subsisting, if only mar-
ginally, and going hungry.

How had this outrage come about? The *World* said it had evidence
that American's president, Charles W. Morse, had received preferen-
tial treatment by giving huge allotments of his company's stock to
higher-ups in Tammany and the city government, who, as a result,
were glad to help him enforce his company's monopoly. Stockholder's in the Ice Trust, as the paper called the combine, not only
included Richard Croker, the truculent, tough-talking Tammany Hall
Boss, and John F. Carroll, Tammany's deputy leader; they also numbered the mayor of New York, Robert Van Wyck, a Tammany hack
handpicked by Croker for the office who reportedly acquired more
than half a million dollars worth of American securities without laying
out a penny. Morse had also lavished stock on members of the Board
of Dock Commissioners, all of whom were Tammany members and
only too happy to let American Ice monopolize the piers.

A week or so later the *World* had an interesting follow-up: Charles
Morse had invited Mayor Van Wyck and Tammany's John Carroll
(Croker was in Europe at the time) to spend a few days with him at
his country estate in Maine. The three men braved the frigid winds of
early spring to tour American Ice's manufacturing facilities along the
Kennebec River in an open launch. It was hardly the kind of sojourn
that would normally excite two city-bred politicos, but the enticement
of money surmounted all.

Although Tammany's past was already littered with peccadilloes,
the Ice Trust Scandal represented Tammany Hall at its most powerful
and corrupt. The scandal also revealed, for all to see, the true nature
of the country's most famous—or infamous—political organization.
The Hall's hold over the city was twofold: Tammany's far-ranging
party apparatus dominated the electoral process—enabling the machine to sustain itself almost indefinitely—and its leadership parlayed
the hall's electoral clout into deals with business interests (such as

American) to influence the city's economic life. In other words, although ostensibly a friend of the poor, Tammany was in bed with the rich. As Tammany historian Morris Werner put it, Tammany was "a singularly effective band of men organized perfectly for political and commercial profit which could not be gained so effectively by individual prowess . . . [its members] were not in business for love, but in business for money."[1]

Boss Richard Croker had said as much himself less than a year earlier. In response to a question from the counsel of an investigating committee, the Boss could not have been more blunt. The counsel, seeking to show how Tammany profited from the sales of judicial offices at the same time that it enjoyed firm control of the nominating process, had asked Croker: "Then you are working for your own pocket, are you not?" The Boss answered: "All the time, the same as you."[2] The statement brought gasps to the hearing room, but few people thought Tammany Hall's avarice would ever affect them personally. The Ice Trust showed how it could.

Tammany Hall's acquisition of such double-barreled power came about in a very piecemeal way, as over the years a succession of wily and sometimes unscrupulous leaders steered and shaped the organization in response to events and opportunities. It all started right after the American Revolution, when some hotheaded members of the Tammany Society, a purely benevolent association, formed a political wing that became known as Tammany Hall, after the place where it met. When political parties began to emerge in the United States, the Hall was quick to join in, becoming an activist wing of the local Republican (later the Democratic) party. Tammany was already earning a reputation for condoning graft.

But not until the middle part of the nineteenth century did Tammany come to be manipulated by the strong personalities historically associated with it. Fernando Wood, the first New York mayor clearly linked to Tammany, showed (after 1854) how an alliance with the police could benefit a scheming officeholder and how money could be coined through shady deals. In the 1860s came the mighty William Tweed, the first true Boss who operated behind the scenes, carrying Wood's notions to a gaudy extreme, plundering the city of untold millions. His successor, Honest John Kelly, tried to bury the Tweed image by denouncing big-time graft and perfecting the "machine" itself, a meticulously crafted device dedicated to swinging elections. It remained for Richard Croker to move Tammany into its most diabolical phase, amassing riches by using the police to elicit payoff's from operators of illegal enterprises such as gambling dens and houses of prostitution while at the same time cementing the Hall's alliances with big business.

Meanwhile, Tammany expanded and solidified its political base by espousing the cause of the huge numbers of immigrants flooding into New York. It helped them get settled, found them jobs (many wound up working for the machine itself), and gave them aid when they were in need—all in return for their votes. In due course, the largest bloc of newcomers—the Irish—took over the Hall and made it their own.

Because Tammany not only reached down into the community to be involved in the everyday life of New Yorkers but boasted good friends on Wall Street as well, it survived downturns in its fortunes that would have wiped out a lesser organization. Whenever a political reform movement came along and, preaching good government and municipal morality, ejected the Hall from power, Tammany just waited for a better day—which always came. While it waited, Tammany generated enough income, legitimately or otherwise, to maintain in fine style a boss who had no other visible means of support.

The Tammany Boss was, in many ways, a law unto himself, responsible only to the Hall's Executive Committee, which appointed him and which he in turn controlled—as long as he continued to win elections and command the party faithful. (Only death or disgrace at the polls was likely to displace him.) To be successful, a boss had to be part folk hero, part intriguer, part technician, and part clairvoyant, and it did not seem to hurt his popularity if he was also something of a rascal. But the type varied: Tweed was the jolly robber, Croker the menacing ex-gang leader, Charles Murphy the quintessence of inscrutability, and the last of them all, Carmine De Sapio, the articulate and suave manipulator.

A juicy scandal, however, could hurt a boss severely, and the Ice Trust affair was too shameful for even blasé New Yorkers to tolerate. The revelation of the American Ice–Tammany tie would have vast repercussions. Mayor Van Wyck, forced to testify in court in response to a suit brought by the *World*, admitted he owned thousands of shares of American Ice and gave such a lame explanation of how he had acquired them that he became the laughingstock of the city. His mayoralty was shattered. American Ice, its motives bared, was forced to rescind the price increase; it gave up its monopoly and eventually faded from the scene. Croker dismissed John Carroll as deputy leader of the Hall. Most important, Croker himself and, by extension, all of Tammany Hall suffered a damaging blow from the incident. Croker's and the organization's ultimate stated aim—to represent the poor and the newly arrived peoples of the city against the powers that be—was shown to be a travesty. Tammany had flourished by marshaling the votes of the underclass, but now it was seen to be making big money off the backs of those same people. In less than two years, Croker would be out, and Tammany Hall, though some of its headiest days still lay ahead, never again displayed its muscle so crudely.

But it did survive, for well over half a century more, until the early 1960s. It was able to operate as brazenly as it did for so long, despite repeated outrages, because, at least in its halcyon days, it actually performed a service to society. It flourished because, in a sense, it was needed. Tammany's minions, its far-flung network of ward heelers, block captains, and district leaders, provided a visible, personal link between the poor immigrant and the otherwise faceless city government, parceling out jobs, helping newcomers cope with the mysterious requirements of the bureaucracy, even functioning as a kind of private welfare service. Whatever its faults, which were many, and no matter how it enriched itself and its leaders, Tammany Hall was above all a personal organization. People knew their local leader and were confident he could help them, which he almost always did. He might even loan them money to tide them over a difficult time. Today that element has largely gone from the scene. In the big cities at least, government has become distant and impersonal, and surely less responsive. No wonder there are still people who long for the days when good old Tammany was around.

Tammany Hall was, of course, far from the only political machine in the United States and perhaps not even the most wicked. Almost every city has had some kind of dominant political organization, or "machine," as opponents habitually label them, adding a sinister element. Other machines might have been more rapacious, for example Tammany's Republican counterpart in Philadelphia. Still others might have challenged it in flamboyance, such as that of Jersey City's Frank ("I am the law") Hague. But Tammany was the longest-running act ever staged in U.S. politics. For a long time it was by far the best known and most successful political machine in the country, its fame enhanced by its identification with the nation's largest and most garish city. So deeply had Tammany embedded itself into the consciousness of New York's voters that even after it had finally been swept away, discredited by its own excesses and crippled by historical forces beyond its control, people could not believe it was no longer there, and politicians continued to run against it, often successfully.

Tammany's disappearance did not end corruption in politics, of course, and it hardly spelled the demise of bosses or political machines, which will always be with us. But Tammany made the mold.

For helping me in the course of this project I would especially like to thank Cynthia Merman, who suggested the subject to me; my agent, Emilie Jacobson; and my editor, Donald Fehr. Thanks also go to the staffs of the New York Public Library and the New-York Historical Society.

1

THE FOUNDING

DURING ALL THE YEARS WHEN TAMMANY HALL was the chief political organization in New York City, an aura of mystery always surrounded it. Just what was Tammany, anyway? In its early years, the last decades of the eighteenth century and the beginning of the nineteenth, this was a particularly difficult question to answer, because from the very beginning, it seemed, obfuscation was a prime Tammany virtue. Was the Hall merely a group of convivial fellows who occasionally dressed up like American Indians and gave themselves strange-sounding titles like sachem or wiskinsky, or was it a close-knit association of conniving politicians? And what was the connection between Tammany Hall and the Tammany Society— and, later on, between Tammany Hall and the city's Democratic party?

If outsiders were confused, Tammany's leaders did not at all mind, either then or later on. In fact, they rather liked it that way. The mystification, the sense of intricacy and enigma, the blurred image and the resulting diffusion of accountability—all these were somehow central to the character (and success) of the organization. The aura of mystery also, for better or worse, helped create a fertile breeding ground for some of the most colorful and outrageous characters to light up New York City politics for the better part of two hundred years. But for most of its history, Tammany Hall was much more than quaint customs and unusual personages. It was the most powerful and insidious political machine in the country. The story of Tammany's first few decades is the story of its conversion, through the pressure of events and the maneuverings of a handful of ambitious men, from a private organization with purely social aims to a fledgling political cabal well on its way to dominating the government of the nation's largest city, thus reaping the riches that accrued to those who could control the vote.

Its beginning, however, was anything but sinister. The Tammany Society, which originated the whole show, was founded during the years immediately following the American Revolution as a benevolent and patriotic fellowship ostensibly dedicated to the memory of an ancient and venerable American Indian chief named Tammany. Right here, however, the confusion begins, for there were actually two Tammanys, one real and one legendary, and the society's members were often happy to mix up the two.

The real Tammany, also known as Tamanend, is believed to have lived at the end of the seventeenth century and the beginning of the eighteenth. He was a sachem, or great chief, of the Delawares, an Algonquin-speaking tribe centered in what is now southeastern Pennsylvania and Delaware. This august personage was evidently present in full regalia in June 1683 when William Penn met with the Delawares to arrange for the orderly transfer of a large tract of land, much of which was to become the Philadelphia metropolitan area. Penn later recalled: "We found him an old man, but yet vigorous in mind and body, with high notions of liberty, easily won by the suavity and peaceful address of the Governor."[1] The Englishman must indeed have been suave, for in exchange for a collection of trinkets, Tammany and his advisers handed over to Penn some three hundred square miles of the opulent surrounding territory. In retrospect it hardly seems fitting that a political body known for wholesale public thievery should have been named after a man who was so easily taken. For his part, Penn later redesigned his coat of arms to incorporate three white balls representing the dumplings that Tammany allegedly baked for him on the occasion. A dozen or so years later, Tammany granted still more territory. The benevolent chief is said by some to be buried near Doylestown, Pennsylvania; others claim he was interred in Princeton, New Jersey, on the site of today's Nassau Hall, but his remains have never been found.

If Tammany himself disappeared, his reputation (such as it was) flourished. In 1732 a fishing club founded by Philadelphia Quakers on the banks of the Schuylkill River honored Tammany by adopting him as its patron saint. Shortly thereafter, two other clubs followed suit. By the time of the American Revolution Tammany had been fully canonized: in the 1770s members of a Pennsylvania organization called the Sons of Saint Tammany proclaimed that they had "adopted a Great Warrior Sachem and Chief, named St. Tammany, a fast friend to our forefathers, to be the tutelar Saint of this Province."[2] Evidently the American colonists, chafing under British rule, needed some kind of native saint to rally around to offset England's Saint Andrew and Saint George; in any event, Sons of Saint Tammany clubs proliferated in the colonies before the outbreak of war, many of them rivaling the superardent Sons of Liberty (the archfomenters of rebellion) in their eagerness to shake off British rule. When the fighting broke out, Pennsylvania troops are said to have carried a flag bearing the image of Saint Tammany. After hostilities ended, many of the societies continued as patriotic clubs dedicated to preserving what they saw as the values for which the revolution had been fought. Out of this movement arose New York's Tammany Society.

So much for the actual Tammany. His mythical counterpart may have been rooted in American Indian lore picked up by the settlers, or he may have been invented by colonists who were tellers of tall tales. But he emerges in glorious hyperbole in a lengthy and well-received oration delivered to the Tammany Society in 1795 on its designated anniversary (May 12) by Dr. Samuel Latham Mitchill. A Tammany member in good standing and an accepted authority on American Indians, Dr. Mitchill was a professor of natural history, chemistry, and botany at Columbia College. In true Tammany fashion, he appears to have given free rein to his imagination during his talk.

The Great Father, Tammany, lived not in the eastern part of the continent, said Dr. Mitchill, but across the Appalachians in the vast space "embraced by the St. Lawrence and the Mississippi." He was a great hunter and warrior whose exploits were known far and wide. So benign and noble were his deeds, in fact, that he was beset by a whole series of challenges from the Evil Spirit that would have wiped out a lesser figure: poisonous plants, swarms of rattlesnakes, man-eating mammoths, floods, murderous rival tribes, even hand-to-hand combat with the Evil One himself that lasted fifty days. Tammany bested them all, and while doing so managed to discover bread and tobacco, teach his people how to make canoes from birch bark, improve the design of the bow and arrow, and create the Great Lakes.

This, then, was the fabled Tammany, whom Society members were glad to accept alongside of or superimposed on the genuine historical figure. Even if he wasn't real, he did bestow an air of nobility on their organization. But note the subject matter, far removed from politics. Mitchill later confessed that he had intended his oration to be "a sort of moral romance" and was genuinely astonished to "find it considered by both political parties a deep Political Allegory!"[3] He had not meant it that way. For the Tammany Society in its earliest days was thought of as a kind of brotherhood of men from all walks of life and political persuasions, wellborn as well as lowly, rich as well as poor, professional leaders as well as artisans and tradesmen—almost an eighteenth-century version of today's Rotary. Political contriving was not in the picture. But by the time Mitchill delivered his oration, Tammany had already acquired a distinct political caste and was on its way to becoming almost a party in itself.

The framers of the U.S. Constitution, of course, had neither desired nor expected the formation of political parties, much less political machines, in the young country. Government was to be in the hands of educated men, who would endeavor to be impartial. Factions—minority groups fighting for special causes—were to be discouraged. Though well-meaning, this sentiment was surely naive. Even before the Revolution, citizens had taken sides on the pressing issues of the day. There were Tories (pro-British and conservative) and Whigs (less Anglophile and more moderate), and despite the decidedly anti-Tory outcome of the war, the same rough divisions of sentiment persisted when peace came. But the framers made no allowance for the development of political parties, let alone political campaigns and elections.

Yet some form of party organization was bound to crop up in any case. In New York, which by 1780 was America's second largest city after Philadelphia (New York would become number one in the next generation), the natural tendency of citizens to form into groups with common interests yielded a proliferation of clubs and societies, some political and some not. One such group was the Society of the Cincinnati. Composed of former officers in the Revolution, it included both George Washington and Alexander Hamilton. Because the Cincinnati had aristocratic leanings (membership could be handed down only by primogeniture), it was only natural that a counterpart would evolve that opposed such undemocratic restrictions. This was the Society of Saint Tammany, a spiritual descendant of the prewar Sons of Saint Tammany. For a while it had several branches in the young republic, notably in Philadelphia, where the veneration of Tammany had first flourished. But gradually all of them declined except the New York chapter, which eventually gave birth to Tammany Hall.

Holding its first meetings in 1786 (although not officially organized until May 12, 1789, its patron's alleged birth date), the Society was envisioned as a generally nonpartisan body. Its membership was made up primarily of tradesmen, artisans, and workmen but included a significant portion of more affluent citizens who subscribed to its anti-aristocratic tenets. As the Tammany archivist Edwin Kilroe wrote, it was "instituted primarily as a social, fraternal and benevolent organization, based on democratic principles, that its membership was not determined by caste, but that all might mingle on the basis of manhood rather than on that of wealth or culture."[4] The initiation fee was $2 to $8, based on ability to pay, and quarterly dues were 24 cents. By the fall of 1791, the new body had more than three hundred members.

The Society's first Grand Sachem, or leader, was an upholsterer and paperhanger named William Mooney, an ex-soldier who, it was rumored, had deserted the Continental forces in 1776 and gone over to the British. The charge was never proved, and anyway by the late 1780s Mooney was claiming to be avidly patriotic. Besides, he was a willing and convivial sort. In the great parade staged in New York by Alexander Hamilton in 1788 to celebrate the ratification of the U.S. Constitution, Mooney represented the city's upholsterers by appearing on a float while preparing a chair to be used by the president of the United States.

Quite possibly, though, Mooney was just a figurehead and not the real guiding spirit of the Society, for the evidence indicates it was a prosperous, liberal-minded merchant and philanthropist named John Pintard who gave Tammany its initial and special stamp. A modest man content to let others take the spotlight, Pintard drew up the Society's constitution and, more important, summed up its most salient tenet: an aversion to upper-class privilege and a belief in the common man. Tammany, he said, is "a political institution founded on a strong republican basis whose democratic principles will serve in some measure to correct the aristocracy of our city."[5] It was this desire to "correct the aristocracy" that eventually contributed to the Society's veering from its strict nonpartisan path.

It was Pintard, also, who seems to have invented much of the complex array of Indian-style offices, titles, and ceremonies for which Tammany became widely known. Tammany members, or "braves," each year elected thirteen sachems to rule the Society, plus a scribe (secretary), a treasurer, a sagamore (master of ceremonies), and a wiskinsky (doorkeeper). The sachems chose one of their group to be Grand Sachem, or head of the Society; the president of the United States was ex officio considered the Great Grand Sachem. Each of the thirteen sachems in turn was to rule a "tribe" within the organization, and each tribe had its own okemaw (warrior), mackawalaw (hunter), and alank (clerk); these subsidiary groupings, however, did not last long and were little more than vehicles for planning social events and ceremonies.

Initiation into the Society was replete with torches, mystical symbols, Indian incantations, and voices raised in song. Braves liked to greet one another with secret handshakes and obscure code words. The calendar was unbelievably arcane: Society events were officially dated as counted from the year of the Society's founding, the year the Declaration of Independence was adopted, and the year Columbus discovered America. Each year was divided into four seasons, spring being the Season of Blossoms; summer, the Season of Fruits; autumn, of Hunting; and winter, of Snows. Months were moons. Thus, as the writer Morris Werner computed in his study of Tammany, a perfectly ordinary monthly meeting of the Society sometime in the nineteenth century would have been chronicled as having occurred in the "Season of Fruits, 17th day of the 7th moon, Year of Discovery 361st, of Independence 78th, and of the Institution the 65th."[6]

John Pintard was also godfather to the Tammany Museum, a collection of artifacts of American Indian history and other Americana originally housed in a room in City Hall (then on Wall Street). The museum was a popular tourist attraction at first, but the Society soon lost interest and in 1795 sold it to its director, Gardiner Baker, a man described as a "snub-nosed, pock-pitted, bandy-legged, fussy, good-natured little body" said to be "a greater curiosity than any in his museum."[7] Unfortunately, Baker died in 1798 and the collection was again sold, eventually winding up in the hands of the great showman P. T. Barnum, who mixed it in with his other collections. Pintard's disappointment in the fate of this institution may have been responsible for his becoming the principal founder, in 1804, of the New-York Historical Society, which has since kept better track of its possessions.

Members of the Society met monthly for an evening of conviviality, with much drinking and storytelling, but they were particularly noted in the city for their parades. These they staged on May 12 (the Society's founding date), July 4, Washington's birthday, Evacuation Day (November 25, the anniversary of the departure of British troops from New York in 1783), and, starting in 1792, on Columbus Day, having decided a year or so earlier—again at Pintard's urging—to elevate Christopher Columbus to patron saint status on a par with Tammany. Thus, the Society's official title became The Society of St. Tammany or Columbian Order in the City of New York. Indeed, Tammany could justifiably claim to have originated America's annual celebration of Columbus' discovery long before there was any significant Italian minority in the United States. Along about 1792, incidentally, Tammany ceased being referred to as Saint Tammany, perhaps to underscore the Society's desire to be democratic. "We have lately uncanonized him," Pintard wrote to a friend.[8]

For each parade the braves dressed up in American Indian costume, heads covered with skullcaps to simulate hairlessness, faces painted. Carrying tomahawks or bows and arrows, they walked as if on the trail, in single file through the city streets. Admittedly, some members were loath to appear in "savage" garb, in which case they dressed in ordinary jackets and breeches but adorned their hats with a bucktail, a symbol of liberty. (Tammany members would later be referred to in the political arena as Bucktails.) In addition to the parade, there would usually be a "long talk" on a patriotic note delivered by a prominent Society member (for example, Dr. Mitchill). The day culminated in a lavish banquet topped off with thirteen toasts. A typical toast would be to "the Grand Sachem of the Thirteen United Fires—may his declining sun be precious in the sight of the Great Spirit that the mild luster of his departing beams may prove no less glorious than the effulgence of the rising or transcendent splendor of his meridian greatness."[9] The American Indian dress was abandoned during the War of 1812, when it was revealed that Indians siding with the British had committed atrocities against Americans. But the banquets, "long talks," and other trappings continued into modern times, as did the sachem title for members of the organization's ruling board. And throughout its history, newspapers unendingly referred to the Hall's members as "Tammany braves."

During its first few years, the Society met in downtown watering spots, most notably Barden's Tavern on lower Broadway near Bowling Green. In 1798, however, it acquired more substantial quarters at the rear of "Brom" Martling's Tavern at the corner of Nassau and Spruce streets (near today's City Hall), in a long room that it proudly called its Wigwam. Although the Society controlled the space (Martling had been a sachem), it would permit the Long Room, or Wigwam, to be used by any responsible political organization that asked; by the same token the Society reserved the right to refuse the room to any group it considered irresponsible or unworthy. The space soon became known as Tammany Hall. Thus did the nebulous Hall come into being, though it was still just a place to meet. And thus was also born the Society's key power, which throughout its history it rarely hesitated to invoke: the power to grant legitimacy to any political force in the city by controlling the place that symbolized authority. Time and time again it would turn aside threats to its hegemony simply by padlocking the doors.

Because Tammany later became known for staunchly befriending the immigrant, it may be surprising to learn that in its earliest years it was a one hundred percent American nativist organization whose members shared a common antipathy to the British. The constitution drawn up by Pintard stated that Tammany was for "American brethren," and only American-born persons could be elected to its offices. Those born elsewhere were considered "exotic." When large numbers of Germans and Irish began arriving in the city in the early nineteenth century, Tammany at first viewed them with alarm. The Society was also anti-Catholic, and for some time it refused to support any Irish Catholic candidate for political office. Only the press of political expediency would prompt it many years later to completely reverse its policy and deliberately seek the support of ethnic peoples just in from the docks.

But there was also a moralistic element to this xenophobia. The backbone of Tammany's membership consisted of true American tradesmen and other workmen who valued the respectability that membership in the Society conferred. It was their club, and they took it seriously. "The austere tone of people in modest circumstances," wrote the political scientist Moisei Ostrogorski, "earning an honest living by hard work . . . found an echo naturally enough in the grave personages of the Tammany society, and more than once its spokesmen uttered warnings, on the solemn occasions of its anniversary, against the bad habits and the vices which were invading the country. . . ."[10] In time, the "bad habits" and "vices" invading the country would no longer be viewed as threatening elements and would become ingredients of Tammany power.

Partly because of its nativist stance and also in deference to the spirit of its patron saint, the Society in its early years was eager to promote friendships with American Indians, and in this capacity, in 1790, it performed a useful service for the new U.S. government, still in residence in New York City. Following the Revolution, the Creek

Indians, who occupied large tracts of land in Georgia and Florida, became engaged in a running dispute with the United States and resisted all efforts to sign a peace treaty. President Washington thought the Tammany Society might help in their conciliation, and so a prominent Tammany member, Colonel Marinus Willett, a revolutionary war hero, was dispatched southward to invite the Creek chief, a half-breed named Alexander McGillivray (whose father had been a Scotch trader), to visit New York. McGillivray arrived in due course with a retinue of twenty-eight warriors and was cordially welcomed by New York's make-believe tribe, the Tammany braves. Society members wined and dined the Creeks, showed them about the city, and got them an audience with Washington, who unnerved his guests by showing them a just completed portrait of himself by the artist John Trumbull; only with difficulty could the Creeks be persuaded there were not two George Washingtons in the room. But a treaty was signed, the calumet (peace pipe) was passed around, and the Creeks departed amid promises of mutual amity. Just possibly the Tammany Society at that moment, just one year into its official existence, enjoyed a higher level of respect and appreciation in the community than it ever would later.

But even now pressure was building to make Tammany less of a unifying, cohesive community force and more of a partisan one. Four developments would combine to convert the organization permanently into a political force linked to, and often synonymous with, the new Republican party (which later metamorphosed into the Democratic party that we know today). Two of these developments produced pronounced shifts in public opinion; the others were outside events that had a critical impact on the local scene and hastened the development of the two-party system.

The first was the forgiveness the U.S government extended to former pro-British Tories, a move engineered by Alexander Hamilton. The pardon angered all still resentful of those who had sympathized with the enemy forces during the American Revolution. Although many in the community felt it was time to forgive and forget, the majority of Tammany members considered Hamilton's move unconscionable—and they would make him pay for it later.

An even sharper dispute arose at the time of the ratification of the U.S. Constitution in 1788. Those who wholeheartedly backed the document were called Federalists and their leader was Hamilton, while the anti-Federalists, who at this time were becoming known as Republicans, expressed grave concern over the document's emphasis on strong centralized rule, which they feared would diminish state and individual rights; their guiding light was Thomas Jefferson. The Tammany Society contained members of both parties, but the Federalists were clearly in the minority, and the time would come when they would withdraw from the organization entirely.

For the moment such differences, while significant, lay under the surface of day-to-day politics, which tended to revolve around the personal predilections of three prominent families: the Clintons, the Livingstons, and the Schuylers. The high-born Clintons happened to be strongly anti-Federalist, and for this they were accepted by the anti-aristocracy Tammanyites. Their most prominent personage in New York State was Governor George Clinton, who had vigorously opposed ratification of the Constitution; he enjoyed strong support among Tammanyites. The Livingstons and Schuylers tended to be Federalists, especially the Schuylers, whose behind-the-scenes leader, Hamilton, was son-in-law of the family's patriarch, General Philip Schuyler. But alignments were fluid, and during the 1790s the Livingstons deserted the Federalists and came over to the opposing camp. In any case, the future local parties would evolve out of these allegiances.

For the Tammanyites, the first outside event to polarize the membership was the French Revolution, which erupted in 1789. The Society had always been partial to the French, who, after all, had helped the colonies oust the British. The news of the revolt was greeted with joy by the anti-Federalist members and with alarm by the Federalists, and arguments between the two camps disrupted Tammany meetings. Nevertheless, successive celebrations were mounted that reached a peak in 1793 with the arrival in New York of Edmond Charles Edouard Genét, better known as Citizen Genét, the representative of the new French Republic. Genét, lionized and entertained by Tammany leaders, brought with him an admirer, Mrs. Ann Julia Hatton, who penned an opera titled *Tammany, or the Indian Chief,* which was a hit at least among Republican Tammanyites. Federalist members of the Society were not so appreciative and expressed their anger at the pro-French Tammanyites, aggravating the split between the two camps. (Citizen Genét, after the start of France's Reign of Terror in the 1790s, was forced to remain in the United States and ended up marrying Governor Clinton's daughter.)

But it was the outbreak of the so-called Whiskey Rebellion in western Pennsylvania in 1794 that brought the most critical rupture within the Society's membership, putting it unmistakably in the anti-

Federalist (hereafter Republican) camp. Settlers in the remote region objected to the excise tax that the Washington administration levied on their whiskey, saying it discriminated against them and infringed on their rights. When they rioted, the president (abetted by Hamilton) sent troops to restore order. Republicans, including many Tammanyites, strongly criticized the move as an unreasonable use of the central government's power, whereupon Washington exacerbated the dispute by lashing out, in a message to Congress, against "self-created societies"—he obviously had Tammany in mind—that fomented trouble for his administration. But Tammany's Federalist members strongly approved of Washington's policy and issued a paper condemning all those who opposed it. That was too much for Tammany's Republicans, who at the Society's next meeting voted (by a margin of 100 to 65) to repudiate what their Federalist brethren had published. Shocked, the Federalists resigned en masse from the organization. Now the Tammany Society, although still a fraternal organization officially outside politics, was considerably reduced in size but composed overwhelmingly of persons strongly committed to one political viewpoint.

Given such a body of articulate and, for the most part, convinced citizens, it was only a question of time before someone moved in to manipulate them for personal or political gain. The man who did so, Aaron Burr, was not out to control Tammany; in fact, he was not even a member of the Society and never, as far as is known, set foot in Martling's Long Room. He had larger aims than those contained by local politics; the Society was simply one of a number of tools he used to further his purposes. But some of the techniques he employed to achieve his immediate aim—maneuvering the Republican party in New York State so as to control the 1800 presidential election—would eventually become central to Tammany's way of operating. So for many Tammany members the experience was a kind of baptism of fire. Furthermore, Burr's chief aides in the 1800 campaign (men such as Matthew Davis and William Van Ness) became the nucleus of the group that only a few years hence—after Burr fatally shot Alexander Hamilton in a duel and fled the city in disgrace—would convert Tammany once and for all into a political organism that would one day become a true machine.

Urbane, brilliant, a consummate political operator but evidently bereft of any controlling viewpoint or philosophy other than his own advancement, the forty-four-year-old Burr was by 1800 already a potent figure on the New York scene. He had been a state assemblyman, state attorney general, and, from 1791 to 1797, a U.S. senator. Now out of office and back practicing law (which earned him high fees but could not keep him out of perennial debt), he had just pulled off a coup that still amazes historians. Anti-Federalists and other Republicans in New York had long chafed under the virtual banking monopoly the Federalists wielded. In addition to the federal government's Bank of the United States, the city had only one principal bank, the Bank of New York, founded by Alexander Hamilton. Both banks catered to large business concerns and the more affluent members of society. If banks less partial to the moneyed classes could be founded they not only would benefit small businessmen (like so many of the Tammanyites) but would facilitate the forming of tontines, groups of citizens that banded together to borrow money and purchase property. The tontines were a way to get around the property restrictions that in New York State still limited the right to vote. And if the property limitation could be weakened, the Republicans, whose strength lay principally among the less advantaged, would almost certainly pick up votes. But all attempts by Tammanyites to start rival banks had been snuffed out by Hamilton and his allies.

Burr's tactic, while a bit underhanded, was undeniably adroit. New York City had long needed a dependable water system, and Burr took advantage of this lack to get what he wanted. He announced a proposal to set up a publicly chartered body called the Manhattan Company that would build a reservoir and lay pipes to supply potable water to everyone. The scheme was widely applauded. But just before the charter was to be approved by the state legislature, Burr quietly added an outwardly innocuous amendment authorizing the new company to invest surplus funds in any manner that did not contravene the laws of the state. In the rush of legislative business, no one paid much attention to the addition, but after the bill passed the truth became known that the wording enabled the company to found a bank—which it soon did. The resulting institution became known as the Bank of the Manhattan Company, which lives on today in the "Manhattan" of New York's Chase Manhattan Bank. The Republicans had their bank, and Burr, while causing eyebrows to be raised among his fellow politicians, enjoyed great popularity among the voters.

Along with other prominent Republicans, Burr saw the 1800 election as an unexampled opportunity to wrest control of the federal government from the Federalists, who had dominated it from its inception. He might also, of course, boost his own career. The administration of President John Adams was particularly unpopular because of the Alien and Sedition Laws he had pushed through Congress in 1798. A reaction to the threat of war with the revolutionary French regime, the laws established severe restrictions on political dissent. Many republicans were aghast, especially the more zealous Tammanyites; even while the new laws were being debated in Congress, Tammany, in conjunction with similar societies in the city, staged a massive Fourth of July parade followed by a stirring address by George Clinton, who at the moment was out of office. Clinton called upon his listeners to "resist the first appearance of usurpation. . . . While with cheerfulness you obey the constitutional acts of the constituted authorities, evince to your country and the world, that you are resolved to *live free or die*."[11] His talk was well received, and popular sentiment in New York State was clearly on the side of the Republicans, whose candidate in the upcoming election would almost certainly be Thomas Jefferson. But the outcome was far from certain. New York, because of its large electoral vote, was considered a critical state in the election—it could swing the decision either way. The question was, how could a win be assured?

What made the situation especially complex was the fact that, at that time, New York's presidential electors—whose vote was so important—were chosen not by the people in direct voting but, as in a number of other states, by the state legislature. A majority vote in the legislature (meeting as a unit) would determine whether the state's electors would be Republican or Federalist. So the way New York voted in the presidential contest would be determined not in November but in the legislative elections the previous spring. Moreover, although upstate New York was partial to George Clinton and thus dependably Republican, the Federalists were still strong in New York City and the lower Hudson River area, which combined to represent the preponderance of power in the state. Aaron Burr clearly saw the opportunity, as did the Federalist party's chief strategist, Burr's archrival Alexander Hamilton, with whom Burr already enjoyed less than cordial relations. Whoever took the city and its environs would probably take the state and thus the nation. Burr resolved to capture New York by capturing control of its legislature.

To assist him in the effort, he had at his side a handful of politically astute cohorts who had helped him in his various campaigns for office. Known as the Burrites, and also as the Little Band, they were for the most part members of the Tammany Society. The key member of the group, a businessman and sometime newspaper editor named Matthew L. Davis, was at the time serving as a sachem of the Society. He was a slick operator, almost a prototype of the Tammany politician to come. In the words of historian Jerome Mushkat, Davis was "a man who could never resist a shady deal or a dishonest dollar, a man whose political acumen was constantly available for sale to the highest bidder."[12] But Davis's fidelity to Aaron Burr never wavered; indeed, he became Burr's authorized biographer. After Burr's death in 1836, Davis aroused the ire of scholars by destroying a huge stock of apparently incriminating letters Burr had written to or received from women with whom he had carried on tempestuous affairs.

Almost as influential was the lawyer William P. Van Ness, who would be one of Burr's seconds in the duel with Hamilton in Weehawken, New Jersey—the other was Matthew Davis—and who would go to jail briefly for refusing to answer a grand jury's questions about the encounter; another was the businessman John Swartwout, whose family would later loom large in Tammany annals. "These men would do anything for the colonel [Burr]," says a recent Burr biographer, Milton Lomask, "and everything was what he had them do."[13]

In past elections, the Republicans had formed three-men ward committees throughout the city whose members constituted a General Committee to run the campaign; but the apparatus was loose and not always effective. Burr tightened it up and appointed a steering committee made up of his followers to ride herd on the larger group. (These groups were the predecessors of the Tammany General Committee and, within it, the Tammany Executive Committee that many years hence would acquire great power and influence.) But this arrangement was only the beginning. Burr ordered the Little Band to prepare a roster of every voter in the city—the list numbered up in the thousands, despite property restrictions—and to specify in each case how the person had previously voted, how interested he was in the Republican cause, his temperament, his financial profile, whether he might work as a volunteer, and any other relevant information. Burr further appointed canvasing committees to go door-to-door to raise funds, and he drew up a list of wealthy Republicans who could be counted on to contribute large sums, with their assumed gift specified. No one had ever seen such a meticulous and thorough job of political organizing. Davis and the other future Tammany leaders would remember what Burr taught them.

Burr knew, however, that he could not defeat the Federalists with a mediocre ticket. He would have to put together a slate so impressive that it would be attractive even to dedicated Federalist voters, which is what he proceeded to do, exhibiting a daring that no one would have believed if they did not know Aaron Burr. He also decided to keep his list secret until Hamilton had publicly revealed the Federalist candidates, so that Hamilton would be trapped and unable to upgrade his own slate. It is said that one of Burr's lieutenants happened to acquire an advance copy of the Federalist ticket in March and promptly brought it to his chief. Burr looked at it, calmly folded it up and stuck it in his pocket, and said, "Now I have him all hollow."[14]

He was right; Hamilton's ticket was for the most part made up of nonentities. Burr at that point, however, did not actually have his own slate, for several on it had balked. His blue-ribbon list had led off with former governor Clinton; next was the aging retired hero of the Battle of Saratoga, General Horatio Gates. Other possibilities Burr was pursuing included Brockholst Livingston of the Livingston clan; John Broome, the president of the New York Insurance Company and a former U.S. postmaster general; and a number of other estimable citizens including John Swartwout, who would represent the Burrites. Burr was also a candidate himself, but not from the city; he chose to run from a safe upstate district so that his controversial role in the Manhattan Company chartering would not intrude.

Most of the gilt-edged names on his list eventually agreed to run, but outright refusals came from Clinton, for whom election to the state legislature hardly seemed a career advancement; Gates, who pleaded advanced age; and Livingston, who said he was too busy. Burr and his associates went to work on them. Livingston was the first to cave in; reluctantly, he said he would accede if both Clinton and Gates would serve. Gates, after much persuading by the Burrites, finally agreed, providing Clinton said yes. Clinton was adamant. He said he was too old and that his political days were over (they surely were not—he would later be governor once again, and then vice-president of the United States). Furthermore, he did not really trust Thomas Jefferson, whom he considered "a trimmer who would change with the times and bend to circumstances for personal promotion."[15] Just possibly he also did not trust Burr, whom he regarded as an upstart. But after Burr's continual pleading, Clinton finally said yes. That is, he said he would consent to his name being on the ticket, but he would not campaign. That was enough for Aaron Burr. The ticket was complete. As could be predicted, its announcement confounded the Federalists.

Campaigning was furious, both before and during the three-day balloting that got under way at the end of April. Burr, said an observer, kept open house for nearly two months at his country estate, Richmond Hill, an imposing abode (located just west of today's SoHo) that had been the residence of John and Abigail Adams when the federal government was in the city. "Refreshments were always on the table," recalled a participant, "and mattresses for temporary repose in the rooms. Reports were hourly received from subcommittees, and in short, no means left unemployed."[16] Burr instructed his followers to maintain the pressure without stint and, another participant later remembered, urged them to "keep up frequent meetings at Tammany Hall until the election."[17] This did not mean Burr was using Tammany directly in the campaign, but that the meetings should be held as often as possible in Martling's Long Room, which was of course available to all comers, to drum up popular support for the ticket. Many Tammany members were in the thick of the fight, but the Society itself still prided itself on its neutrality.

It was probably during this campaign that Matthew Davis, who was well aware of the power of publicity, is said to have introduced a technique that has long since become a political staple, especially among the likes of Tammany Hall. Newspapers were told that nightly meetings were being held in every ward of the city, that the meetings were well attended, that speeches were wildly cheered, and that spirited resolutions passed unanimously. The papers dutifully reported what they were told. Only later would it become known that those present almost invariably consisted of Davis and two of his friends.

As the balloting began, Burr crisscrossed the city visiting polling places to harangue the voters. On more than one occasion he met up with Hamilton, with whom he would carry on an impromptu and vigorous debate. All manner of carriages and wagons were commandeered to get people to the polls (another election technique that was to become standard), and in the predominantly German Seventh Ward a group of Burrites spoke to the voters in their native tongue. Shortly after the polls closed on May 1 the results became known: Burr and the Republicans had swept New York.

The strange outcome of the national election of 1800 need not be dwelled on here except as it affected the fortunes of the Tammany Society. Because of an anomaly in the Constitution, vice-presidential candidate Burr almost stole the top office from Thomas Jefferson: the electoral vote for the two men was tied, throwing the election into the House of Representatives, where Burr showed unexpected strength. Burr's cryptic behavior almost won him the election and did bring him the vice-presidency, but it effectively robbed him of almost all his political allies—except his loyal band of friends from Tammany. The Federalists scorned him as a Republican parvenu. Jefferson would not forgive him for stubbornly and, he surely felt, needlessly protracting the election process. And George Clinton began to believe that Burr had acted dishonorably in edging him out of the vice-presidential nomination. All at once Burr was isolated and without influence, as were his followers, who were seen as apostles of expedience and seekers of power at the cost of all else. (Not long after Jefferson's inauguration, Matthew Davis called on him in Washington—where the federal government had just moved—and made bold to boast of the immensely valuable role played by Tammany members in the campaign. "Jefferson listened," recounts the historian Gustavus Myers. "Then reaching out his hand and catching a large fly, he requested Davis to note the remarkable disproportion in size between one portion of the insect [perhaps meaning its head] and its body. The hint was not lost on Davis, who, though not knowing whether Jefferson referred to New York or to him, ceased to talk on the subject."[18])

Davis was unluckier than he knew. Patronage being a prime motivating force in politics even in those days, Davis, along with the other members of the Little Band, had assumed their hard campaign work would be rewarded by appointments to important federal posts. None came. Burr, from his supposedly high and influential position, submitted a list of names to Jefferson with the recommendation that Davis be named chief of the federal customhouse in New York, a job Davis desperately desired. But the president was evasive and after many months appointed someone else. Other Burrites were similarly frozen out.

Worse yet, Jefferson was not only bypassing Burr but was funneling all patronage matters for New York State through Albany, which meant by way of George Clinton, who was back as governor (having resigned from his newly won post in the legislature shortly after being elected). Clinton and his associates were not fond of Burr and his Tammany minions. But public attention was no longer focused on this one member of the Clinton family. It was increasingly directed toward a thirty-two-year-old rising politician who was already showing great promise and who for the next quarter century would be an implacable enemy and goad of Tammany: the governor's nephew, De Witt Clinton.

Over six feet tall, with a strong, broad face, curly hair, and a commanding mien, De Witt Clinton seemed ticketed for greatness. The son of a revolutionary war general who was George's brother, he had been the first student admitted to Columbia College after the war and had graduated at the head of his class at the age of seventeen. After being admitted to the bar he devoted a number of years to working for his uncle as confidential secretary. In 1797, still in his twenties, he was elected a state senator. In his early years, he had been a member of the Tammany Society and had once served as scribe, or secretary, of the organization but had drifted away and was no longer active in it. Stubborn, imperious, quick-tempered and contemptuous of political maneuvers (though not above manipulating the levers of power himself to good effect), he was immensely creative and understandably ambitious. On behalf of his uncle, he now proceeded to turn his wrath on the Burrites.

He did so through the Council of Appointment, a governmental body that George Clinton named him to head. The council was authorized at that time by the state constitution to dispense the state's patronage, which included thousands of public positions, from county sheriff all the way up to and including the mayor of New York City (not yet an elected office). Because the council was overwhelmingly Republican and beholden to the Clintons, De Witt suddenly became the most powerful politician in the state. And he saw to it that Davis and his colleagues were denied any state political plums.

The Little Band, Burr's Tammany cohorts, were not helped by their leader's personal problems. Burr had never been able to control his own financial indebtedness, and in 1802 he was forced, along with his henchman John Swartwout, to withdraw from the directorate of the Manhattan Company, the water concern he had founded that also functioned as a bank. It was De Witt Clinton, a fellow director, who engineered the ouster. Swartwout accused Clinton of trying to destroy Burr to advance his own career, whereupon Clinton called Swartwout "a liar, a scoundrel and a villain."[19] Swartwout challenged Clinton to a duel and the two met across the Hudson in New Jersey (dueling being outlawed in New York) with inconclusive results— Clinton wounded his opponent but Swartwout refused to apologize or yield (nor would Clinton), and the affair was halted by the principals' attendants, or seconds.

The following year De Witt Clinton received another boost from his uncle the governor. The mayor of New York, Edward Livingston (a member of the far-flung Livingston family), had resigned from his post, and the governor persuaded the Council of Appointment to name its chief, De Witt Clinton, to succeed him. The young man seemed more powerful and influential than ever.

It was shortly thereafter, in 1804, that Burr fought his celebrated duel (again across the Hudson in New Jersey) with Hamilton. The ostensible provocation had been remarks Hamilton evidently made about Burr at a dinner party, which Burr was convinced robbed him of a chance to become state governor in the 1804 election. Hamilton's death shocked the city and the nation; the Tammany Society, even though many of its members had been implacably opposed to the Federalist former secretary of the treasury, joined in the mourning. When Burr was subsequently tried for treason for his alleged involvement in a plot to overthrow the U.S. government, it was doubly disadvantageous for anyone in New York to call himself a Burrite. Tammany activists such as Davis seemed to be suffering irrevocably from their association with the mercurial former vice-president.

So it was all the more remarkable, then, that over the next several years Matthew Davis was able to rescue his group of Tammany operatives from near-oblivion and lead them in a dramatic recovery of influence within Tammany, mainly at the expense of the Clintonians. Davis and his followers acquired control of Tammany, completing its transformation into a politically effective body. It was a feat whose audacity makes Davis the true founder of Tammany Hall as we know it. The recovery was also the first of many occasions over the next century and a half when Tammany, having suffered egregiously and been given up for dead, rebounded to new triumphs.

Davis was aided in his struggle by a new alignment within Tammany that came into existence in 1805. In that year the Society, perhaps recognizing that some of its members' partisan activity might seem inappropriate for a body that had always seen itself as nonpolitical, sought to clarify its position for the record. It applied for and was granted (by the state legislature) official recognition as a benevolent and charitable organization "for the purpose of affording relief to the indigent and distressed members of said association, their widows and orphans and others who may be proper objects of their charity."[20] So the Society proper was now ostensibly walled off from the political arena. At the same time, however, the Society's sachems, undoubtedly urged on by Sachem Matthew Davis, organized the General Committee of Tammany Hall, making permanent the apparatus that Burr had used so effectively in the 1800 election. The General Committee, which Burr had set up as a council of his followers, was to operate now as an elected organ of the city's Republican party (now sometimes called the Democratic-Republican party); and before very long it seemed that Tammany's General Committee was, in fact, the

party's General Committee: Tammany had co-opted the party and
was acting in its name. What's more, although members of the General Committee were in theory chosen by Republican party members
in wards throughout the city, in actual fact they were almost always
largely handpicked by the sachems of the Tammany Society, that
outwardly nonpolitical outfit; when a vacancy occurred, there tended
to be only one candidate (designated by the sachems), and his election was virtually automatic. Thus, wonder of wonders, the benevolent and politically neutral sachems were at this point—by the end of
the first decade of the nineteenth century—in firm control of the
party's General Committee, which directed the fortunes of the party
as a whole. The arrangement, masterminded by Davis, could not
have fooled many, but it more or less persisted to the end of Tammany's days. When pressed for explanations, the Society's sachems
always proclaimed their innocence, but everyone knew they were ultimately giving the signals.

So the rudiment of a large-scale political organization, or machine,
was established: a disciplined and tightly held central directorate capable of using a multitude of sophisticated election techniques to stay in
power. But who was taking Davis's Tammany coterie seriously? Once
again, events in the world outside the city were responsible for bringing about a change in the local situation. In 1807, with the Napole-
onic Wars raging in Europe and threatening to involve other parts of
the world, President Jefferson persuaded Congress to pass the Embargo Act, which halted all international trade in and out of U.S.
ports. Cries of dismay rang especially loud in New York, whose merchants depended heavily on foreign commerce. The Clintonians
came out against the act by enlisting George Clinton (who became
vice-president in 1805, succeeding Burr) to run for president in 1808
against Jefferson's chosen successor, James Madison. But other
Republicans, the Livingstons for example, espoused the embargo.
Matthew Davis, for tactical reasons, decided to ally himself (and
therefore Tammany) with the Livingstons and the other pro-embargo
forces, backing up his commitment with a series of slashing editorials
in New York paper friendly to the Jefferson administration's cause.
All at once Davis and his cohorts, now part of a larger political alliance whose members called themselves the Madisonians, were back
in the good graces of the president and well on their way toward
eradicating the stigma of Tammany's previous association with Burr.

Having adopted a jingoistic stance (the Embargo Act was a decidedly anti-British measure), Davis was able to persuade other Tam-

many sachems to join him in a public relations maneuver that could hardly fail to remind New Yorkers of the Society's commitment to ardent patriotism. Ever since the revolutionary war the bones of some 11,500 soldiers and others who had died aboard British prison ships anchored in Wallabout Bay (later the site of the Brooklyn Navy Yard) had rested in shallow graves along the shoreline. It happened that one of the Tammany sachems, John Jackson, owned property nearby. Davis (with Jackson's approval, of course) proposed that the Society organize a campaign to bury the martyrs' bones properly on the Jackson land and erect a suitable monument at the site. The bones were accordingly reinterred. On April 13, 1808, Society members marched from Martling's Tavern down to the waterfront and embarked for Brooklyn in thirteen large open boats, each craft carrying a symbolic coffin draped in black. At Wallabout a proper dedication ceremony was held, and soon thereafter the state legislature voted to give Tammany $1,000 to erect a suitable monument on the spot. The grateful Society, having pulled off its public relations coup, seems to have pocketed the $1,000, because the monument was never built. But Davis and Tammany came out of it looking like responsible, public-spirited citizens.

Favorable publicity, as a matter of fact, was exactly what Tammany needed at this point and would continue to need, because incidents of malfeasance involving its members seemed to crop up with increasing regularity. A number of Tammanyites who had jobs with the city were not exactly pillars of probity, a circumstance that would become all too familiar in future years. Just why Tammany produced such malefactors at this early stage is hard to say; some of the blame can perhaps be ascribed to the memory of Aaron Burr, who was anything but a paragon of propriety. It should also be borne in mind, of course, that during these years the United States was still experimenting with local government and was far from developing a strong tradition of political morality or from imposing constraints that would limit improper municipal behavior. New Yorkers in particular, accustomed to a certain level of political buccaneering on the local scene, had no reason to be shocked by a certain level of transgressions by officeholders.

Nevertheless, for Tammany, which still stood for some degree of rectitude, the news of wrongdoing was not good. Benjamin Romaine, for example, once a prominent sachem, had to be removed from the office of city controller in 1806 for allegedly acquiring valuable land in the center of the city without paying a cent for it. The following

year Philip Arcularius, superintendent of the almshouse, and Cornelius Warner, superintendent of public repairs, both of them Tammanyites, were dismissed for irregularities. Jonas Humbert, another
sachem, decided to resign from his post as inspector of bread when he
was found to have extorted a significant portion of the fees collected
by his office. But the most noteworthy malfeasance involved the original Tammanyite himself, William Mooney, who had succeeded
Arcularius as head of the almshouse. Mooney's annual salary was
$1,000, in addition to which he was permitted to charge $500 a year
for the support of his family. Very soon it became evident that he was
making use of far more money than that. An investigating committee
found that he had spent nearly $4,000 on himself and his family, and
had swiped numerous supplies that totaled some $1,000. In account-
ing for some of these items, he listed them as "trifles for Mrs.
Mooney," a phrase that in years to come would become a popular
staple of local political lore. Though beloved by many, Mooney was
asked to relinquish his office.

Such revelations were the result of investigations launched by
Mayor Clinton, who thereby dropped even lower in Davis's estima-
tion. In fact, Davis himself came under critical scrutiny at this time,
for even while defending the Embargo Act he had evidently been
smuggling flour out of the city in large quantities, racking up handsome profits. But the charges were never substantiated, and he was
not prosecuted.

Davis's escape from trial, ironically, provided him with a rare opportunity. He was now able to advocate his cause at the expense of
those who had been caught and penalized. For when the other Tammanyites were forced by their legal difficulties to suspend activity in
the Society, Davis and like-minded Tammanyites were able to move
in and take over the vacant Society positions. Davis became scribe, or
secretary, but more significantly he became chairman of the Society's
Committee on Organization, which directed the group's everyday
affairs. He was thus in a better position than ever before to manipulate the Society for his own purposes, which he did to great effect.

For instance, while the Embargo Act was still in effect (it was superseded after fifteen months), the Madisonians, led by Davis, called
a meeting of the Republican General Committee at Martling's Long
Room to denounce the Clintonians for their opposition to the act. A
band of Clintonians arrived to break up the meeting but were outvoted and expelled from the room. By dint of this move, Davis and
his allies—who now had a new label, "Martlingmen"—gained practi-

cal control over the Republican General Committee, which thereafter reflected their point of view.

The Martlingmen also found ways to extend their control from the top down to minimize the threat of grass-roots rebellions. This in itself was a shift of immense significance for the future development of Tammany Hall. In theory, the party's General Committee reflected the desires and views of the ward committees, who responded to the mass of party members. But Davis and his colleagues, drawing on their experience with Burr, became adept at calling meetings with less than adequate advance notice, packing the meetings with their followers, and speeding through the agenda so as to provide the minimum chance for dissent. The same techniques pervaded the nomination process. Only persons "friendly to regular nominations," that is, willing to act as party regulars faithful to Tammany, were permitted to run for office. Such methods seem almost old hat today, but they were considered radical at the time.

From his new strategic eminence Davis directed a full-scale new membership drive for the Tammany Society that stressed patriotism and Americanism as he and his friends saw it. The drive was a success and marked the completion of the Society's shift from a nonpartisan, fraternal organization to a partisan political vehicle. As Jerome Mushkat has observed, Davis had "restructured the Society. . . . Because of [his] masterful politicking, Tammany Hall absorbed the key political techniques of Burrism—the ability of a few men to control the ward committees, the nomination process, and the means to turn out the voters—and by so doing laid the groundwork for the organization's amazing victories in the future. Later Tammany bosses such as Tweed and Richard Croker owed more than they knew to Matthew Davis."[21]

During all these maneuvers the Society proper still maintained, as it always would, that it was merely a fraternal body, far removed from the disorderly world of politics. It held its meetings on evenings other than those when the General Committee or other party organizations gathered; there was, the Society insisted, no connection. But the sachems controlled the Republican party's officially accepted meeting place and could deny its use to any group they did not approve of. And over time more and more of the top leaders of the Republican party (which would formally metamorphose into the Democratic party in the 1820s) happened to be sachems of the Tammany Society; conversely, the way to become a sachem was to be an influential politician. The Wigwam—the Society's meeting place—became the symbolic center of party loyalty. By the 1830s, when the Democratic party consolidated its position as the dominant political force in the city, the erstwhile fraternal Society, with its odd titles and quaint customs, would develop a virtual hammerlock on the city government. That degree of control did not occur in Davis's time, but all the groundwork had been laid.

As if to mark its newfound role, the Society in 1812 moved into its own building. It had long chafed at the limitations of Martling's Long Room, the "pig pen" that critics had also described as "the Den where the Wolves and Bears and Panthers assemble and drink down large potations of beer."[22] The new Wigwam, at the corner of Nassau and Frankfort streets, was just a few doors up from Martling's Tavern and only a block or so from New York's brand new City Hall. (The site is now occupied by the Manhattan approaches to the Brooklyn Bridge.) A five-story structure costing $55,000, it contained a large area (often referred to nostalgically as the Long Room) for social or political events that could hold up to two thousand braves; the rest of the building operated as a hotel. The Society was to occupy the building for fifty-five years, until a new structure was dedicated uptown on Fourteenth Street in 1867. For the first time, "Tammany Hall" meant a structure that was readily identifiable.

Davis had thus not only changed Tammany but burnished its image with a fine new building. He was riding high. De Witt Clinton, however, remained a thorn in his side. In 1810 the Federalist party, in an unlikely resurgence of power, briefly recaptured control of the state legislature. Tammany plotted circuitously with its leaders to have the Council on Appointment remove Clinton from the mayoralty. The move succeeded, but Clinton was only temporarily sidetracked. Out of office for the first time in more than a decade, he began marshaling support for the huge project that would later become his own triumph, the Erie Canal that led across New York State from Albany to Buffalo. The idea had not originated with Clinton, but from now on he was its principal (and highly energetic) sponsor. Tammany, at this state, opposed the entire scheme, which it said was simply a vehicle for Clinton's personal advancement and would bankrupt the state. The following year the Republicans won back the legislature and Clinton returned to City Hall.

The War of 1812 found Tammany at its most patriotic, zealously supporting President Madison and condemning all those who harbored doubts about the conflict. The Society had to make its own adjustments: marching in American Indian costume was abandoned because of bad feelings toward Indians, and even using Indian titles was shelved for the duration (sachems and wiskinskies came back after hostilities concluded). De Witt Clinton, who was less than enthusiastic about the war, ran for president against Madison and even carried New York State, but Madison won enough other states to take the election and subsequently rewarded his Tammany allies with a number of high appointments (John Swartwout and his brother Robert both became generals) and lucrative government contracts. Davis, though declining public office, profited hugely as a businessman. Among other things he purchased government bonds directly from the Treasury Department at a discount and sold them to the public at a large markup. But he also became involved in a conspiracy to raise the price of goods purchased by the army. Such questionable exploits took much of his time; more important, they disenchanted many of his erstwhile political followers, who were not quite as ready to tolerate graft in a top Tammany leader as later members of the Hall would be. As a result, Davis lost influence in the Society and its control now passed to others, although no strong leader would emerge for a number of years. Davis's great days of political power, despite his sizable contributions to Tammany's fortunes, were at an end.

But Tammany Hall's influence was stronger than ever. During the war a number of prominent Federalists, disgusted by their party's opposition to the hostilities, came over to join the Society. In 1815, with the war over and the Democratic-Republicans firmly ensconced in the legislature, Tammany persuaded the Council of Appointment to remove Clinton once and for all from the mayoralty, and to appoint in his stead the Society's Grand Sachem, John Ferguson, who thereby became the first Tammany mayor of New York. A faithful Tammanyite, Ferguson was true to his calling: removing Clintonian city jobholders in wholesale fashion, he replaced them with loyal Tammany ward heelers. Thus was the dispensing of patronage (and the edging out of opponents' officeholders en masse) firmly established as a Tammany tradition.

Tammany had come a long way in a quarter of a century. The innocently nonpartisan social club had evolved, in a mere twenty-five years, into a sharply focused political force angling to steer the affairs of the largest city in the nation. But more changes were to come. The Society's—and the Hall's—membership had up to now been made up primarily of white Anglo-Saxon males who, although largely anti-aristocratic, were well enough off to own some property and thereby enabled to vote. Two new developments to take place over the next generation would have a marked effect. One was the arrival of universal male suffrage, which by greatly expanding the voter rolls would extend Tammany's reach to the great mass of poorer citizens. The other was the beginning of large-scale immigration to the United States, which would bring entirely new groups into Tammany's sphere—most notably the Irish, whom up to now the Society had regarded with suspicion and distaste.

2

GROWING PAINS

ON APRIL 24, 1817, AN EVENT OCCURRED IN Tammany Hall's Wigwam that seems particularly surprising today in view of the organization's later reputation as a bastion of Irish Roman Catholics. A group purporting to represent New York City's Irish Catholic voters, irked by Tammany's refusal to give Irish Catholics proper representation among the party's nominees for public office in an upcoming election, broke into a meeting of the Hall's General Committee and demanded to be recognized. The group had a candidate for Congress, the Irish-born orator Thomas Addis Emmett, a lawyer of note in the city and brother of the Irish revolutionary leader Robert Emmett. It had previously asked Tammany to endorse Emmett because the Hall's political clout virtually guaranteed success at the polls. But the Tammany leaders rejected Emmett not just because he was a friend of their archenemy, former mayor De Witt Clinton, but because they suspected most Irish of being less than one hundred percent American patriots. When the insurgents, having marched into the Wigwam on the appointed evening, were refused recognition they exploded. As Tammany historian Gustavus Myers put it, "Eyes were blackened, noses and heads battered freely. The invaders broke the furniture, using it for weapons and shattering it maliciously; tore down the fixtures and shivered the windows. Reinforcements arriving, the intruders were driven out, but not before nearly all present had been bruised and beaten."[1] The Irish had given notice, and although Emmett failed in his bid for office the shaken Tammany sachems were moved to question their traditional anti-immigrant stance. The Society and its political arm, Tammany Hall, would never be the same again.

During its early years, the Society had been a strictly one hundred percent American organization. Its rigidity was reflected in its constitution, which provided that "No person shall be eligible to the office of Sachem, unless a native of this country." Not until 1809 could the Society bring itself to back an Irish New Yorker for public office; he was Patrick McKay, a candidate for the state assembly. But that was as far as the sachems were willing to go at the time, and they certainly did not accept McKay as a member of the Society. But the Emmett affair forced them to ponder. Political realists, they began to see the perils of flouting such a formidable and growing block of potential voters, not to mention the potential electoral benefits to be had if one could establish a degree of control over the newcomers. Thus began a momentous shift in policy: Tammany began courting the newcomers.

That change was only one of many in the years between 1817 and the early 1840s that caused growing pains for Tammany Hall. Matthew Davis and his cohorts had made Tammany a political organism; the question now was, just what kind of political organism would it be? Who would control the Society and its political offshoot, Tammany Hall, and for whose benefit? The answer mattered because New York, already the most powerful city on the continent, was entering a boom period in which commerce was thriving and bringing in great wealth. The city's population, fed by increasing immigration from Europe (particularly from Ireland), was almost doubling every decade. Between 1820 and 1840, for instance, the city's population rose from 123,700 to 312,000, and by 1860 it would leap to an incredible 813,000. Whoever controlled the politics of the incipient colossus would reap great gains, not only in power but financially as well. Expanding northward up Manhattan island, New York seemed in a constant state of building and rebuilding. Tammany, too, was perforce almost constantly in the throes of rebuilding as it adjusted to the new realities. During the next decades it would be fought over, divided, and continually reshaped by forces and personalities intent on bending it to their will.

Up until now, politics in New York, as elsewhere, had been a gentleman's occupation, a calling dominated by the well-to-do merchants and the upper classes content to maintain the status quo. A key element of their defensive stance was the limitation of the right to vote to property owners. That would not suffice in the new era, however, with new groups of would-be voters—such as the emerging Irish population—demanding to be heard. Political life in New York City, already rough and ill-mannered, was becoming even more so, and Tammany Hall would be a leader among organizations endeavoring to control elections by illegal or forceful means. Although the great days of the Tammany bosses had not arrived, the Society was lurching in that direction. As the historian Leo Hershkowitz has written, "It was an era of experiment, of vociferous debate, of the raucous, rambunctious Young Americans, of tenuous party lines, and of flexible politics not yet hardened to machine-controlled regularity."[2]

One prominent member of the old elite who failed to see that politics were changing was De Witt Clinton. The former mayor left City Hall for the last time in 1815 but did not stay out of power very long. His painstaking work in marshaling support for the Erie Canal project finally paid off in 1817 when the state legislature authorized the start of construction on the waterway. Later that year a rejuvenated Clinton, age forty-eight, swept in as governor. Once again he was in a position to bedevil Tammany by steering the actions of the legislature's Council of Appointment to control patronage throughout the state.

But he found himself more and more annoyed and frustrated by what he considered Tammany's increasingly slick and unprincipled methods, techniques he felt were unacceptable in a decently run government. In 1819 he inveighed against what he deemed the sachems' secret tactics and their disregard for public opinion in a series of anonymous articles in a party newspaper. The articles, collectively titled "The Martling-Man" (a reference to Tammany's former meeting hall), were later published as a pamphlet. "I have attended round the door of this Nominating Committee," he wrote, "to try and learn something of what was going on. But none who were on the outside could tell me anything; and if any one of the committee by chance popped out, he always looked mysterious, put on his wise face, and said the proceedings were confidential. . . . Says I to myself, how is this? why not nominate in the old way, where we can all have a chance? . . . Why are the old Republicans kept out of the room until these grandees settle the affair, and then ask us all to come like humble slaves and vote them into office?"[3]

The answer was that the old way was out of date. Clinton, despite his many extraordinary accomplishments, represented a world that was disappearing, a world in which gentlemen felt they had a right to guide public affairs for the presumed benefit of all.

Among those who felt it was time for the political system to become more open was a young man from upstate, Martin Van Buren. An ally of Tammany Hall who would become a powerful player on the national political scene, Van Buren was a cagey operator who typified—if he did not actually pioneer—the new breed of professional politician, a person whose sole aim was to organize and direct political events. Van Buren would soon best the governor in a campaign of great significance to both the state and the city and to Tammany Hall itself: the battle to rewrite the state constitution and thereby expand the franchise. In doing so, and in his subsequent masterminding of Andrew Jackson's presidential campaign, he would become a key formative influence on Tammany.

Known as the Little Magician for his astonishing ability to work the most unexpected political deals, Van Buren was the son of a tavern keeper in Kinderhook, New York, not far from Albany. Instead of attending college he began working at age fourteen in the office of a local attorney, who taught him to dress nattily to impress clients. In 1801, not yet twenty-one years old, Van Buren came to New York City to practice law and immediately started winning cases. Short (five feet six inches) with reddish hair (he would also become known as the Red Fox), he liked to appear for work in white trousers, a snuff-colored broadcloth coat, pearl vest, and orange tie. His demeanor was unfailingly ingratiating and cheerful. His high forehead gave him somewhat of a resemblance to Aaron Burr, whom he admired and for whom he worked briefly. At the same time he became a member of Tammany. But he did not stay long in New York City. In 1803, after only two years, he moved back to Kinderhook, where he opened his own law practice. In no time he was enmeshed in local politics. In 1808 he was appointed county surrogate and in 1812, at the age of twenty-nine, he was elected to the state senate in Albany, where he rose rapidly to the leadership of the Democratic-Republican party in New York State. Opponents were often unaware he was plotting against them—one remarked that he had no idea Van Buren was not on his side until the votes were counted and he found that the Little Magician, a smile on his face, had vanquished him.

Throughout Van Buren's rise in politics his chief rival remained De Witt Clinton. Both had been recognized early on as gifted young Democratic-Republicans. But Clinton was contemptuous of party fealty and repeatedly crossed up members of his own party in order to advance his own political agenda. To Van Buren, that was a cardinal sin; party regularity was sacrosanct. For his part, the patrician Clinton believed that Van Buren and his ilk were degrading the political system.

One way to get around Clinton, Van Buren and his colleagues decided, was to change the rules of the game by altering the state's constitution. There had been agitation for some time by radicals both within Tammany Hall and elsewhere to amend the document to expand the right to vote, but Tammany's leaders were at first reluctant to back the idea; many of them were property owners themselves who benefited from the status quo that favored their continuance in power. Nevertheless the clamor could not be stayed, and Van Buren persuaded Tammany to join him in recommending a constitutional convention. For even if the right to vote was not widened, the new constitution could do away with the Clinton-dominated Council of Appointment and thus directly benefit the Hall.

In 1818 a Tammany legislator accordingly introduced a resolution calling for the convention. It passed, but Governor Clinton vetoed it. "I am in favor of a convention properly and fairly called," he said, "but not for one got up precipitately for bad purposes, under bad auspices, and with a view to shake society to its foundations in order to sustain bad men."[4] Much political maneuvering ensued, and the upshot was the decision to submit the convention resolution to a popular referendum. When the referendum was held early in 1821 the vote was so overwhelmingly in the affirmative that Clinton decided not to object. The resulting convention, held later that year with Van Buren calling the shots, not only abolished the Council of Appointment but to all intents and purposes introduced universal male suffrage in New York State. Any white male over twenty-one who had lived in his election district for six months and who had either paid property taxes, served in the militia, or worked on public roads could vote, as could black males if they held property. High state officers such as comptroller and state treasurer would be appointed by the legislature, while most lower positions, such as sheriff, would be elected directly by the people, a marked innovation. New York's mayor would no longer be appointed by the governor but at least for now would be chosen by the city council (a decade later the mayoralty would also become subject to popular vote).

News of the document's passage was greeted with rejoicing in New York City, and following its ratification by the voters in 1822, Tammany threw a large banquet in celebration. The sachems had good cause to raise a glass: the greatly widened suffrage meant a far bigger world for Tammany to operate in. And because New York City was growing at such a rapid rate compared with the rest of the state, Tammany's influence was bound to increase statewide.

Governor Clinton, temporarily set back, decided not to run for reelection in 1822. He would be returned to power in 1824 by a political fluke: some of Van Buren's colleagues in the state legislature misguidedly introduced a resolution removing Clinton from his one remaining post, that of unpaid member of the Canal Commission. The move seemed completely gratuitous since Clinton's name was closely bound up with the Canal project, and the ensuing public outcry was so great that he was swept back into office. The following year Clinton triumphantly presided over the canal's opening. He remained the state's chief executive until 1828 when, on February 11 of that year, he was stricken with a heart attack and died. His passing, though universally mourned, removed a prominent obstacle from Van Buren's path. From now on the Little Magician's influence went unchallenged in the state.

Van Buren's ideas about political organization were already having a decisive effect on his party statewide and on Tammany Hall in particular. Having been elected to the U.S. Senate in 1821 but desiring to retain control of the state Democratic-Republican party, Van Buren had summoned his aides and empowered them to act for him in his absence. It was their duty, he told them, to maintain party discipline and order. Except when back in Albany between sessions, he would advise them from Washington. So skilled were these men and so extensive was their influence that they first became known as Van Buren's cabal or the holy alliance, but after a while they came to be called the Albany Regency. Van Buren and his aides had a profound effect on the development of U.S. political parties, and it has often been said that they functioned as America's first true political machine.

Tremendously potent throughout the 1820s and still a strong force in the 1830s, the Regency influenced and even controlled Tammany policy on all federal and state issues, and even on some local ones. Its members usually made their desires known through an associate on the scene. Although the Tammany leaders might sometimes resent being dictated to from the outside, they went along with most of the directives because the potential rewards were great: control of all state and, in the event their party captured the White House, federal patronage. The day would come, decades hence, when Albany politicians would kowtow to Tammany. But during the 1820s and into the 1830s, Tammany Hall produced no dominant leader, so the Regency called the shots from upstate. The tutelage widened Tammany's horizons and had a lasting effect; the apparatus put in place by Matthew Davis was, under Van Buren's guidance, moving into an infinitely larger arena.

The Regency code, which sprang direct from the brow of the Little Magician, was rigorous. The party must be totally organized statewide from county committees all the way down to ward committees, with no blank spots; thus Tammany Hall, representing the party in New York City with its own array of ward committees, was but a single link (if a vital one) in an extended network. Party discipline was rigidly enforced and there were to be no backsliders; growled one Regency member when told of a group that threatened to provide only lukewarm support, "Tell them they are safe if they face the enemy, but that the first man we see step to the rear, we cut down."[5]

The reward that made up for all the drudgery and obedience was patronage, which was deemed a worthy exercise in its own right. The principle was summed up in an oft-quoted speech on the floor of the U.S. Senate by one of the Regency's most noted members, William L. Marcy. The speech, made in 1832, was in response to Henry Clay's criticism of President Andrew Jackson's appointment of Van Buren as minister to London. Marcy replied, "It may be that the politicians of New York are not so fastidious as some gentlemen are. They boldly preach what they practise. When they are contending for victory, they avow their intention of enjoying the fruits of it. If they fail, they will not murmur. If they win, they expect to reap all the advantages. They see nothing wrong in the rule, that to the victors belong the spoils of the enemy."[6] From these very words came the great pejorative phrase "the spoils system," which in later days became eternally associated with Tammany Hall and other boss-ridden political machines.

The culmination of everything Van Buren and the Regency embodied came in the election of 1828, in which the Little Magician directed the campaign that sent Andrew Jackson to the White House. Jackson had declared himself a candidate in 1824, but Van Buren, unsure of where the general stood on major issues, had favored another man, and the resulting split in the Democratic-Republican party sent John Quincy Adams to the White House. Four years later Van Buren resolved to unite the party behind a single strong candidate, and he was now satisfied that Jackson was that man. Van Buren

thereupon became Jackson's unofficial campaign manager. His work
was so successful that he ranks as perhaps the key architect of the
Jacksonian revolution and one of the principal founders of what now
became the Democratic party.

To bring off his triumph, however, he first had to make sure that
Tammany Hall was behind him, as control of the New York City vote
was vital. In September of 1827 he traveled to New York to persuade
the sachems to back the general—a task more difficult than expected.
He found Tammany's General Committee split, with a majority favoring Jackson but a determined minority holding out for John
Quincy Adams. The Adams men would not budge. So the Hall's
Jacksonians, assuring Van Buren that they would put matters aright,
decided to use force. At the ward primary elections in October they
seized the meeting rooms and controlled the agenda, preventing the
Adams forces from being heard. Retaliating a few days later, the Adams men found a way to lock the Jacksonians out of Tammany's
Long Room and proceeded to name a slate of local candidates favoring the president. Whereupon the Jacksonians retreated to a room in
the cellar known as the Coal Hole and approved a competing ticket of
their own men partial to Old Hickory.

That left matters to be decided in the November election that year,
which functioned as a kind of primary contest among the candidates.
It is not known who was in direct control of election activities in the
Hall at this time (possibly Van Buren guided them from afar, or at
least made recommendations to the local forces), but the 1827 election was the first in which Tammany resorted to outright fraud on a
large scale. It induced—and this was significant in view of their recently altered policy on immigrants—recent arrivals and other inter-
lopers to vote illegally. Such transgressions were easier in those days
because registration was highly inexact and all voting was in the open.
Ballots were preprinted, so a party worker need only hand a voter a
premarked printed ballot to be sure he voted correctly. Cartloads of
immigrants, many of whom had been in the United States less than
the time required for proper naturalization, were carried from ward to
ward to vote the straight pro-Jackson ticket over and over. One group
of six hirelings boasted that they had cast ballots at six different polling
places. Many voters who tried to vote for the Adams slate had their
ballots seized and replaced with Jackson tickets. Tammany guards
wielded stout hickory branches (connoting their partiality to the general) to discourage anyone from protesting. The dubious tactics
worked: the Jackson slate rolled up a handsome majority.

By the beginning of 1828 the Hall was totally under the control of the Jackson men, directed from afar by the Regency. During the presidential campaign the Little Magician used every tactic on the national scale that had ever worked locally in the past—parades, buttons, campaign songs, banners, press releases, handshaking tours— plus a few new ones. Banquets were held to commemorate the anniversary of Old Hickory's victory at New Orleans, and clubs were formed to plant hickory trees; in New York City the planters would conclude their ceremonies with a trip to the local barroom to toast the general's health. Van Buren adroitly supervised fund-raising, a new art on the political scene.

On election day the same suspect techniques that were used in the primary were trotted out by Tammany to shape the vote, but with two new wrinkles. One was using underage boys (nineteen and twenty years old) not just to electioneer but to add to the voting total. The other was handing out cash. In 1828, says the Tammany chronicler Gustavus Myers, "For the first time in city elections money was used to influence voting."[7] The election was a rout. Jackson easily defeated Adams.

The 1828 election represented the birth of the Democratic party as it is known today, but it also saw the beginnings of another grouping, a coalition of onetime Federalists and other anti-Democrats, led by Henry Clay, who called themselves National Republicans. Within a few years they would abandon that name and call themselves Whigs because they opposed what they saw as Andrew Jackson's tyranny (as pre-revolutionary Whigs had opposed George III of Britain). For the next quarter of a century, the Whigs constituted the main party vying with the Democrats both in New York City and nationally.

For Tammany Hall, the election represented the final working out of the policy shift brought about by the Emmett affair more than a decade earlier. It was Tammany's first full-scale effort to enlist in its cause the many thousands of immigrants now flooding into the city. By 1828 the sachems had abandoned all hostility to foreigners, seeing them now as a handy means of increasing the Hall's power base. Moreover, they were prepared to cultivate them in a variety of ways. Immigrants would be met at the dock, given assistance in finding lodging, tutored in United States customs and in the requirements for filling out naturalization forms, provided with jobs (especially in the city government), and hustled through the citizenship mill. Eventually, having been duly proclaimed as citizens (or before), they would be shepherded to the polls on election day where they could return

Tammany's kindnesses. Especially prominent among the arriving immigrants in New York (as well as in other cities) were the Irish, closely followed by the Germans. Although the Germans were only moderately concerned with political matters, the Irish had a talent for politicking honed through generations of opposing the British back home. Recently arrived Irishmen were soon to become a major force in Tammany affairs, and the corner saloon, where many of them liked to pass the time of day (or night), began to serve as a favored meeting place for politicians.

Without question, many immigrants willingly took part in some of the unscrupulous tactics now adopted by Tammany and other political groups. Tammany was especially adept at getting the inmates of New York's almshouse, the majority of whom were Irish, to the polls. As one account put it, "The morning of the election was a busy time at the Alms House. Officers hurrying to and fro—getting together inmates of the establishment, clad in their new [clothes]—distributing to them tickets to vote and tickets for grog—putting into their hands nice pieces of silver coin, that they might solace themselves after the arduous labor of depositing their ballots."[8] Such irregularities, to be sure, did not escape the notice of the general public. While there was no well-defined reform movement to oppose Tammany deeds just yet, there were indications of growing resentment on the part of native New Yorkers toward the newcomers. By the 1827 and 1828 elections, the first signs of organized nativism appeared in the city, whereby American-born citizens began talking about limiting the rights of the newly arrived.

Another innovation of the 1828 election was the Jackson administration's wholesale adoption of the spoils system, four years before Marcy uttered his famous lines. Jobs at every level changed hands, and in New York City the Tammany chiefs were given the pick of the appointments. They proceeded to exercise their rights to the full, supplanting large numbers of incumbents. No apologies were forthcoming: this was the reward they had awaited so long at the behest of Van Buren and the Regency men. When asked about what was going on, the Little Magician replied, "We give no reasons for our removals."[9] He himself, after putting in a short stint as state governor in the early months of 1829, advanced swiftly, becoming Jackson's secretary of state and serving as one of Old Hickory's chief advisers. From such an exalted position it was difficult for him to maintain his close watch on New York politics, and from this point on his connection to Tammany grew remote. The Regency, however, continued to influence the Hall.

The 1828 election has come down in history as the triumph of the Jacksonian revolution, supposedly a reaffirmation of the principles enunciated by Thomas Jefferson but with broader opportunities for the common people. Just how this would be put into practice was a question that now moved to center stage and directly challenged Tammany to its core, even as it luxuriated in all its newfound power and influence.

For the Hall itself remained anything but democratic. In spite of its espousal of the rights of man and its talk about befriending the lowly, it had always been controlled by men with money. A great many of them had joined the organization because it could show the way to amassing wealth. A well-placed and well-heeled—even law-abiding— Tammany member might have the inside track on all sorts of municipal projects and other lucrative schemes. The less affluent Tammany-ites had nothing against opportunity as a general principle, but some of them began noticing that it was the rich members who became sachems and directed the policies of the organization. These leaders also tended to stifle debate and brooked no dissension from their edicts. As the historian Jerome Mushkat has observed, "The Hall operated as if the popular will set party policy while in reality the organization did little more than follow the wishes of a small, wealthy clique."[10] That clique was made up of well-to-do merchants, bankers, and lawyers.

More to the point, these men were constantly persuading the state legislature not only to grant them monopoly city franchises of one sort or another, which brought no financial benefit to the city as a whole, but to grant them charters for new banks, an arrangement resented by many members within Tammany itself, as well as by many of New York's working population, who mistrusted banks and thought there should be fewer rather than more of them. For banks, instead of circulating old-fashioned coinage (which had a nice solid ring to it), liked to issue paper money; businesses would then pay their workers in paper, which always seemed to depreciate. So the rich were getting richer while the workers felt they were getting no-where—and Tammany seemed to be a major cause of the problem. Workers also objected to the age-old custom of imprisonment for debt, which they claimed hurt the poor far more than the rich, and to the swindling of mechanics and other workmen by contractors who would erect buildings, get paid for them, and then vanish without paying their laborers. A group of less well-off Hall members resolved to fight these inequities, and the resulting struggle absorbed the Hall's attention off and on for the next decade, until the early 1840s.

Into this discordant situation stepped a number of reform-minded radicals: Frances Wright, an eloquent and fiery spokesperson for the emancipation of women and sexual freedom; Thomas Skidmore, an imperious New Yorker who had written a book entitled *The Right of Man to Property!* that advocated an end to private land ownership; and Robert Dale Owen, whose newspaper, the *Free Enquirer*, urged free, universal education. Soon some of Tammany's own discontented were talking to the three reformers, and together, in October 1829, they formed an alliance called the Workingmen's party. It issued a broadside condemning inherited wealth, the unequal distribution of property, chartered monopolies, banking privileges, and imprisonment for debtors. It also endorsed Owen's educational ideas. Bankers were branded "the greatest knaves, imposters and paupers of the age,"[11] and the banking system was criticized because its encouragement of speculation "leads to intemperance and despair."[12]

If the Workingmen's party had limited its activity to the spoken and written word, Tammany's leaders would have had little cause for alarm. But the group proceeded to run a full ticket of candidates in that year's November elections for the City Council. Instantly, the Hall's leadership opened a campaign of abuse denouncing the new party, and a substantial number of New York's merchants and bankers joined the sachems in the attack. But when the votes were counted it was discovered that the Workingmen had not only drawn six thousand votes to Tammany's eleven thousand, a dangerously high proportion of the normal Democratic showing, but had prevented the Wigwam from dominating the Council as it customarily did.

The sachems were seriously concerned. Clearly it was necessary to do something to turn the threat aside. Accordingly, they secured passage through the City Council of a mechanics' lien law, which required the owner of a building to withhold from his payments to a contractor the money that would be due the laborers on the project, who thus would be guaranteed their wages even if the contractor skipped responsibility. They also introduced legislation to abolish imprisonment for debt and persuaded a number of bankers in the city to relax their credit requirements so as to enable more workers to obtain loans. But they rejected the Workingmen's more general assertions that all wealthy citizens were to be denounced; rich and poor should work together, they intoned, for the common good. The following year the Workingmen again fielded a full ticket of candidates for the City Council, but this time they polled only half as many votes as in 1829. The losses split the party into a number of factions, and within a few months it went into eclipse. Some of the rebels hived off to join the new National Republican (Whig) party, but most returned to the Hall. The issues the Workingmen had raised, however, could not be so quickly dismissed. Despite the concessions that Tammany had made to them, the discord they introduced into the Hall remained strong. Tammany still seemed to be run largely for the benefit of the wealthy.

Two years later, in 1832, the Hall entered enthusiastically into the campaign to reelect Andrew Jackson. The sachems' zeal for Old Hickory was not without a certain irony, however, for the conflict within the Society's ranks had not been resolved: a surprisingly large number of prominent Tammany members disagreed (if privately) with the administration on one of the major issues of the campaign—Jackson's determination to kill the Bank of the United States. And when some of them turned out to have been financially beholden to the Bank, the revelation, by reopening the difficult question of where Tammany stood on favoritism to the rich, proved embarrassing to the Hall in no small degree.

The Bank—technically the Second Bank of the United States—had been founded more than a decade earlier by Congress to succeed the First Bank of the United States, which had been created by Alexander Hamilton as a central depository of capital funds for the young country. The idea of a central bank, today embodied in the universally accepted Federal Reserve system, was highly controversial in the early years of the country: Federalists claimed it was vital to the country's economic future, but Jeffersonian Republicans insisted it was undemocratic, unconstitutional, and a threat to liberty. The First Bank went out of existence in 1811 during Madison's presidency, but economic chaos during the War of 1812 revived the idea, and in 1816 Congress authorized the Second Bank, which, like its predecessor, was headquartered in Philadelphia. Although in theory it had been acknowledged as essential to the United States, it was still controversial. Among those who detested it, none brought to the subject as much venom as Jackson; indeed, as a product of the rural southeastern United States he suspected all banks (since their interests seemed to favor merchants and other city groups over farmers) and felt they wielded far too much power.

During the summer of 1832, just as the presidential campaign was getting under way, Congress, acting under the strong influence of Jackson's archenemy Henry Clay, voted to extend the Bank's charter, and Jackson, in a dramatic move, vetoed the bill. The campaign was suddenly in an uproar. And nowhere did the clamor reverberate more acutely than in Tammany Hall. Some months previously, a congressional investigation had revealed that the Bank's president, Nicholas Biddle, who had resolved to fight Jackson for his institution's survival, had made "loans" (that is, bribes) totaling $50,000 to the owners of the *Courier and Enquirer*, an outwardly pro-Tammany newspaper edited by Mordecai Noah, a sometime sachem of the Society, and James Watson Webb. Biddle's object was to persuade the paper to stop backing Jackson and to come out in support of the Bank and the anti-Jackson candidates. And so it did, citing the "fearful consequences of revolution, anarchy and despotism" that would ensue if the president were returned to office.[13] The unmasking of Biddle's act, although it did not deter Congress from renewing the Bank's charter, was decidedly bad for his cause, and he was accused not only of attempting to bribe the editors but of plotting to subvert the nation's free press. And since the *Courier and Enquirer*'s editor, Noah, was a Tammany sachem, this did not make the Hall look good.

Hard on the heels of the revelation came the report that quite a large number of other Tammanyites had also been the beneficiaries of Biddle's largesse. Congressman Churchill C. Cambreleng, for example, a key member of the Albany Regency and Van Buren's personal representative in Tammany's power structure, turned out to have received payments from the Bank for supporting its cause on Capitol Hill, as had another New York representative and Tammanyite, Gulian Verplanck.

Moving to repair the damage, the Tammany Society and the Hall's General Committee issued statements reiterating and strengthening their endorsement of Jackson and his anti-Bank policy. They also severed their ties to the *Courier and Enquirer*, ceasing to recognize it as an official party organ. The sachems renewed their backing of the Jacksonian ticket despite the pro-Bank feelings of so many of their members partly because many other members were officers of New York State banks, who reasoned that in the absence of the Bank of the United States the government's deposits might be transferred to their own institutions. When the president vetoed the Bank charter bill, Tammany's Jacksonians staged an enormous rally in celebration.

The Hall had further cause for rejoicing because of what happened to its friend in Washington, Martin Van Buren. In 1831 Jackson appointed Van Buren minister to England. Vice-President John Calhoun, jealous of the Little Magician's rising power, suspected Van Buren was plotting to become Old Hickory's heir apparent and decided to block his confirmation in the Senate. When the voting resulted in a tie, Calhoun, as presiding officer, cast his vote in opposition, defeating the nomination. He was jubilant. "It will kill him, sir," he was heard to remark, "kill him dead."[14] Jackson naturally was enraged. Far off in London Van Buren, who had moved there immediately after his appointment, was not bothered when he got the news. "It is an advantage to a public man," he said, "to be the subject of an outrage." In the United States the press attacked Calhoun for his vindictiveness. Senator Thomas Hart Benton commented to a colleague, "You have broken a minister, and elected a Vice President."[15] And so it was. Jackson formally chose Van Buren as his running mate in 1832, replacing Calhoun, and in 1836, after Jackson's second term was up, the Little Magician moved on to the White House—the first machine politician in U.S. history to do so.

If anything, Jackson's bank veto had increased his nationwide popularity coming into the 1832 election. The campaigning was boisterous. In New York, Tammany held rallies almost daily in and around the Wigwam, and on October 30 the sachems, in a jubilant ceremony, planted a hickory tree out front, moistening its roots with a barrel of beer. On election day both sides were guilty of fraud, although this time the Whigs, with Henry Clay at the top of the ticket, outdid Tammany, buying votes for $5 apiece and managing to distribute faulty Jackson tickets to Tammany supporters that were designed to be invalidated. The trick cost Jackson an estimated one thousand votes, but he carried the city anyway by a majority of 5,620. For several nights thereafter, the Wigwam rang to the sounds of alcoholic rejoicing. And soon afterward Jackson withdrew the government's funds from the Bank of the United States (depositing them largely in state banks as the Tammanyites had hoped), and the Bank gradually withered.

When a local election the following year (1833) produced more irregularities, a committee of assistant aldermen (members of the City Council) was appointed to investigate. Not surprisingly, several members of the committee were connected to Tammany. Its report expressed the appropriate degree of dismay. "That frauds have been practised at the polls, the committee are convinced," it proclaimed.

"At any rate, a universal and deep conviction prevails among our citizens that tricks have been resorted to for the purpose of defeating the election of one candidate and securing that of another."[16] It also noted that many persons were allowed to vote who were not citizens and that many voted more than once. The tone of righteousness was not followed by any remedy, however—the aldermen, after all, were part of the system they were supposedly excoriating—and the city went on to experience the grim local election in the spring of 1834, which set a new low and presaged the many fraudulent contests that Tammany would dominate in the next half a century.

What made the 1834 election special was that it was the first to give New Yorkers the chance to choose a mayor by popular ballot. All signs indicated a close contest. Tammany Hall, staunchly supporting Jackson, had decided not to renominate the current mayor, a banker (and Tammany sachem) named Gideon Lee, as he had been partial to the Bank of the United States. Instead, it was running a genial politico named Cornelius Lawrence. The Whig party, although a minority in the city, fielded a strong candidate in opposition, the widely respected Gulian Verplanck, who had defected from Tammany ranks.

Balloting was to take three days, and despite a heavy rain on the first day, April 8, the turnout was large from the moment the polls opened. As an observer later wrote, "To such a fever heat had the public feeling been carried, that no one seemed to heed the storm. . . . The stores were closed, business of all kinds suspended. . . . Men stood in long lines, extending clear out into the street, patiently enduring the pelting rain, waiting till their turn came to vote."[17] Many of them, however, found they were prevented from actually voting, for in many precincts Tammany had posted hefty guards at the main doors to the polls who barred entry to everyone—approved voters were hustled in via a backdoor and allowed to cast their ballots. In heavily pro-Tammany districts these tactics drew few objections, but in the Sixth Ward, already known as the Bloody Sixth for its potentially divisive racial mix, its squalid tenements, and its profusion of gangs, the Whigs decided to protest. During the day, they established themselves there in force. Not to be outmaneuvered, a band of Tammany toughs armed with clubs and knives broke into the Whig command post and fell upon its occupants, severely wounding many of them and stabbing one to death. Having laid waste their opponents, they wrecked the premises, tearing down banners, destroying ballots, and smashing furniture.

The following day the Whigs, bent on revenge, gathered in force at their headquarters in Masonic Hall. When Tammanyites attacked one of their campaign floats as it passed the building, they rushed out and gave battle, whereupon a far larger crowd arrived and turned the tide against them. The lame-duck mayor, Gideon Lee, arrived and, standing on the steps of the hall, tried to restore order; he was pelted with stones and staggered back. Soon the surrounding streets were awash with people slugging each other and yelling. A rumor suddenly went the rounds that the mob might attempt to storm the state arsenal at Franklin and Elm streets and help themselves to its weapons, and a group of rioters did set off toward it; but a posse of Whigs beat them to it and held them off. Eventually an infantry detachment and two cavalry squadrons, swords bristling, arrived in response to the mayor's plea and dispersed the crowds. The military also moved in to guard the polls and ballot boxes, and when the polls closed on the third day the Sixth Ward's ballot box was taken under guard to City Hall and locked up. Late that evening, as crowds milled around the streets, it was announced that the Tammany stalwart, Lawrence, had squeaked through with a slight plurality although the Whigs had captured a majority on the City Council.

Such hard-won electoral victories made satisfactory headlines and bolstered the image of Tammany as a potent force. But the outward show of power concealed the divisions that still plagued the organization. Within the Hall itself and in the day-to-day business that occupied it when elections were imminent—procuring jobs for the faithful, tending to citizens' needs, lobbying for favorable legislation in the City Council as well as in Albany—there were still signs of discord. Little had been done to remove or quell the dissension that had given rise to the briefly lived Workingmen's party. In 1833 resentment against the more privileged members of the Hall worsened when Tammany legislators in Albany succeeded temporarily in amending a recently passed and much-touted bill outlawing imprisonment for debt. The amendment reinstituted imprisonment for debts under $50—an obvious blow to the poor, whose debts were often under that minimum but large enough to warrant prosecution. Once again, the poor would be suffering while the rich would not be. The bill did not actually become law, but the bad feeling remained. Many other ills that the Workingmen had noted went unalleviated, such as the sachems' refusal to give ordinary members any voice in the Hall's doings.

It was also becoming clear to many rank-and-file Tammanyites that the organization's higher-ups were increasingly involved in all sorts of unsavory schemes to line their own pockets without benefiting the Hall or anyone else. In 1831, when the Harlem Railroad Company applied to the city for an exclusive franchise to use Fourth Avenue for its trains free of charge, the request was denounced by only one member of the City Council, Alderman George Sharp, who said it constituted an unnecessary giveaway, as all franchises should be paid for; he was given word that Tammany Hall would read him out of the party if he persisted. In 1833, a state investigating committee found that the Seventh Ward Bank, which had recently been founded with Tammany's backing, had distributed thousands of shares of its stock among more than a hundred state and city officeholders, including a large number of Tammanyites; every Tammany member of the legislature had been on the take. Such revelations served to turn up the heat within Tammany's ranks.

So it was that in 1834, after the bitter spring election, the Hall split once again when a group of Tammany dissidents founded the Equal Rights party, a well-organized revival of the Workingmen's movement but with a much bigger base. Besides laborers and artisans, the new group attracted small businessmen, professionals, and many other educated members of society. It advocated the equal right of every citizen to own and manage property, the abolition of bank notes as a circulating medium (they would be replaced by coins), and the doing away with all monopolies (as in transit franchises) created by legislation.

Early the following year, the group attracted widespread attention for its tactics. A meeting had been called at the Wigwam to discuss the granting of ferry franchises between New York and Brooklyn. An organization known as the Peaconic Company had for years possessed the only franchise for the route. The City Council, dominated by members with landholding interests (and Tammany backing) who did not want to encourage people to leave Manhattan for Brooklyn where rents were lower, had just extended the franchise. The Equal Rights spokesmen pointed out that both cities were growing rapidly and so should get the benefit of competing franchises, and they backed a plan to give all franchising power to a state board of commissioners, which would likely grant new routes. When Tammany's leaders tried to smother the plan at the franchise meeting, the Equal Righters howled down the Hall's spokesmen and took over, running the meeting to suit their own purposes and adopting resolutions favoring a board. Later in the year the state legislature bowed to their logic and created the new body, which soon granted a second ferry route.

By the fall of 1835, the Equal Rights party, emboldened by its victory earlier in the year, decided to prevent Tammany's conservatives from nominating a slate of local candidates whose views were not acceptable to them. The Hall's official nominating committee had called a meeting for October 29 to ratify its slate. When the Equal Righters arrived at the Wigwam, they found the conservatives had gotten there early and packed the Long Room with their supporters, and were in the process of endorsing their ticket. The insurgents demanded to be heard, and upon being ruled out of order stormed the dais, took over the meeting, and, amid much shouting and catcalls, ejected the conservatives. Out on the street, the conservatives retreated to a nearby tavern to complete their nominations, but one of their group stole back into the Hall, went to the basement and turned off the gas, plunging the Long Room into darkness.

The insurgents were ready for that. Suspecting that something of the sort might be attempted, they had come equipped with a supply of loco-focos, a new kind of self-igniting match, and plenty of candles. In no time at all the place was ablaze with twinkling lights. The meeting was again called to order and a slate of candidates partial to Equal Rights tenets was quickly voted, each name greeted with cheers. To another round of hurrahs, the party adopted a platform that called for an end to exclusive privilege and chartered monopolies, approved Jackson's actions against the Bank of the United States, and endorsed his denunciation of "shinplaster" paper money. Finally, the triumphant group marched out of the Wigwam and, with flags flying and torches held high, paraded through the streets. As news of their meeting spread through the city in the next few days they were dubbed the Loco-Focos.

The revolt thus far seemed outwardly to be merely an echo of the Workingmen's movement. But this challenge was different. In the years since the Workingmen's movement dissolved, there had been no real changes from Tammany higher-ups, and so the anger among the rank and file was keener. The Loco-Focos had better leadership, including the trade-union official and congressman Ely Moore, and Van Buren's old friend Congressman Churchill Cambreleng. They also had the solid backing of the influential New York *Evening Post*, whose editor, William Leggett, became a persuasive apologist for their program.

Events also underscored the urgency of the Loco-Focos' program. During these years, New York City was undergoing rapid expansion and unheralded prosperity stemming from its commanding role as the nation's number one port. But the increasing inflow of immigrants brought on housing shortages and other ills, contributing to the development of slums, where many of the newcomers were congregated. All of this lent even greater urgency to the Loco-Focos' demands. Then in December 1835 a terrible fire gutted much of lower New York, destroying $20 million worth of property and rendering large numbers of people homeless. The response of the City Council, again dominated by Tammany Hall, was almost insulting to the poor. It authorized loans totaling $6 million at 5 percent to banks and insurance companies hurt by the fire. After all, they reasoned, these institutions were the cornerstones of the city's financial solidity and warranted swift recompense. Nothing was done for poor people who had suffered so egregiously. True, at Christmastime Tammany ward leaders distributed firewood, clothing, food baskets, and money to the hard-pressed in their neighborhoods—the start of a great tradition for which the Hall would become famous—but it was hardly an adequate response. Officialdom, abetted by Tammany, was again turning its back on the city's poor.

Seething over the city's and Tammany's response to the fire, the Loco-Focos sought help and reassurance elsewhere, specifically from Tammany's presumed friend in high office, Martin Van Buren. After Van Buren was nominated for the presidency in 1836, the Loco-Focos challenged him to comment on the Declaration of Principles they had adopted. But the Little Magician had other things on his mind now. When he replied with evasive generalities they were incensed, and they showed their irritation by naming candidates for public office throughout New York State; in New York City they fielded a full ticket for the November election. When the votes were counted it was learned that Tammany had taken a licking, and that many Equal Rights candidates had triumphed. Van Buren barely carried the city, with a margin of only 1,124 votes, although he won nationally.

On top of this came the Panic of 1837, a severe downturn caused partly by the failure of many businesses despite the City Council's first aid measures following the 1835 fire. The city was filled with the unemployed and the homeless. Early in February an incident occurred that gave further pause to the city fathers and Tammany. A mass meeting in City Hall Park had been called by the Loco-Focos to protest what were considered undue profits by bankers and merchants at the expense of workingmen and shopkeepers, and a large crowd assembled. The rally started with a long and erudite address by a

Loco-Foco speaker on the subject of hard and soft money, causing the crowd to murmur restlessly. But then another speaker mounted the platform and accused local flour merchants of hoarding. "Go to the flour stores and offer a fair price," he said, "and if refused, take the flour."[18] At this, someone yelled, "To Hart's flour store!" and some two hundred persons broke away from the crowd and surged toward the warehouse of Eli Hart & Company on Washington Street, just a few blocks from the park. As the Hart employees stood by helplessly, the crowd battered down the doors, seized nearly five hundred barrels of flour and one thousand bushels of wheat and, heaving or rolling them out of the building, emptied them in the street, where others gathered up the contents and made off with them. Nearby a similar establishment was also ransacked until the police arrived to restore order.

Now genuinely worried, Tammany's sachems realized that the deeply entrenched divisions within the Society could not persist without destroying the Hall itself. Many of the sachems felt that the organization's future probably lay more with the Loco-Focos than with their opponents; but before they had an opportunity to move toward a resolution, another bomb dropped. Martin Van Buren, who was now president, announced that in an attempt to restore the economy he was transferring the federal government's funds from the state banks, where they had lain for several years, to federal subtreasuries in key cities. The conservatives within Tammany, its banker members who had been prospering from their custody of the federal deposits, howled in disapproval. When the sachems and the Hall's General Committee voted to back the president, the conservatives succeeded in derailing the action by means of parliamentary maneuvering. Tammany seemed more deeply divided than ever.

Seeing an opportunity to mediate, a group of Tammany moderates known as the Democratic-Republican Young Men's Committee seized the initiative and proposed a compromise. The Loco-Focos, they said, stood for the principles that would best assure long-run success for the Democratic party; Tammany Hall would lose all its influence if it turned its back on them. At a general meeting at the Wigwam in September 1837, the committee declared itself in general agreement with the thrust of the Loco-Foco Declaration of Rights and with Van Buren's decision. The conservatives were clearly in the minority now. Throughout the fall a solid block of support was building behind the more moderate proposals of the committee, with the result that by the turn of the year the Tammany sachems put the full weight of their support behind the moderates, thereby, in effect, rejecting the conservatives. Furious, the conservatives resigned from Tammany en masse—and did not return. The Loco-Focos, relieved that their ideas had been accepted by the Tammany power structure, promptly voted to dissolve their party and return to the Hall. The nasty, destructive fight was over. In a contest between the banking interests of Tammany's more moneyed members and those of the people at large, the people had won out.

Although the discord within the Hall had been dispelled, Tammany still operated as ruthlessly as ever at election time. In the 1838 election for state governor, fraud by both parties was widespread, though actually the Whigs taught the Democrats some new tricks. Not only did Whig ward leaders pay directly for votes at the polling places, but the party imported voters wholesale from Philadelphia at $22 a head and painstakingly instructed them on the proper casting of ballots. Ships tied up along the wharves were scoured for potential voters, legally eligible or not, who were rushed to the polls. Inmates of the House of Detention were set loose for the day to vote the Whig ticket and ex-convicts were hired to distribute party literature. A tremendous amount of money was spent, but the ruses worked. The Whigs carried the day, sending their man William Seward to Albany to dislodge, at long last, Van Buren's old friend, William L. Marcy, from the governorship.

Nor had the absorption of the Loco-Focos' idealistic beliefs made any change in the seemingly inevitable tendency of Tammany operatives to get involved in unsavory attempts to fleece the city or the federal government. Indeed, the phenomenon would keep resurfacing throughout Tammany's history, reflecting perhaps the natural tendency of inventive (or at least unscrupulous) politicians to seek out money-making opportunities in the corridors of power. This time—in 1839—the culprit was the former collector of the Port of New York, Samuel Swartwout, the third of the brothers who had been originally allied with Aaron Burr (another brother, Robert, had been caught a few years earlier siphoning government funds). When Andrew Jackson appointed Samuel Swartwout to the collector's post in 1829, Van Buren warned Old Hickory that the man might not be totally trustworthy, but Jackson went ahead anyway. It was not long before Van Buren's concerns proved justified. Swartwout found speculation irresistible. In 1833, after a group of merchants refused to loan him $7,000 on the strength of his interest in some questionable real estate holdings in New Jersey (part of the so-called Jersey Meadows, then considered of little value), he issued an ultimatum: pay up or I will move the custom house uptown to a location less convenient to you. They maintained their refusal, and he did not carry out his threat. Three years later he was known to be involved in a less than ethical attempt to corner the stock of the Harlem Railroad, and he also participated in the manipulation of Commercial Bank funds.

But these acts paled next to discoveries made after he departed the collector's office in 1838. Because his accounts there did not seem quite in order, an investigation was launched, and before long it was revealed that from the very first months after his appointment he had been "borrowing" substantial sums from the government and manipulating customhouse receipts to hide his transactions. He was found to be deeply involved in land speculations in Texas. The total amount that had somehow disappeared came to nearly $1,250,000, a mind-boggling sum in those days. (Multiply it by twenty to arrive at a roughly comparable figure today.) By the time the news came out, Swartwout had fled to England, allegedly to see about selling some coal and iron holdings in those parts. In the words of the Tammany historian Gustavus Myers, "The community was so impressed with the size of this defalcation that a verb, 'to Swartwout,' was coined, remaining in general use for many years thereafter. A defaulter was generally spoken of as having 'Swartwouted.' "[19] Myers adds that several years after Swartwout's flight an American met up with him in Algiers and reported that Swartwout had cried like a child over his enforced absence from his homeland. Oddly enough, his transgression gave a black eye not only to Tammany but to the Whigs as well, as Swartwout (for reasons that are not clear) had switched over to that party just a short while before he was found out.

But the opportunities available to collectors were evidently quite seductive to anyone in the post. Swartwout's successor, a Tammany sachem named Jesse Hoyt, was soon found to have defaulted to the tune of $30,000 in dealings with Wall Street brokers. Had he not been caught, he might have been well on his way to emulating Swartwout's monster achievement.

All these unsavory feats had been financial. What would happen when one person, or group, tried manipulating Tammany's power for outright political gain? That power was well worth cultivating, because by 1840 the Hall was a very different organization from what it had been a quarter of a century earlier. No longer select in its membership, it was reaching out to the vast numbers of newcomers crowding the New York docks and welcoming them; no longer confining its appeal to an electorate of limited size, it was amassing strength from the far larger base of voters made possible by universal male suffrage; no longer directed by businessmen who operated it as a sideline, it was coming under the sway of full-time politicians who modeled themselves after the likes of Martin Van Buren; no longer deeming itself an agency for the betterment of bankers and merchants (though they would continue to wield some influence within it), the Hall had placed itself solidly in the camp of the middle and lower classes. The organization's most visible activity, running campaigns and winning elections, was becoming rougher and more unprincipled all the time.

The answer to the question of what might happen when a strong individual took over the Hall and shaped it to his ends was not long in coming. As it happened, the chairman of the Tammany Young Men's General Committee, which had led the way in patching up the Hall's wounds, was a young and ambitious businessman named Fernando Wood. In due course, he would show the city what could be done.

3

FERNANDO

NO ONE COULD EVER QUITE FIGURE OUT WHAT TO make of Fernando Wood. Some were awed by the ease with which he commanded the office of mayor of New York; a few close followers adored him for his flamboyance and seeming commitment to civic betterment; but many more New Yorkers regarded him with loathing as a liar and demagogue. Certainly it was impossible to be neutral about the man. One observer called him a "brilliant desperado,"[1] and Wood was undoubtedly as wily and deceitful a political manipulator as ever rose from the ranks of Tammany Hall. Another remarked, "I have seldom seen a more passionless individual than Wood. . . . Nothing seems to move him and he appears as if nothing could. His cold, sardonic smile . . . tells of a soul apparently uninfluenced by the common impulses of humanity."[2]

Yet this elusive individual, who has been called New York's first modern mayor, played a crucial role in the development of the Tammany machine. Unlike Aaron Burr and Martin Van Buren, who maneuvered the organization from the outside, Wood was the first strong citywide leader produced by Tammany itself. And while he was not a true boss in the sense of having unequivocal power, he laid all the essential groundwork for the predatory giants, Tweed and Croker, who soon followed. Although Wood ultimately failed in his attempt to unify and dominate the Hall, he led the way in using techniques that were to become virtual Tammany staples, such as catering to the urban lower-class voter and the immigrant, manipulating the police for partisan purposes, stealing elections, and artfully using bribes and other financial skulduggery for political gain.

To make any sense of Fernando, as he was widely called during the years he held power, it helps to understand the burgeoning, wide open New York City of the 1840s and 1850s, the years when Wood loomed so large. They were a turbulent time for the city. Its population was growing at an astonishing rate: from 312,710 to 515,547, for example, in the single decade from 1840 to 1850. Much of the increase came from immigration, Irish and German in particular. A large number of the immigrants were uneducated and knew little about the ways of their new homeland. Many of the newcomers, unable to find work in a city still recovering from the financial troubles of the late 1830s, joined the growing ranks of the unemployed. This massive influx brought on huge changes in the city, and for many New Yorkers the city's problems seemed unsurmountable: fearful crime in the streets, poor sanitation, meager public education, deficient housing, overburdened public transportation, and inadequate health care, among many other ills. The city's government, kept weak by a charter imposed on it by the rural-dominated state legislature that limited the powers of both the mayor and the City Council, was hard put to cope.

A strong Tammany Hall might have thrived under such circumstances, but its leaders were too bogged down in their own disputes to offer much in the way of constructive suggestions. Although the basic character of the organization was set in the late 1830s when the conservative mercantile minority was driven out, no strong single personality emerged to provide a clear sense of direction—that is, until Wood made his play for power. Although Tammany was potentially the strongest political organization in the city—the rival Whigs had nowhere near as wide a network of local workers—this meant little as long as its members could rarely agree on what to do. A schemer and manipulator could go far in such a turbulent, shifting atmosphere. Although Wood was not elected mayor until 1854, by 1840 he was already well known on the local scene.

Born in 1812 in Philadelphia of Quaker parents, he was given his unlikely name because during her pregnancy his mother had been reading a popular novel entitled *The Three Spaniards*, whose hero was a dashing fellow named Fernando. Fernando's father was a cigar maker who speculated in dry goods, got heavily into debt and went bankrupt in 1819. Two years later, the family moved to New York, where the father opened a tobacconist store that failed. He died soon after. In the opinion of Wood's biographer Jerome Mushkat, the father's failings instilled in Fernando a fierce drive to attain three things: respectability, money, and power. The last two he achieved, but genuine respectability was to elude him.

His early attempts to scratch out a living in the commercial world were hardly promising. Leaving school at age thirteen, he tried his hand at several occupations throughout the eastern states without much success. In 1832 he was back in New York City, where he opened a wine and tobacconist store that brought meager returns. A ship chandlery firm that he started in 1835 collapsed in the recession of 1837. The following year, he opened a grocery and grog shop (a kind of general food store plus bar) near the waterfront; by 1840 business was so poor he was forced to suspend operations.

In the meantime, however, he had become one of Tammany Hall's rising stars. Attracted to Jeffersonian-Jacksonian ideals perhaps because they represented the longings of small entrepreneurs like himself, Wood saw Tammany as a pathway to recognition and public approval. In 1836, because he had turned out to be a capable ward worker, he was invited to join the Tammany Society, a great honor for someone only twenty-four years old. Soon he became a key member of one of the Hall's most influential groups, the Young Men's Democratic-Republican General Committee. It was as the leader of that group and because of his skilled arbitration of the dispute between the Loco-Focos and the conservatives that he first became known to the public. In 1840 the Hall showed its approval of Fernando by nominating him for a seat in the U.S. Congress. He was only twenty-eight.

Respectability was at hand . . . almost. Four days before the election a Whig newspaper came out with what would become the first of many allegations of shady or suspect business or political conduct on Wood's part that swirled around him throughout his career. In 1836 a clerk in the Merchants' Exchange Bank, where Wood held a small account, mistakenly credited Fernando's account with a check for $1,750.62. The money was not Wood's, yet he drew on it until it was gone. When the error was discovered and the bank requested payment, Wood refused, saying he was not responsible for someone else's mistake, but when the bank demanded to see his books he said somewhat vaguely that a fire had destroyed them. The dispute went to three referees, who ruled that he must repay the amount together with interest. Whigs trumpeted that Wood "dishonestly appropriated to his own use moneys that he knew did not belong to him."[3]

Wood knew he was in a crisis, but he responded promptly, with affidavits from two of the referees who said that although he did owe the money he was blameless. He also repaid the bank—minus the interest due. Evidently this was enough to assuage the public, since he won his election. Yet in the years to come he was never able to shake the suspicion of many New Yorkers that he had been guilty.

As a congressman, Wood won a reputation as a persuasive orator; according to one story, after one of his speeches in the House the aging former president, John Quincy Adams (who had returned to Congress), came up to him and said, "Young man, when I am gone, you will be one of the foremost men in this country."[4] While he was generally well regarded on the Hill, he also evidenced the kind of political double-dealing for which he would later become well known. Two prospective candidates for the 1844 Democratic presidential nomination, U.S. Senator John C. Calhoun and former president Martin Van Buren (who had lost his 1840 reelection bid), both coveted New York's support; Wood secretly gave assurances to each that he would work for him and against the other. Calhoun seems not to have found out he was double-crossed, but Van Buren did, and thereafter he never trusted Wood. Through some lack of moral sense that became characteristic, Wood had needlessly made an enemy.

Fully expecting reelection in 1842, Wood was stunned to discover that redistricting based on the 1840 census, together with new House rules, pitted him against another highly popular incumbent. Fearing he might not win, he tried running in another district, but lost. Suddenly he was out of a job, and his resources were almost nonexistent.

Desperate to succeed, he decided to abandon politics for the time being and, while retaining his membership in the Tammany Society, try his hand again at business. This time he was luckier. He revived his old ship chandlery firm, built it up carefully, and was soon leasing ships and trading profitably with southern markets. Later he moved into real estate where he also did very well. For almost a decade he stayed more or less uninvolved in the local political scene.

That was just as well, for the local scene was fraught with turbulence. Into the vacuum produced by Tammany's inability to speak with one voice rushed all manner of independent political parties. More notably, several unofficial groups resolved to take matters into their own hands if the city's leader would not, or to have their own way in spite of what the city (or Tammany) told them. Many of these groups, or gangs really, were concerned with control over little more than their own neighborhood, but others were large, well-organized bodies of young toughs prepared to use violent means to accomplish their aims.

The organizer of one such group, an entertaining and highly capable workingman's advocate named Mike Walsh, took delight in exposing what he called the "insulting farce" of Tammany Hall's nominating procedures. Walsh criticized the sachems to their faces in speeches delivered at the Hall (of which he was careful to remain a member), a bit of daring that in the future would cease to be tolerated. "I know perfectly well," he proclaimed during one meeting, "and no man who knows anything about the matter will dare question the truth of the statement, that the delegates to nominating committees are chosen not by the electors of each ward, but generally by a few unprincipled blackguards, usually office-holders or office-seekers, who meet in the back room of some low groggery, where they place upon a ticket for the support of their fellow-citizens a number of wretches of their own moral calibre, whose characters and consciences have been so long buried that they have become putrid. . . ."[5]

With such strong talk, Walsh was obviously unable to build a political base for himself within Tammany, and so in 1840 he created his own organization, which he called the Spartan Association. It consisted essentially of young laborers from the Sixth and Fourteenth wards on the East Side, two of the roughest areas in the city. The Spartans were soon having their way at ward meetings, where they would forcibly remove the opposition and dominate the proceedings. Tammany leaders tried to make a deal: if Walsh would give up the Spartans they would nominate him for the state assembly. Walsh refused and directed his band of "shoulder-hitters" to take over the Hall's nominating session on November 1, 1842. Intimidated, the delegates meekly complied by including him on the ticket. Walsh went on to win his election, and served not only in the legislature but later in Congress. More to the point, however, he had introduced a new element into New York politics. For the next several decades—certainly until after the Civil War—organized gangs were an all-too-visible feature of New York politics. Strong-arm methods, moreover, while not new to city elections, were coming to be seen as almost mandatory in mounting a successful candidacy. Not that New Yorkers were instinctively more violent than other Americans; but in a rapidly changing and expanding city the firm but dispassionate enforcement of law and order often seemed to go by the board.

Many of the gangs were centered in the Sixth Ward, especially in the area known as the Five Points, a vice- and crime-ridden slum district populated mainly by Irish immigrants and located just a few blocks north of City Hall on the edge of what is now Chinatown. It was a fearfully crowded part of town: a midcentury study of the Five Points revealed that more than three thousand people lived along one short stretch of Baxter Street, while one 25-by-100-foot lot on Baxter contained a total of 286 persons. The whole neighborhood was awash with dance halls, saloons, and brothels. Two rival gangs held sway here, the Dead Rabbits—whose name came about during one of their meetings when someone tossed a dead rabbit into the center of the room—and the Bowery Boys. For a while in the 1850s, the Dead Rabbits were allied with Fernando Wood, invariably glad to be of service to him in storming polling places. Other groups sported such piquant names as the Roach Guards, the Plug Uglies, and the Wide-Awakes, and all were prepared for violence at a moment's notice. Some gangs were organized around colorful personalities, most notably the Empire Club, which was headquartered in a bar on Park Row across from City Hall and led by Captain Isaiah Rynders, a onetime gambler and pistol-and-knife fighter along the Mississippi River who had come to New York in the 1830s. Rynders was the Tammany leader of the Sixth Ward and a longtime member of the Hall's General Committee. He was said to coordinate all gang activities that had to do with politics.

Another rough-cut character who was to become a formidable power in Tammany circles was John Morrissey, a beefy barroom brawler and Hudson riverboat deckhand from Troy, New York. Soon after his arrival in the city in the 1840s, Morrissey began working for Tammany as an immigrant "runner," rounding up new arrivals at the downtown docks and shepherding them to chosen boardinghouses courtesy of Tammany Hall. He was also proving valuable to Tammany as a protector of ballot boxes on election day. He eventually became one of the Hall's key members, earned a fortune operating a gambling house on Broadway near Tenth Street, then moved his gambling operations upstate to Saratoga Springs, which he eventually represented in Congress and the state senate.

As for Isaiah Rynders, he directed his operations from his saloon, for neighborhood bars were becoming increasingly known as centers of political activity and would be key focuses of Tammany power in later years. Many of these saloons, which were typically Irish, as this was the largest immigrant population during these years, tended to become social clubs for an entire neighborhood. From there it was but a small step to the saloons becoming the meeting places of political groups. The bar owner himself—who could readily assemble from among his customers a phalanx of shoulder-hitters to help influence the outcome of an election—often became a Tammany ward leader of considerable power.

Many New Yorkers inveighed against what was considered the corrupting influence of the saloons. There were periodic attempts to close them down, or at least to limit their hours of operation, but restrictions were hard to enforce, since the police—by now increasingly Irish—were generally disposed to ignore what went on there. After all, the average cop most likely owed his job to the saloon owner's political influence. And as Mike Walsh once remarked, the saloons served a real need in lower-class districts: "So long as it is looked upon as indecent, if not criminal for persons to run, sing, dance, and skylark in the public streets and squares, so long will the greater mass of the poorer portion of people, who have scarcely room enough to turn around in, continue to seek excitement and amusement in public places."[6] While New York's well-to-do neighborhoods might be quiet and orderly, areas such as the Bowery and the Five Points never seemed to shut down.

To large numbers of New Yorkers, however, the saloon culture represented a general breakdown in civic affairs and was a symptom of the rampant political corruption that many were beginning to blame directly on the immigrants and, by inference, on Tammany Hall, which was associating itself more and more with the new arrivals. The Irish were a particular target because so many of them belonged to the dreaded gangs. But all newcomers were suspected of having been naturalized illegally in order to vote and were accused of taking jobs away from the native-born by working for lower wages. By 1843 this growing anger and resentment by native-born New Yorkers reached a political head when a good number of members from both the Democratic and Whig parties (and from the Tammany membership itself) broke away to form a citywide nativist organization called the American Republican party. The new group pledged, among other things, to increase the naturalization period for immigrants to twenty-one years, a waiting period they claimed was necessary for the preservation of honest government, and to close the saloons on Sunday. Armed with such reform notions, they not only established branches in other

American cities but in 1844 attracted enough support in New York to elect as mayor one of their number, James Harper of the newly successful publishing firm of Harper and Brothers.

Harper's one-year term (so set by the state legislature in one of its periodic tinkerings with the city's charter) was a flop. A political novice, he proposed not only to padlock the saloons on Sunday but to ban sidewalk peddling throughout the city. He also wanted to bar fast and dangerous driving. Closing the saloons was attacked by workingmen's representatives as discriminating against those who had only Sunday off, while the antipeddling ordinance was said to injure widowed apple sellers and other impoverished street vendors; the speeding law was merely greeted with amusement. The schemes all came to naught, as did the nativists' attempts to persuade Congress and the state legislature to extend the naturalization period. In 1845 Harper and his party were swept from office, and two years later the American Republican party expired in New York and nationwide.

Harper's brief tour was nevertheless highly significant in New York's political history. He had been elected in a citywide protest against what Tammany Hall was thought to stand for: corruption, lawlessness, and favoritism toward the newly arrived. It was the first of many so-called reform administrations that would periodically come to power with the announced aim of weeding out corruption and ending the evil influence of the Tammany machine. As time went on, in fact, city politics would become less and less a struggle between the Democratic and the Whig (later the Republican) parties and increasingly a fight between Tammany bosses (almost synonymous with the overwhelmingly more populous Democrats) and reformers (usually Republican), with the reformers rarely surviving for long. Harper thus began a noble if often quixotic tradition.

Furthermore, although Harper's party dissolved, nativism did not die. In the 1850s, the movement was to come alive again throughout the United States in the form of the Native American party, the outgrowth of a secret organization whose members were popularly called the Know-Nothings because they habitually responded to questions about the organization by saying "I know nothing." In 1855, a Know-Nothing almanac listed the party's principles as "Anti-Romanism, Anti-Bedinism, Anti-Papistalism, Anti-Nunneryism, Anti-Winking-Virginism, Anti-Jesuitism."[7] This time New York's nativists were unable to elect a mayor, but for several years the movement stayed strong enough to complicate the city's already fractured politics.

Not only was Tammany Hall rent by discord over such local concerns as saloon closings and the treatment of immigrants, but the Democratic party as a whole was almost continually split during these years by the great national dispute over slavery. The first division, during the 1840s, was between two groups known as the Barnburners and the Hunkers, whose disagreements complicated the local scene. The Barnburners, radical Democrats who felt slavery should not be extended to the country's free territory, got their name from the remark of a contractor who said of them, "These men are incendiaries; they are mad; they are like the farmer, who, to get the rats out of his granary, sets fire to his own barn."[8] The more conservative Hunkers, whose name connoted squatting down and refusing to move, were mainly officeholders (both in New York and elsewhere) who saw no reason to be concerned about the slavery question, as it did not affect them. Not only could the two factions rarely agree on candidates for local office; on more than one occasion they sent competing delegations to state political conventions, necessitating all manner of tricky formulas to ensure that both viewpoints were represented.

The Barnburner-Hunker feud yielded in the 1850s to a somewhat equivalent division, between Softshells, known as Softs and roughly comparable to the Barnburners, and Hardshells, known as Hards, successors to the Hunkers. On one occasion the two factions, coincidentally, held rival meetings in Tammany Hall's Long Room. Each side duly elected a chairman, passed resolutions and the like, and tried to shout down the other side. On another evening, the proceedings of a committee summoned to decide between the two factions became so animated and loud that a group of Tammany revelers in the bar downstairs, who had been playing a contemporary version of the game Simon Says and paying their forfeits in drink, decided to ascend and settle matters. Bursting into the committee room, they proceeded to upset tables, throw chairs about, and create general mayhem. In the process, the committee members became so terrified that a number flung themselves out the windows—which unfortunately were not open. Among the badly injured was the committee chairman, whose head had intercepted a flying chair.

Amid all this discord came a favorable development: the city's economy in the early 1850s started booming again. There was plenty of money and plenty of opportunities around as well as plenty of chances to take dubious advantage of those opportunities. Along with the booming economy came a booming population; hence there was a great need for new transit lines and other urban facilities whose financing and construction could be manipulated for great profit. So it was that during these years New York acquired a City Council that established a very special record: it was the most corrupt in the city's history up to that time, and perhaps even worse than any that came after. Such manipulation was all too easy, inasmuch as there were few controls over a public servant's behavior. In 1851 the Council had been in the hands of the Whigs, who had accomplished little, and so there was an impatience to get things done—at any cost. The new body, which took office in January 1852, included a generous number of Tammanyites and got so many things done so crookedly that it has been known ever since as the Forty Thieves. Its shoddy example was not lost among current and future Tammany politicians like Fernando Wood.

The Council at that time, it should be noted, was made up of two boards of twenty members each, the Board of Aldermen and the Board of Assistant Aldermen. Although the assistants had only modest power, the aldermen were in effect petty despots. Each alderman appointed the police in his district, including all the precinct officers. He licensed all the saloons. With his fellow aldermen he granted all franchises for streetcar lines and ferries. Furthermore, he sat as a justice in what was known as the Mayor's Court, which tried all persons accused of poll violations. Since the alderman was himself a politician subject to the whim of the voters, this judicial prerogative was a particularly juicy plum that could make for all sorts of conniving and fraud. But there was another judicial prize: the alderman also sat as a judge in the criminal courts, and as such also helped pick the members of grand juries, and so had a hand in deciding what cases came to trial, truly a heady privilege.

Finally, the alderman received no salary—a holdover from the days when public service was considered a proper duty for the well-to-do, who theoretically had no need for extra compensation and who considered pay corrupting. Among the aldermen of the 1850s, this was a virtual license to steal. Given these peculiar conditions, it is no surprise that the post of alderman was greatly coveted. (One of the aldermen elected in 1851 was a twenty-eight-year-old chair maker and Tammany fledgling named William M. Tweed, just now getting his public career under way. At this point, however, Tweed was just one of a number of connivers.)

One of the Council's first acts was to purchase land for a potter's field, or burial ground, for paupers. A reasonable estimate of the value of the desired land, located on Ward's Island, was $30,000. The

Council decided to pay $103,450 for it, and the recipient obligingly kicked back the difference to his distinguished benefactors.

Another example of how the spirit of largesse infected even the smallest of affairs occurred on the Fourth of July in 1852, which happened to be the seventy-sixth anniversary of America's independence. The aldermen paid $4,100 for fireworks whose estimated value was $500. A day or so later, money was appropriated for cigars and liquor to be available on a boat carrying dignitaries escorting the body of Henry Clay from New York to Albany; the bill came to $1,400, and another $2,500 was spent decorating the boat with black and white bunting and small flags. There is little doubt that much of the excess, while modest, found its way into aldermanic pockets.

But this was small change. Franchises and street improvements were bigger game. One applicant for the right to operate a ferry between New York and Williamsburgh (a community later annexed to Brooklyn) was told he would have to pay the aldermen $5,000 to "get it through" but was outbid by another who readily forked over $20,000. Bribes to obtain the franchise for the Wall Street Ferry were similarly increased from $5,000 to $15,000, but then were settled at $20,000, which was offered by Jacob Sharp, an entrepreneur who had many friends on the Council. Applicants for a Third Avenue railroad franchise paid at least $30,000 in bribes to various aldermen during the year. And untold thousands of dollars were reputedly paid by applicants for the right to build a streetcar line on Broadway, although the line was never built due to the sustained opposition of the department store magnate A.T. Stewart, who felt streetcars would adversely affect his deluxe establishment at Broadway and Chambers Street.

City-owned land could be sold, too. A nice parcel was occupied by the Gansevoort Market, near the west end of Fourteenth Street; it was said to be the single most valuable piece of real estate in New York. The city received bids of $225,000 and $300,000 for it, but the Forty Thieves decided this was excessive and so parted with the property for $160,000. It was sold to one Reuben Lovejoy, who after an investigation turned out to be fronting for a group headed by James B. Taylor, a good friend of many aldermen, who undoubtedly rewarded the group members for their thoughtfulness. The mayor at the time, Ambrose Kingsland, vetoed the appropriation but the Council promptly overrode him. Ten years later the Council, with a new set of members, saw the error of the transaction and bought the land back—for $533,437.50.

Sometimes the distinguished aldermen needed some quick cash without the waiting required to enact needlessly time-consuming appropriation bills. In such cases, they would resort to what was known as strike legislation. A phony bill, ostensibly meritorious but conveying the possibility of financial loss to someone, would be introduced and the potentially injured party would complain to the legislators. "Oh, I'm sorry," an alderman would say. "I tell you what. Just give me $250 and I'll see that it gets killed in committee." Money would change hands and the bill would vanish.[9]

While the Thieves were siphoning money from the city they were also eating well; they had taken care to vote themselves an official "tearoom" where they could refresh themselves. "After one particularly grueling meeting," wrote Alfred Connable and Edward Silberfarb in their entertaining study of Tammany Hall, "they submitted a bill to the Comptroller which was duly analyzed by [editor] Horace Greeley and his mathematicians at the *Tribune*. It was an open question as to how much padding had gone to the bill and how much to the waistlines of the aldermen, for it seemed that at one sitting *each* alderman had consumed eight pounds of beef, a chicken and a half, 225 oysters, one pound of sausage, two pounds of ham, and more than three loaves of bread, all followed by the smoking of one hundred cigars."[10]

When revelations of this kind began appearing in the press, a ground swell of indignation rose against the Forty Thieves and, more to the point, against the system that made such transgressions possible. A new reform movement sprang up whose leaders urged amending the city charter so that, for example, work and supplies contracted by the city would have to be awarded to the lowest bidder and franchises to the highest, while bribery was to be punished severely. The changes were officially adopted by the electorate in June 1853, and later that year most of the Thieves were voted out of office.

Their extravagances did not reflect well on Tammany Hall, as many of the aldermen were true-blue Tammanyites. The public's rebuff in voting most of them out of office once again exacerbated the bickering and infighting within Tammany itself. But into the maelstrom, just a few years earlier, stepped a man many of the sachems hoped could heal the Hall's wounds. He was Fernando Wood, returning from his decade of self-imposed exile. Although he was known to be controversial, his work in resolving the Loco-Foco controversy led Tammany's sachems to believe that he was the likeliest person to bring their feuding factions together. And he was undeniably attractive. In the words of Jerome Mushkat, he was "the very picture of a chief magistrate: tall and erect in bearing; urbane in manner; intelligent, forceful, and personable, with a commanding, authoritative presence."[11]

He was now also rich. In 1848, he had purchased (with some of his wife's money) a large parcel of land on the Upper West Side of Manhattan. Its value skyrocketed and Wood, using it as collateral, began buying, developing, and selling land all over town. Everything worked for Fernando and money rolled in. By the early 1850s, he was one of Manhattan's wealthiest citizens. Many years later, Boss Tweed, himself something of an operator in real estate, paid Wood a backhanded compliment. "I never yet went to get a corner lot," he remarked, "that I didn't find Wood had got in ahead of me."[12]

Yet even this heady period had a dark side. One episode, when it was revealed, cast a shadow over his character that proved impossible to shake off. When gold was discovered in California in the late 1840s, Wood, like many other New Yorkers, saw an opportunity to cash in. With four partners he chartered a bark, the *John C. Cater*, loaded it with all sorts of goods and equipment, and sent it out to San Francisco, where its cargo sold at what appeared to be great profit to Fernando and the others. It subsequently developed, however, that Wood had obtained the up-front money for the endeavor from his brother-in-law, a retired merchant named Edward E. Marvine, on the basis of a letter purportedly sent by a contact in Monterey, California. Marvine now claimed that Wood had swindled him and others out of $20,000 before the *Cater* sailed, that the letter had been in effect a forgery, and that Wood had thereupon falsified documents to bilk Marvine and his friends. Fernando's defense was unconvincing, and a grand jury indicted him for perjury and "false pretenses." The case would have gone to trial if the court assigned to it had not found, by remarkable coincidence, that the statute of limitations had expired one day before they were to rule on it. Furthermore, Wood was alleged to have paid one of the judges to delay the case. This hardly cleared his name. Several years later a New York Supreme Court ordered him to pay Marvine $8,000 and the other partners slightly smaller amounts. As Jerome Mushkat observes, "These awards meant Wood stood before the legal system and, by extension, the public, as a forger and swindler, a man who apparently escaped prison only with the connivance of a corrupted official."[13]

Before this story broke, however, Wood had already relaunched his political career with a run for mayor in 1850. He campaigned vigorously, seeking support especially among working-class and ethnic groups, but at the last moment several Whig newspapers published reports of the Marvine affair, which hurt him badly. Wood lost. His failure appeared terminal; newspapers all over town declared him a dead politician.

Far from it. Four years later, now still wealthier from his business ventures (and with the Forty Thieves come and gone), he was back again appealing to the Tammany leaders as someone who could bridge the Democrats' destructive gaps. Despite the blots on his record, Tammany leaders persisted in the notion that he was that most valuable of Tammany assets, a proven vote-getter. This time fortune was on his side; there were three other candidates in the mayoral race, and so his opposition was divided. But a new revelation almost torpedoed the whole effort. Several years earlier, it was now made known, Fernando, who prided himself on being a friend of the immigrant, had secretly joined the rabidly nativist Know-Nothing party. He had even become a member of the party's Executive Committee. Wood, in a carefully crafted and notarized statement, appeared to deny the charge, but published affidavits from several Know-Nothings left no doubt in the voter's mind that it was true. His candidacy was badly compromised. But while the revelation doubtless cost him some of the immigrant vote, it also brought him some nativist support. On election day, the Tammany faithful went out in force to work their customary wiles, and among other violations it was reported that six hundred more votes were cast in the "Bloody Sixth" Ward than the number of voters there. When it was all over, Wood just barely managed to squeak through.

His prospects seemed dim. He would have little control over his executive departments because they would (by city charter) all be headed by persons independently elected. His power to act was further limited by the fact that the new Common (i.e., City) Council was controlled by a combination of prohibitionists, Know-Nothings, and Whigs, who were in the process of banding together as members of the new nationwide Republican party. His reputation, too, had been severely damaged. As Horace Greeley wrote in the *New York Tribune*, "No man ever went into higher office under a deeper cloud of ignominy that [Wood] will."[14]

But a surprise was in store, for the irrepressible, unpredictable Fernando Wood began his administration as no mayor had in all New York's history. In his first address, he pointed to the city's massive problems and declared that only a strong mayor could make a start in solving them. But the city charter was stacked against him, he said, as it deprived him of necessary authority over the major departments. The worst example was the Police Department, which should surely be under the mayor's control but was not. The charter should be totally overhauled, he argued. But in the meantime he would simply take what power he felt was needed. "For myself, " he declared, "I desire to announce here, upon the threshold, that, as I understand and comprehend my duties and prerogatives, they leave me no alternative, without dishonor, but to assume a general control over the whole City Government, so far as protecting its municipal interests may demand it."[15] So the newly elected mayor, having satisfied two of his lifetime drives—having acquired money and, superficially at least, respectability—was now going to grasp the third, power.

His first months were a whirlwind. A steady succession of orders and suggestions emanated from his desk—for better streets, for a new city hall, for cutting unnecessary spending, for speeding up the construction of Central Park, for better public health regulations and for myriad other concerns. He forbade all members of his administration from taking any kind of gratuity or gift. When an operator of omnibuses sent him a season pass he made sure the public learned he was returning it. But his greatest public relations stroke was inaugurating a "complaint book" in City Hall in which any citizen could call attention to wrongdoings or lapses of duty on the part of city employees. Not only did this allow citizens to let off steam, but Wood also followed up on many of the gripes. One complaint came from a tailor who said a policeman had not paid the money he owed him. Wood summoned the cop to City Hall for an explanation and learned there had been sickness in the policeman's family; so the mayor paid the bill out of his own pocket.

Beyond all this, Wood announced plans to improve the quality of life in the city by enforcing Sunday closing laws, bearing down on gamblers, and forcing prostitutes off the streets. Soon there were fewer than twenty saloons operating on the Sabbath, in contrast to twenty-three hundred before the crackdown. Prostitutes were carted off at a great rate, and brothels and gambling dens closed in large numbers. It was admittedly true that many of the saloons in the Fourth and Sixth wards, where Wood's political support was very strong, somehow managed to remain open on Sunday, that padlocked gambling establishments reopened at other locations, and that arrested streetwalkers were soon released and merely moved to other parts of town. But a start had been made, and Wood's popularity soared. It was given a further boost when he vetoed a plan passed by the Common Council to cut back on the projected size of Central Park. He was called the "model mayor" and his reputation spread throughout the country. The governor of Ohio reported that Fernando was the most popular American to people who lived west of the Alleghenies, and there was even a report that when a passenger on a train in the Midwest threw a pickpocket who had threatened him off the train, the other passengers shouted, "That must be Mayor Wood!"[16]

The party chiefs in Tammany Hall regarded all these triumphs with mixed feelings. It was good to have produced a winner, but Wood was not playing their kind of game. Specifically, he was not throwing patronage their way. Appointments were made from his own circle of friends rather than from Tammany stalwarts; to the office of city chamberlain, for example, he named Andrew Stout, believed to be a Know-Nothing. The sachems began to suspect that Wood was attempting to create his own machine at the expense of the Hall.

Their suspicion, and that of other New Yorkers, was reinforced when Wood formally asked the Council to amend the 1853 police act, which had vested control of the force in a three-man board that only incidentally included the mayor. To Wood, shared power was no power at all, and he demanded sole control. Only by granting him such power, he said, could the city be assured that the police would not be mired in politics, for only the mayor could be above petty politicking. "As a magistrate and chief executive officer of this city," he intoned, "I know no party and recognize no political obligations."[17] Those who had known the Fernando of the past wondered whether he could ever be nonpolitical, and feared that control of the police might give him power of a kind that could hurt the city. Was he to be trusted? Unsure of the answer, the aldermen ignored his request.

Presently, those who had suspected Wood's untrustworthiness were given pause. For at least a decade, prohibition had been a strong cause not only in New York City but in the state as well, its backers mainly conservative Protestants who equated alcohol with every form of sin. Indeed, a sizable portion of the nativist vote for Harper in 1844 had been made up of prohibitionists, many of whom resented the beer-drinking German immigrants and the whisky-drinking Irish. Such groups applauded Wood's Sunday closings. But in April 1855 the state legislature passed a temperance measure that went far beyond what Wood had done: it banned all sales of intoxicating liquors. The law was to go into effect on July 4. Momentarily stumped by the prospect of trying to enforce a law that tremendous numbers of New Yorkers would revile and evade, Wood consulted with the district attorney, A. Oakey Hall (from whom much would be heard in subsequent years), and the two of them came up with a preposterous solution. The new law, they observed, nullified all existing regulations, yet it would not go into effect until the Fourth. So between May 1 and July 4, they announced, drinking throughout the city would be unrestricted. Perhaps after July 4 the new law would be ruled unconstitutional (as it indeed was), but in the meantime, bottoms up! Out the window went Fernando's Sunday closing rule, along with a large share of his credibility.

Soon thereafter, yet another vestige of the old Fernando seemed to have appeared. A merchant ship, the *Joseph Walker*, carrying a cargo of grain, had sunk next to a city pier. The ship's rotting cargo was deemed a menace to public health. To remove it, the mayor, in his capacity as head of the New York Board of Health, selected one Walter Jones as the lowest bidder. After the work stalled, an alderman charged Wood with having ignored still lower bids to choose Jones, who had allegedly given Wood an $11,000 bribe. The case against the mayor was compromised when the accuser was suddenly charged with bribery himself in an entirely different matter. Wood furthermore announced he was prepared to "make good any money that the City will lose by any act of mine while Mayor. . . ."[18] But the accusation had not been totally disproved. During this time Horace Greeley remarked in the *Tribune*, "Here is a man of decided talent, untiring industry, and considerable executive ability, who might have been anything he chose if Providence had blessed him with a reasonable share of honesty."[19]

Wood was also doing his best to transform the police force into a body more responsive to him. He had persuaded his fellow commissioners to allow him to fire officers who were not performing their duties properly. Opponents charged that he was hiring only Democrats to replace the dismissed officers; Fernando evaded them by citing a technicality that he said invalidated the charge. In the summer, he put the entire force on parade in City Hall Park. The *New York Tribune* expressed approval of the officers' military precision, but there were those who were bothered by the thought that the mayor seemed to possess a virtual private army that might be used to further his political ambitions.

As a new mayoral contest approached in 1856 (the mayoral term having reverted to two years), Wood defied tradition by deciding to run for reelection. Previous mayors had been businessmen who retired gracefully after one term, but not Fernando. Tammany's leaders were lukewarm about him, for although he was unquestionably a member of the Hall in good standing and could claim, as mayor, to be the titular leader of the Democratic party in the city, he had little interest in heeding the sachems' wishes in patronage matters. So he decided to outflank them. First, it was necessary to indicate that he had widespread popular support. He thereafter began by declaring that he had decided not to run. Then he produced a letter signed by nearly one hundred prominent merchants (a document almost certainly manufactured by him) that urged him to reconsider. With feigned reluctance, he condescended to make the sacrifice and become a candidate. Second, he proceeded to take over the party's nominating machinery. He got himself named to the Hall's General Committee and arranged to have a cohort installed as chairman. Then he took over the naming of election inspectors and vote counters, who would run the party's primary for choosing delegates for the local nominating convention. When the day of the primary came, the mayor's henchmen controlled the voting, forcibly barring many persons from casting their ballots, stealing ballot boxes, and resorting to numerous other subterfuges. It was also alleged that members of the police force assisted Wood's operatives in controlling the vote. The outcome was preordained: he won, and the delegates so chosen handed him the nomination.

This showed that the party was unified, or so he claimed, and he staged a parade in which Hards and Softs marched side by side. But a rump group of Tammanyites rebelled and named James S. Libby, a hotel keeper, to run against him as an independent in the general election. When a meeting was announced for October 22 at Tammany Hall to ratify Wood's nomination as the regular Democratic candidate, the Long Room was jammed not only with the mayor's partisans but with Libbyites as well, and the proverbial Tammany fisticuffs quickly broke out. As a reporter for the *New York Times* put it, "A general fight took place in front of the speaker's stand and all around the room. Blows were given and exchanged with great spirit, and not a few faces were badly disfigured." Before very long Fernando's friends had gotten the upper hand. "The great body of Libbyites," the account concluded, "were kicked out of the room and down the stairs with a velocity proportionate to the expelling force behind."[20] There were no further rebellions against Wood's nomination, and Tammany Hall reluctantly swung in behind him.

Having begun on a low note, the general campaign, in which four candidates (including Libby) were pitted against Wood, got even nastier. Although the mayor took the high road, defending his record in orotund phrases, his followers were another story. In previous elections shabby tactics had for the most part been limited to election day itself; now they were in evidence throughout the entire campaign. Roving gangs, in particular Wood's friends the Dead Rabbits, broke up meetings staged by opposition candidates. Street orators on both sides were stoned or hooted down. An anti-Wood pamphlet dredged up every transgression the mayor had ever been accused of and invented a few more; accusations of a similar nature were hurled by the Wood forces at the opposition.

Tammany had long persuaded friendly judges to speed the naturalization of immigrants so that they could vote the straight Democratic ticket. Wood took a special interest in this process and liked to write out notes for each immigrant to take to court which read: "Please naturalize the bearer."[21] It is not known how much the tactic helped his cause, but the effect must have been substantial.

But it was his manipulation of the police for his own purposes that was particularly reprehensible. Policemen became virtual political aides to him—a startling turnabout in view of his earlier declaration that they should be nonpartisan. Wood had already taken to demoting captains who were unfriendly to his candidacy, and he now assessed each policeman a portion of his salary for his campaign chest: captains were assessed $15 to $25 apiece, patrolmen a lesser amount. Anyone who refused to pay was placed on the mayor's list, which meant that he could be dismissed for the most minor offense. One officer who balked was given duty for twenty-four hours without a break. Officers who were particularly enthusiastic about Wood's campaign were released from their regular duties to work for him, in clear violation of the city charter.

On election day, Wood produced yet another twist: he gave large numbers of policemen a few hours off to vote, with specific instructions not to go near the polls until they were ready to cast their ballots. The net effect was to deplete the polls severely of police protection, so that the Dead Rabbits and other gangs doing their bit for Fernando had clear sailing. Fights erupted everywhere. Ballot boxes were destroyed, and voters not known to be partial to Wood were forcibly prevented from casting their ballots. If they insisted on voting, they were beaten up. When the mayor and the chief of police were called upon to quell the disturbances, they refused to act. Needless to say, Wood won the election.

He was now without question the most powerful man in the city. And as a result, says Jerome Mushkat, "Wood was becoming a prototypical modern municipal leader, a professional politician seeking to get, keep, maintain, and expand power. In even a larger sense, Wood verged on being the forerunner of a more important development. Since his [first] inauguration, he had combined in himself divergent and often conflicting strands of urban life as the one man capable of creating a coordinated and cohesive society out of the chaos that was New York City. By sort of a natural progression, Wood was unwittingly laying the basis for a new mechanism in city politics, a political machine under a single 'Boss.' "22

A few weeks later a grand jury, convened at the request of the losers, took testimony on the frauds that had allegedly been perpetrated by the mayor's forces. But despite ample evidence of fictitious voters, multiple voting, and delayed counts that yielded false returns, the jury brought no indictment. Frauds of this kind, said the jurors, had been going on since the earliest days of the republic, so there was nothing new. But Wood's use of the police was undeniably new. Many New Yorkers were now convinced that the erstwhile image of Fernando as a paragon of deception was forever proved. He had fallen a long way since his days as the model mayor.

He had also made more enemies than he thought. As a newly victorious chief executive and the ostensible head of the Hall, he began moving to take over the Tammany Society itself. He got a frosty reception. The sachems instinctively distrusted anyone who tried to upset their special form of collective leadership, and when Wood tried to oust them by running an opposition slate of sachems in the Society's annual election, he was trounced. From this point on, as far as Tammany was concerned, he was a renegade, a man to be tolerated only so long as he did not disturb their way of doing things. If he had ever fancied that he controlled the Tammany General Committee, it was most assuredly no longer so; his influence over the party machinery was a thing of the past.

But that was just the beginning of his troubles. As he began his second term, he repeated the call for a strong, centralized city government. If uttered today, such a plea might be considered sensible, even progressive, but nineteenth-century New York was not prepared to give such power to a single executive, or at least not to Fernando Wood. In addition, the Republicans, although they had lost the re-

cent election to Wood, had made heavy gains upstate and were now
in firm control of the state legislature. (Their sway over most of the
state north of the city presaged the pattern that has held ever since,
with the GOP strong upstate and the Democrats heavily favored in
the city.) The Republican legislators did indeed vote New York City a
new charter, but far from bolstering the mayor's power the new document actually weakened it. A number of independent agencies were
consolidated under the mayor's control, and he was given additional
appointment powers, but the number of department heads and other
key officers elected rather than appointed was increased, and for the
first time the mayor had no say over city contracts. (A popularly
elected and theoretically bipartisan Board of Supervisors was also set
up, to consist of six Republicans and six Democrats; the body was
immensely significant in the career of William M. Tweed, who was
elected to it, but was of little concern to Wood.)

In a separate legislative stroke, the Republicans dealt Wood an
even worse blow by canceling whatever control he had enjoyed over
the police. They had acted partly on the urging of one of Wood's
fellow police board members, a former Republican city judge, who
warned that the existing arrangement could enable the mayor to
wield his power "with tremendous force to promote his own purposes."[23] The city's police were merged with those of Kings (Brooklyn), Richmond (Staten Island), and Westchester Counties and put
under a five-member Metropolitan Police Board appointed by the
state. The mayor would be merely an ex officio member of it and
have no authority whatsoever. Although the new law stemmed partly
from the upstaters' habitual distrust of the "wicked city" and partly
from revulsion over Fernando Wood's blatant misuse of the police, it
was, as the historian Edward K. Spann has observed, "based on the
assumption that New York was too important to be left in the hands
of New Yorkers."[24]

In a final thrust at Wood, the legislature reshuffled election dates
to allow for the mayor to be elected on odd years instead of even. The
next mayoral election would take place in December 1857. Wood's
ill-gotten second term was thus slashed to one year.

Humiliated, shorn of much of his power, and bereft of most of the
influence he had once exercised over his old Tammany political base,
Wood considered resigning but instead decided to fight back. He applied for an injunction to forestall the new law until it had been tested
in the courts; the courts turned him down. The new Metropolitan
Board ordered him to disband the Municipal Police; he refused and

called upon the men to stand behind him. Two thirds of them voted to do so, while the rest joined the Metropolitans. New York now had two rival police forces.

The result was both chaotic and comic. In many areas, there was virtually no law enforcement as the two groups spent all their time arguing over who was in charge. Sometimes the Municipals would arrest someone and the Metropolitans would free him. In one instance, two rival policemen got into a fight over who had the right to arrest an offender. Visitors to the Fifth Ward station house beheld the unusual sight of two rival police captains sitting side by side at the same desk, each unwilling to yield to the other.

The conflict came to a head on June 16, when a Republican omnibus proprietor named Daniel D. Conover showed up at City Hall to be sworn in as street commissioner. He had been appointed by the state governor in conformance with the new city charter. This was no routine appointment: the commissioner's office dispensed a huge number of city jobs and controlled contracts worth an estimated $2 million, both items of great interest to the mayor. Wood not only refused to recognize the validity of the new charter (and thus of Conover's appointment) but had his own candidate for the post, a contractor named Charles Devlin (who was subsequently accused of having paid the mayor $50,000 for the appointment). The mayor refused to see Conover and ordered the Municipal Police, who were present in force, to eject him, which they did while roughing him up a bit.

Conover retreated to the chambers of a Republican city judge, who was pleased to issue a warrant for the mayor's arrest on charges of assault and inciting to riot. The warrant was entrusted to Captain George Walling, late of the Municipals but now resplendent in the frock coat and plug hat of the Metropolitans. Although City Hall was by this time guarded by some five hundred Municipals, Walling was permitted to enter the building. He accosted the mayor, who met him from behind his official desk.

"I have here a warrant for your arrest," Walling announced, holding out the writ.

"You are not an officer," said Wood. "I dismissed you from the force."

"I am an officer. I am a member of the Metropolitan Police."

"I do not recognize the legality of the service or the existence of the Metropolitan police. I will not submit to arrest, or go with you, or concede that you are an officer."

Walling was firm. "I shall have to take you forcibly if you resist."

"I will not be taken!" the mayor exclaimed. "You may consider that answer resistance, if you please."

"No, sir," replied the captain, "that is not resistance—only refusal." And he started around the desk toward his quarry.

"Go away!" commanded the mayor, striking a bell on the desk. With that, a detachment of Municipals burst into the room and seized the captain. He was duly escorted from the building. He made his way back to the judge, who responded with a new order that instructed the county sheriff to make the arrest.[25]

Meanwhile a company of Metropolitans, having heard of Walling's plight, advanced on City Hall. As they approached the front steps of the building they were set upon by several hundred Municipals, who belabored them severely, clubbing, punching, and kicking them until the intruders, more than twenty of them badly injured, were driven from the field. Just at this moment, however, New York's Seventh Regiment, the state militia, happened to come marching down Broadway on their way to the docks to embark for a ceremonial event in Boston. The defeated Metropolitans appealed to them for assistance and their commander obliged, detaching a body of militiamen to escort the sheriff into the mayor's office. This time the Municipals did not resist, and the sheriff entered and arrested Wood for contempt of court. The mayor submitted without objection. New York's newspapers were indignant, the *Times* calling the whole episode "Civic rebellion."[26]

When his case came to trial, the mayor pleaded he was a "law-abiding and order-loving citizen," and after much maneuvering by Tammany lawyers intent on damage control, the charge was dismissed. Some time later, a civil court held that the governor did not have the right to appoint the city's street commissioner, and so Wood's man Devlin ended up getting the job. But that was the extent of the mayor's good news. On July 2 the state Court of Appeals upheld the constitutionality of the Metropolitan Police Act, wiping out Wood's faithful Municipals. Fernando disbanded them, and the great police war was over.

Not its repercussions, however. Early in the morning of July 4 in the Sixth Ward, the Dead Rabbits, whose fondness for Fernando Wood was now well established, decided, after imbibing copious amounts of liquor, to attack a detachment of Metropolitans who were patrolling the streets. When the police fled, the Rabbits resolved to go after their old enemies, the Bowery Boys, whose main meeting place was a bar at 40 Bowery. Only a few of the Boys were inside at the time, and when the Dead Rabbits attacked the bar with paving stones, wrecking it, the Boys retreated and fled the area. But that afternoon, seeking revenge, the Boys assembled their whole gang—more than two hundred young rowdies—and erected on Bayard Street a massive barricade of wagons, drays, mattresses, and assorted junk, just inside what was considered Dead Rabbit turf (and in the center of today's Chinatown). Not to be outdone, the Dead Rabbits constructed a similar barrier just to the west on Bayard, and the two sides began blazing away at each other with guns. Although the noise was considerable, the normal cacophony of the Fourth was such that the Metropolitan Police did not detect the battle for some time. When they finally dispatched a detail of twenty-five patrolmen to the scene, the Dead Rabbits routed them, aided by an avalanche of bricks and stones hurled at the cops from the windows and roofs of nearby tenements. The fighting continued, with reinforcements from both gangs arriving until there were more than a thousand gang members rioting through the streets of the Lower East Side. CIVIL WAR IN THE BLOODY SIXTH roared a newspaper headline the next day.

Order was finally restored on the evening of July 5, when a far greater force of Metropolitans returned to the scene, backed up by two militia regiments. At least ten people had been killed during the rioting, and more than a hundred wounded. Further eroding public respect for Wood was the discovery that large numbers of former Municipals had taken part in the fighting to discredit the Metropolitans. Such was the state of law and order courtesy of Fernando.

Because of what the mayor had allowed to happen, there was widespread fear in the city that the civic fabric had broken down completely. True, poverty and slum conditions were likely to breed violence no matter who was in power. Still, Wood could not escape blame. The *New York Times*, calling attention to the "terrible increase in crime" in the city, said the rise was "only to be accounted for under a system when the police force is perverted from its proper calling and made the political machine that it notoriously has been and still is."[27] The mayor, it said, had induced the climate of lawlessness by his "disorganizing and reckless opposition to the laws of the State."[28]

Yet the mayor could not be counted out quite yet. Despite his shoddy record he was evidently still popular among many Democratic voters, and in the fall of 1857 Tammany Hall, perhaps not wishing to split the party further, surprised everyone by backing him once again for renomination. But then two things happened that diminished his prospects. One was the revelation that he and his brother Benjamin Wood had made an illegal profit on the sale of four thousand glass ballot boxes to the Metropolitan Police Commission. Ben had bought the ballot boxes for $20,000 and then turned around and sold them to the commission (of which Fernando was an ex officio member) for $60,000. The two brothers presumably split the difference.

While this hurt him among the rank-and-file voters, a message that Wood delivered at about the same time to the Common Council further damaged what was left of his reputation among civic leaders. In mid-October of 1857, the city was hit by a severe economic downturn, part of a nationwide collapse resulting from the overextension of credit that had come about during years of headlong manufacturing expansion. Some thirty thousand New Yorkers were thrown out of work. Wood commendably proposed to the Council a vast work-relief program that would pay the workers in food. That was fine, but then he added, "Truly may it be said that in New York those who produce everything get nothing, and those who produce nothing get everything."[29] This was too revolutionary a notion for midcentury New Yorkers to abide. The *New York Times* said in an editorial that "Mr. Wood raises the banner of the most fiery communism."[30] Many city dwellers were horrified when radical workingmen, after the Council rejected the mayor's proposal, held a series of noisy protest rallies.

It was also too much for Tammany Hall, whose leaders now withdrew their earlier campaign endorsement and turned on Wood. Many of them joined with Republicans and Know-Nothings to nominate the fusion candidate Daniel F. Tiemann, a German-American paint manufacturer. Tiemann, a popular and effective campaigner, won the December mayoral election.

Wood did not accept his defeat meekly. He vowed revenge on the Hall. In late December he showed up at a Tammany General Committee meeting and angrily demanded the ouster of those who had backed Tiemann; as a report of the meeting related, he "resolved to carry the war to the knife, and should he fail in the struggle, with his hands on the throats of the traitors, he would drag them down with him."[31] But the Committee rejected his plea, and when Wood formed a rival General Committee, the Society's sachems padlocked the Long Room, denying legitimacy to Fernando's group. His followers jammed a subsequent Tammany meeting, shouted down the speaker, and started a furious fight. As the *New York Tribune* reported, "On all sides men were knocking down the next man to

them. Similar scenes are not uncommon at Tammany Hall, but rarely
has Tammany seen such a scene as this."[32] The dispute was quieted
only with the arrival of forty Metropolitan patrolmen.

In a final effort, Wood tried once again to capture Tammany's
Council of Sachems at its April 1858 election. This time the leaders
packed the meeting room by rounding up every single surviving
member of the Society they could locate. Some, tottering in from as
far away as Boston and Cincinnati, had not set foot in the Wigwam
for years, and many were no longer Democrats. But they all voted. As
a writer for the *Tribune* put it, "Old Injuns, young Injuns, lame In-
juns and blind Injuns, wounded Injuns and whole Injuns, Injuns with
gold-headed canes, and Injuns with red shirts on, whisky Injuns and
Injuns who came in carriages, Injuns with political aspirations, Injuns
without political aspirations, and Injuns with no aspirations, except
aspirations eternal—in short, impossible Injuns of all varieties turned
out and congregated within the bounds of the wigwam."[33] They
added up to a massive denunciation of Fernando, turning back his bid
by a two-to-one margin.

Refusing to give up, Wood started a rival organization. Gathering
his die-hard followers around him—and there were many who still
admired his political cunning and personal magnetism, not to mention his wealth—he formed what was in effect a third party, known as
the Mozart Hall Democracy, or simply Mozart Hall, from the hotel
where it met, near the corner of Broadway and Bond Street. "I am,
henceforth and forever against Tammany Hall," Wood thundered.
"Every man who strikes at it is my friend; every man who will support
it is my enemy. . . . They have me at bay now . . . and now let them
beware!"[34]

There was more to the Mozartians than bluster. Wood, ever the
meticulous craftsman, drew up an organizational plan based not on
wards, as was Tammany Hall's, but on the smaller election districts;
each district sent one of its members to the Mozart General Committee, which could thus claim to be more representative than Tammany's committee. Wood actively invited community participation.
Workingmen's clubs were set up in each ward and were encouraged
to enter candidates in school board elections in addition to larger
political contests. "Here," observes the historian Amy Bridges, "was
the beginning of the clubhouse as a social institution independent of
the saloon and liquor grocery."[35] Despite the show of democracy,
however, no one ever doubted who was in charge. The whole Mozart
Hall apparatus was a Fernando Wood juggernaut, not only directed

but largely financed by him. So it was hardly a surprise when, in 1859, Wood declared his candidacy for mayor.

Tiemann had run a lackluster administration, and during the 1859 mayoral contest Fernando's undiminished abilities as a campaigner made up for the poor reputation he had acquired in office. His Mo zart Hall machine worked with great efficiency. A rally staged at Cooper Union drew an audience of five thousand, and fifteen thousand more packed the streets outside. Wood was still popular among the many recent immigrants grateful to him for easing their naturalization. He also came down forthrightly on the side of slavery, an institution quite popular in New York at the time because of the city's profitable trading links with the South. Tammany Hall, for its part, still possessed weak leadership, and this time it was unable to unite with the Republicans against Fernando. When it was all over, Wood proved an easy victor.

It was a stunning triumph, and some new Yorkers were even saying that Mozart Hall had superseded Tammany as the city's premier Democratic organization. Yet Wood's mayoral power was limited. The Common Council was in the hands of Tammanyites and Republicans, and the state legislature at this point threw him off the Metropolitan Police Commission. And as a politician, Wood was running out of ideas. He spent much of 1860 unsuccessfully dabbling in the Democratic party's presidential nominating process. Then, in January 1861, he committed a monumental blunder in his annual address to the Common Council. With the nation drifting toward civil war, New York's merchant community was in something of a quandary: although many businessmen might have disapproved of slavery, they depended heavily on southern markets, and so were hardly sympathetic toward Unionists' efforts that were pushing southern states toward secession. In addition, Wood had been smarting for years over the success of upstate Republicans in limiting the city's home rule powers. He now proposed that New York consider separating itself from the state and becoming a "free city" with full sovereign powers equal to those of the other states of the union. That way it could trade with anyone, even with "our aggrieved brethren of the Slave States."[36]

He had badly misjudged the temper of the great majority of New Yorkers, who, no matter what their feelings about trade and slavery, fundamentally believed in the necessity of preserving the union. Condemnation rained on the mayor from all sides. "Mayor Wood's secessionist message," declared the *New York Sun*, "has sounded the bathos of absurdity."[37]

When war broke out in April, Wood was quick to change course and soon sponsored a Mozart Regiment that trained on property he owned in Yonkers. (Tammany Hall also raised its own regiment, commanded by Sachem William D. Kennedy.) Yet the damage was done. For the majority of New Yorkers, Wood was merely reverting to his old two-faced behavior.

Later that year, he became embroiled in a scandal that further reminded New Yorkers of his seemingly unquenchable predilection for sleaze. Some months previously, the Common Council saw fit to award a five-year street-cleaning contract at $279,000 a year to one Andrew V. Hackley, even though twenty-three other contractors had underbid him; the lowest bid was $84,000 less than Hackley's. What made the deal all the more bold-faced was that Hackley didn't seem to be doing the job: the streets were filthy. But Wood had reportedly been eager to sign the Council's bill that named Hackley the contractor and stayed in his office until nearly midnight on the evening of the vote to affix his signature to it. The reason, it was alleged, was that Wood had arranged for his brother, Ben, to be paid one quarter of the contract amount, or $69,750 a year, as a bribe from Hackley. (Some of the money would presumably end up in Fernando's pocket.) Council members had also been bribed a total of $40,000 to pass the bill. After lengthy litigation, Wood was finally absolved of the bribery charge, but he could not escape blame for breaching city ordinances that banned closed bidding, or for cutting his brother in on the deal.

It was almost anticlimactic when in December 1861 Wood lost his reelection bid to Republican candidate George C. Opdyke. Down again, he was once again not out. Although he would not return as mayor, he ran for Congress in 1862 and, backed by both Mozart Hall and Tammany (whose sachems were glad to help move him out of town), won easily. He would bedevil Tammany no longer. He served in the House of Representatives, with one interruption, until his death in 1881.

In the wake of his departure, Mozart Hall flourished for a while but, with Fernando increasingly concerned with national issues, gradually declined. In 1868, Wood resigned from Mozart and rejoined Tammany, which had no further reason to oppose him. Soon thereafter, Mozart Hall dissolved. Tammany Hall had survived its most formidable intraparty challenge and was preparing itself for new adventures.

Soon a new Tammany strongman would emerge. Wood's excesses and deceptions had been highly instructive to the up-and-coming politician William M. Tweed, who detested Wood but had learned much from him. Wood had changed Tammany in ways that would prove valuable to a resourceful operator like Tweed. His constant involvement in shady deals helped bolster the presumption that those in elected or appointive office had a right to line their pockets. His use of the police to assist in his campaigns and his close ties to gangs such as the Dead Rabbits had the effect of legitimizing (among like-minded politicians) the use of force to consolidate power. His single-minded lust for personal power and his desire to dominate the very organization—the Hall—that had created him in the first place helped usher in the era of Tammany autocrats who would forever make the Hall, to most Americans, synonymous with dictatorial boss rule.

4

THE RING

STARING MALEVOLENTLY OUT OF THOMAS NAST'S political cartoons of the 1870s, Boss Tweed's image gleams and glowers. The leering, menacing brute, a fat and corrupt monumental rogue, embodied all that could seem threatening and evil in urban America. Surrounding him in many of the cartoons are his key henchmen who formed the core of the Tweed Ring: the thickset, bushy-haired political schemer Peter Barr Sweeny; the slick, round-faced money manager Richard B. Connolly; and the droll, wispy Mayor Oakey Hall. But the hulking Tweed is always dominant, and the telling cartoons established him once and for all as the quintessential big-city boss. He was the man who put Tammany Hall on the U.S. map. For all Americans, Tammany Hall came to symbolize the ultimate manifestation of predatory machine politics.

Tweed put it on the map by controlling it completely, almost submerging it. Although the Tweed Ring and Tammany were to become almost synonymous in the minds of the American people, Tammany played a distinctly secondary role—Tweed used it as a mere stepping-stone to personal power. It was the Ring—the conspiratorial cabal within the Hall—that was in charge. And so during the years when Tweed and his fellow plotters were on the ascendant, the Tammany apparatus was to all intents and purposes the boss's personal machine. And when Tweed fell from power, gravely wounded, Tammany, too, was wounded.

The enormity of Tweed's transgressions is hard to grasp today. The amount of money he and his cohorts are believed to have stolen from the people of New York City is almost beyond belief, even when viewed from the inflationary world of the late twentieth century. The most conservative estimate during Tweed's time placed it at $30 million, but there is good reason to believe the total was upwards of $75 million, and some pegged it as high as $200 million. Furthermore, those were nineteenth-century dollars, worth at least ten times their equivalent today. Tweed masterminded his gargantuan thefts by accumulating political power on a scale that rendered him virtually unstoppable. By dint of clever manipulating as well as by showing how illicit profits could be maximized, he united a Tammany organization that under Wood and his predecessors had been rent by internal feuds for a generation, and he accomplished the same for the state Democratic party. For the brief period between 1868 and 1871, he was without question the most powerful figure in both the city and the state. It sometimes seemed, though, that he acquired power merely as a convenient pathway to make more money. Under Tweed, Tammany changed from an organization primarily dedicated to winning elections to one brazenly employed for wholesale thievery. The way was open in the 1860s to manipulate the system for extraordinary personal gain; Tweed saw the opening and plunged in with beguiling gusto.

But Thomas Nast's portrayal of Tweed is, in a way, misleading. The man is far more impressive and intriguing than the cartoons imply. Though physically immense—close to six feet tall and weighing almost three hundred pounds—he was nimble and far from lazy. Nast reveals the Boss as a drunken oaf, yet Tweed was a virtual teetotaler, adept at keeping his wits about him by making a single glass of wine last an entire evening while others around him became increasingly besotted. Although guilty of epochal wrongdoing, he did not seem malicious to those about him; unfailingly courteous and possessed of a wry humor, the man had no personal enemies and almost never lost his temper. Unlike Fernando Wood, he never doublecrossed anyone: a Tweed promise could be relied on. Indeed, he seemed to sail through his rapacious career with a smile on his face, enjoying himself to the hilt during one of the most amoral periods in U.S. history.

Finally, Tweed was anything but stupid. To have accomplished what he did took a first-class mind and formidable organizing abilities. In 1877, many years after he had been shorn of power, with his health broken and most of his former allies turned against him, he calmly and painstakingly described to an investigating committee the inner workings of the Ring he had masterminded, producing the facts and figures that make up much of what we now know of his plunderings, as well as of his achievements. This was no ordinary politician.

The times were ripe for a man like Tweed. The post–Civil War United States was a boom era in which the nation, tired of crusades and emotionally spent by the recent strife, wanted to put sectional discord behind it and concentrate on expanding and making money. Industry burgeoned and the country was growing by leaps and bounds; wages and prices were rising, and there seemed to be plenty of cash around. The flush times bred political apathy; people were too busy making money to worry about the morality of public servants. In New York, rapid growth and urbanization brought massive dislocation and pressing social needs. The demand grew for all sorts of expanded services, such as mass transit and help for the poor. In such a bewildering situation, a machine like Tammany Hall was prepared to play middleman between the powerless individual and the huge, baffling city.

Doing so, furthermore, could bring rich rewards, as New York City's government was imbued with corruption and waste. In 1866, a writer named James Parton, taking it on himself to explain the city, decided to visit City Hall and was appalled by what he found. Almost no one was working and a noxious cloud of cigar smoke hung over every room. The City Council was irresponsible, passing measures of dubious value without debate, and its members hardly merited respect: the "absolute exclusion of all honest men" and the "supremacy in the Common Council of pickpockets, prize fighters, emigrant runners, pimps, and the lowest class of liquor dealers, are facts which admit of no question."[1] Among the excesses, Parton was astonished to learn that there were 131 clerks in the city comptroller's office and 60 employed by the street commissioner. A city manual listed 12 persons who were, in theory, serving as "manure inspectors," 22 as "health-wardens," and 7 as "inspectors of encumbrances," but on further inquiry Parton learned that the majority of these people "were bar-keepers, low ward politicians, nameless hangers-on of saloons, who absolutely performed no official duty whatever except to draw the salary attached to their places."[2] Everyone was on the take.

It would take a tough, capable, and self-assured man to rise above such a morass and organize it for outlandish profit, and William M. Tweed proved himself up to the task. Contrary to what many have assumed, he was of Scottish, not Irish, descent; his great grandfather came to the United States in the middle of the eighteenth century from a town on the river Tweed near Edinburgh. Tweed's father was a chair maker. William was born in 1823 in the family home on Cherry Street, a spot now occupied by the Manhattan approaches to the Brooklyn Bridge. Because of Tweed's later notoriety, someone once imagined that his middle initial stood for Marcy, in remembrance of the Albany Regency politician William L. Marcy, who was known for giving rise to the notion of the "spoils system," and even today the Boss is still referred to as William Marcy Tweed. But as the historian Leo Hershkowitz has pointed out, this error was merely another manifestation of the legend that was to grow up around Tweed, because in 1823 Marcy was hardly known outside Albany, Tweed never signed his name that way, and the M almost certainly stood for Magear, Tweed's mother's maiden name. "Marcy was surely tacked on by newspapermen as a clever thought," writes Hershkowitz, "a nickname befitting a 'corrupt' politician."[3]

Tweed's father hoped Bill would follow him into the chair-making business, which he did after a few years of schooling, but he did not like working with his hands and in due course left to become a bookkeeper for a brush-making concern in which his father had an interest. He was good at keeping figures straight, and by the age of nineteen became a part owner of the company. In 1844, at the age of twenty-one, he married the daughter of the head of the firm. (They were to produce ten children, eight of whom survived to adulthood.) From all outward signs, Bill was headed for a solid career in business.

But his heart was elsewhere. To the big, hearty, strapping young man, who already weighed more than 250 pounds, the volunteer fire company he had recently joined offered more excitement. Tweed loved the fun and companionship Engine Company No. 12 offered. In 1848, a state assemblyman named John J. Reilly invited Tweed and others to help form a new engine company, No. 6, and Bill happily assented. They decided to name it the Americus Engine Company, perhaps after Americus Vespucci, and further to adopt as its symbol the likeness of a ferocious Bengal tiger that the members copied from a French lithograph. It is not known for sure whether Bill Tweed suggested the tiger, which was soon emblazoned on the company's engine, but a decade or so later, when Tweed became Tammany Hall's undisputed leader, Tammany politicians began wearing pins portraying the tiger. Shortly thereafter Thomas Nast in his anti-Tweed cartoons used the tiger to symbolize a predatory Hall.

In the ensuing years, Tammany's leaders—despite the scandals surrounding Boss Tweed—adopted the symbol officially. Tammany Hall was the Tiger.

Tweed loved the fire company. It came to be known as Big Six, and in 1849 he became its foreman. Hurrying through the streets to reach a fire could be perilous, as street gangs often attacked the volunteers, and fire companies might even fight each other for the honor of dousing a blaze. But Tweed did not shrink from the danger. In fact in 1850 he was suspended for three months by the city's chief engineer for directing Big Sixers to attack Hose Company 31 with "axes, barrels and missles" as they sped to a fire. The penalty did him no harm among his fellow volunteers. He also relished the company's social life. A friend later recalled that at Big Six's first ball, Tweed appeared resplendent in a blue coat with brass buttons. He "was young and good looking then, with dark brown hair and clear, gritty eyes. He was a tip-top dancer and never wanted a partner."[4] In April 1851, Tweed led the company, by this time renowned in fire-fighting circles, on a triumphal tour of Philadelphia, Baltimore, and Washington that culminated in a visit to the White House, where he presented the men, proud in their bright red shirts, to President Millard Fillmore.

Most important for Tweed, Big Six, with its devoted, tight membership that could be counted on to vote as a block, provided an entree to politics. It is not known when he joined Tammany Hall, but in 1850, at age twenty-seven, popular, a recognized leader from a good family, he was invited by the Democrats (and thus by Tammany) to run for assistant alderman. It was not a good year for the Democrats, and he lost. The following year, however, having established his credentials, he was nominated for alderman. This time, says his biographer Denis Lynch, Tweed gave evidence of the political savvy for which he was to become known. Realizing the odds were against him, as he was competing with a well-regarded Whig candidate, he prevailed upon an old friend who was president of the East Broadway Seminary, a school for young girls, to do him the favor of coming into the race as an independent Whig. The friend, Joel Blackmer, got only 206 votes, but this cut down the other Whig's vote enough to enable Tweed to win.

As an alderman representing the rough-and-tumble Seventh Ward on the eastern flank of the Lower East Side, Tweed was exposed for the first time to the seamy side of city politics—but he caught on quickly. The new Democrat-dominated Council, or Board of Aldermen, which replaced a predominantly Whig body, pursued graft so assiduously that its members soon became known as the Forty Thieves (see chapter 3). It is not known exactly to what extent Tweed was in on the take, but he rapidly became one of the Board's leaders, and it is believed that he represented the city in its purchase of land on Ward's Island for a potter's field; although the plot was worth no more than $30,000, Tweed obtained it for $103,450; the huge markup was presumably kicked back and divided among the Thieves. Transit franchises provided a rich source of ill-gotten money. When applicants for the Third Avenue Railroad franchise distributed some $30,000 among the aldermen in 1852, William Tweed was said to have pocketed $3,000 of it. As the Boss himself observed in later years, "There never was a time when you couldn't buy the Board of Aldermen."[5]

Deals of this kind were certainly more enthralling than manufacturing chairs or brushes. After only one year as an alderman, Tweed decided he was ready for a bigger arena, specifically the U.S. Congress. In 1852, while still an alderman, he wangled a congressional nomination in an interesting manner. His district happened to include, besides New York's eastern section, the city of Williamsburgh across the East River, which was not yet a part of Brooklyn. Williamsburgh's Democratic leaders were at this time applying for a franchise to operate a ferry to Manhattan. Tweed offered them a deal: support him for Congress and he would get the Council to vote them the franchise. It worked—almost. Williamsburgh's backing was enough to gain Tweed a tie in the nominating convention, and no more. But the young man had an answer to that one. He had arranged to be appointed chairman of the convention, and he now cast the deciding vote in his own favor. "Tweedie never goes back on Tweedie," he remarked.[6] He went on to win his election in November.

But Congress turned out to be the wrong move for him. Tweed disliked Washington, missed his old pals, and found the daily congressional grind boring. He introduced no meaningful legislation and made only one speech. The prospect of going on to the Senate hardly seemed better; as he remarked to a reporter, "If I wanted to go to the Senate, I'd go; but what for? I can't talk, and I know it. As to spending my time in hearing a lot of snoozers discuss the tariff and the particulars of a contract to carry the mails from Paducah to Schoharie, I don't think I'm doing that just now."[7] Returning to New York in 1855—the year Fernando Wood took office as mayor—Tweed discovered that after a two-year absence he no longer counted for much. He tried to regain his old seat on the Board of Aldermen but was defeated by a candidate of the Know-Nothings, the anti-immigrant, anti-Catholic group who at this point enjoyed great success. Although he would later turn this defeat to his advantage in a successful play for the support of New York's Catholic foreign-born, right now he was at a standstill. He had even lost control of the Seventh Ward, his home base, to the implacable Tammany strongman Isaiah Rynders. Tweed was barely thirty-two years old and going nowhere. He was just a little-known businessman, a maker of chairs and brushes. But perhaps he was the wiser for his travails. His experience as one of the Forty Thieves evidently gave him a clear insight into the telling relationship between power and money in city politics. Political clout could bring money, which in turn could be used to win greater power. The one built on the other. The prospect was a heady one.

There was only one thing to do: change direction and adopt new tactics. Elective office, at least for the moment, was not for him. He decided to focus on building up his reputation within Tammany by throwing himself back into Seventh Ward politics and cultivating some key associates. It was better to work from the inside, making friends and achieving power by directing others. The strategy worked. In little more than a decade it would place William M. Tweed at the summit.

Late in 1855, he was named to the city's Board of Education, a minor post that held little challenge. Yet it provided a revealing look at the way the city awarded contracts, and it may have allowed him to share in kickbacks from the sale of textbooks to the schools. Less than two years later, however, in 1857, having demonstrated conviviality and hard work for the Democratic party, he received the break he was waiting for, and he proceeded to exploit it to the fullest. New York's Republicans, who had succeeded the Whigs as the main opposition party to the Democrats, thirsted for a way to curb the power of Mayor Wood, who had been reelected in 1856. In 1857 they tried to thwart him by ramming a new city charter through the state legislature, which they dominated. In addition to removing the city police from the mayor's control, the new charter gave formidable new authority to the appointive Board of Supervisors, hitherto a virtually powerless organ in the New York county government. Under the new charter, the supervisors were to audit all county (that is, city) expenditures, appoint election inspectors, and oversee not only public improvements and local taxation but the operation of certain city departments. Only the mayor would hold more power than the supervisors.

By law the Board was to be composed of six Democrats and six Republicans to make it bipartisan and to assure the Republicans of representation. Because of his strong position in the party, William Tweed was one of the six Democrats named.

There were two reasons why this appointment represented such a windfall for Tweed. First, it gave him a chance to build a power base separate from that of Fernando Wood, whom he correctly viewed as his chief rival in the struggle to control not only Tammany Hall but the city itself. Working from this base, he could derail Wood and shunt him aside. Second, any truly astute operator could tell that the "bipartisan" requirement was a joke: all that was necessary to upset the equilibrium was to buy off just one Republican, thereby creating a majority to control the Board. Tweed sensed that anyone capable of bringing that off could attain real power.

For the moment, he lay low and consolidated his own position. By 1858, he had not only become a member of the Tammany Hall General Committee, the organization's principal governing body, but had edged Rynders out of the Seventh Ward leadership. He had also helped maneuver some friends into key positions. By all odds the most important of these was Peter Sweeny, a short, beetle-browed man with a large head of bushy black hair, a walrus mustache, and black piercing eyes. The son of a Jersey City saloon keeper, Sweeny was a bachelor who lived with his sister and her husband, a state senator. He had few personal friends and seemingly no private life, subsisting entirely on politics. Crafty and subtle, he was, as one observer put it, "a completely cynical man to whom exercising the arts of politics came as naturally as breathing."[8] A Roman Catholic of Irish descent, he had become a lawyer and a devoted Tammany hand and worked in Albany as a lobbyist for railroads, gas companies, and stagecoach lines. His ability to gauge the exact strength of a candidate became legendary among Tammany hands. Although he became district attorney of New York in 1857, he recoiled from public appearances and could hardly bear to appear in court, preferring to work behind the scenes, where he was brusque and domineering. Sweeny was to become Tweed's chief adviser and political strategist. Although Tweed usually deferred to Sweeny's judgment, he was not personally fond of him. "Sweeny is a hard, overbearing, revengeful man," Tweed said during an extended and revealing appearance before an investigating committee after his fall from power. "He wants his way. He treasures up his wrath. He has considerable ability of a kind. . . .

We were so opposite and unalike that we never got along very well."[9]
Sweeny's cunning earned him many nicknames: Brains Sweeny, the
Great Democratic Warwick, Spider Sweeny, and Peter the Paragon.

Not as politically savvy as Sweeny but of immense eventual importance to Tweed for his mastery of financial detail was Richard B.
Connolly, who was to become the Ring's money man. Born near
Cork, Ireland, Connolly had immigrated to Philadelphia and then to
New York, where he worked in the customhouse and later in a number of banks. He became county clerk in 1851 and was reelected
three years later. A large, portly man (though not as huge as Tweed)
with a handsome nose on which he perched gold-rimmed spectacles,
Connolly habitually wore a stovepipe hat, even indoors, which exaggerated his height. Besides his ability to keep track of all the extraordinary sums the Tweed Ring would eventually be juggling during its
monumental thievery, he was initially of special value to the Ring
because he was highly popular among New York's Irish population.
He could persuade them to declare their allegiance to Tweed rather
than to Fernando Wood, and this helped assure Wood's downfall.
Connolly was the least attractive of all the Ring members. As the
Tammany historian Morris Werner wrote, "Connolly was said to be
obsequious to Tweed and Sweeny and arrogant to his clerks. His
manner was crafty, insinuating, but somewhat cowardly, and he was
popularly known to his friends as well as to his enemies by the sobriquet of "Slippery Dick.' "[10]

Another key friend whom Tweed helped promote during these
years was a tall, swaggering, mustachioed lawyer named George G.
Barnard, who in due course would perform signal service to the Ring
as a readily corruptible judge. Unlike Sweeny and Connolly, Barnard
was well-born—from a proper New York family—and a Yale graduate. But aside from those qualifications, he was quite unusual. Arrogant and witty, Barnard had been a gold prospector in California, a
"shill" in a gambling house, and a member of a minstrel troupe before returning East to practice law in New York and engage in Tammany politics. In 1858, when Barnard decided to run for recorder,
a judicial post, Tweed's way of helping his nomination provides
good evidence of the future Boss's imaginative way of controlling a
meeting.

A prominent Tammany sachem, Elijah Purdy, had been scheduled
to chair the event, but as Tweed later recalled, "So I went that night,
and behold! no Purdy came. 'Come on,' said I, 'I'll preside!' So I took
the chair, and wasn't very comfortable in it, either. A man from Cali-

fornia, by the name of Doyle, was running for Recorder against Barnard. . . . I saw, as the roll call proceeded, that Doyle had the majority of delegates. Said I to a secretary, 'Have a motion made to dispense with calling the roll!' It was done. 'All in favor of Mr. Barnard as the nominee of this body say aye. Carried! The meeting is adjourned!' Well, there was a riot and I was driven into one corner; Isaiah Rynders had a pistol as long as my arm drawn and cocked. Said he, 'I'll pay you for this!' I was scared, but I didn't say so. 'I'm not afraid of a whole ward of you fighting villains,' said I, and we all got out."[11]

As recorder, Barnard did not disappoint his Tammany backers, but it was not until Tweed got him named to the New York Supreme Court in 1860 that he came into his own. Courtrooms presided over by Barnard were always good theater. He habitually wore a tall white hat while on the bench and sat with his feet up in front of him. He would spend the entire session whittling pine sticks, which court attendants were ordered to keep in copious supply. From time to time, he would take a swig from a brandy bottle, and he constantly interrupted the proceedings to make bawdy jests, provoking loud laughter. Young lawyers loved him not only for his repartee and his tolerance of their occasional lapses due to inexperience but also for his knowledge of the law, which shone through his antics. Barnard was no fool: he could see where the power lay. In years to come he would amply repay Tweed for his support by handing down a multitude of rulings favorable to the Ring and its members, as would other Tammany judges. But when events turned against Tweed, Barnard was one of the first to desert his old friend.

Allied with characters such as these, Tweed in the fall of 1859 was ready to make his first overt grab for power. By this time he had become a member of the Tammany Society itself, having been admitted to that sacrosanct organization on September 5, 1859, and was thus privy to the organization's central power structure. Tammany felt it was essential in the upcoming election to defeat Fernando Wood, who had lost reelection in 1857 but was attempting a comeback under the aegis of his own organization, Mozart Hall. Tammany Hall, which had expelled Wood, knew that he posed a serious threat and was prepared to go to any lengths to beat him. The key was the Board of Supervisors, which had the authority to appoint election inspectors. A few days before the Board was scheduled to make the appointments, five of its Democratic members met at the home of member John R. Briggs, and during the meeting the sixth member,

New York postmaster (and Tammany sachem) Isaac Fowler, arrived in his carriage, entered, and said he wanted to speak to Tweed privately. The two conversed in whispers and Fowler departed. Tweed reported to his colleagues that Fowler had raised $2,500 to be given to one of the Republican supervisors, a coal dealer named Peter P. Voorhis, in return for Voorhis's absenting himself from the Board on the day the inspectors were to be chosen. Briggs gave the money to Voorhis, who dutifully stayed away while the Democrats drew up a list of inspectors—many of them gamblers, strong-arm men, and other unsavory souls—who could be counted on to do Tammany's bidding. And so they did; the election was rife with repetitive voting, false registration, and the like. Unfortunately, Wood won the election. But the Board of Supervisors had been compromised.

"From that time out," Tweed later testified, "it was all combination on every subject, most, that came up."[12] Quite aside from having their way on partisan matters, the Tammanyites on the Board—generally marshaled by Tweed—found they had a wondrous source of graft, petty at first but gradually assuming significant dimensions, that came from the Board's authority to audit expenditures. Thus was created the so-called Supervisor's Ring, the predecessor of the better-known Tweed Ring. The supervisors' caper hinged on city contractors inflating (by permission of the supervisors) their bills and then kicking back the increase to their friends on the Board. "Pretty nearly every person who had business with the Board of Supervisors," Tweed recalled later, "or furnished the county with supplies, had a friend on the Board . . . and generally with some one member of the Ring. And through that one member [those who sold supplies to the county] were talked to, and the result was that their bills were sent in and passed, and the percentages were paid on the bills, sometimes to one man, sometimes to another."[13] Contractors were usually advised to tack on 15 percent, but in the future this would increase.

The core of the Ring consisted of Tweed and two other supervisors, John Briggs and Walter Roche. "Mr. Briggs, Mr. Roche and myself used to meet together nearly every day," said Tweed, "at my office in 95 Duane Street; I had an office there; we were all members of the various committees before which bills were brought . . . and we agreed what bill we would go for; there was hardly a time when our three votes wouldn't carry 'most anything."[14] But more than three supervisors were usually delighted to take part, and the Ring at one time even included a Republican, Henry Smith. There were times, it is true, when some supervisor afflicted with a surfeit of honesty would show signs of upsetting the arrangement and revealing it to the public. But Tweed knew how to handle that threat. As Alexander Callow has related, "On one such occasion, Supervisor Smith Ely, Jr., later Mayor of New York, had been talking to the newspapers and to the reform-minded Citizens' Association [which had just come into existence] about possible transactions in graft among the Supervisors. The day of an important meeting arrived, but Ely was told by the clerk that no meeting was to be held. He went home. At four o'clock that afternoon Tweed, with the troublesome Ely safely out of the way, held the meeting which passed some expensive appropriations and a tax-levy involving several millions of dollars. And that was that."[15] Ely's suspicions could not be documented and the public remained in the dark. Even if reform-minded citizens thought something was going on, there was no proof.

Just to be on the safe side, however, Tweed decided to buy off a key officer of the Citizens' Association, its secretary Nathaniel Sands, by arranging for his appointment as a tax commissioner at $15,000 a year. The association gave him no further trouble.

Machinations of this kind ate up so much of Tweed's time that his family's business interests suffered. At the end of the 1850s, his father-in-law died and the brush-making concern closed; meanwhile, the chair-making firm languished. His father had retired. Tweed's brother Richard was said to be spending too much time gambling, and with William preoccupied with politics there was no one else to mind the store. By 1860 the chair-making firm went bankrupt. Tweed was now a full-time politician.

At this juncture, the supervisors turned their attention to a construction project just under way on Chambers Street, behind City Hall. A new county courthouse had been authorized in 1858, to be designed by the distinguished architect John Kellum. The budget was set at $250,000, surely an adequate price for such a structure. It appears that Tweed sensed the project might lend itself to the kind of collusion between contractors and supervisors that had already yielded such happy returns. In any event, the initial appropriation was soon deemed insufficient, for in 1864 the city added a whopping $800,000 to the outlay. But that was only the beginning of the increases, as New Yorkers would one day learn to their amazement and sorrow.

Meanwhile Tweed moved to increase his influence within Tammany Hall. The opportunity he was waiting for came with the revelation that Grand Sachem Isaac Fowler, the man who had produced the $2,500 to pay off Supervisor Voorhis, had stolen $150,000 in post

office receipts. Although this did not reflect well on Tammany, the
Hall minimized the damage by an ingenious device: the warrant for
Fowler's arrest was given to Isaiah Rynders, who at that time was
serving as a United States marshal. When Rynders went to Fowler's
hotel to arrest him he made so many loud declarations of his task that
Fowler was tipped off and escaped, fleeing to Mexico. Then Tweed,
as a member of the Council of Sachems, came up with a recommen-
dation that turned the whole affair around. He moved that Fowler be
succeeded as Grand Sachem by James Conner, who was both Irish
and Roman Catholic. Conner's elevation was a milestone, for no Roman Catholic had ever headed the Tammany Society. Instantly, the
Hall's image improved, and untold numbers of immigrants and
Catholics, who had been disillusioned by Fernando Wood's connection with the Know-Nothings (which had rubbed off on Tammany),
returned to the fold. No longer could the Hall be accused of bigotry.
And the tactic made Bill Tweed look very good.

Most notably, in returning to Tammany the immigrant groups deserted Wood. In the mayoral election of 1861, Tammany went all out
to defeat him, and Tweed himself pitched in by running for sheriff.
Although Tweed failed in his own race (which hardly bothered him as
he had more pressing concerns), the bigger prize was won: Wood
went down for the last time. William Tweed was now recognized
throughout Tammany as a skilled operative, and not long after the
election he was named chairman of the New York County Democratic General Committee. Just over a year later, on January 1, 1863,
he became head of Tammany Hall's General Committee—largely by
dint of the intense lobbying efforts of Peter Sweeny, who packed the
committee with Tweed partisans. That April, with Conner and two
successors having rotated in and out of the office of Grand Sachem,
Tweed took that top prize as well.

The achievement was noteworthy for two reasons. First, the society's Grand Sachem had often been considered a nonpolitical post;
now it was most assuredly not—not as long as Tweed held it. Second,
never before had the Grand Sachem also been the chairman of the
Hall's General Committee. But Tweed had concentrated all power in
his own hands.

He had simultaneously unified the Hall, something Fernando
Wood had tried to do but could not, and that no one had achieved for
decades. Yet it must be admitted, however, that historical events were
on Tweed's side. Tammany had been split over the same issues that
had torn the United States apart—slavery and states' rights. With the

advent of the Civil War, these issues were no longer debatable in a city like New York; the die had been cast. But Tweed's charm and his unusual political acumen—as evidenced by his winning back the immigrant groups—tended to minimize conflicts and bring together those under him who might otherwise be at each other's throats. As long as he was successful, few people would stand in his way.

It was at this time that Tweed began to be referred to as the Boss. The title betokened not only his unexampled status but also his peremptory way of conducting meetings. Opposition was not to be condoned. What he had attempted years earlier in railroading Barnard's nomination now became the norm. Once when he declared the nomination of a certain judge unanimous and adjourned the meeting, a rump group stayed in the room hoping to make a counter-nomination. Tweed had the gas turned off. (This time there were no Loco-Focos with matches to carry on.)

His mastery of the entire Tammany apparatus was by now complete. In every ward in the city he had his own representative as ward leader, someone totally subservient and removable at Tweed's whim. Below this leader were subleaders and district captains who likewise responded to his every command. Each of these underlings had a number of responsibilities, all vital to the organization. He must supervise the payment of protection money by businesses engaged in marginal or illegal activities that Tammany was in a position to shelter; he must monitor all patronage requests, referring them to Tammany headquarters; he must make sure the needy were taken care of in one way or another; and he must be ever sensitive to the subtleties of the local political scene, alerting the Boss to any shift in the wind. Ward leaders and district captains *must* deliver their precincts on election day; no backsliding was permitted. They also had to be popularly accepted; anyone who lost his popularity would be quickly replaced. The vast network was in effect Tweed's private army.

He further cemented his control by creating a new elite body, the Tammany Executive Committee, to be composed of the city's twenty-two ward leaders—all of whom owed their jobs to Tweed. Henceforth, the much larger Tammany General Committee, the historic unit whose members were ostensibly elected in their local districts, played a decidedly minor role. From now on, it was the Executive Committee, or the Boss himself, who made up the true driving force of Tammany Hall.

And now that he was indisputably the chief, Tweed felt it was appropriate that he dress the part. He took to wearing a large diamond in his shirtfront, a stone so impressive that there was no mistaking the eminence of its wearer. Power being what it is, the style rapidly caught on among New York politicians, though lesser lights were careful not to rival the Boss's stone. Recalled a contemporary, "The politician who had not got a diamond in his bosom was of little account among his followers, and was looked upon as having neglected his opportunities."[16]

By this time in his life—he was now forty—Tweed was an awesome persona. Not only was he extremely large, but everything about him seemed outsize—large head, large nose, huge hands, massive shoulders, and a vast protruding stomach across which was draped a gold watch chain given to him by his old fire-fighting buddies in Big Six. His manner was usually genial if not boisterous; he had a booming laugh and loved to tell stories. Wrote the English historian James Bryce, who had the pleasure of seeing him in action, "Tweed had an abounding vitality, free and easy manners, plenty of humor, though of a coarse kind, and a jovial swaggering way which won popularity for him among the lower and rougher sort of people."[17]

Many of those rougher sorts would have a new reason to respect him after he had himself appointed deputy street commissioner in 1863. Note that he was not the commissioner—that position was too exposed and Tweed preferred to work behind the scenes. But the top man knew he should defer to Tweed, and as a result the Boss commanded a force of thousands of laborers and street cleaners, all of whom owed their jobs to Tammany patronage. All were available for whatever dirty work needed to be done on election day. The general now had an additional army to supplement his Tammany minions.

By this time he had money, too, and not all of it was coming from the supervisors' bill-padding system. One neat transaction came about when Tweed learned that a building in Harlem was to be converted into a church and had three hundred benches to dispose of. He bought the lot at five dollars apiece; sold seventeen to a friend, at cost; and then sold the remainder to the city for use in county armories, not at cost but at the unconscionable price of $600 apiece, for a total of $169,800. His profit on the deal: $168,385.

Such returns could buy many a diamond, but Tweed also put the money to more constructive uses. In 1864 he bought controlling interest in the New York Printing Company, which began to do all the city's official printing at inflated rates. Tweed also advised railroads, ferries, and insurance companies to have their printing done at his company lest they find the city looking on them with disfavor, and most felt constrained to comply. He acquired the Manufacturing Stationers' Company and through it sold—again, at inflated prices—blank books, paper, pens, and ink to the city's schools as well as to many of the city's departments. With some friends he paid $3,080 for a marble quarry in Sheffield, Massachusetts, which before long was doing a brisk business selling marble to the city for the new courthouse. Initially, the quarry was put under contract in 1864 to deliver $1,250 worth of marble; by 1867, it had shipped $220,000 worth. In other words, Tweed had it both ways. Sitting on the Board of Supervisors over which he usually presided, he approved inflated bills to be paid by the city and then took his cut. At the same time, operating on the other side of the process, he profited as a contractor, enjoying inflated returns.

Two other activities occupied him. Although Tweed had only rudimentary knowledge of the law—he had no formal training—in 1860 his friend George Barnard was pleased to repay old favors by certifying him as an attorney. Tweed soon hung out his shingle at 95 Duane Street. Over the years he was to earn high fees from companies anxious to benefit from his political influence. One notable example was the Erie Railroad, which paid him upwards of $100,000. The Boss was also putting much of his excess cash into real estate. By the late 1860s he had become one of the largest landowners in the city.

Because he was moving up in the world, moreover, he felt it was fitting that he possess a suitable home. Until the mid-1860s he and his wife had lived on the Lower East Side not far from where they both grew up, but with a growing family they needed more space. So in 1866 Tweed purchased a handsome brownstone residence at 41 West Thirty-sixth Street, on the edge of the city's most fashionable district. No one seemed concerned about how he had paid for it.

Up to now, Tweed had not counted the mayor of New York as an ally, but that changed in 1865 with the election of John T. Hoffman to that office. Hoffman, who had been recorder following Barnard, was a handsome, estimable descendant of an old Dutch family, a member of a fine New York law firm and a Tammany sachem. Attractive and personally above reproach, though politically ambitious, he was to become extremely useful to Tweed by exemplifying probity while studiously ignoring any corrupt activities taking place in his vicinity. He was, in other words, a good front man. As the journalist Horace Greeley wrote of him in 1868, "His humble work is to wear good clothes and be always gloved, to be decorous and polite . . . to repeat as often as need be, in a loud voice, sentences about 'honesty' and 'public welfare,' but to appoint to rich places such men as Mr. Sweeny."[18] The smoke screen worked. Although there might have been murmurs here and there in the city that something fishy was going on, specific evidence of wrongdoing was not to be had. In a study of the Boss, a Massachusetts paper, the *Springfield Republican*, could find nothing amiss and merely expressed wonderment at Tweed's spectacular rise.

With Hoffman in City Hall, a pleasant social custom developed whereby Boss Tweed would come across the street from Tammany Hall at lunchtime to dine in the basement with the mayor, to be joined most days by Street Commissioner Charles Cornell and Comptroller Matthew Brennan. From time to time Peter Sweeny stopped by. As Tweed later recalled the sessions, the talk "was all politics; no money was ever mentioned there. . . ."[19] As time went on, however, the group's membership changed. Cornell dropped out and Brennan gave way to Slippery Dick Connolly when the latter became comptroller in 1867. Sweeny became a regular. And it is probably safe to say that whenever Mayor Hoffman was not present, there would be talk of money and how to produce it. Thus, the nucleus of the Tweed Ring came into being: the Boss, Sweeny, and Connolly. But a fourth man also began to drop by from time to time, and he would eventually become the fourth member of the fabled group: the district attorney and future mayor, the irrepressible Abraham Oakey Hall.

By all odds the most entertaining character who ever served as New York's chief executive, Oakey Hall (as he called himself) was a short, wiry slip of a man with a thick head of dark hair, drooping black mustache, luxuriant beard, and sharp eyes that peered out through pince-nez glasses attached to a long ribbon. As his biographer Croswell Bowen wrote, "He had the look of a professor—benign, knowledgeable, and full of jokes which, in his case, were chiefly puns."[20] Born in the city, he claimed to be descended from a Britisher, one of the officers responsible for trying and executing Charles I—a fact Hall liked to bring up whenever an Irish voter was within earshot. He had been a newspaper reporter, successful lawyer, and lobbyist, had written plays and acted in them, and was a much sought-after lecturer and after-dinner speaker. He liked reciting Shakespeare and packing his prose with Latin quotations. In court, someone said, "His legal arguments abound in coruscations of vivacious fancy."[21] Aside from his atrocious puns (called upon to discuss the "Chinese question" on a hot night in June, he remarked it was a good time to talk about coolies), he was a master of the quick rejoinder. Once while he was mayor, attending the funeral of an alderman, a job seeker approached him and managed to say to Hall that he hoped very much he could take the man's place. "I'm willing," Hall shot back, "but you'll have to apply to the undertaker."[22]

What really set Hall apart, however, was his clothing, which was flamboyant. He wore a different necktie and different cuff links every day and on special occasions could be counted on to turn himself out in spectacular fashion. For a key Tammany ball, a newspaper related, Hall "was faultlessly attired in a bottle-green fly-tail coat, with half sovereigns of pure guinea gold for buttons and a green velvet collar and lapels, a waistcoat and a light unwhisperable of the same material and color and a new satin necktie of large dimensions. . . . He wore a pair of eye glasses with rims of Irish bog-oak and attached to a green silk cord."[23] On St. Patrick's Day he would be similarly turned out in riotous green, and at German functions he would sport the colors of the fatherland, leading the *New York Sun* to call him the Honorable Abraham Von O'Hall. But to New Yorkers he was universally referred to as the Elegant Oakey.

Behind the razzle-dazzle was a sharp and inquiring mind. As district attorney under Mayor Fernando Wood, Hall had come up with an outrageous opinion that enabled Wood to slide out from under an unpopular prohibition law, endearing the mayor to every barfly in the city. Hall's opinions on the treatment of criminals were enlightened, and he possessed one of the city's finest collections of books on crime. Yet he craved the spotlight and the crowd's applause and would seemingly do anything to preserve his job, and this allowed him to wink at the Ring's excesses and even partake of them. Tweed, in turn, liked to have Hall around because he brought an air of respectability to the Ring. Oakey belonged to most of the city's best clubs and was accepted in society. That was enough for the Boss. "Hall's all right," he once said. "All he needs is ballast. . . . Politics are too deep for him. They are for me, and I can wade long after Oakey has to float."[24]

All the while the Boss was putting together the combination that would constitute the Tweed Ring itself, shoring up the support he wanted from the judiciary. Barnard had been promoted to the New York Supreme Court in 1860, and in the ensuing years four others would be counted as particularly faithful devotees of Tweed's cause. Albert Cardozo, a quiet, courteous, hardworking jurist from a New York Portuguese Jewish family, had none of the pomposity or dash of Barnard, but his vaulting ambition led him to do Tweed's bidding when asked. He was pleased to appoint whatever commissioners or court officers the Ring wanted, and he arranged to pardon or free countless criminals whom the Ring wanted released for various illegal tasks. (When the Ring fell, Cardozo resigned from the bench just before his impeachment, sullying his family's name. It remained for his son, Benjamin Cardozo, to bring honor to the family many years later by serving with distinction on the U.S. Supreme Court.) Totally unlike either Barnard or Cardozo was Judge John McCunn, a rough-cut Irish immigrant who had worked on the docks before going to law school. Along with Barnard, McCunn rendered valued service to Tweed in the late 1860s by ignoring the niceties of U.S. citizenship requirements, thereby naturalizing astonishing numbers of recent im-migrants, the better to swell Tammany's vote totals.

Two other members of the judiciary rounded out the shabby crew. John Hackett, who became city recorder in 1866 on the recommen-dation of Oakey Hall, specialized in doing favors for ward chiefs—he would suspend or discharge convicted criminals who were friends of theirs. During one period lasting a year and ten months he dismissed 170 cases, 28 of whose suspects had been found guilty of grand larceny and 15 of burglary. But he could be vindictive: he once sentenced a man to twenty years in prison for entering his mother's room and taking $8.00. The city's corporation counsel, Richard O'Gorman, a huge, gruff onetime Fenian leader in Ireland, allowed friends of the Ring to file fraudulent claims against the city. Instead of fighting the claims, as his office should have, O'Gorman recom-mended they be paid in full—at which point he collected a healthy commission.

In undisputed command of Tammany Hall, Tweed was now in total control of a powerful political machine based on patronage that benefited not only the Hall but himself and others personally. The city payroll, comprising at least twelve thousand jobs, was a rich source of funds, as officeholders were expected to express their grati-tude by returning a percentage of their salaries to those who had appointed them. In the mayor's office, to cite one area, there were six marshals, a record clerk, a copying clerk, an interpreter, two messen-gers, a private secretary, several sergeants at arms, and five miscella-neous clerks. Furthermore, as many as a third of these officeholders were no-shows: though collecting full salary they did no work. Sala-ries could total substantial amounts when one man held down a large number of positions. Cornelius Corson, for example, a boyhood friend of Tweed's and the Boss' partner in the New York Printing

Company, received $25,000 a year in salaries from the city: he got $10,000 as clerk to the commissioners for a Ninth District courthouse; $5,000 as head of the Bureau of Elections; $2,500 as clerk to the Board of County Canvassers; another $2,500 as a clerk to the Board of Supervisors; yet another $2,500 as official reporter for the Board of Aldermen; and a final $2,500 as a court stenographer. Yet most of these jobs required very little of his time, if any.

Some of the jobs passed out to the faithful seem to have been thought up with a high degree of creativity. One Tammany stalwart, state Senator Mike Norton of the Eighth Ward, in addition to serving as commissioner of two county courthouses, including the new one on Chambers Street, also drew a salary as corporation livery stable keeper and another as baggage agent at Castle Garden, the city's immigration station. He also received $30,000 a year as contractor for the sprinkling of Harlem Lane, a service that probably cost him no more than $5,000. Because the manifold holders of these city jobs liked to wear tall sleek hats to set them apart from their fellow citizens, they became known as the Shiny Hat Brigade.

The Brigade had plenty of room, too, for members of Tweed's ample family. A son, William M. Tweed, Jr., enjoyed employment as an assistant district attorney and as a commissioner of street openings; the Boss also got him appointed to a receiver position in the Pacific Railroad, and the young man served as a general in the state militia. The Boss's brother, Richard Tweed, was a tax assessor, and Richard's son was a first assistant clerk in the Department of Education. Another son of the Boss, Alfred Tweed, could be found clerking in the district court, while a nephew, William H. King, Jr., in time became a deputy commissioner of public works. Tweed's associates also distributed largess: Sweeny's brother, brother-in-law, and uncle were on the city payroll, as were John Hoffman's father-in-law and brother-in-law.

The sudden affluence of Tammany under Tweed was additionally reflected in the Society's decision to build a new, grander headquarters to replace the old Hall on Nassau Street. The new Wigwam was to be located on East Fourteenth Street between Third and Fourth avenues, a good solid address, and was to include not only a large meeting hall capable of seating one thousand but, to crown its facade, a greater-than-life-size statue of Saint Tammany. The laying of its cornerstone on July 4, 1867, was accompanied by speeches, a parade, and an elaborate banquet. Two months later, the sachems found that the money they had raised proved inadequate and that $250,000 more would be needed. No problem: the Society held a meeting and raised $175,000 on the spot, fifteen members accounting for $10,000 in instant pledges apiece.

Another sign that money was accruing to the Ring came when Hoffman named Peter B. Sweeny to be city chamberlain in the fall of 1867. This was a key post because it controlled the depositing of the city's funds in bank accounts. Heretofore the chamberlain had been allowed to pocket the interest payments derived from the deposits, but Sweeny surprised everyone by announcing, after his appointment had been ratified by the Board of Aldermen, that he would renounce that form of payment—estimated at $200,000 a year—in favor of an annual salary of $10,000. The city's newspapers, swallowing their incredulity, showered Sweeny with praise, the *Herald* likening him to the patriots of ancient Rome who had sacrificed all for their country. Only later, when the Ring had been exposed, was it shown that Sweeny's declaration had been pure grandstanding, for the amount of money he was able to make illegally as chamberlain far exceeded the sum he had renounced. Indeed, it was revealed (by Tweed, in his famous latter-day testimony) that he paid the Board of Aldermen $60,000 in bribes to ensure his approval for the post. Yet for the moment, none of this was publicly known. And with prosperity continuing, most New Yorkers were too busy to care.

At this point William Tweed dominated all the major sources of power in city politics: Tammany Hall, City Hall, the municipal financial structure, and much of the judiciary. What was missing? Surely nothing locally. But the Boss saw that ultimately New York City was always going to be at the mercy of the state legislature in Albany for the form of its government and for the way it handled its finances. It would pay to have a strong representative in the state legislature. And what better candidate could there be but himself? So it was that in 1867 Tweed thought better of his aversion to elective office and decided to run for the state senate. Given his exalted status, it was hardly a contest, and in January 1868 he arrived in Albany prepared to do battle in a new arena.

That he was no ordinary freshman senator was made known by his quarters in the state capital, a suite of seven thickly carpeted rooms in Delevan House, Albany's preeminent hostelry, replete with cages of his favored canaries as well as conveniently placed porcelain cuspidors. It was amply stocked with liquor for the pleasure of fellow legislators and other potentates, who could come and go via a private elevator to avoid public scrutiny. Among his guests were bankers and industrialists courting his favor, as well as legislators from rural districts who had traditionally regarded city politicians as the ultimate in evil, but in whose pet local projects Tweed proceeded to take great interest, to their gratitude. Other guests undoubtedly included the presumed members of the Black Horse Cavalry, a group of some thirty legislators whose votes were said to be purchaseable by the highest bidder. Frequently in attendance at Delevan House also was Peter Sweeny, always ready to plot a new strategem or help the Boss win over an indecisive legislator.

Tweed's massive frame caused an unsuspected problem: when he presented himself on the senate floor on the opening day of the new session, the seat assigned to him was not strong enough to support him. Accordingly, recalled one observer, "he had to hold a sort of levee in the cloakroom . . . while the Clerk . . . ordered and had ready for the next day's session a special seat, larger, stronger, and in every way adapted to the emergency."[25]

But there were more important things to be concerned about. It was essential, Tweed felt, to demonstrate his power early. His prime antagonist, he was sure, was not anyone in the legislature itself or even the governor, the Republican Edwin D. Morgan. It was Samuel Jones Tilden, a successful New York City lawyer originally from the small upstate village of New Lebanon, who had been a disciple of Martin Van Buren and active in Tammany affairs from the early 1840s. Although Tilden had renounced public office in 1846 to concentrate on the practice of corporation law (at which he was extremely successful), he had become a Tammany sachem in 1856 and had agreed to be state Democratic chairman in 1866. This was no minor personage.

Because he was an insider well acquainted with Tammany's ways, Tilden harbored the deepest suspicions of Tweed and his sudden power. He would one day emerge as the Ring's most prominent antagonist. As of early 1868, however, he had no direct evidence against the Boss and, being a cautious man (though highly ambitious), was reluctant to speak out against him. But he did have his own candidate for speaker of the assembly, a post of great influence. His choice was a very capable assemblyman from Rensselaer County named John L. Flagg, who was also mayor of Troy. Tweed's candidate was William ("Billy") Hitchman, a former carriage painter, fireman, and policeman from New York's Upper East Side, a true Tammany hack. Tilden thought it was no contest. He was wrong. The Boss, wrote a reporter for a Republican paper, "slipped around like a porpoise among the small fishes of the Assembly, varying the performance, now and then, by reverently raising his hands and blessing his dearly beloved Democratic children."[26] Among those on whom he worked with special care were those upstate assemblymen whom he had already cultivated. Billy Hitchman won in a walk, and Tilden was totally stymied. Tilden was not an unforgiving sort, however, and he would be heard from again.

With his predominance assured, Tweed backed a piece of legislation that he had good reason to consider of great importance, and that of course passed easily. It was the Adjusted Claims Act, which empowered New York City's comptroller—Slippery Dick Connolly—to perform two new functions. One allowed him to adjust claims against the city, which meant he could reduce some claims and increase others: if a contractor was not charging enough, the comptroller could up the man's fee—the better to exhort kickbacks. The second gave him the authority to raise money by bond issues, a power taken for granted today but virtually unheard of at that time. In the Ring's terms, it was a license to print money, and Connolly was quick to take advantage of it. But there was no public outcry, and the press seemed strangely muted, having been bought off—it would later be learned—by the Boss.

Moving to Albany for part of the year did not mean that Tweed ignored New York City. Urgent problems simply had to follow him there. In 1868, the men financing the building of the Brooklyn Bridge found themselves in a dilemma. The city of Brooklyn (still an independent entity) had already subscribed to $3 million worth of stock to pay for the bridge, but New York's share, amounting to just half of that, or $1.5 million, had not been approved by the City Council, which had to okay the comptroller's issuing the necessary securities. The head of the bridge company, Henry Cruse Murphy, who happened also to be a state senator from Brooklyn, knew where to go to break the logjam. He called at Delevan House and conferred with the Boss, who after protesting that he had no direct line to the Council agreed to make inquiries. He reported back to Murphy that, as he put it later, "the appropriation could be passed by paying for it" to the tune of $55,000 or $65,000 (the exact amount is not recorded) in bribes to the aldermen.[27] Murphy evidently agreed (although he steadfastly denied to the end of his days that he had done so); a bag containing the necessary cash was brought to Tweed for transfer to his contact on the Board of Aldermen, and the project went forward. It should be added that Tweed did not make the arrangement without getting something out of it for himself and his friends. A year later, an official list of stock owners in the project revealed that Tweed, Sweeny, and another man each possessed 560 shares of Brooklyn Bridge stock, worth $56,000 apiece. The evidence is that none of them paid a cent for their shares. Such was the cost of doing business with the Boss.

In Tweed's circle of power one piece was still missing: the governorship. Mayor Hoffman had tried for the office once before but failed; Tweed resolved to bring every force to bear to elect him in 1868. First, however, it would be necessary to make sure Hoffman would not step out of line. The mayor had recently shown an unwonted independence, vetoing an ordinance passed by the Common Council for "opening, regulating, and improving the avenues or boulevards north of Central Park." It was a measure close to the heart of the Boss, as it was sure to generate plenty of work (that is, patronage) for the Street Department. But Hoffman had been swayed by a group of taxpayers opposed to it. Tweed, in Albany at the time, sped back to the city and stopped in at City Hall to talk with His Honor. That same evening the newspapers reported from Albany, seemingly by coincidence, that Tweed would shortly announce his own candidacy for governor in the next election, opposing Hoffman. The mayor, shaken, was relieved when the Council passed the ordinance over his veto, taking him off the hook, and he never transgressed the Boss again. That summer, after Tammany had proudly hosted the Democratic National Convention in its newly completed Wigwam on Fourteenth Street and had seen Horatio Seymour nominated for president (to run against Ulysses S. Grant), Tweed was happy to stage the state convention in the same hall and to bring about the naming of Hoffman as a candidate for governor.

He had meant to pull out all the stops to throw the election to Hoffman, and he delivered. The 1868 election was almost certainly the crookedest in the city's history, either before or since. So blatant were the frauds, in fact, that the U.S. Congress ordered an investigation that proved an eye-opener. In preparation for the event, Tammany Hall had opened up its treasury and allotted $1,000 to each election district (of which there were 327 in the city, for a total of $327,000) for electioneering. More than six weeks before the election the Hall embarked on a massive campaign to naturalize recent immigrants, a drive that was for the most part illegal and that yielded a total of 41,112 new voters—of whom probably 85 percent dutifully voted the straight Tammany ticket in November. In preparation for the drive, Tweed's New York Printing Company ran off 105,000 blank application forms and 69,000 certificates of naturalization. The Hall opened offices throughout the city where foreigners could fill out their applications and where witnesses were available to swear to anyone's eligibility on receipt of a token fee. "There are men in New York," said one investigator, "whom you can buy to make a false oath for a glass of beer."[28] One witness for hire, James Goff, swore to the "good moral character" of no fewer than 669 applicants; two days later he was arrested for stealing.

So eager was Tammany Hall to bring in new citizens that it authorized free-lance naturalization brokers to act in its name. One man operating out of a saloon on Chatham Street would fill out hundreds of blank applications using names previously given to him, walk the papers through the system, return with them approved (illegally, of course), and sell them for five dollars apiece. He paid his court costs using special certificates given to him by Tammany Hall. Another operator told an undercover agent that he alone had obtained citizenship papers for seven thousand persons.

Tweed's friends in the judiciary were glad to oblige him in the campaign. In 1866 Judge Albert Cardozo had performed nobly for Tammany, often granting naturalization papers to as many as eight hundred persons a day, most of them sight unseen; most of the citizenships were questionable (in one five-minute period he naturalized thirteen persons). By 1868, he had been promoted to a new bench and could no longer render such fine service, but judges Barnard and McCunn were ready for the challenge. During the first week in October, Barnard announced that he would devote the rest of the month exclusively to naturalizing aliens. He held court daily from 6:00 P.M. to midnight to process applications, putting through 140 or 150 at a time, initialing each application without reading its contents. By election day Barnard had provided citizenship papers to 10,093 men. McCunn's record was equally impressive; on one day alone he naturalized 2,109 persons, sometimes processing three a minute.

New citizens had to register, and many of them were listed at preposterous addresses: no fewer than forty-two newly made voters were said to be residents of 70 Greene Street, which was a well-known brothel. Meanwhile, ordinary Americans were earning good money by registering in several places under fictitious names: one John J. Mullen got himself listed as a voter in ten different polling spots during a single day, using such names as James Gannon, James Gray, John Murphy, and John Moran, in addition to his own.

On election day, finally, the usual instances of repeating occurred. One man testified that he had been told he voted twenty-eight times, but he was not sure about the number because he had been drunk most of the day. Tammany's election inspectors paid little attention; those who tried to enforce the rules found they would be beaten up if they did so. At the end of the day, poll clerks tallied the vote by virtually inventing the totals. As Tweed himself described the process in his testimony years later, the technique was to "count the ballots in bulk, or without counting them announce the result in bulk," One estimate held that more than fifty thousand illegal votes were cast in New York City. But it did not really matter how big the number was. "The ballots made no result," Tweed said. "The counters made the result."[29] Suffice it to say that Seymour carried New York State (while losing to Grant nationwide), and Hoffman was handily elected governor.

As for the congressional investigation that unearthed all the excesses, the investigating committee drew up a report condemning the frauds and also made sure that the necessary legislation to prevent future transgressions was introduced into the New York state legislature. The bill, which passed easily, called for tightening voter registration requirements and giving election inspectors more clout. Did it become law? Not at all. Hoffman, the brand-new governor, refused to sign it, and it passed into limbo.

On the local scene, Horace Greeley of the *New York Tribune* wrote an open letter to Samuel Tilden accusing him of being "at least a passive accomplice" in the frauds because of his role as state chairman, and challenged him to put a stop to such deeds in the future.[30] The supercautious Tilden chose not to respond.

There was one other victor in the election: Oakey Hall, who moved up to succeed Hoffman as mayor. His arrival in City Hall was universally applauded. As the *New York Herald* expressed it during the campaign, "It will be a refreshing novelty to have for Mayor of New York a strictly upright, honorable, capable man, and at the same time one who writes a drama or a farce with equal success, acts a part as well as most professionals on the stage, conducts the most difficult cases on the calendar, sings a good song, composes poetry by the yard, makes an effective stump-speech, responds to a toast with remarkable eloquence and taste, mixes a lobster salad as well as Delmonico's head cook, smokes the best cigar in New York, respects old age, and admires youth, as poets and orators invariably do."[31]

Charles A. Dana of the *Sun* speculated that Hall might go much further than just City Hall; he could end up in the White House. Though insuppressible, Hall over the next many months was careful not to do anything Tweed would disapprove of.

And Tweed seemed invincible. In addition to serving as state senator, he was still president of the Board of Supervisors of New York County, chairman of New York County's Democratic General Committee, and Grand Sachem of the Tammany Society, and there was no important power center in the state that did not do his bidding. He seemed to be able to do anything he wanted.

Furthermore, criticism of the Boss in the press was muted, as he made it his policy to reward members of the Fourth Estate who overlooked Tammany misconduct. For years, City Hall had doled out annual "Christmas presents" of $200 apiece to reporters covering local political doings and the courts, but Tweed in addition subsidized six or eight key newspapermen to the tune of $2,000 or $2,500 apiece, a practice likely to discourage any attacks on his moral rectitude. Newspapers were paid large sums for carrying "city advertising," which should actually have cost only a fraction of the money provided. One Albany paper received, through Tweed's efforts, a legislative appropriation of $207,900 for a year's printing when the true cost was not more than $10,000. Another Albany journal, a Republican one at that, regularly allowed the Boss to read and censure articles that were highly critical of him in return for regular payments. As he later recalled, it was "sometimes $5,000, sometimes $1,000, sometimes $500. It was a general dribble all the time."[32]

Behind this veil of silence, or censorship, or apathy—or all three— Bill Tweed and his fellow Ringmates proceeded to raise the level of graft in the city's business. Now the Boss, Peter Sweeny, Dick Connolly, and Oakey Hall were each taking 20 percent of the kickback from every inflated bill submitted, with the fifth 20 percent set aside for contingencies and to reward minor players in the combine.

The group had found a surefire conduit for fraudulent payments: the renting and repairing of National Guard armories. Far from being the large, solidly constructed affairs usually associated with the military, these were mostly dingy rooms reached by rickety stairs in run-down buildings—but the city was paying heavily for them. The Fifth Regiment's armory was a single room over a saloon on Hester Street that rented for $10,000 a year, while that of the Seventy-Ninth was a fifth-floor walkup at the corner of Greene and Houston streets that cost the city $8,000 annually. Eight of the armories were actually stables that rented for a total of $85,000 a year. Most of these inflated payments, it goes without saying, found their way back to the Ring. But Tammany Hall directly benefited, too, as its top floor was in theory rented as an armory and several other rooms were similarly leased out for military activities for a total annual stipend of $36,000.

If rents for the armories were sky-high, repairs were in the stratosphere. Waxing rich on repair work while paying over huge sums to the Ring were a small band of contractors whose names only a few years hence would be well known to New Yorkers. One was a well-connected plasterer named Andrew Garvey who, between 1869 and the end of 1871, received $197,330.24 for work done on armories; the New York Times dubbed him the Prince of Plasterers. During the same period John H. Keyser was paid $142,329.71 for plumbing, George S. Miller got $431,064.31 for carpentry, and James H. Ingersoll took away $170,729.60 for "furniture and accessories." On just one day in 1870, it was later revealed, four men were paid $163,992.66 just for repair work.

The money spent on armories, however, was nothing compared with that shelled out by the comptroller for the new county courthouse. The $800,000 added in 1864 to the original appropriation of $250,000 for the building had been followed by a grant of $300,000 more in 1865, to which was shortly added yet another $300,000. Even this turned out to be inadequate, and another half a million dollars was paid over to the project in 1866. Still, the building was nowhere near completion. A group of reformers, alarmed at the runaway costs, demanded an investigation. They were told that the Board of Supervisors already had an investigating committee looking into the project. So the reformers appointed a committee to investigate the investigators. The upshot was a report declaring that the granting of contracts for the courthouse was entirely free from fraud. (Those issuing the report showed that they, too, were on the take when they submitted a bill for expenses totaling an unbelievable $18,406.35, including $7,718.75 to Tweed's New York Printing Company.) The city continued to sink money into the courthouse project until, some estimates said, it had cost more than $13 million, approximately four times what England had recently spent for its Houses of Parliament, and nearly twice what the United States had just paid for Alaska.

In truth, the same contractors who were fleecing the city for armory work were earning even greater sums on the courthouse, with the Ring benefiting in the same way. Before the building was finished, Andrew Garvey had been paid a princely $531,594.22 for plastering, John Keyser had received almost $1.5 million for "plumbing and gas light fixtures," and James Ingersoll had gotten a mind-boggling $5,691,144.26 for furnishings. Someone did some figuring and announced that the amount spent for carpets, which was part of Ingersoll's fee, if computed at $5 a square yard, would buy enough carpeting to cover City Hall Park (eight and a quarter acres) three times over. There was also a charge of $41,746.83 for awnings, of $41,190.95 for "brooms, etc.," and of $2,676.75 for door locks. Eleven thermometers—admittedly large framed ones five feet long—were obtained for $7,500. Cuspidors were purchased for $190 apiece, and there were $404,347 worth of safes. But not all the expense was for new construction; even before the building was completed it had cost nearly $2 million in repairs; half that amount went to Andrew Garvey. It has been estimated that at least half of the entire $13 million outlay went straight into the pockets of the Tweed Ring and its friends.

Given such astonishing graft, one might expect that some lowly member of the Hall would betray the Ring, if only because he was not being cut into the profits. But as yet no one came forward. For one thing, the Ring's veil of secrecy was tight; very few people knew what was going on. For another, most rank and file Tammanyites, if informed of the stealing, would have simply been jealous. Tammany higher-ups like Tilden who suspected wrongdoing felt they had insufficient evidence to go on. Press inquiries into the excesses got nowhere. When the New York Times questioned Ingersoll's fee of $350,000 for carpeting, he replied indignantly, "There is one thing you people down in the Times don't seem to take into account. The carpets in these public buildings need to be changed a great deal oftener than in private houses." The Times figured the city had been overcharged $336,821.31, but it let the matter drop for the time being.[33]

As the payments went up, moreover, the Ring was taking a bigger cut of them. At first the cut had been 10 percent of every bill, then 55 percent, and by the end of 1869, the amount skimmed off had climbed to 65 percent. In other words, a contractor would have to charge a whopping amount for a job because he was only going to get 35 percent of it himself. The Ring's rules were strict: payments were to be made either to the city auditor, James Watson, who was Connolly's assistant, or to E. A. Woodward, clerk to the Board of Supervisors. They would in turn skim off the Ring's take (keeping a portion for themselves) and deliver it to Tweed (when he was in town) and the others. Few people, amazingly, were aware of the vast sums being transferred. One day, it is said, Andrew Garvey arrived at Tweed's office in the Street Department carrying a sizable parcel stuffed with bills, only to find the commissioner himself, George McLean, talking with the Boss. McLean, who was not in the loop, had no idea why Garvey had entered. As Garvey tried to slip the parcel to Tweed it fell to the floor. Tweed swiftly clamped his foot down on it, and when McLean was not looking, managed to toss it in a drawer. The commissioner apparently suspected nothing.

As if so many political plots and financial shenanigans were not enough to keep any one man more than busy, Tweed was also operating on an entirely different level as an adviser, lobbyist, and power broker for the Erie Railroad. The Erie was under the control of the wily financier Jay Gould and his colorful, high-living sidekick Jim Fisk, but the rail magnate Cornelius Vanderbilt was trying to gain control of the line so that it would not undercut his own New York Central Railroad. For a while Tweed had acted as Vanderbilt's agent in Albany, and Judge Barnard, at the commodore's behest, had dutifully issued an arrest order for Gould and others for illegally issuing securities, an order they successfully evaded. But Gould and Fisk persuaded Tweed to change sides and work on their behalf, offering him a seat on the Erie board and a large block of stock. Sweeny— whose moves throughout these years are hard to plot but who was always Tweed's right-hand man—also became an Erie director. Tweed said later that his profits from just three months of working for the Erie were $650,000.

The Erie's disreputable proprietors, Gould and Fisk, got their money's worth. In the legislative session of 1868, with Tweed calling the shots and Gould (plus the Boss himself, and Sweeny) handing out bribes said to total at least $500,000, the Albany lawmakers passed the Erie Classification Bill, which legalized the Erie's fraudulent stock and thus greatly enriched its owners. Not long afterward, after Jay Gould on September 24, 1869, had mesmerized Wall Street by coming within a hairbreadth of cornering the gold market through an elaborate conspiracy, Judge Cardozo did him a favor on Tweed's behalf: he allowed him to escape most of the huge debts he had incurred during his cornering gambit.

Tweed also developed a fond friendship for Jim Fisk, who in many ways was like him—big, gruff, vulgar, and exuberant. Fisk, though married, had left his wife behind in Boston and was openly consorting

with Josie Mansfield, a tall, handsome woman for whom he had
bought a house on Twenty-third Street. Tweed and Judge Barnard
spent many an evening at the Mansfield establishment playing poker
with Fisk, and when Fisk was shot and killed some years later by a
rival for Josie's affections, Tweed was one of the most prominent
mourners.

In addition to all the politicking and socializing, Tweed was careful
never to forget his strongest constituency, the foreign-born or first-
generation poor of New York City, the majority of whom were Roman Catholics. He prodded the city government to provide more aid
to orphanages and shelters for the homeless as well as to other private
charitable institutions, and he was instrumental in setting up the
Manhattan Eye and Ear Hospital. In the spring of 1869, he introduced a bill into the legislature calling for public support of parochial
schools. Republicans immediately denounced the measure, saying
they "smelt a savor of Popery" in it,[34] and so Tweed withdrew it but
attached an equivalent appropriation onto a tax-levy bill, which
passed, and the schools got the money. The following year the special
appropriation was killed; but Tweed managed to assure that all the
schools that had benefited would get one more year of funding, with
the result that between 1869 and 1871 they received nearly $1.5
million. As the historian John Pratt has noted, "This was the only
time in New York's history that Catholic parochial schools received
regular public grants avowedly intended for general instructional
purposes."[35]

Assistance to the Erie's chiefs and aid to charitable and parochial
institutions were mere sidelights for the Boss, however. Already potent beyond imagining, Tweed hatched a plan to reorganize New
York City's government via a new charter, centralizing control in the
mayor's office, and incidentally providing himself with even greater
leverage over the city's affairs. Before pushing the charter through the
legislature, however, he had to quell a dangerous revolt brewing in his
own party.

The rebellion was founded on jealousy and resentment. For although most Democrats were pleased that Tweed had wrought so
many victories at the polls, a number of key party members felt the
Boss had acquired altogether too much power and had robbed them
of the independence and status they had once enjoyed. And if booty
was being won, even illicitly, why weren't they being allowed to share
it? The three leaders were Henry Genét, Mike Norton, and Thomas
Jefferson Creamer, all of them state senators and prominent Tam-

manyites, but the group also included John Fox, a waterfront leader
who thought the Ring kept him from becoming sheriff; John Morrissey, the ex-pugilist and latter-day gambling casino owner, who resented Tweed's high-handed ways; and Jimmy O'Brien, an ex-sheriff
who claimed the Ring owed him money. There was also a smattering
of reformers. The motley group called themselves the Young Democracy, and they drew up a rival charter that differed little from
Tweed's but that the leaders hoped would bring them increased
power and prestige. What made the group especially dangerous, however, was a well-rehearsed plan to unseat Tweed as the head of Tammany Hall's General Committee by capturing one of its meetings and
voting him out. If they were successful, they would capture the Hall.

Tweed got wind of their plot and was ready for them. On the
evening of March 28, 1870, the insurgents were to march on Tammany Hall and take over a meeting of the Committee that the Boss
was scheduled to chair. They were confident they had enough votes.
But when they arrived at the Wigwam, they found it surrounded by
policemen who blocked their entry. More policemen filled the Hall,
staring out the windows. What the leaders of the Young Democracy
had forgotten, in their zeal, was the age-old rule of Tammany: he who
controls the sachems controls the Hall and can deny its use to those
he considers unsuitable or unfriendly. For Tweed was still in control
of the sachems. Just for good measure, he had informed New York's
police commissioner—who happened to be a Republican—that a
meeting in the Hall that evening might lead to a riot and should be
prevented. It is said that the following morning, when reporters accosted Tweed in a corridor of the state capitol, he raised his fist over
his head and said, "By ———, I'll show them that the Boss still
lives!"[36]

Its plan scotched, the Young Democracy folded. Tweed declined
to press charges against the rebels, preferring to move swiftly to enact
his charter. There was plenty of opposition, especially in the upper
house, but the Boss and his henchmen distributed large batches of
cash among the dubious senators to carry the day. Some of them
demanded $5,000, while others could be had for $500 or $1,000; a
handful of Republicans were said to have received $40,000 apiece;
estimates of the total amount of money that changed hands range
from $200,000 to more than $600,000, some of it supplied by Garvey, Ingersoll, and other contractors, some of it by Jay Gould, the rest
undoubtedly out of Tweed's deep pockets. One prominent man,
Samuel J. Tilden no less, tried to voice some reservations about the

charter; Tweed, chairing the Senate Committee on Cities that was considering the legislation, humiliated him by remarking angrily, "I am sick of the discussion of this question."[37] Tilden did his best not to notice Tweed's insult, but he was clearly offended. The charter passed, and Hoffman dutifully signed it into law.

There was actually much good in it, and in such provisions as beefing up the mayoralty, the charter was ahead of its time. Many reformers, including the editor Horace Greeley, praised it. Department heads were made directly responsible to the mayor, who could remove them for malfeasance. Many overlapping jurisdictions were straightened out. The Board of Aldermen could vote money only by a three-fourths vote of its members. All this was estimable. But the system lost most of its checks and balances. And there was another hitch that, while seemingly making for greater efficiency, could only—if one looked closely—give the Ring even more power than it already had. The Board of Supervisors was abolished and replaced by a Board of Audit whose duty it was to manage the city's financial affairs. This body was to consist of the mayor, the comptroller, the commissioner of public works (a new post), and the president of the Parks Department. All well and good, but who were they? Well, the mayor was Oakey Hall, the comptroller was Slippery Dick Connolly, Tweed himself was shortly named commissioner of public works, and the incoming head of parks was the former chamberlain, none other than Peter "Brains" Sweeny. The new Board, pure and simple, was the Tweed Ring.

At its very first meeting, on May 5, 1870, the Board of Audit okayed $6,312,000 worth of bills that had been submitted to the city, most of them for work allegedly done on the new courthouse. Of these, it was subsequently learned, perhaps 10 percent were legitimate. Of the excess skimmed off by the Ring, as Tweed later recalled, the custom called for 25 percent to go to him, 20 percent to Connolly, 10 percent to Sweeny, 5 percent to Hall, and 5 percent to the likes of Watson and Woodward.

But how could the city afford such egregious expenditures? The taxes it collected plus all other sources of income would cover little more than the city's running expenses; the courthouse and other such projects were capital expenditures. The ever resourceful Connolly had the answer in the wondrous Adjusted Claims Act that Tweed put through in 1868 that enabled him to float bond issues. As Alexander Callow puts it, "He created a litter of stocks and bonds raised for every conceivable project, ingenious in wording and intent. There were Accumulated Debt Bonds, Assessment Fund Bonds, Croton Aqueduct Bonds, Croton Reservoir Bonds, Central Park Improvement Fund Stocks, . . . Tax Relief Bonds, Bridge Revenue Bonds, New Court House Stock. . . . As a result of Connolly's various enterprises, the city groaned under a debt which increased by nearly $70 million from 1869 to 1871."[38] To obscure his trail, Connolly also resorted to devious accounting techniques, setting up fictitious accounts, rigging phony warrants, and forging affidavits.

Still, amazingly, there was no real outcry. Rumors were beginning to circulate that something was terribly wrong, and many well-informed citizens were aware that the Ring was breaking laws right and left. Wrote the diarist George Templeton Strong, a lawyer well versed in the ways of the city, "People begin to tire of holding their noses, and are looking about in a helpless way for some remedy. . . . Law protects life no longer. Any scoundrel who is backed by a little political influence in the corner groceries of his ward can commit murder with absolute impunity."[39]

But thanks to Connolly's sleight of hand there was still no direct evidence on which the Ring could be stopped. Thomas Nast was beginning to issue his searing cartoons in *Harpers Weekly* attacking the Ring, but they were as yet having little effect. Of the New York newspapers, only the *New York Times*, a staunch Republican journal, appeared interested in attacking the Boss. But for a while the *Times* was inhibited from an all-out attack: one of its directors, James B. Taylor, was Tweed's partner in the New York Printing Company and was acting to restrain the paper. But Taylor died on September 20, 1870, and within a few days the *Times* opened its editorial attack. How did it happen, the paper asked, that William Tweed, who only half a dozen years back had virtually no funds, was now worth a reputed $10 million? What was the true story behind the Tweed charter? Why had the city's debt escalated?

The *Times* demanded that Connolly throw open his books. Very well, the comptroller would be happy to oblige. Oakey Hall, with his pipeline to society, was able to assemble a blue-ribbon investigating committee of distinguished New Yorkers headed by John Jacob Astor III (grandson of the founder of the family fortune), and Connolly went through the motions of revealing all to them. The Astor Committee found that there was no evidence of wrongdoing, that the account books were "faithfully kept, that we have personally examined the securities of the department and sinking fund and found them correct."[40] As to how such an astonishing whitewash could have occurred, one theory holds that the committee members were all threatened with huge increases in their tax assessments if they were to find blame. Another and more likely reason was that Connolly had practiced his customary legerdemain, and the group was denied the real figures. Perhaps both were true. In any event, the Ring had once again eluded detection. And the *Times*, though it continued its attacks, had no hard proof, no smoking gun as it were, that would wake up the public and drive it to act. In the fall elections of 1870, both Hoffman and Hall easily won reelection, and all Tammany candidates to Congress triumphed. The Ring seemed invincible.

Success prompted large thoughts in the Boss's brain. In 1872, he surmised, Hoffman would become president of the United States, the Elegant Oakey would move into the governor's mansion in Albany, and Tweed himself might enter the U.S. Senate. On the other hand, as he had long ago dismissed the senatorial idea, maybe a more pleasing role would be U.S. ambassador to the Court of St. James's. In that case Sweeny, although he still professed to dislike public office, might go to Washington as senator. Connolly should probably stay in New York to keep an eye on things.

It was all glorious, and Tweed, even though he told friends he was working too hard and needed a change, was living like a monarch. He had bought a large mansion on the southeast corner of Fifth Avenue and Forty-third Street, the very center of the city's most fashionable neighborhood. His stable on Fortieth Street glittered with fine carriages and sleighs and gold-plated harnesses. When he traveled to Albany it was in a luxuriously fitted Wagner parlor car. At Delevan House in Albany, wrote an observer, "when he came into the great dining-room at dinner-time, and looked at all the tables thronged with members of the Legislature and the lobby, he had a benignant, paternal expression, as of a patriarch pleased to see his retainers happy. . . . And he never doubted that he could buy every man in the room if he were willing to pay the price."[41]

But the sheer opulence of Tweed's life was best demonstrated by the gaudy Americus Club in Greenwich, Connecticut, over which he presided. The club, founded in the city in 1849 for fun and sociability by a group of politicians, businessmen, and volunteer firemen (Tweed was not a member at first, but the group appropriated the name of his fire company), would hire a launch in warm weather to ferry members to a beach in Greenwich, where they could fish and clam and camp out. But in the late 1860s, with Tweed's ascent to power, the Connecticut operation changed radically. In 1867, with the Boss recently elected its president, Americus rented a spacious structure on Greenwich's Indian Point that soon was as sumptuous as almost any other club on the eastern seaboard.

The clubhouse's 90-foot-long parlor and 100-foot dining salon were lined with imported carpeting "as thick as a beefsteak,"[42] and the library was filled with finely bound books (which nevertheless showed few signs of use); there was also an ample reception room (known as Tweed's Room), a billiard room, a barbershop and, of course, a well-stocked bar. Upstairs were sleeping rooms whose beds were made up with blue silk sheets. Surrounding the house was a broad veranda from which members could look down at the club's prized possessions in the harbor: three yachts, the largest of which, the steam-driven *William M. Tweed*, was a luxurious affair equipped with Oriental rugs and a library. It required a crew of twelve. For large parties, an orchestra would be brought onboard.

Members, limited to one hundred, paid a $1,000 initiation fee and monthly dues of $250, and included most of the Tammany leadership and such other lights as contractors Andrew Garvey and James Ingersoll, and financiers Jay Gould and Jim Fisk. Peter Sweeny and Oakey Hall did not belong, possibly because they were accepted in more lofty circles, and Dick Connolly was also absent for reasons that are unclear. While on the premises, the members were required to wear the club uniform, which was of "blue cloth, navy pantaloons with gold cord down the sides, blue sack cloth of navy cut, white cloth vest cut low, and navy cap."[43] Most also sported the club badge, a round metal pin covered in blue enamel on which was set a solid gold tiger's head, the club's symbol (and soon to be Tammany's as well). For Tweed and a few other club potentates, the tiger's eyes were set with rubies; those pins were reported to cost $2,000 apiece. There was also an Americus club belt with the tiger's head surrounded by diamonds.

At club events, the Boss might show up in the company of a small blond woman, who barely reached his shoulder. She was his mistress and was rumored to be ensconced in a small nearby dwelling that passed for the home of the Boss's coachman. Tweed's wife spent the summer months in the couple's regular home in Greenwich, which they had purchased in 1865. Tweed also owned several other houses in the town, whose total value was said to be $60,000.

Already a major investor in New York real estate, Tweed was by 1871 also a significant stockholder in iron mines, gas companies, and many other kinds of corporations, many of which had made stock available to him purely to protect themselves or advance their own interests. He was on the board of directors of the Harlem Gas Light Company and the Third Avenue Railway Company, in addition to the Brooklyn Bridge Company, and was president of the Guardian Savings Bank. So much money was coming to Tweed and the other Ring members that they organized their own bank, the Tenth National, in which to keep their funds and those of the city as well. Its directors were Tweed, Connolly, Hall, James Ingersoll, and Jim Fisk.

Tweed also liked to present gifts to his associates and to favored Tammany leaders. On one occasion or another he gave state Senator Mike Norton a $1,000 watch and chain, police Justice Edward Shandley a "gold hunting case watch, chain and locket" worth $1,000, and the retiring president of the Board of Aldermen a diamond stud said to have cost $1,500. In addition, it must be conceded, he gave substantial gifts to the poor of the city, gestures that greatly enhanced his popularity in slum neighborhoods. (Maybe Tweed stole all that money, people were saying, but it didn't matter as long as he was passing it along to them.) In the winter of 1870–1871, for example, he gave each of the city aldermen $1,000 to buy coal for the poor. His most celebrated benevolence was made that same winter when police Justice Edward Shandley, who handled such matters for him, approached the Boss for his usual $5,000 Christmas contribution for poor relief in the Seventh Ward, Tweed's home base. Tweed wrote out his check for the amount, whereupon Shandley reportedly said to him, "Oh, Boss, put another nought to it." The Boss instantly got the point. "Well, well, here goes!" he said, and changed the amount to $50,000.[44]

So heroic a figure should no doubt be memorialized, and in March 1871, the *New York Sun* followed up on what was evidently a joke going the rounds by suggesting, tongue in cheek, that the citizens of New York erect a statue of the Boss at some suitable location. Other papers rose to the challenge and had a field day with the idea, suggesting appropriate poses and settings for the monument, some ridiculous. Tammany Hall, however, did not consider it a lighthearted matter and formed a fund-raising committee under police Justice Shandley. When $7,973 had been collected, Tweed—who some claimed had gone along with the idea only to see who liked him enough to contribute—decided to scotch the whole scheme. "Statues are not erected to living men," he wrote. " . . . I claim to be a live man, and hope (Divine Providence permitting) to survive in all my vigor, politically and physically, some years to come."[45] The plans were quietly dropped.

If the entire Tweed era had a high point, a culminating event, an occurrence that people looked back on in later years with both wonderment and disbelief, it certainly was the wedding of the Boss's daughter, Mary Amelia Tweed, to Arthur Ambrose Maginnis of New Orleans on May 31, 1871. Without question the marriage was the most splendid social event New York had seen in years. The ceremony itself took place at seven o'clock in the evening at Trinity Chapel, but long before that, one newspaper reported, the chapel "was crowded with a richly dressed audience, who awaited in speechless expectation. . . ." The ladies were "aglow with rich silks and satins and flashing with diamonds."[46] But the bride herself was far more splendidly got up, in a lavish gown that had cost $4,000, and she sparkled from tip to toe with diamonds, outshining even the diamond-fronted Boss as he escorted her down the aisle.

After the ceremony, the guests repaired to the Tweed home on Fifth Avenue, which was ablaze with light and fragrant with the aroma of numberless flowers. "Imagine all this," a reporter gushed, "lighted up with the utmost brilliancy, and hundreds of ladies and gentlemen in all the gorgeousness of full dress and flashing with diamonds, listen to the delicious strains of the band and inhale in spirit the sweet perfume which filled the atmosphere, and some inadequate notion can be formed of the magnificence of the scene."[47]

Dinner was catered by Delmonico's, and there was dancing until all hours. It was the wedding presents displayed in a room on the second floor, however, that got everyone talking. There were forty complete sets of sterling silver. Jim Fisk sent a huge frosted silver iceberg, for serving ice cream. Peter Sweeny had given diamond bracelets. Another diamond-studded object was known on good authority to have cost $45,000. James Gordon Bennett of the *Herald* stared at the display and estimated that the total value of all the presents came to $700,000. "Seven hundred thousand dollars!" he wrote two days later. "What a testimony of the loyalty, the royalty, and the abounding East Indian resources of Tammany Hall!"[48]

Those resources did, indeed, seem endless and Tweed's power uncheckable. But there were disturbing events afoot. One evening more than four months earlier, City Auditor James Watson had chosen to go sleigh riding in the snowy cold, and there had been an accident. The world of William M. Tweed, the man who had risen so alarmingly to grasp awesome power and amass stunning riches—the tactician of the ballot box, the canny conspirator, the astute manipulator of his fellow man, America's first truly rapacious political boss—was beginning to come apart.

5

THE COLLAPSE

HARDLY ANYONE COULD HAVE PREDICTED THAT James Watson's sleighing accident would prove to be the event that triggered the swift downfall of the Tweed Ring. For Watson was nothing if not prudent.

He was a quiet, unobtrusive man, careful not to give any indication of his status in life or of the immense power he wielded within the city government. As the low-salaried ($1,500 a year) county auditor in the office of Comptroller Dick Connolly, he was to all intents and purposes a mere functionary, notable only for his neat penmanship. True, Watson and his family inhabited a handsome mansion on Madison Avenue at Forty-second Street, but no one took particular notice of this or of the fact that Watson owned a stable of five fast trotters, including the well-known bay Charlie Green, reputed to be worth $10,000. Insiders, however, were quite aware of Watson's key role. He was the Tweed Ring's paymaster, in charge of the secret records listing all the exorbitant sums being charged to New York County for construction of the new county courthouse and other spurious projects, and he personally saw to the paying of the monstrous kickbacks that were lining the pockets of his superiors. His books were under lock and key, accessible only to a few of the faithful. Skillful, discreet, and well-nigh indispensable, Watson had become a millionaire.

Given his importance, it was probably a mistake for him to have taken Charlie Green out for an exercise sleigh run on the snowy evening of January 21, 1871. Snow had fallen all day long, a biting wind whipped across the city, and the going was treacherous even for top-notch rigs like Watson's. But the bracing air obliterated all caution. Watson and his coachman sped up Fifth Avenue with the auditor handling the reins, and in no time had reached Harlem Lane, a popular racing site. After a brief spin on the lane they turned around and, with the coachman now driving, started home. At 138th Street a northbound sleigh suddenly turned out of its track and crashed into Watson's rig, and as its horse reared at the impact, one of its hooves struck Watson's head, bashing in his skull. He died a week later.

Tweed was well aware of the threat posed by the loss of Watson. Two days after the accident, when he was informed of it in Albany, he hastened back to New York and ordered a twenty-four-hour guard placed around Watson's house so that no unfriendly soul would be present if the wounded auditor happened to make a deathbed confession. But the Boss's concern, though genuine at the time, somehow did not extend to further damage-control measures. What turned out to be far more destructive to the Ring in the long run than immediate concern over Watson was the almost casual manner in which the auditor was replaced. Perhaps the Boss and his fellow plotters were mistakenly overconfident. Some years later, after Tweed and the others had been routed, the plasterer Andrew Garvey testified that just three days after Watson's death Dick Connolly remarked to him, "Garvey, I have done the best day's work today I've done in my life. I have succeeded in getting hold of Watson's book, giving a list of his payments, and I have put it out of the way."[1] Connolly should have known that Watson's "book" did not constitute the entire record. There were other paper trails, as New Yorkers would soon learn.

Watson's job was at first filled by the city bookkeeper, Stephen C. Lynes, Jr., but he soon proved unfit and was replaced by Matthew J. O'Rourke, a seemingly innocuous auditor who had been a military news editor for a New York paper. Although the Ring did not envision O'Rourke taking over Watson's secret role as paymaster to the conspirators, the appointment would prove a fatal error. A little checking might have revealed that O'Rourke was a cohort of former sheriff James O'Brien, who spelled bad news to the Ring. For O'Brien, originally a faithful Tammanyite, had previously broken with Tweed over the Ring's refusal to pay him some $300,000 in claims he had allegedly collected while sheriff in the 1860s; and as one of the founders of the erstwhile Young Democracy, he was also fuming from the drubbing that Tweed administered to the group in 1870 when it tried to oust him from the Tammany Hall leadership. Embittered, O'Brien was prepared to do anything to destroy the Boss. So it was that O'Rourke's appointment was to lead to the passing of massive amounts of incriminating information on the Ring's operations to the *New York Times*, and this in turn led with remarkable swiftness to the bringing down of Tweed and his partners in disgrace and disorder. What the Boss had put together over a decade with such ruthlessness and daring blew away in a period of just a few months, although the legal and financial repercussions were felt for years to come.

Until the *Times* got its historic break, its editors were almost coming to suspect that their crusade against the Ring, launched the previous year, might be in vain. Boss Tweed gave every appearance of being invulnerable. Yet the paper did not let up. It had reason to despise Tweed, for it was the only solidly Republican major newspaper in the city, and so the only one that viscerally opposed the Democratic Boss on party grounds, rejecting all attempts to be bought off. Its earnest Republican tilt had been instilled at its founding in 1851 by its first editor, the opinionated, strong-willed Henry Raymond. When Raymond died in 1869, the journal's publisher and co-founder, George Jones, moved into the editor's office, but still retained his previous duties. Jones hardly seemed like a giant-killer; in the words of the *Times* historian Meyer Berger, he was "a grave, lush-bearded, ponderous man close to 60, who peered through thick-lensed gold-rimmed spectacles."[2] Yet it was Jones who ordered the *Times*'s all-out attack on Tweed that began in September 1870, and once having set that course he never let up. In his campaign, he had the expert assistance of a brilliant, temperamental Britisher, Louis J. Jennings, whose editorials could be searing.

The problem was, no one was paying much attention to the paper's rantings and scoldings. Virtually everyone in New York knew, or at least suspected, that the city was corrupt and had long been so; what could be so special now, and what was so bad about politicians who kept everybody happy and gave off such an air of success and prosperity? The *Times* was unable to produce the proof of wrong-doing that would make people sit up and take notice.

The *Times* was not alone in attacking the Ring, however. In the pages of *Harpers Weekly*, the endlessly inventive and trenchant political cartoonist Thomas Nast was publishing a remarkable series of drawings that could amuse the reader while at the same time inspire loathing for the subject—in this case Tweed and company. A native of Germany who had been brought to the United States by his parents in 1846, Nast had grown up in lower New York. He made a name for himself drawing cartoons for *Harpers Weekly* during the Civil War. But it was his anti-Ring drawings that built his reputation as one of America's greatest practitioners of the cartooning art. In them, Tweed is always the bloated, gross corruptionist, Sweeny the crafty confidant with gleaming eyes and spiky hair, Connolly the smooth, rotund, oily hanger-on, and Oakey Hall the lightweight buffoon dominated by his absurd pince-nez spectacles, which Nast invariably showed as drooping pitifully. New Yorkers laughed at the cartoons, but Boss Tweed did not. "I don't care a straw for your newspaper articles," he was heard to remark. "My constituents don't know how to read, but they can't help seeing them damned pictures."[3]

Tweed was even prepared to punish the *Weekly* by ordering the city's schools to cease purchasing textbooks issued by Harper & Brothers, its publisher. The Harper owners winced but told Nast to keep going. As for the *Times*, Ring officials claimed the paper's only reason for opposing them was that the city had refused to pay it $13,764.36 for city advertising on technical grounds; they also ordered city employees to stop using the cafeteria in the *Times* building and threatened to confiscate the newspaper's building, claiming its title was defective. Jones produced proof that his title was perfectly in order, laughed at the other charges, and continued his attack.

But the public was not listening. In early April 1871, a group of eminent citizens, including the celebrated preacher Henry Ward Beecher and former mayor William Havemeyer, staged a mass rally at Cooper Union to protest what they called "the alarming aspects of public affairs generally."[4] Calling attention to the mammoth increase in the city debt from $36 million in 1868 to more than $80 million at the end of 1870, they urged their fellow New Yorkers to rise up and throw the Tammany rascals out. There was little response. Until someone was caught red-handed, New Yorkers refused to get excited.

Meanwhile, Tweed was still unscathed. That same month he was in Albany working his customary wiles on the state legislature. One day in the assembly chamber a rough-cut Tammanyite assemblyman from New York City, Jimmy Irving, found reason to stage an unprovoked attack on an upstate Republican member, Smith Weed, felling him with a blow to the side of the head. Legislators on both sides of the aisle were outraged, and Tweed, to contain the damage, was forced to order Irving to resign. As this loss to the Democrats threatened the party's majority in the assembly, the Boss resorted to a tried-and-true tactic. He found a docile Republican who could be bought, Orange S. Winans of Chautauqua County, and paid him $100,000 to vote with the Democrats. Other Republicans cried "Shame!" and "Traitor!"[5] But Winans was glad to be of service.

And at the end of May the stellar wedding of Tweed's daughter Mary Amelia to Arthur Maginnis went off without a hitch.

The Boss did not know, of course, that the recently appointed city bookkeeper, Matthew J. O'Rourke, had for some time now been committing espionage in the comptroller's office. Suddenly privy to the Ring's closely guarded records, O'Rourke was astonished to find confirmation of the long-heard rumors of gross overcharging and kickbacks in the outfitting and repairing of city armories, and he quickly reported as much to Jimmy O'Brien, the former sheriff. O'Brien advised him to copy the figures surreptitiously and give them to him.

Copying the figures was slow and dangerous, and so O'Brien wormed another mole into the system: an accountant named William Copeland. Now there were two spies.

Some time in the late spring of 1871, Jimmy O'Brien took his file of incriminating documents and began to make the rounds of the city's newspapers. Oddly enough, he did not start with the *Times*, his reason presumably being that a scandal involving Democrats would be far less damaging to the party if it appeared in a Democratic paper rather than a rabidly Republican one. But none of the Democratic publications were interested. So one torrid evening in early July he presented himself in the newsroom of the *Times* and found Louis Jennings's office.

"Hot night," he said.

"Warm," said Jennings. There was an awkward silence.

"You and Tom Nast," O'Brien finally said, "have had a tough fight."

"Still have," responded Jennings.

"I said *had*." And O'Brien laid his envelope of documents on the desk. "Here's proof to back up all the *Times* has charged. They're copied right out of the city ledgers."[6]

Jennings glanced at the envelope but did not touch it. Mustering all the calm he could, he thanked his visitor, and O'Brien departed.

Only then did Jennings tear the package open. He could hardly believe his eyes. Excitedly, he found Jones and showed it to him and reporter John Foord, who had written many of the Ring articles. They were overjoyed, and their happiness increased still further when Matthew O'Rourke came in a day or so later with additional material rounding out what O'Brien had supplied. Now for the first time the newspaper could back up its rage with some facts.

A few days after that, on July 8, 1871, the *Times* broke the story—but not all at once. There was too much. The paper began by revealing just the moneys misspent on armories. GIGANTIC FRAUDS IN THE RENTAL OF ARMORIES cried the headline, while tables revealed the outlandish sums paid on rents and repairs of what were clearly wretched and inadequate quarters. It constituted, wrote Jennings in an accompanying editorial, "a chapter of municipal rascality which in any other city but New York would bring down upon the heads of its authors such a storm of public indignation as would force them to a speedy accountability . . . or compel them to take refuge in flight. . . ."7

A storm of indignation did indeed begin to build throughout the city; at last there was some truth to all the rumors. Quite by chance an event took place just four days later that further undermined the confidence of New Yorkers in their Tammany overlords. The city's Protestant Irish had applied for a parade permit to commemorate the Battle of the Boyne, but Peter Sweeny and Richard Connolly, evidently fearing that Catholics would foment violence along the route, issued an order under Oakey Hall's authority rejecting the permit. At this many of the city's newspapers, Protestant-owned, cried out that Sweeny and Connolly, both Catholics, had deprived the Orangemen of their civil rights. Whereupon Tweed's handpicked state governor, John Hoffman, countermanded the Hall order and directed the superintendent of police to allow the parade to proceed, protected by state militiamen. It did, but along the way a shot rang out, the militia fired into the crowd, and more than one hundred people were killed or wounded. The performance did not speak well for the Ring or its minions.

One thing was certain: Boss Tweed and his cohorts were feeling the heat, for they tried to meet with Jones. He refused to see them. One day, however, Jones got a request from a lawyer whose office was in the *Times* building asking if he would stop by. Jones went to the man's office, and as he entered he found himself face-to-face with Slippery Dick Connolly.

"I do not care to see this man," Jones told the lawyer.

Connolly blanched, then blurted out, "For God's sake, Mr. Jones, let me say a word or two. Listen for just a moment. Wouldn't it be worth, say, five million dollars, Mr. Jones, to let up on this thing? Five million dollars, sir!"

Taken aback, Jones hesitated for a moment and then declared, "I don't think the devil will ever make a higher bid for me. My answer still stands."

The comptroller pleaded with him. "With that money, Mr. Jones, you could go to Europe—anywhere—you could live like a prince. . . . You could—"

Jones interrupted him. "True, sir, all true. But I should know while I lived like a prince, that I was a rascal. I cannot consider your offer— or any offer. The *Times* will continue to publish the facts."[8]

But there was a far more dangerous threat closer to home. One day as a *Times* editor was strolling through City Hall at lunchtime, he chanced to hear Mayor Oakey Hall say to Dick Connolly, "I think that deal with Mrs. Raymond will go through." The editor, startled, rushed back to his office to inform Jones—for "Mrs. Raymond" must be Henry Raymond's widow, who held a substantial portion of *Times* stock, and this must mean that the Ring was well along in a covert attempt to acquire her shares and thus gain control of the paper. Jones immediately wired one of the original investors in the *Times*, a well-heeled businessman named Col. E. D. Morgan, and the colonel, checkbook in hand, visited Mrs. Raymond and bought her out. The editors breathed a sigh of relief.[9]

And they proceeded to trot out their biggest guns. Having told the story of the armories, they now unveiled the figures behind the most monstrous boondoggle of all, the county courthouse project. The July 8 story had run on the paper's inside pages, but on July 22 a huge headline, THE SECRET ACCOUNTS, stretched across three columns of the front page; it was the first time the paper had ever run a head-line wider than a single column (not even Lincoln's assassination had received such treatment). "Proofs of Undoubted Frauds Brought to Light," ran the subhead. "Warrants Signed by Hall and Connolly Under False Pretenses."[10] The listings of payments made to contrac-tors made for juicy reading, and all over New York people alternated between hilarity and wrath. Andrew Garvey, for example, had been paid $45,966.99 for a single day's plastering, on July 2, 1869; for one month he had collected $153,755.14, and he had once received $945,715.11 over a two-month period. Two days after this block-buster story, the *Times* published additional figures, following up with still more accusations a day or so later; and at the end of the month the paper wrapped up the entire series by putting out a booklet summarizing the revelations, printing it both in English and in German—to make sure of reaching New York's large German population.

It was about this time that Tweed apparently made the remark that has ever since been irrevocably associated with him. A reporter was reputed to have asked him to comment on the *Times* stories, whereupon the Boss turned on him and snarled, "Well, what are you going to do about it?"[11] But there is no evidence from any newspaper or other contemporary publication that Tweed ever actually made the remark. The same provocative line had appeared more than a month previously as the title of a Nast cartoon, suggesting that people had simply assumed Tweed said it. But whether or not he actually spoke the words, in the summer of 1871 they seemed appropriate for the Boss and an angry population was firmly convinced they were his.

Nast himself, who was turning out a new anti-Ring cartoon almost every week, was getting some odd attention. He was told that a group of wealthy gentlemen wanted to send him abroad to study under European masters, but he declined the offer. Soon he was visited in his home by an officer of the Broadway Bank, the institution in which the Ring kept its funds. The banker told Nast that the wealthy men were prepared to pay him $100,000 if he would go. Tantalized, Nast asked half-humorously if the fee could be raised to $200,000. Yes, came the reply, and the banker added, "You need study and you need rest. Besides, this Ring business will get you into trouble. They own all the judges and jurors and can get you locked up for libel. My advice is to take the money and get away."

This was getting to be amusing, and so Nast asked, "Don't you think I could get five hundred thousand dollars to make that trip?" Without hesitating his visitor agreed, saying, "You can get five hundred thousand dollars in gold to drop this Ring business and get out of the country."

"Well, I don't think I'll do it," Nast stated. "I made up my mind long ago to put some of those fellows behind the bars, and I'm going to put them there." The banker got up to go, but then remarked, "Only be careful, Mr. Nast, that you do not first put yourself into a coffin."[12]

It was the Ring members, however, who were beginning to panic. In August, just a few weeks after the *Times* began its exposé, Tweed very quietly and secretly began to transfer his real estate holdings and

other investments to others, principally his son Richard. (By the end
of the year, very little remained in his name.) Early in September,
Connolly's wife signed over half a million dollars in U.S. bonds to a
son-in-law, although she retained bonds worth three and a half million in her own name. Only Hall, of all people, professed to take it all
in his stride, responding with his usual avalanche of jokes. "We are
likely," he said, "to have what befell Adam—an early Fall." When a
reporter noted that Hall seemed cheerful, he responded, "Oh yes, I
am always cheerful. You know the true philosophy of life is to take
things just as they come. How was the clever definition—let me see, I
forget his name—of life? What is mind? No matter. What is matter?
Never mind. That's my philosophy."[13]

Unique among the Ring members, the mayor, however, did respond with a constructive move. In view of his presumed ties to the
whole web of wrongdoing, it is hard to know why he acted as he did,
but toward the end of August he suggested to the boards of aldermen
and supervisors that they appoint a nonpartisan investigating committee to examine the *Times* charges. The resulting body, known as the
Booth Committee after its chairman, was to have a decided impact on
the unraveling drama months hence.

For most New Yorkers, shocked by the revelations in the *Times*,
the mere naming of a committee was not enough. With the specially
deep resentment that is felt by those who belatedly realize they have
been conned, they were furious, and when the same esteemed citizens—truly New York's upper-class business, financial, and social
leaders—who had called the ineffectual meeting of the previous April
issued a new call for a gathering at Cooper Union on September 4,
the response was well-nigh explosive. The hall was packed and the
overflow was so vast a companion rally had to be held outdoors in
Astor Place. Inside, the atmosphere was charged. One of the speak-
ers, Judge James Emmott, briefly summed up the list of excesses
allegedly perpetrated by the Ring. "Gentlemen," he proclaimed,
"there is no denial of these fraudulent payments, and there is no
fabrication of their amount. Now, what are you going to do with
these men?" A voice rang out from the floor, "Hang them!" at which
loud applause broke out.[14]

The evening's high point came when the highly regarded lawyer
Joseph H. Choate, vigorous and sharp-featured, strode to the center
of the stage and, holding up a scroll of paper, yelled, "THIS is what
we are going to do about it!"[15] Unfurling the scroll, he read to the
assembled throng a long list of prearranged resolutions that called for

a full accounting of public receipts and expenditures by the city administration, the repeal of the Tweed charter of 1870, the reform of the city government, and the appointment of a Committee of Seventy to follow up on these demands. The resolutions were carried by acclamation.

The public clamor brought another uncharacteristic outburst from Boss Tweed. Despite his alleged earlier sign of irritation ("What are you going to do about it?"), he had generally held his temper, and when a reporter from the *Missouri Republican* asked him if it was true he had stolen money he merely said, "This is not a question one gentleman ought to put to another."[16] But after the Cooper Union rally he blurted out to a *New York Sun* reporter, "The *Times* has been saying all the time I have no brains. Well, I'll show Jones I have brains. . . . You know if a man is with others he must . . . take care not to do a rash act. . . . If this man Jones would have said the things he has said about me twenty-five years ago, he wouldn't be alive now. But, you see, when a man has a wife and children, he can't do such a thing." Clenching his fists, the Boss added, "I would have killed him."[17]

Bravado was no longer sufficient to protect him, however. For it was at this point that some of his most trusted and faithful aides began to defect. The first was perhaps the unlikeliest: the swaggering Ring judge, George Barnard. The Committee of Seventy, resplendent with personages bearing such distinguished names as Roosevelt, Steinway, and Pierrepont, had sought to put teeth into the resolutions adopted at the Cooper Union meeting by taking legal action. They chose one of their number, the wealthy pen manufacturer John Foley (picked because of his fine Irish name), to bring a taxpayer's suit against the city, prohibiting the mayor and all other officers from raising any more money through taxes and from making any further expenditures. The suit came before Judge Barnard, who was asked to issue a restraining order but who, in view of his record, was not considered likely to do so.

The first sign that Barnard would surprise everyone came when he listened with unaccustomed respect to the arguments presented to him. Then when the lawyers had finished, instead of picking up the papers and announcing that he would issue his ruling on a later occasion, he simply said, "The facts presented warrant an injunction. I will grant the order."[18]

There are two possible explanations for Barnard's apostasy. One is that he simply felt it was a good time to leap from a sinking ship. A

more likely theory is that he was offered a major reward—for example, the chance to run for governor—by someone of commanding
influence who had reason to want to sink William Tweed. Many
observers at the time felt, and others have since agreed, that the
mover in question would have been that major figure in the state
Democratic party as well as in Tammany Hall, the man who had
patiently been biding his time, Samuel Jones Tilden. From this moment on, in fact, Tilden was to move rapidly to the leadership of the
forces opposed to the Ring. His work would eventually take him to
the governor's mansion in Albany and almost to the White House.

Plenty of people wondered why Tilden had waited so long. This
short, circumspect man surely had ample reason to despise Tweed.
There was the Boss's shellacking in 1868 of Tilden's handpicked
choice for speaker of the assembly, John L. Flagg, whom Tweed
brusquely shunted aside. Two years later, when Tweed was shoving
his new charter through the legislature, Tilden showed up to deliver a
long-winded critique of it and was insulted by the Boss. But in all his
long and highly remunerative career as a corporation lawyer, Tilden
had never been one to act rashly. Every move by this cold and cautious man, of whom it was once said that "he treated his friends as
though at some time they might become his enemies,"[19] was carefully
thought out. Even after the humiliation of the charter, he had been
reluctant to break publicly with the supersuccessful Boss. Nor had the
Times bombshells moved him immediately to action.

Two interrelated things combined to bring him finally into the
fray. One was a desire to minimize the damage the scandal would
inevitably do to the state (not to mention the local) Democratic party;
it was necessary for the party itself, which he felt he personified, to be
on the side of throwing the rascals out. (Tammany Hall would of
course suffer severely, but that was a secondary concern to him.) The
other was the sense that if he himself had ambitions for high office, as
he surely did, he must move now or be forever condemned as indecisive. It must also be conceded that this intensely self-interested man
probably felt an overriding sense of responsibility toward the city in
which he had achieved such personal success.

But Tilden also knew that newspaper stories, no matter how damaging, could not by themselves do the job. To blow the Ring away, it
was necessary to defeat Tweed and his cohorts politically at the polls
and legally in the courts. And fighting them in the courts would require the painstaking marshaling of evidence. As a politician, Tilden

could direct an anti-Ring electoral campaign, and as a lawyer, he could help prepare the legal attack. That is what he now set out to do.

At this point, hard on the heels of the stinger from Judge Barnard, a windfall appeared in the shape of another defector, Slippery Dick Connolly. The comptroller might not have parted company with his associates if they had not first ganged up on him. Tweed, Sweeny, and Hall, it was said, had gotten together and decided to make Connolly the scapegoat for their misdeeds; as the Ring's moneyman, after all, he was the most obviously culpable. Let him take the heat. One night, in what appeared to be a deliberately planned action, the comptroller's office was broken into and a large number of vouchers and warrants, needed as evidence for the Ring frauds, were stolen. It is not clear how and why the burglary took place, and in any event the stolen items turned out to be duplicated elsewhere, but the theft gave Oakey Hall an excuse to follow up on his colleagues' decision by demanding Connolly's resignation. "Our constituents will have a right," the mayor wrote, "to hold you responsible. . . . With great personal reluctance I officially reach the conclusion that the exigency requires your retirement from the head of the Finance Department, in order that I may place there another gentleman who will be enabled thoroughly to investigate its affairs, and restore public confidence."[20]

Connolly refused to go along. He told Hall he would not resign. "My official acts," he explained, with some logic, "have been supervised and approved by your superior vigilance," and so "equal responsibility attaches to yourself."[21] But even before Connolly sent the letter, he presented himself to Samuel Tilden and pleaded for mercy. He promised to do anything to save his own neck.

His acquiescence gave Tilden a unique opportunity. The injunction that Judge Barnard had granted was momentarily paralyzing the city, as it ordered the comptroller to stop all payments; someone must therefore be put quickly into authority who was not bound by the court order. But it was essential that Connolly not resign, as that would enable Mayor Hall to name his successor, who would be accountable only to the Ring, not to the public. Tilden proposed to Connolly a devious solution: that he remain in office but that he appoint as his deputy, with full power to act in his name, someone acceptable to the Committee of Seventy. "It was represented to Connolly," a chronicler of the event wrote, "that if he threw himself upon the mercy of the public and assisted the reformers, he would have less to fear than he would from his confederates."[22] The comptroller assented, and Tilden promptly named Andrew Haswell Green, his law partner and a widely respected civic figure in his own right, to fill the critical spot. Tilden now had his own man strategically placed at the center of the city's finances.

The coup reduced Mayor Hall to spluttering indignation. The move was patently illegal, he asserted, and he wrote another letter to Connolly saying he regarded the delegation of authority to Green as "equivalent to a resignation, and I hereby accept your resignation." It happened that the letter arrived in Connolly's office just as Tilden was meeting there with Connolly, Green, and several highly placed members of the Committee of Seventy, and their reaction was one of the first and most welcome signs that a revolution had just taken place in the government of the city. They greeted it with laughter.[23]

Oakey Hall was not quite done. In desperation, he asked the former Civil War general, George B. McClellan, to accept the comptroller post; with his well-known excess of prudence that had brought him notoriety in the war, McClellan said no thanks. (This news prompted further laughter from Tilden and Green.) Tilden now saw that the question of legality could well stand clearing up. He accordingly asked Charles O'Conor, a leading figure in the New York bar (and once again the possessor of a good Irish name), for an opinion. O'Conor issued a public statement declaring that Connolly certainly had the power to name a deputy, and the question was not raised again. Tilden then asked O'Conor if he would take over as chief prosecutor of the Ring members, and he agreed.

Tilden's acceptance of Connolly's plea for help and of the comptroller's willingness to cooperate was significant, given Connolly's unalluring reputation. From this point on, those in charge of prosecuting the Ring showed themselves willing to make deals with lesser Ring members and to grant them conditional immunity in return for their help in nailing the number one man, Boss Tweed. Let the small-fry go, they reasoned; the important thing was to get the big fish, as that would have the maximum effect on public opinion. The policy, while controversial, seemed to Tilden and others the only realistic one.

Meanwhile, Andrew Green had been grappling with the city's fiscal mess. The situation was parlous. Interest payments were due on many of the bond issues that Connolly had been floating with such abandon, but there was hardly any money left in the city's bank accounts, not even enough to meet the city's payroll. Green got through the first few weeks by actually borrowing money on his own good name. Besides persuading friends to contribute, he appealed to every kind of public and private institution. For example, as the *New York Tribune* of September 23, 1871, reported, "Acting Comptroller Green visited the Clearing-House Association yesterday and requested a loan of $500,000, to enable him to meet payments now pressing. It was readily granted."[24] By dint of such maneuvers, the crisis was allayed. Green also moved swiftly to cut the city's Ring-bloated payroll, for example firing eighteen unnecessary supreme court attendants who had been earning $1,200 a year apiece.

Green was helping to unravel the mysteries of the Ring's financial legerdemain as well. Observing that there were irregularities on the warrants covering payments for work on the county courthouse, he recommended that the Ring's accounts in the National Broadway Bank be examined, and he urged Tilden to oversee the search personally. What Tilden found showed not only exactly how much Boss Tweed had pocketed out of every inflated payment made by the city (he got 24 percent of the money theoretically paid to the plasterer Andrew Garvey, and an incredible 42 percent of that paid to the furniture maker James H. Ingersoll), but also how the payments were covered up through a series of money launderings. The fraudulent payments to Garvey and Ingersoll totaled more than $6.3 million.

Tilden summed up his findings in a document entitled "Figures That Could Not Lie." He released the document to the press in late October 1871, and it caused quite a stir. Public sentiment for moving against the Ring gathered momentum. New reform organizations sprang up throughout the city, and Republicans were being urged by their leaders to vote for reform candidates in the upcoming election. Tilden began to hear from people who had previously hesitated to speak out but who now were ready to provide facts about the Ring. A group of students at New York University who had recently applauded a speech made to them by Oakey Hall tore down his portrait from the wall. Letters flooded into Tilden's office cheering him on. "Push the scoundrels to the wall!" said one writer. Another declared, "Speed and vigor for God's sake and the Republic's."[25] But no comment came from Tammany Hall's rank and file, who were in a state of shock.

Just at that moment, another telling report was issued, that of the nonpartisan Booth Committee which Mayor Hall had innocently brought into being back in August. Interestingly enough, the committee's members had initially been hostile to the *Times* disclosures, calling them "libels so gross and attacks so false and exaggerated" that they hardly needed to be taken seriously.[26] Barely two months later, after being confronted with the facts (readily offered by Green), they made a complete about-face and provided a neat, dispassionate verification of everything the *Times* had alleged. They reported that the city's debt was indeed doubling every two years; that more than $3 million had been paid for repairs to armories and drill rooms where the true cost was less than $250,000; that more than $11 million had been spent on the courthouse for work that should not have cost more than $3 million; that furnishings for the courthouse that had cost more than $7 million were actually worth $624,180; that $460,000 had been paid for $48,000 worth of lumber; that printing and advertising for the city had been grossly overpaid; that many persons had been placed on the city payroll "whose services were neither rendered nor required"; and that the records showing these transactions had been "fraudulently altered." As a result, "frauds and robberies of the most infamous character have been committed with the connivance and cooperation of some of the officials who were appointed to guard the interests of the people."[27]

The marshaling of facts was thus going well. The political campaign, surprisingly enough, seemed at first to be bogged down. Tilden had been putting great stress on the need to recapture the state legislature by ousting Tweed's Tammany henchmen from it in the November 1871 election. He thus wanted the Boss's candidates frozen out of the state Democratic convention that convened in October in Rochester. To all outward signs, Tweed's political standing had by now been fearfully shaken. Yet his old friends in Tammany Hall were not so quick to dump him. They could not believe the charges the *Times* and others had leveled at their leader, and they felt that somehow Tweed would rally to defeat his tormenters. Just a few days before the state convention, the tarnished Boss was, amazingly, re-elected chairman of the Tammany General Committee. He arrived at the Rochester convention surrounded by traditional Tammany shoulder-hitters, who threatened the reformist delegates and bribed others and ended up nominating all the Tammany candidates. Tweed himself was renominated for state senator, and returning in triumph to New York City, he was cheered wildly at a rally in his district that attracted an estimated twenty thousand. "Mr. Tweed took off his little Scotch tweed cap," reported one newspaper, "and made his bow to the boisterous and noisy multitude."[28] Samuel Tilden was abashed.

But if the Democratic party could not be so quickly cleansed, the voters of New York were ready to be, particularly after absorbing

Tilden's Broadway Bank discoveries and the Booth Committee's broadside accusations. The Tilden candidates ran as independents in the fall campaign. Almost all of them won. Notable among the victors were former sheriff Jimmy O'Brien, who was elected to the state senate, and Samuel Tilden himself, who had decided he must become a member of the assembly in order to ensure the passage of reform programs. Of all the Tammany candidates, astonishingly, only Tweed won, a reflection of his personal popularity in his own Seventh Ward. He had campaigned as never before, denying all the charges against him and calling attention to the many favors and benefits he had won for his constituents in the past. "I feel I can safely place myself and my record, all I have performed as a public official before your gaze," he declared to one audience. He only asked, he said, for "the justice and fair play that have been denied me by bitter, unrelenting, unscrupulous, prejudiced and ambitious partisan foes."[29] The crowd loved it.

But this final moment of glory was worth little to him. The election had spelled the political end of the Ring. Even before the voting, state Supreme Court Justice Wilton Learned, acting on the basis of the Broadway Bank information that Tilden had furnished him, signed an order for the Boss's arrest, with bail set at $1 million. The order was handed over to O'Brien's successor, Sheriff Matthew Brennan, an old friend of Tweed's who had recently gone over to the reform forces. On October 26, Brennan, accompanied by a large crowd of reporters and onlookers, called on Tweed at his office in the Department of Public Works. The Boss was waiting for him. He seemed to have aged considerably in the past few months, looking as if he were well over sixty, although in reality he was only forty-eight.

"Good morning, Mr. Tweed," said the sheriff.

"Good morning," Tweed replied in a quiet voice.

"Mr. Tweed, I have an order for your arrest," said Brennan.

"I expected it," Tweed said, "but not so soon. However, I have my bail ready, and you can take it here if you will."

A number of Tweed's close friends who had joined to provide the necessary bond sureties were present, among them the slight, notorious financier Jay Gould, and after some time the formalities were concluded. Brennan emerged carrying the documents, the crowd dispersed, and Tweed rode off to catch the afternoon train to Greenwich.

An observer might have felt that nothing much had taken place. But the Boss well knew that a milestone had been passed. From this point on, William M. Tweed, formally accused, would be at the mercy of the complex, devious workings of the law. Although he would triumph at the polls in the election a week or so hence, the victory would be a hollow one, for he would never return to Albany to take his seat in the senate. The Ring was smashed.

In December Tweed received the first of many criminal indictments, causing him to be rearrested, and at the end of the month a crowning indignity took place. At long last the extraordinary weight of evidence against Tweed and his cohorts broke down the doors of the Tammany Wigwam on Fourteenth Street; the sachems of the Society were forced to take action, if reluctantly. Their bigger-than-life leader, they now had to admit, had led them to disaster. At a meeting of the Council of Sachems, Tweed was not only deposed as Grand Sachem but expelled from the Society. Oakey Hall, Slippery Dick Connolly, and Peter B. Sweeny were also removed as sachems and expelled. Tweed was succeeded as Grand Sachem by Augustus Schell, a businessman and former port collector; Sweeny was replaced by Tilden, and Connolly by the attorney Charles O'Conor. Hall's spot was taken over by a quiet, unobtrusive man who would soon acquire unexpected fame: he was John Kelly, who would succeed Tweed as Boss of Tammany Hall.

Although the Ring was now removed from the political scene, two questions remained: how would the culprits be punished, and how much of the stolen money would the city be able to recover? The questions and their answers had surprisingly little impact on Tammany Hall, which managed to pick itself up with surprising aplomb after its ignominious role in condoning the Ring's plunder, as will be seen. But the questions of punishment and reimbursement were of consuming interest to the people of the city, and their outcomes are worth relating as a commentary on the wages of political and financial sin. In brief, only two of the major figures, Tweed and Hall, were ever brought to trial, and only one of them, Tweed, was convicted. And of the untold millions of dollars taken illegally, less than one million was paid back.

Most of the malefactors either attempted to strike a deal with the prosecutors, confessing all in return for immunity, or skipped town to avoid trial, or both. Slippery Dick Connolly, who thought he had received a firm guarantee of immunity from Tilden back in September, formally yielded his office to Andrew Green on November 20. From force of habit, or for sentimental reasons, he still tended to come into the office every day in the weeks that followed. But on January 2, 1872, he received a rude shock. There he was, chatting with Tilden, when Sheriff Brennan suddenly appeared, tapped him on the shoulder, and said he had a warrant for his arrest.

"Mr. Tilden!" Connolly exclaimed. "I'm arrested."

"No!" said Tilden, trying to look surprised. "What is the bail, sheriff?"

"One million dollars," replied Brennan. Tilden made a show of examining the arrest warrant and remarked quietly, "I am surprised at this—the bail is really one million." Connolly was crushed. Although he was reputed to be worth more than $6 million, he felt he could not put up any of that amount as bail, for doing so would enable the prosecutor, O'Conor, to attach his entire estate. So Brennan led him off to the Ludlow Street Jail.[30] Connolly's lawyer formally protested to Tilden, but without success. Connolly later learned that his arrest had come on an affidavit signed by none other than Tilden himself, who thus can be said to have worked a double cross. It showed, says the historian Alexander Callow, that "reformers could play as hard as Tammany Hall."[31]

A few days later, Connolly's bail was reduced to half a million. This he was able to furnish, and he walked out of jail. Shortly thereafter, he left for Europe with his $6 million, never to see New York again. An American reported seeing him many years later on the veranda of a hotel in Egypt, looking sad and lonely, "shunned by everybody, with trembling hands and vacant eyes."[32]

Peter "Brains" Sweeny proved hard to nail. Throughout the golden days of the Ring, he had arranged to have all his illegal payments sent to his brother James, who held a sinecure as a clerk of the superior court, and so linking the frauds to Peter proved difficult. In October 1871, James scuttled away to France, and a couple of weeks later Peter, after decamping to Canada, joined him there—ostensibly on "doctor's orders." Several years later, after James died from alcoholism, Peter struck a deal with the city, whereby he paid $150,000 (out of his brother's estate) as retribution for his malefactions, and another $250,000 for the chance to return to New York, where he lived out his days in obscurity. There were many who felt Sweeny should not have gotten off so lightly. In 1878, a report from an investigating committee of the Board of Aldermen—the body that would be examining William Tweed—stated that there was no doubt whatsoever "that Peter B. Sweeny had not only been a member of the Ring and a participator in all the Ring frauds, but that he had been perhaps the most despicable and dangerous, because the best educated and most cunning, of the entire gang."[33]

The two major contractors who had been in on the take also fled town, though only briefly. Chair maker extraordinary James H. Ingersoll found his way to Europe but stayed only a few months, returning to New York where he was arrested, tried, and sent to jail, then pardoned in return for giving testimony about others; he paid back nothing to the city. Andrew J. Garvey, whom the *Times* had dubbed the Prince of Plasterers, similarly escaped to Europe, where his nervousness at being caught approached paranoia. As his ship was approaching Bremerhaven a German pilot came aboard; Garvey thought the man was a cop and tried to bribe him in the best Tammany fashion (the pilot tossed the money overboard). Garvey returned in 1872, and made surprise appearances in the trials of both Hall and Tweed, testifying for the prosecution; he himself was never tried; he, too, paid back nothing.

Except for the payment made by Peter Sweeny, the only significant sums the city collected from Ring members came from the two paymasters, the late sleigh rider James Watson and Elbert A. Woodward. Watson's widow settled with the city for $558,237, by far the largest amount paid back—although surely this was just a fraction of what her husband must have siphoned. Woodward, after hiding in Connecticut for many months, emerged to settle with the city for slightly more than $150,000, after which he went free. Many years later, in 1877, when Tweed was at last providing extremely valuable testimony to a Board of Aldermen investigating committee, Woodward showed up and, on the witness stand, revealed himself to be totally without remorse about what he and others had done. He felt he had earned every penny that had come his way. Asked whether he would do it all over again if he had a chance, Woodward replied, "I don't think there's one in this room who wouldn't do it if they had a chance." He added, "If you ask my opinion of politicians, I can only say I never met an honest one, and I don't believe there's an honest politician in the world."[34]

The fates of three other subsidiary characters—the Ring-bought judges—are worth mentioning. If Judge George Barnard thought his granting an injunction against Tweed and the others had cleansed his reputation, he was in for a disappointment. In the early part of 1872, he fell under the scrutiny of the state assembly's judiciary committee, which recommended his impeachment for favoritism, conduct unbecoming to the bench, and many other offenses, and in July Barnard was convicted and removed. (Years later, when he died, $1 million in cash and securities was found among his effects.) The same committee also investigated judges John McCunn and Albert Cardozo, recommending that both be impeached, but while McCunn was convicted, Cardozo chose to resign from the bench rather than undergo the final ordeal. His son, Justice Benjamin Cardozo, as a member of the U.S. Supreme Court, would clear the family name in the twentieth century.

As for Oakey Hall, he never once considered resigning his office (which he had been elected to hold through 1872) or leaving town, and he continued to entertain the people of the city with jokes, innuendos, and wry posturings through a succession of court trials. When a grand jury in October 1871 considered whether or not to indict him, the evidence was impressive: as mayor he had signed thousands of vouchers and warrants over the years, many of them obviously fraudulent. But right at the outset Hall's defense was made clear. He had been too busy running the city, he said, to check on each and every paper put before him. If there were frauds, it was the work of Tweed and Connolly, not the overworked mayor. Anyway, he had not intended to perpetrate anything corrupt. The grand jury dismissed the charges.

A second grand jury in February 1872 saw things differently and returned an indictment. The mayor professed to be unperturbed. "A friend asked if I had given bail," he told reporters. "I replied that I did not wish to exert a baleful influence." This was too much for the *New York Sun*, which asked in a headline, WILL MAYOR HALL CRACK A HIDEOUS JOKE AT HIS OWN FUNERAL?[35] His Honor arrived at his trial jauntily on horseback and exhibited no concern. (Ironically, the trial was held in the new county courthouse, whose cost had so enraged the city.) As the proceedings began, Hall revealed his strategy: he would sway the jury by bedazzling it. Whenever possible he made quips, pranced about, struck poses and exhibited bizarre behavior—anything to confuse the twelve jurors. A few days into the trial, the prosecution unveiled a surprise witness, Andrew Garvey—who had actually been present at the trial up to that time, wearing a disguise. His appearance startled the courtroom. "Had Garvey risen from the dead and appeared in his grave clothes," said a bystander, "he could not have carried greater consternation into the ranks of the defense."[36] "Michelangelo" Garvey, as the papers were calling him, told how the vouchers for work performed were scandalously inflated and how he paid large sums to Tweed, but he provided no information about any payments to Hall nor anything concerning Hall's having signed the vouchers. After two weeks one of the jurors died, and the judge declared a mistrial.

A second trial, later in the year, ended in a hung jury. Many months after that, on December 22, 1873, with Hall no longer in office, the third trial began; it lasted only two days. The jury, after deliberating for a few hours, asked the judge for clarification of a technical matter. The judge responded to their question and then remarked that if they did not return a verdict soon they would have to be locked in their chambers all night. It just happened that the date was December 24—Christmas Eve. The jury shortly voted to acquit. Hall wept.

Though technically exonerated, Hall was never able thereafter to dispel the cloud of suspicion that hung over him. His law practice languished. For a while he helped manage a theater, then wrote and starred in a play about a man unjustly accused of stealing; the play did poorly. He put in a stint as city editor of the *New York World*, and in the 1880s went to London where he worked as a newspaper correspondent. Back in New York, he once again practiced law, and on March 25, 1898, made news again by being baptized into the Roman Catholic Church; one of his sponsors was a figure from the past, Peter B. Sweeny. A few months after that, Oakey Hall died.

Given his reputation as a lightweight who was probably not central to the Ring's machinations, Oakey Hall's avoidance of jail was hardly a surprise and did not cause the prosecutors any special grief. Boss Tweed was another matter. It was essential that he suffer—and he did.

Bringing him to trial took longer than expected because the chief prosecutor, Charles O'Conor, chose for tactical reasons to bring the action in the name of the state rather than the city. O'Conor's reasoning was that the city's legal officers might be biased in favor of the Boss and might not press hard enough. But his tactic turned out to be a mistake. Tweed had surrounded himself with expert defense counsel; headed by David Dudley Field (brother of the entrepreneur Cyrus Field), it included John Graham, one of the country's premier criminal lawyers, and a young man who would years later win fame as U.S. secretary of state, Elihu Root. They objected so tellingly to O'Conor's tactic that an appeals court eventually sided with them, requiring the state's case to be merged with that of the city, and this delayed the trial for almost a year (as Field had hoped it would).

During the trial itself, which got under way on January 7, 1873, the star witness once again was Andrew Garvey, who was far more nervous on the stand than he had been during Hall's trial. As he testified, Tweed glared at him, and when Garvey said he had fled to Europe because he feared the Ring might kill him, Tweed became visibly angry. During a recess, Tweed found him and said something to him, and when Garvey was asked about it he said, "His language was blasphemous."[37] After three weeks, the case went to the jury and it failed to agree. Said the Boss the next day, "I am tired of the whole farce. No jury will ever convict me." But there were those who claimed that the jury had been bought, and the prosecutors resolved to make another attempt.

For Tweed's second trial, which began on November 19, 1873, special care had been taken in selecting the jury. This time Garvey did not testify, but the prosecution presented a formidable array of vouchers, warrants, and other documents to prove the Boss's guilt, and after just four days the jury withdrew, to return after several hours of deliberation with a verdict of guilty—on 204 of the 220 counts in the indictment. Judge Noah Davis gave Tweed a cumulative sentence of twelve years in prison and a $12,750 fine, a surprisingly small monetary amount but acceptable to the prosecution in view of the stiff prison sentence. In delivering the sentence, the judge addressed the prisoner in tones that New Yorkers had waited long to hear: "Holding high public office, honored and respected by large classes of the community in which you lived, and, I have no doubt, beloved by your associates, you, with all these trusts devolved upon you, with all the opportunity you had, by the faithful discharge of your duty, to win the honor and respect of the whole community, you saw fit to pervert the powers with which you were clothed in a manner more infamous, more outrageous, than any instance of like character which the history of the civilized world contains."[38]

Taken to the Tombs prison, Tweed upon entering was asked by an officer what his occupation was. "Statesman," he responded.[39]

A year later he walked out, after an appeals court had ruled Judge Davis's cumulative sentence excessive. But he was not free, for he was immediately rearrested on a civil action whereby the state sought to recover $6 million in stolen funds that had been traced directly to him. Bail was set at $3 million, an astronomical amount, and Tweed forthwith repaired to the Ludlow Street Jail.

While awaiting the start of the new trial, the vanquished Boss was given certain privileges, such as the chance to take brief outings in the company of a guard. On the afternoon of December 4, 1875, he and a keeper and the warden of the jail set forth in a carriage and, after a spin around upper Manhattan, stopped in at the Tweed home at Madison Avenue and Sixtieth Street (he had sold the Fifth Avenue mansion), where Mrs. Tweed was to have dinner ready. After sitting for a while in the parlor, Tweed said he'd like to go upstairs to visit his wife, who was sick, and he left the room. Soon thereafter, the warden asked Tweed's son, William Tweed, Jr., to fetch his father, and young Bill went upstairs, only to return and announce, "Father's gone."[40]

What Tweed did, it appears, was mount the stairs, then tiptoe back down, don a soft black hat and black cloak, and quietly leave the house. No one saw him depart. By prearrangement, a carriage picked him up a block or so away and sped him to the Hudson River, where he was rowed across to New Jersey and taken to a farmhouse some- where back of the Palisades.

His escape caused a sensation. It also dismayed his legal counsel, who realized the public would see it as tantamount to a confession of guilt. While he hid out in New Jersey, he awaited the outcome of his civil trial; if he won, he could presumably return to the city free from imprisonment. But the trial, beginning in February 1876 and lasting a month, resulted in a verdict of guilty and a judgment of $6 million. He panicked. Transferring to a fisherman's hut on Staten Island near the Narrows, he was taken onto a small schooner that took him to Florida. There, using the name John Secor, he was joined by a man named William Hunt, and the two sailed to Cuba and from there embarked for Spain, which Tweed understood had no extradition treaty with the United States.

He had bet wrong, however. The American consul general in Cuba (then a Spanish possession) had guessed Tweed's identity, con- firming it after Tweed's departure, and the Spanish authorities said they had no objection to the United States capturing Tweed upon his arrival in Spain. A U.S. warship was accordingly waiting for him there, and he was apprehended and brought back to New York. A family friend noted that although the Boss was tanned from his expe- rience and much thinner, he was quite ill, suffering from pleurisy and a number of other ailments. On November 23, 1876—he had been free for almost a year—he was once again incarcerated in the Ludlow Street Jail.

There he took to sitting by the window and calling out to friends who passed by. It was reported that "he could give details of [the friends'] business, residence, relations, and events in their lives to the few intimates who dared to visit him."[41] By this time he was ready to tell all. Contacting the state attorney general, Charles Fairchild, he offered to provide a full confession of his criminal activities and surrender all his remaining personal property in return for his release. Fairchild said yes, providing the confession was thorough and revealed new information. Tweed drew up the document, enumerating all manner of swindles, payoffs, bribes, and other illegalities not heretofore made public. He waited. Fairchild returned the paper saying it did not provide enough new information to justify Tweed's release.

Clearly, Fairchild had gone back on his word. As to why he did so, there are two theories, both perhaps true. One is that Tweed's document went too far—that it incriminated too many people high up in the state's power structure. One of those who might have been uneasy about it, ironically, was Tweed's old nemesis, Samuel Jones Tilden, who had ridden the surge of popularity that had come to him from his anti-Ring efforts to run successfully for governor in 1874 (and unsuccessfully for president in 1876). At this date, Tilden was no longer in public office but was considering another run for the presidency in 1880, and the theory held that some undisclosed dealing between him and Tweed before 1870, or simply his acquiescence in the Boss's rise to power, might have proved embarrassing to him, and so he may have joined in the efforts to suppress the report.

The other theory is that at this stage, with so many other members of the Ring unpunished, it would have been political suicide for anyone to pardon the Boss. The people of New York would not have accepted it.

Among those dissatisfied with the Fairchild decision were the members of the city's Board of Aldermen, who now appointed a special committee to examine Tweed and others who might shed further light on what had really happened. Its hearings were held during the latter part of 1877, and they yielded voluminous testimony from the Boss, much of which, quoted herein, has provided posterity with the most complete story of the Ring's frauds. Tweed was in remarkably good form, recalling great amounts of detail when given sufficient advance warning. He could wax indignant, as when he angrily attacked the credibility of the Tammany politician John Morrissey, who had turned against him: "This man has taken me when I am at a disadvantage. . . . I shall fight back at everybody that fights me. I can't be crushed out because I am unfortunate."[42] He was eager to correct any misapprehensions about the Ring: when an alderman stated that it was through the instrumentality of Tammany Hall that the Ring got its power, Tweed interrupted him: "Not at all. Tammany Hall got all its powers from us—not we from them."[43] This was something of an exaggeration, of course, as Tammany had possessed formidable power, at least potentially, even before Tweed took it over; but the Ring, without question, put that power to use—if invidiously—to an unimagined extent.

Except for the light shed on the recent past, however, the aldermen hearings accomplished nothing: there were no further arrests, trials, or money judgments. (The city, it was felt, was tired of the whole affair.) The committee's report bewailed the fact that so few of the guilty had been brought to justice and so little of the stolen millions of dollars recovered. Tweed ended up paying nothing; his legal expenses had come to more than $400,000, and all his other assets had been transferred or had disappeared. The state and city, too, had incurred high legal costs, and when these were subtracted from the amounts paid back by Sweeny, Woodward, and Watson's widow, the net to the citizenry—which had suffered frauds amounting to at least $50 million (equivalent, conservatively, to $500 million in today's currency)—came to just $876,241.84.

Tweed died in prison on April 12, 1878, after saying, "I guess Tilden and Fairchild have killed me at last. I hope they will be satisfied now."[44] He was fifty-five years old. The funeral service was modest. An old friend of the Boss observed that if Tweed had died in 1870, the whole city would have been festooned with black. As it was, when the funeral cortege proceeded downtown on its way to the cemetery in Brooklyn, hardly anyone noticed. New York's current mayor, Smith Ely, Jr., who years earlier had served with Tweed on the Board of Supervisors and, though not sharing in the graft (he was independently prosperous), had freely connived with the Boss, refused to fly City Hall's flag at half-mast.

It was a chastened city that noted Tweed's passing. The Ring's larcenies had wrought a fierce financial toll, for during its hegemony the municipal debt—testimony to Connolly's unchecked borrowing—had soared, tripling, for example, from 1869 to the end of 1871, and reaching $118 million by 1874. Taxes had gone up by a similar degree. The thefts constituted an expensive object lesson to New Yorkers, demonstrating how deeply the city could be compromised and corrupted if the people paid no attention to what their elected officials were doing. As for Tammany Hall, its reputation was changed for all time: not for the rest of its days would it ever shake off the memory of Tweed's brazen exploits, for they were deeds in which it had gladly shared.

Given the city's great energy and fundamental prosperousness, however, the sense of guilt hardly lasted. In a commentary on the Tweed era at the time of the Boss's death, the editor of the *Nation* noted that Tweed rose to power because the people had allowed him to do so, and that many of them felt no rancor toward him. "A villain of more brains would have had a modest dwelling and would have guzzled in secret," the editor wrote. "[Tweed] found, however, the seizure of the government and the malversation of its funds so easy at the outset that he was thrown off his guard. His successors here and elsewhere will not imitate him in this, but that he will have successors there is no doubt."[45]

Indeed, they were already on the scene.

6

HONEST JOHN

THE TWEED RING SCANDALS ALMOST KILLED TAM-
many Hall. By the end of 1871, with the Boss in disgrace and his
friends scrambling for cover, the Hall, even though the majority of its
members had been mere observers of the Ring's shameful excesses
and were probably untainted, stood discredited and tarnished. Many
New Yorkers predicted that Tammany was finished as a political force
in the city. They were wrong. Not only did it recover, it emerged
stronger than ever. That it did so was due to the wiles and expertise of
one man: Tweed's successor as the Boss, John Kelly.

Many times in the ensuing decades Tammany Hall would be declared dead or dying, only to rise again. But the renewal that Kelly
brought about was by far the most important of Tammany's many
rebirths. Far more than breathing new life into the organization, Kelly
transformed it and gave it new direction. Tweed's methods had
proved a disaster; new ways would have to be found, and Kelly found
them. He overhauled Tammany's structure, tightened discipline, and
recast the Hall's public image. The Tammany Hall that survived and
flourished during the next century, leaping from one political triumph to another under powerful bosses such as Richard Croker and
Charles Murphy while never ceasing to entertain and outrage the
citizens of New York, was Kelly's Tammany. He gave it the shape
that enabled it to endure. Kelly, someone once said, found Tammany
a horde; he left it a political army.[1]

Not by coincidence, Kelly also gave Tammany its Roman Catholic cast, which it would keep to the end of its days. William Tweed and his predecessors at Tammany's helm had all been Protestant and Anglo-Saxon. But by 1850 large-scale emigration from Ireland had made the Irish New York's largest minority—a very vocal one at that—and Tammany Hall had long since counted them among its most faithful supporters. Kelly was a devout Catholic, as were the Tammany chiefs who succeeded him. In the words of the scholar Arthur Genen, Kelly "laid the foundation for an 'Irish Tammany' which controlled New York City politics until the New Deal era of the 1930s."[2] In this sense, he can be seen as the most important Boss of all.

But this stolid, heavyset man, whose resolute demeanor and square, bearded jaw caused more than one observer to liken him to Ulysses S. Grant (who at that time was president), did not enjoy unalloyed success as Tammany's guiding light. Intelligent, forthright, efficient, and a supreme organizer, he was also stubborn, vain, and unduly susceptible to flattery. Above all, he was vindictive. Those loyal to Kelly and to Tammany he defended and protected, but anyone who crossed him, challenged his way of doing things, or threatened the well-being of Tammany Hall would not be forgiven, and an enemy once made was an enemy forever. In the world of politics, such inflexibility can be costly, and although Kelly's rule of the Hall brought lasting internal benefits to the organization, it was also marked by ruinous quarrels with key politicians, most notably those potent Democrats Samuel J. Tilden and Grover Cleveland, who for Tammany's benefit should have remained his friends. More than once, Kelly's defeat at the hands of such adversaries gravely wounded the Hall, and it was only the Boss's tight grip on the smooth-running Tammany machine that enabled him to survive.

The New York City that Kelly's Tammany Hall operated in continued to grow at a rapid pace, as it had during the days of the Tweed Ring. Its population, which stood at 942,292 in 1870, climbed to 1,206,299 in 1880, and building was expanding up both sides of the new Central Park. The city was now uncontestably the nation's premier manufacturing center, and its port was handling more than 70 percent of all imports into the United States. It was also handling an ever increasing number of immigrants; in 1874 alone, almost four hundred thousand arrived. And a large portion of these newcomers stayed in the city. Up to the 1870s, the great majority of them came from northern Europe, principally England, Ireland, Germany, and

Scandinavia, but at this point a shift began to occur: the great surge of arrivals from southern Europe (principally Italians) and Eastern Europe (especially Polish and Russian Jews) was getting under way. Many of the newcomers perforce settled in the already congested tenement areas of the city, especially the Lower East Side, where Tammany was already strong. The Hall accordingly picked up further strength by befriending and assisting them—in return, as always, for their support at the polls. If Tammany's influence had been temporarily reduced by the Ring debacle, its potential for even greater power was undeterred.

Although John Kelly achieved his renown by repudiating most of the things Tweed had stood for, his early life was quite similar to that of his predecessor. The son of Irish immigrants who had come to the United States in 1816, Kelly, like Tweed, was born on the Lower East Side, in 1822 (Tweed was a year younger). As a young man, Kelly too became a volunteer fireman and a hardworking member of Tammany Hall. Also, like Tweed, he served as an alderman in the city government and later as a congressman. But there the resemblance ends. Unlike Tweed, who was raised in comfortable circumstances, Kelly grew up in poverty. His father, a grocer, died when John was only eight, and the youngster was forced to leave his parochial school and look for work to help support his family. For a while he toiled as an office boy at the *New York Herald*, whose owner, James Gordon Bennett, took a liking to him, but he quit in his teens to apprentice to a grate-setter and soapstone cutter, a trade he thought might be profitable. He was a plodder and said little, but when a neighbor remarked on his taciturnity to Mrs. Kelly, she replied that John "thinks a great deal more than he talks, but be sure he is not dumb."[3]

He certainly was not. Upon completing his apprenticeship he opened his own grate-setting concern on Broome Street. The firm did so well that by age twenty-one Kelly expanded to a larger store on Elizabeth Street. In his spare time he took part in amateur theatricals and became known for his ability to move effortlessly into such demanding parts as Hamlet, Macbeth, and Othello. He had grown to six feet and weighed 200 pounds. In addition to serving as a volunteer fireman, he acquired a solid reputation as an amateur boxer, which made him a popular member of various gangs on the Lower East Side. He was also captain of the Carroll Target Guard, a target-shooting club, whose members would later be of great service to him during election campaigns. Taking part in Tammany affairs, he was particularly vigilant in combating the anti-Irish, anti-Catholic Know-Nothing party that became so strong during the 1840s. Twice he ran for alderman in his district and lost. But on the third try, convinced that Know-Nothing election inspectors were voiding proper Kelly ballots, he arrived at the polling place at the corner of Elizabeth and Grand streets accompanied by a group of impressive-looking supporters and found that a partition hid the inspectors from view. Voters—who Kelly had reason to believe were heavily favoring his candidacy—were required to hand their ballots through a window in the partition, but there was no way of knowing what happened to them after that. Kelly and his friends tore down the screen and drove the inspectors from the hall. The Know-Nothings brought in reinforcements from nearby shipbuilding yards and counterattacked. For a while, Kelly's forces were outnumbered, but in the nick of time more Kelly supporters arrived and carried the day. This time, when the votes were counted, Kelly had been elected.

As a thirty-one-year-old alderman, he dutifully supported Tammany-backed measures but otherwise attracted little notice. He had his eyes on higher office. That autumn, he ran for the U.S. Congress against the celebrated Tammany maverick Mike Walsh, and to everyone's surprise pulled it off, winning by just 18 votes out of 8,199 cast. Stunned, Walsh announced he would contest the election, but Kelly countered by threatening to reveal that Walsh, for all his bluster, had never become an American citizen, at which point Walsh gave up. In Washington, Kelly stood out as the only Catholic member of Congress. In speech after speech, he vigorously defended the rights of Catholics and the Irish. His fellow legislators barely listened. In 1856, he was easily reelected and began speaking out on other topics. But the Tammany Hall sachems had different plans for him; in 1858, he was invited to run for the lucrative office of sheriff of New York. He agreed and easily won election.

The post of sheriff was unsalaried but officeholders were entitled to retain all the fees they collected in the line of duty, which could add up: sheriffs transported criminals to jail, impaneled juries, and issued reports on the identity of those convicted. They were also responsible for arrests and executions. Kelly's efficiency paid off, and the money rolled in, so that by 1860 he moved with his wife, son, and two daughters from Elizabeth Street to a more prominent house on Lexington Avenue. Many years later, after Kelly had become Tammany Boss, allegations were made (though never proved) that he had inflated the number of cases handled and thus profited unduly, allegedly pocketing as much as $30,000 that was not legally his. At this stage, however, no one suspected such a thing; Kelly's assumed probity was so well established that he was dubbed Honest John, a label that stuck. Sheriffs were not permitted to succeed themselves, and so in 1861 Kelly returned full-time to his grate-setting business. But in 1864 William Tweed, already established as Tammany's leader and well aware of Kelly's strong following among the Irish, invited him to serve again as sheriff. This time Kelly expanded the office by hiring as deputy sheriffs such dubious underworld characters as Isaiah Rynders and John Morrissey, but no irregularities were reported. Kelly was now successfully investing in real estate and also became part owner of two New York newspapers, the *Star* and the *Evening Express*. His wealth increased.

In 1866, Kelly endured two blows: his wife and his son both died of tuberculosis. He, too, was suffering from a bronchial ailment and decided to retire from politics. He had also, despite Tweed's favors, come to believe that the Boss's methods were bad for both Tammany and the Democratic party, and had decided to disassociate himself from him. But in 1868 a Democratic reform group opposed to Tweed's choice of Oakey Hall for mayor asked Kelly to run for that office on its slate and he agreed. Nine days after his nomination, however, he abruptly withdrew, citing poor health, and left for Europe with his two daughters. There were rumors that he actually feared disclosure of irregularities stemming from his tenure as sheriff, but no allegations surfaced. Oakey Hall, in surprisingly (for him) poor taste, quipped, "I am the medical adviser who drove Kelly to Europe."[4]

So it was that just as the Tweed Ring was gearing up to engineer its most outrageous municipal thefts, Kelly had removed himself from the scene. He was gone until the fall of 1871, traveling about Europe and the Holy Land, studying church antiquities often in the company of Roman Catholic priests who acted as guides and interpreters. At the very moment he returned (bearing with him four large religious paintings that he had commissioned and that he presented to New York's brand-new St. Patrick's Cathedral), the Ring was in a state of collapse—Connolly had already defected—and Tammany Hall was, through association, nearly as badly off. It would lose heavily in the November 1871 elections. In such circumstances, with Tammany seemingly on the ropes, it must have appeared that John Kelly's self-imposed retirement would become permanent.

But a number of leading Democrats, principally Samuel J. Tilden, Ring prosecutor Charles O'Conor, the venerable sachem Augustus

MATTHEW L. DAVIS.

Matthew L. Davis, the true founder of Tammany Hall as we know it and a Burr disciple, combined with other Burrites to take over the Hall and then, by manipulating party gatherings, made Tammany's General Committee synonymous with that of the Democratic-Republican party as a whole. Henceforth, for the better part of a century and a half, Tammany spoke for the party. (*Culver Pictures*)

Potent mentor of Tammany from afar, Martin Van Buren after 1820 made the Hall a key part of his statewide political machine (the nation's first), which his followers directed from Albany. Van Buren's firm beliefs in party discipline and in the value of patronage became central features of Tammany dogma and practice. (*The Bettman Archive*)

Aaron Burr, though never a member of Tammany Hall, helped propel the organization into partisan politics by involving its members in his expertly crafted—and successful—campaign to win the 1800 national election for the young Democratic-Republican party. (*The Bettman Archive*)

Tammany's first true Wigwam, or clubhouse, was dedicated in 1812 and stood at the corner of Nassau and Frankfort Streets, a block from City Hall. Although the Society used only the first floor of the building (the upper floors were rented out as a hotel), this was "Tammany Hall" for fifty-five years. (*The Bettman Archive*)

The controversial but imaginative mayor of New York in the 1850s, Fernando Wood (*left*), never seemed able to shake accusations of fraud and deceit. A member of Tammany Hall but often at odds with it, he nevertheless demonstrated how control of the police could lead to control of elections. (*Culver Pictures*)

Masters of deception, the Tweed Ring was portrayed in a celebrated cartoon by Thomas Nast published on August 19, 1871. The rotund Boss Tweed stands at left; next to him is the shaggy-haired Peter ("Brains") Sweeny, then Comptroller Richard ("Slippery Dick") Connolly and the bespectacled mayor, "Elegant Oakey" Hall. Beyond Tweed are the chairmaker James H. Ingersoll and Andrew Garvey, whom the *New York Times* nicknamed the "Prince of Plasterers." (*Courtesy of the New-York Historical Society*)

William M. Tweed was Tammany Hall's best known Boss. His name came to symbolize civic deceit and corruption, but he never seemed as diabolical in person as his monstrous thefts from the city treasury would imply. Courtly in public (until finally caught), he exuded affability and confidence. From 1865 to 1871 he was unquestionably the most powerful man in the city and state, if not the nation. (*The Bettman Archive*)

Tammany's most famous Wigwam was this building on Fourteenth Street, which it occupied for more than sixty years, from 1868 to 1929. Crowned by a statue of the Society's patron saint, St. Tammany, it is shown as it was being readied for the 1868 Democratic National Convention, which took place in its Long Room. (*Courtesy of the New-York Historical Society*)

Honest John Kelly, who rescued Tammany Hall from the disgrace of the Tweed Ring scandals, perfected Tammany's organization from the lowliest party worker up to the Executive Committee and made it a model of efficiency and accountability. (*Culver Pictures*)

Tammany's bard and philosopher, George Washington Plunkitt, sits in his "office," the bootblack stand in the New York County Courthouse, from which he liked to expound on party matters to anyone who would listen. Plain-talking but deceptively smart, Plunkitt at one time served simultaneously as a magistrate, alderman, county supervisor, and state senator. (*Photo from* Plunkitt of Tammany Hall *by William L. Riordon*)

New York's mammoth chief of police in the Croker era, William S. Devery (*below*), reputedly co-directed (with Big Tim Sullivan) one of the most prosperous gambling rings in the nation. When questioned about payoffs to the police he would reply, "Touchin' on an' appertainin' to that, there's nothin' doin'." (*Culver Pictures*)

The swashbuckling Richard Croker (*center, in derby*), who led Tammany during its most notoriously corrupt years, arrives back in New York in 1899 from a vacation on his estate in England. Unsalaried and without any other visible means of support, Croker managed to own a house on Manhattan's fashionable Upper East Side, estates in Florida and England, a racing stable worth at least $100,000, and securities amounting to several million dollars. (*Museum of the City of New York*)

Big Tim Sullivan (*left, at center*), though never a Boss of Tammany Hall, exercised so much power as a district leader that county bosses like Croker or Murphy often had to defer to him. Personally ruling most of the Lower East Side, he grew rich from the gambling syndicate that he and Devery headed, which earned an estimated $3 million a year. (*Culver Pictures*)

Charles Francis Murphy, Tammany's far-sighted Boss from 1902 until his death in 1924, strides the Atlantic City boardwalk during a convention in 1917. Realizing that the Hall after Croker had to stand for more than corruption and handouts, he put it squarely behind the most advanced social legislation. (*UPI/Bettman*)

Two of Tammany's most noted sons, Mayor James J. Walker (*second from left*) and former Governor Alfred E. Smith (*second from right*), line up with other dignitaries during the dedication of the Hall's new Wigwam in 1929. At center is 100-year-old John R. Voorhis, Grand Sachem of the Tammany Society; at far left, New York Surrogate James A. Foley (Charles Murphy's son-in-law), a Tammany sachem; and at far right, John F. Curry, Tammany Boss at the time. (*UPI/Bettman*)

At the height of the so-called Seabury investigations in 1932, Mayor Jimmy Walker responds spiritedly to the relentless questioning of former Judge Samuel Seabury (*left*) during the mayor's second day on the stand. Although the courtroom crowd cheered the mayor, the evidence unearthed by Seabury proved fatally damaging to Walker, who resigned a few months later. (*Wide World Photos*)

Tammany's last building, an impressive structure on Seventeenth Street and Union Square, served as headquarters for the organization from 1929 until 1943, when the beleaguered Society was forced to abandon it for lack of funds. (*UPI/Bettman*)

The last Boss of what was still called Tammany Hall, Carmine De Sapio (*left*) shakes hands in 1953 with his candidate for mayor, Robert F. Wagner, Jr. Although Wagner's victory gave De Sapio great power and influence, ironically it was the mayor's decision in 1961 to run for a third term on an anti-Boss platform that brought an end to De Sapio's leadership. (*UPI/Bettman*)

Schell, and the financier August Belmont (although they had been working alongside the civic reformist Committee of Seventy to defeat Tammany's candidates in the 1871 fall elections and thus deal the Ring a death blow) felt it was important not to destroy the Hall itself in the process. A renewed and reformed Tammany, after all, could be good for their party, as it had often been in the past, providing candidates, operating the party machinery, and, in most cases, determining party policy. The Hall must be saved. But who could direct it? The ideal man would be experienced in Tammany affairs yet certifiably honest and unblemished by the recent horrors. Because the Irish were such a strong force in the party, it would also be good if the new man were Irish. Their gaze swiftly fell on the newly arrived Kelly, who fit the formula precisely, and they asked him if he was available. He said he was and, as he remarked later, "threw my whole heart into the work."[5]

At the outset, at least, he exhibited a humble and self-effacing air toward his new responsibilities. The men who had approached him had asked him to do a job, he said, and if he were to lose their confidence "it will be an easy matter for them to dispense with me. I am not commissioned as a leader by any constituted authority. . . . I am wholly in their hands, and they can keep me or reject me any day."[6]

To reestablish Tammany, he would first have to clean out all those who had shared in Tweed's rule and surround himself with the most respected Democrats in the city. He therefore persuaded former general George McClellan, former governor Horatio Seymour, and Peter Cooper's son-in-law, Abram S. Hewitt, to become Tammany members. Augustus Schell took over Tweed's post as Grand Sachem in December 1871. The following April, a completely new Council of Sachems was duly elected by the Tammany Society and included, besides Schell and Kelly, Belmont and, most important, Tilden. By that time, Tilden had acquired the reputation (not entirely deserved) as the man who brought down the Tweed Ring. For this reason—and because he was an astute political operator in his own right—he was rapidly becoming not only a key member of the Council of Sachems but the most influential Democrat in New York State. Tilden and Kelly, at this point, got along well.

Having cleansed the Tammany leadership, Kelly now proceeded to make sure the Hall, despite its past sins, was recognized as *the* representative of all New York Democrats. His only potential rival was a group called Apollo Hall, led by "Jimmy the Famous" O'Brien—the man whose incriminating evidence, handed over to the *New York Times* earlier in 1871, revealed the Ring's crimes. But this insignificant rivalry was short-lived, for at the state party convention in May 1872, all of Tammany's delegates were seated and Apollo's were frozen out. The Hall's legitimacy was assured, at least for now.

But were any of Boss Tweed's allies still around to make trouble? That October a dissident Tammany faction led by former state senator Henry Genét—a friend of the old Boss's—tried to get one of their number, Samuel B. Garvin, nominated for district attorney. Kelly recognized the threat and strongly opposed the nomination. When the dissidents became obstreperous at a Wigwam gathering, Kelly asked Augustus Schell, who was presiding, to adjourn the meeting until the next day. And when the Genét group arrived the following day they found the doors barred to them. The Tammany toughs controlling access were under the command of John Kelly's good friend Richard Croker. The restricted meeting nominated Kelly's candidate, . Charles Donohue.

The first sign that not everything might go as Kelly hoped came in the fall elections of 1872. The Republicans made a virtual clean sweep of state offices (including the governor's) and won the mayor's office, too. Admittedly, it was a Republican year—the GOP ticket was headed by the popular Ulysses S. Grant, who was seeking reelection, and the memory of Tweed's excesses was still strong—but both Kelly and Tilden had counted on electing one of their own to succeed the discredited Oakey Hall. They prevailed on one of their most presentable colleagues, the businessman Abram Lawrence, to run for the post. Lawrence had the advantage of being a onetime Apolloite and so could presumably help unify the Democrats. But the irrepressible "Jimmy the Famous" O'Brien insisted on running as an independent. With the Democratic vote thus split, the winner was the reform candidate, William F. Havemeyer, who had the backing of the Republicans. A wealthy sugar magnate, Havemeyer had presided over the Committee of Seventy's massive September 1871 anti-Tweed rally at Cooper Union that had so roused public support for the drive to oust the Ring. Oddly enough, he had also been a long-time member of the Hall, had served as a Tammany mayor twice in the 1840s, and had even helped Tilden in the fall of 1871 persuade Slippery Dick Connolly to appoint Andrew Green as deputy city comptroller, a key step in bringing down the Tweed Ring. Kelly and Tilden nevertheless did not want him for mayor; for their purposes he was too old (sixty-eight now) and too tied to the reformist Committee of Seventy, which was fundamentally anti-Tammany. But as the committee's candidate (and blessed by the GOP), he won.

A blunt, pugnacious man, Havemeyer spelled plenty of trouble for Kelly. Their conflict was perhaps inevitable. As Tammany historian M. R. Werner put it, "Havemeyer considered the government of the City of New York a business which should be run efficiently for the purposes of the corporation, just as the sugar business was run for its corporation, and to Kelly the government . . . was a business which should be run efficiently for the purposes of the men who held subordinate positions under it; the one believed in corporate finance for the good of the corporation, and the other believed in prosperity for the greatest number of officeholders."[7] On top of this, Havemeyer doubted that Kelly really represented a change in Tammany; the Hall, he felt, had merely been reshuffled, not genuinely reformed. Kelly, in turn, chafed under Havemeyer's reluctance to go along with Tammany's patronage recommendations.

For the next year, however, the two men avoided open conflict. In the fall elections of 1873, in which local offices were at stake, Tammany was triumphant. On election night, after the returns were in, grateful Tammanyites paraded under torchlight from the Wigwam to Kelly's home and serenaded him. In less than two years, he had brought success back to the Hall. He was now unquestionably the Boss.

Mayor Havemeyer, on the other hand, was not happy with the results of the election. Among those elected was Richard Croker, whom Kelly had nominated for coroner, and whom Havemeyer abhorred because of Croker's background as a gang leader. Kelly had assured the mayor that Croker was an honest man but Havemeyer did not believe him, and he said later that on hearing that Croker had won he was "overwhelmed with a torrent of indignation."[8] Even the *New York Times*, which had been sympathetic to Kelly, had objected to Croker's nomination and opined that Tweed's spirit was still alive: "There is no longer any doubt that Tammany is controlled by the same spirit and to a large extent by the same men by means of which and under whom it became infamous and dangerous as a political organization. There have been vast pretenses of reform but it is clear that the only change is in the 'Boss.' "[9]

On the contrary, there had been great change at Tammany Hall, although it could not necessarily be classified as reform. Kelly had completely revamped the place: it was a new machine. In the past, he felt, the Hall had been too loosely structured, its procedures too haphazard. Any cohesiveness had depended too much on the personal magnetism of someone like Fernando Wood or William Tweed, and that was risky. A more tightly bound organization was needed to resist the unexpected onslaughts of politics. To ensure Tammany's endurance, the organization needed better discipline and more centralized control, which Kelly had already moved to implement.

The core of the apparatus was its thirty-three district leaders. Kelly insisted that these leaders be both efficient in producing satisfactory election results and obedient in responding to his dictates. In theory, the leaders of these districts made up Tammany's Executive Committee, which had the power of naming the county leader (or Boss) of the organization. Actually, however, the Executive Committee was totally within Kelly's control and consisted of his favorite district leaders plus a handful of the Tammany Society's sachems. Kelly dismissed unsatisfactory or uncooperative leaders. Every district leader and many other subordinate ward leaders belonged to the Tammany General Committee (generally synonymous with the New York County Democratic General Committee), and theoretically this body directed party affairs, but in effect the General Committee was mere window dressing. The Boss and his friendly Executive Committee ruled all, which meant the Boss's word was law. Low-level Tammanyites exercised almost no independent power at all. Not that they disputed this state of affairs: as long as the Boss was successful, they were perfectly happy to do his bidding.

The principle business of the organization, of course, was to win elections. Great care was given to choosing proper candidates and to making sure they were ratified by the appropriate conventions or briskly approved in carefully managed primary elections. Care often meant muscle. Any renegade faction attempting to send an opposing delegation to a nominating convention might have its meetings disrupted by Tammany shoulder-hitters friendly to Kelly; primary elections, if closely contested, could be controlled by stuffing the ballot boxes or simply by preventing the opposition from voting. Strong-arm methods were to be applied with some restraint, however, and extreme violence was frowned on. "Blood's news," warned a Tammany stalwart. "It gets into the papers."[10]

The payoff was patronage. Passing out jobs by a newly elected party had been accepted practice for decades, but it tended to be an informal, hit-or-miss affair. Certain jobs might be dispensed by an alderman, a state senator, or a city department head, others by Tammany itself; there was no single method. Kelly, however, centralized the entire system and brought it under his control. Henceforth all jobs (except for high-ranking ones) were handed out by the Tammany district leaders—and the number of jobs each leader could dispense depended on the number of votes he had produced in the last election. A poor showing at the polls meant fewer jobs for the leader to hand out. Then entire process was monitored by another Tammany group, the Committee on Organization (dominated by Kelly, of course), which, after reviewing the situation, would inform the district leader how many jobs he could fill. Only then could he award the coveted posts.

But to keep itself in business, the machine needed not only jobs to hand out but a continuing inflow of cash to cover its day-to-day expenses and to finance election campaigns. In the past, to meet campaign costs Tammany relied largely on contributions from friends. And those who were running for office often attempted to meet their own expenses. Kelly systematized the process by automatically assessing every candidate a sum of money proportionate to the office he sought. Every office had its price—the stipend for a job paying only $1,000 a year might be as high as $250—and Tammany counted on the candidate to pay his assessment promptly. The money thus collected was held in a general fund until the day before the election, at which point it was doled out to the district leaders to pay for poll watchers, transporting infirm voters to the polls, and so on. This was known as Dough Day.

But much more money was needed to keep Tammany going beyond the expense of running campaigns. In the past, as in the present, a great deal of money was produced by extralegal levies—known as protection money—exacted by district leaders, party functionaries, or even the police (generally acting for Tammany) from neighborhood saloons, gambling dens, houses of prostitution, and other businesses whose owners for one reason or another needed to evade the law or who simply wanted assurance that they could live and work peaceably without interference from the authorities. A grocer might want to obstruct the sidewalk for a special display that was technically forbidden, or a builder might hope to violate the regulations to cut his costs; money would be paid over and at least part of it would end up in the Tammany treasury. Tammany would see to it that the payer was protected. This practice continued under Kelly.

Beyond this was a huge gray area represented by the continuing phenomenon of city funds somehow ending up in Tammany pockets. That this was taking place during Honest John Kelly's rule might have surprised many New Yorkers, for Kelly not only disapproved of the Ring's outlandish thefts but (despite rumors to the contrary) was personally above reproach. Furthermore, the unmasking of Tweed and his friends made it unlikely that anyone in the future could get away with masterminding so bald-faced a swindle as the Ring had organized. The city simply would not let that happen again. Yet there were subtler and more devious paths to aggrandizement—surely known to Kelly but conveniently overlooked by him—known as honest graft. Just what this was and how it worked was explained in an utterly delightful manner by a Tammany district leader named George Washington Plunkitt, whose highly successful career was already well advanced by the time Honest John became Boss of the Hall.

Like Kelly, Plunkitt was born and raised in the poor Irish neighborhood of the Lower East Side. As a teenager, he started working in a butcher shop and then opened his own store. In the early 1870s, he became a contractor specializing in harbor work. From the outset he worked for Tammany Hall, rising through the ranks to become an election district captain and finally an assembly district leader. Gregarious and loquacious, Plunkitt was highly intelligent and an especially hard worker. At one point he served simultaneously as magistrate, alderman, county supervisor, and state senator. Not only did he acquit himself creditably on all these assignments, but he managed to do so without maintaining a formal office. Instead, he transacted all his business from what he called his office, the bootblack stand in the New York County Courthouse, where he also held forth at length on all manner of political topics. His remarks were recorded by a newspaper reporter, William L. Riordon, who published them (after reworking them somewhat) just after the turn of the century as *Plunkitt of Tammany Hall: A Series of Very Plain Talks on Very Practical Politics*. In the course of his remarks, Plunkitt made clear his scorn for the crude methods employed by the Ring.

"The politician who steals," he said, "is worse than a thief. He is a fool. With the grand opportunities all around for the man with a political pull, there's no excuse for stealin' a cent.[11] . . . There's the biggest kind of difference between political looters and politicians who make a fortune out of politics by keepin' their eyes wide open. The looter goes in for himself alone without considerin' his organization or his city. The politician looks after his own interests, the organization's interests, and the city's interests all at the same time. See the distinction?"[12] Plunkitt conceded that he was a fine example of the benefits of honest graft. "I might sum up the whole thing by sayin': 'I seen my opportunities and I took 'em.' Just let me explain.

. . . My party's in power in the city, and it's goin' to undertake a lot of public improvements. Well, I'm tipped off, say, that they're going to lay out a new park at a certain place. I see my opportunity and I take it. I go to that place and I buy up all the land I can in the neighborhood. Then the board of this or that makes its plan public, and there is a rush to get my land, which nobody cared particular for before. Ain't it perfectly honest to charge a good price and make a profit on my investment and foresight? Of course, it is. Well, that's honest graft."[13] There were no conflict-of-interest laws to stand in Plunkitt's way. By the time he died in 1924, he was a millionaire.

But it wasn't through honest graft that Plunkitt achieved his key position in the Tammany hierarchy; he obtained that through sheer hard work, providing all kinds of help to the people of his district. For by Plunkitt's day the local Tammany district leader had become a "fixer" who could cut through red tape, provide any number of helpful services, and act as the citizen's friendly link to a fearsome and impersonal city government. "What tells in holdin' your grip on your district," he said, "is to go right down among the poor families and help them in the different ways they need help. I've got a regular system for this. If there's a fire in Ninth, Tenth, or Eleventh Avenue, for example, any hour of the day or night, I'm usually there with some of my election district captains as soon as the fire engines. If a family is burned out I don't ask whether they are Republicans or Democrats, and I don't refer them to the Charity Organization Society, which would investigate their case in a month or two and decide they were worthy of help about the time they are dead from starvation. I just get quarters for them, buy clothes for them if their clothes were burned up, and fix them up till they get things runnin' again. It's philanthropy, but it's politics, too—mighty good politics. Who can tell how many votes one of these fires bring me? The poor are the most grateful people in the world, and, let me tell you, they have more friends in their neighborhoods than the rich have in theirs. . . . The consequence is that the poor look up to George W. Plunkitt as a father, come to him in trouble—and don't forget him on election day." A district leader could also serve as a one-man employment bureau. "I know every big employer in the district and in the whole city, for that matter, and they ain't in the habit of sayin' no to me when I ask them for a job."[14]

For Plunkitt, taking care of his constituents' problems could be a virtual around-the-clock affair that would exhaust all but the most energetic of politicians. Riordon chronicled a typical day in Plunkitt's life: It begins at 2 A.M. when a bartender knocks on his door asking him to go to the police station to bail out a saloonkeeper who had been arrested on a minor violation. At 6 A.M. a fire rouses him again. From 8:30 A.M. to 11 A.M. he is in court helping to ease the penalties handed out to persons in his district who were found guilty of various minor offenses. From 11 A.M. until lunchtime he is busy getting jobs for people. By 3 P.M. he's at the funeral of a Catholic constituent, followed immediately by attendance at a Jewish funeral. At 7 P.M. he presides over a meeting of his election district captains at which the needs and political views of individuals in the district are thrashed over; at 8 P.M. he attends a church fair, buying ice cream for the children, kissing babies while flattering the mothers, "and [taking] their fathers out for something down at the corner";[15] at 9 P.M. he is back at the clubhouse attending to myriad small problems; at 10:30 P.M. he stops in at a Jewish wedding, having previously sent a handsome present to the bride. At midnight, finally, his day is over and he can fall into bed.

Of course there is another side to the impression that Tammany's district leaders were the soul of benevolence and nothing more, as Plunkitt claimed. For every $100 that Tammany distributed for charitable reasons it received at least $1,000 from some special interest to refrain from alleviating the underlying condition that caused the suffering. The district leader, as one observer noted, "helps the widow, whose suit for damages was blocked under a system he was paid to perpetuate."[16] Plunkitt would be aiding the victims of a fire while Tammany would be doing nothing to improve housing conditions that brought on such tragedies. Indeed, Kelly, Plunkitt, and their like had contempt for well-meaning reformers who battled to improve life in the city. The reform administrations that he had observed, said Plunkitt, "were mornin' glories—looked lovely in the mornin' and withered up in a short time, while the regular machines went on flourishin' forever, like fine old oaks."[17]

Given this kind of attitude, it was only a matter of time before a full-scale collision occurred between Kelly and the reformist mayor Havemeyer. The first confrontation came when two police commissioners appointed by the mayor—Oliver Charlick and Hugh Gardner—removed two Tammany election inspectors on election day in 1873 without giving them formal notice. Kelly was already resentful because the Republican-controlled 1873 state legislature had given the mayor the power to appoint such commissioners, putting them outside Tammany's lucrative patronage domain. But what these men did was to him inexcusable. He brought charges against the mayor through the Tammany-dominated Board of Aldermen, which in April 1874 obediently passed a resolution demanding that Havemeyer fire Charlick and Gardner. The mayor refused. Kelly took the matter to court, which fined the men but did not remove them. Then the two resigned. This might have solved the problem, but Havemeyer confounded everyone by pulling a silly switch, appointing Charlick to Gardner's post and Gardner to Charlick's. Kelly was livid. "This is extraordinary," he said. "It is only adding fuel to the flame."[18] He formally requested the Republican governor, John Dix, to remove Havemeyer from office; the city's Board of Aldermen echoed Kelly's demand; the governor, while roundly criticizing the mayor, declined to oust him. Charlick and Gardner resigned again and Havemeyer appointed two unknowns to the posts. Several New York newspapers agreed that the mayor was making a fool of himself.

In September Havemeyer boiled over. In an open letter to Kelly released to the press, Havemeyer accused him of dishonesty, corruption, and fraud during his tenure as sheriff years back. Havemeyer concluded his letter by saying, "I think that you were worse than Tweed, except that he was a larger operator. The public knew that Tweed was a bold, reckless man, making no pretensions to purity. You, on the contrary, were always avowing your honesty and wrapped yourself in the mantle of piety. Men who go about with the prefix of 'honest' to their names are often rogues." Accompanying the mayor's letter was one from a former city judge, who said, "I know that every statement contained in the Mayor's letter is true and that Kelly is the public robber the Mayor has depicted him to be."[19]

Kelly replied to the mayor's charges in October, saying the "official" court records Havemeyer had cited were wrong. After the mayor reiterated his charges, Kelly sued Havemeyer for libel, and a trial date was set for November 30. But the seventy-year-old mayor, who had been forced that morning to walk two and a half miles to City Hall in the cold after his train broke down, collapsed in his office and died. Kelly abandoned his suit.

In 1874, there was more good news for Kelly. If 1872 had been a Republican year, 1874 was the opposite: the Democrats and Tammany Hall made a virtual clean sweep of the fall elections. Winning the race for mayor was an old friend of Kelly's and a lifelong Tammanyite, diamond merchant William H. Wickham, who could be counted on not to make trouble for the Boss. And into the governor's mansion in Albany, riding the crest of his popularity as a foe of the

Ring, went Samuel Jones Tilden, still a firm friend and staunch political ally of Kelly. Few could have guessed that the two men were to
have a disastrous falling out, and surprisingly soon at that. For the
moment, however, Kelly was riding high, his power was absolute, and
Tammany Hall had no effective competitors in the city.

Just a few months into the new year, however, Kelly's sway over
the Hall was challenged from within by none other than John Morrissey, the colorful and outspoken ex-pugilist and gambling house operator who until this time had been a good friend of the Boss. As the
Tammany historian M. R. Werner put it, Morrissey's "personal following was large, and his tendency was toward eccentricity rather
than obedience, for his personal experience as prize fighter and gambler had taught him independence."[20] Early in the fall of 1874 Morrissey had voiced doubts about the desirability of Wickham's
candidacy for mayor. To win Morrissey's backing, Kelly reluctantly
agreed to nominate for the office of city register Morrissey's friend
James Hayes, a former Tweed associate who allegedly made
$500,000 from Ring swindles. Hayes paid a $15,000 assessment for
the campaign, but when he lost his race—the sole Tammany candidate who did not win that year—Kelly did not return any of his assessment fee, nor did he appoint Hayes to any other post in the
Wickham administration. Hayes was indignant. So was Morrissey,
who decided to get even with Kelly by spreading the word that the
Boss and Wickham had lost touch with the common people, especially the Irish. Just a few weeks after Wickham had taken office, it
seemed, Morrissey stopped in to see the mayor but was refused entry
by a uniformed attendant who asked him for his card. Morrissey was
especially irked at being stopped because a number of his friends were
nearby. "By whose orders are you acting?" he asked. "By order of His
Honor Mayor Wickham," the guard replied. "Is that so?" said Morrissey. "Well, give my compliments to His Honor Mayor Wickham
and ask him to tell 'Billy' Wickham that when John Morrissey has
time to put on French airs, he may call again. Good day, sir!"

A few days later Morrissey showed up in City Hall Park conspicuously gotten up in swallowtail coat, patent leather boots, and white kid
gloves, and carrying a thick book. To a friend who asked him if he was
going to a wedding he replied, "No, I've just bought a French dictionary to help me talk to our dandy Mayor. I'm going in full dress
to make a call, for that is now the style at the Hotel Wickham. No
Irish need apply now."[21] Inside City Hall, Morrissey was welcomed
by the mayor, who laughed and apologized for the affront, saying it

had all been a misunderstanding. But Morrissey made sure the story got around.

John Kelly, who could not abide jokes made at his expense, did not think it was funny. He set out to show that anyone taking him lightly would feel the consequences. He ordered Tammany's Committee on Discipline, an otherwise innocuous body that he had brought into being, to investigate Morrissey. When the committee found that Morrissey had secretly been working against certain Tammany legislative bills in Albany, Kelly had him expelled from Tammany. The Hall was well rid of him, Kelly said: Morrissey's past life and present gambling operations had "rendered him odious to many in the Tammany organization and repelled many other good Democrats."[22] For his part, Morrissey was not about to accept such treatment, and he soon organized a rival political group, the Irving Hall Democracy (as with such groups, it got its name from its place of meeting).

Before very long Irving Hall could count among its members a large number of well-heeled Tammany dissidents, and it became a major anti-Kelly force within the Democratic party. Morrissey himself decided to challenge Tammany directly. In 1875, running for state senator in New York's Fourth District (which Tweed had represented in Albany) against a highly favored Tammany candidate, John Fox, Morrissey won by 3,377 votes. In the state legislature he continued to work against Tammany's interests. In 1877, responding to taunts that he could only get elected in the kind of district that had backed Boss Tweed, he deliberately switched to another district to run against the distinguished Tammany sachem Augustus Schell—and won again. This time, however, his triumph was brief, for in May 1878, he died. Irving Hall, on the other hand, remained in operation for many years to bedevil Kelly.

The Boss's refusal to yield on any patronage matters, which had brought him into early conflict with Mayor Havemeyer, won him more headaches in the case of John H. Hackett, the city recorder, who was also a judge of the court of general sessions. When job openings occurred in his court and Kelly attempted to fill them with Tammany appointees, Hackett politely but firmly told him to forget it. The judiciary, he said, must be free from political influence; he alone would name his court attendants. Kelly persisted but the answer remained no, and the editorial pages of newspapers all over the United States (which had been alert to Tammany excesses ever since the exposure of Boss Tweed) rang with praises for the judge. The Boss countered by spreading the word that Hackett was not only a poor judge but had been connected with the Tweed Ring (he had held office during the period but was not known to have had any dealings with the Ring). The voters showed how they felt about the matter by reelecting Hackett by a substantial margin in the 1875 election.

The Boss's comeuppance in the 1875 elections, when both Morrissey and Hackett trounced their opposition, might have hurt Kelly's public image, and, indeed, there were calls for his resignation in the press, but within Tammany Hall his backing remained solid. When he defended his record at a big postelection meeting at the Wigwam, the assembled four-hundred-odd braves cheered him.

More troubling, however, was Kelly's deteriorating relationship with Governor Tilden. It is not known what specifically caused the break, and certainly the two men were close for a while during Tilden's governorship. Tilden, after all, had been one of those who had persuaded Kelly to take over direction of the Hall, and Kelly surely respected Tilden's abilities and political sagacity. It made sense for the two to work closely: Tilden needed to retain a strong power base in the city, and Tammany's cause would always benefit from having the state's chief executive as an ally. In addition, Tilden was already being talked about as a likely Democratic presidential candidate in 1876. If he won with Tammany's help, the rewards could be dazzling.

For the first few months of Tilden's governorship, the two men cooperated cordially. Kelly was a frequent guest at the governor's mansion and Tilden went along with almost all of Kelly's recommendations in patronage matters. One man Kelly backed was William C. Whitney, a well-to-do lawyer and Tammany member who was in line for the post of corporation counsel, a state appointment. The Boss described Whitney as "an honest, high-toned gentleman, who will cooperate with you and do credit to himself."[23] (Whitney got the job, but, ironically, would later become one of the strongest leaders of Irving Hall.) At this early stage, says his biographer Alexander Flick, Tilden would frequently unburden his worries and concerns on Kelly. The Boss once responded by writing to him, "May God spare you . . . until you have finished your tasks. Most men would have become disheartened at the many repulses."[24]

Both of these potentates, however, were fiercely proud, ambitious (Tilden for himself, Kelly for the Hall), jealous of their prerogatives, and likely to be unyielding if put to a test. What might have triggered their estrangement was the case of New York City's comptroller, Andrew H. Green, whom Tilden had helped install as Connolly's deputy during the height of the Ring revelations and who subsequently succeeded to the post itself. Green, an old friend and associate of Tilden's, was the soul of integrity. But he was also an overly prudent, prickly, and obstinate administrator. His reorganization of the city's finances had won him deserved praise, but when a severe depression hit New York in 1873 his reaction (and that of Mayor Havemeyer) was to cut back on public works and relief programs, which made him widely unpopular—especially to Kelly, who felt expanding public works projects would help the city as well as provide many jobs for Tammany to hand out. Green, in fact, had a visceral dislike of anything connected with Tammany, which hardly endeared him to the Boss. At some point in 1875, Kelly must have decided, with Mayor Wickham agreeing, that Green must go. As the comptroller could be removed only with the consent of the governor, whom Kelly did not want to embarrass, the Boss had a bill introduced into legislature that transferred removal power to the New York mayor. Tilden stalled and equivocated in his attitude toward the bill; an unsuccessful attempt was made by newly elected Congressman Abram Hewitt to persuade Green to pull out on his own; in the end Kelly's bill was defeated. Although Tilden had not killed it, the autocratic Kelly took it as a personal affront. Any man not with him was by definition against him—it was as simple as that. Asked to explain Kelly's sudden enmity, Tilden merely hazarded, "Kelly sees in me an obstacle to his ambition."[25]

By 1876, their relationship deteriorated to such an extent that Kelly made it known he was neutral on Tilden's possible presidential candidacy, which meant, essentially, that he was against it. Granted, there were reasons to believe that the governor, who was petulant, indecisive, and lacking in a popular touch, would be a weak candidate, but for Kelly to be openly trying to thwart a onetime ally was nevertheless astonishing. In May the *New York Express*, the paper partly owned by Kelly, bitterly attacked the governor. At the Democratic National Convention in St. Louis that summer, where both Abram Hewitt and Mayor Wickham were supporting Tilden, the Boss actively opposed him. When Hewitt tried simply to deliver a message to him on the convention floor Kelly said to him, "I don't choose to receive any message through you, sir, or any letter from your hands."[26] After Tilden won the nomination on the second ballot, Kelly grudgingly announced his support for him. Back home, at a meeting in the Wigwam, a number of Tammanyites severely criticized the Boss's conduct during the convention, but the Hall's General Committee went on record expressing "unlimited confidence in the leadership of the Honorable John Kelly."[27]

Just before the election that fall, a huge parade in New York City celebrated the entire Democratic ticket. On the reviewing stand in front of Tammany Hall on Fourteenth Street, Tilden appeared alongside Kelly and other dignitaries, everyone wreathed in smiles for public consumption. The election itself was another Tammany triumph: not only did the Hall's mayoral candidate, Smith Ely, Jr., win, but so did the gubernatorial nominee, Lucius Robinson, whose candidacy had been agreed on in a pact between Tammany and Irving Hall. Tilden carried New York City as well as the state, but he did not quite reach the White House. Although he won the popular vote, a dispute over the electoral vote sent the election into the Republican-controlled Congress, which appointed an electoral commission that gave the presidency to Rutherford B. Hayes. Ironically, Tilden's loss redounded to Kelly's credit, for although he had predicted the governor's defeat, he had helped deliver the state to him.

In the aftermath of the election, Kelly basked in power that seemed practically complete. As the historian Arthur Genen has pointed out, the mayor was Kelly's man, Tammany had a three-to-one majority on the Board of Aldermen, most of the city judges were Tammany members, and both the Police and Fire departments were solidly behind the Boss. The *New York Herald* called him King of Gotham, and he was now signing his letters "John Kelly, The Tammany Boss."[28] It was ironic that a man who came to power as an antidote to the unchecked power of the Tweed Ring was now himself a virtual autocrat.

Two developments at this point brought Kelly immense personal gratification. One was his marriage, on November 21, 1876, to Teresa Mullen, the niece of New York's Cardinal McCloskey. The other was Kelly's appointment by outgoing Mayor Wickham (who chose to ignore the enmity the Boss had shown him at the convention) as comptroller of the city, succeeding their old nemesis Andrew Green, who was finally retiring. One reason Kelly sought the comptrollership may have been a desire for still more power; another may have been a longing for the respectability that only a high government office could bring. But a third was surely his hope of erasing, once and for all, the stigma of venality that had dogged him since his days as sheriff. In any event, he had a good record as the city's finance officer: he was not charged with any irregularities during his four-year term, and he reduced the city's debt by $2 million.

But the glory that Kelly enjoyed from these two developments did not last long. In late 1877 Tilden, who had taken an extended vacation in Europe following his loss of the presidency, returned to New York and decided that Kelly had become much too powerful. He and his closest admirers, who included William Wickham, Abram Hewitt, William Whitney, and Edward Cooper (Peter Cooper's son and Hewitt's brother-in-law), walked out of Tammany and began holding their meetings at Irving Hall, the headquarters of Tammany's dissident minority. It was the beginning of a split that would weaken the Democrats for years to come. That fall, the Irving Hall Democracy ran Edward Cooper for mayor against Kelly's Tammany candidate, the aging Augustus Schell. Cooper won. The loss was a real setback for Tammany, a presage of things to come. On election night a defiant Kelly proclaimed, "John Kelly is not dead yet, but fights the harder when he has been defeated."[29]

His vindictive streak now manifested itself in brand-new hostility toward Governor Lucius Robinson. The governor had become anathema to him, partly because he was a Tilden man but also because he had vetoed one of Kelly's plans (as comptroller) to use New York's sinking fund to help reduce the debt. Furthermore, Robinson had been involved in the decision to refuse a final pardon to Boss Tweed, who during all the years of Kelly's rule had been under trial or in prison. But what finally made Kelly turn on the governor was Robinson's decision to remove a Tammany man, Henry A. Gumbleton, from the office of county clerk. That would not be tolerated; Kelly resolved to destroy Robinson. "He is like a mad bull," he said of Robinson. "If you were to speak to him of Tammany, he would fly at you." And he added, "We would rather be politically killed by our enemies than be politically and treacherously assassinated in the house of our friends."[30]

When state Democrats met in September 1879 to choose a candidate for governor, Kelly tried everything he could think of to prevent Robinson's renomination. When the pro-Robinson–Tilden forces proved too strong, Kelly announced that he would not support the governor and marched out of the convention with his delegation. The next day, the Tammanyites met in a nearby hall and nominated the Boss for governor. The party's split was now complete.

Kelly knew that he was unlikely to win the gubernatorial race and that he was also taking a dangerous risk: if he succeeded in derailing Robinson, it would prove that the party could not get along without Tammany Hall, but if Robinson won Kelly would be finished. He was also acknowledging that, for him, the preservation of the Hall was more important than the success of the Democratic party. He had also flouted the age-old Tammany principle of party loyalty. No matter: his vindictiveness drove him to do it. The Boss ran a well-organized campaign throughout the state. When election day came, the result was as he had hoped. His 77,756 votes were more than enough to deflect Robinson and elect the Republican candidate. Kelly was delighted. He had proved that Tammany support, which he controlled beyond question, was crucial to the Democrats; anyone who took Tammany lightly would be in jeopardy. Furthermore, Tammany could deal with a Republican governor far more easily than it could with Robinson. Wrote the *New York Herald*, "The election disposes of the Tilden effort to kill off John Kelly. . . . Henceforth, for local politics, and within the close corporation of the Democratic machine, John Kelly is a bigger man than old Tilden."[31]

That might have well been true, but old Tilden was still a threat. Convinced he had been cheated out of the presidency in the 1876 election, Tilden assumed he would be renominated in 1880, and although he had not announced his candidacy, his followers avidly promoted his cause. Kelly was implacable in his opposition: Tilden must not be the nominee. If he ran, said the Boss, Tammany would bring about his defeat. Actually Tilden was nowhere near as likely a candidate now as he had been four years earlier: his health, which had never been very good, was deteriorating, and his image as a reformer had been tarnished by irregularities to which he was linked in the 1876 race. At length, the party's national convention, meeting in Cincinnati, nominated another man, former Civil War general Winfield Scott Hancock. Once again, Kelly had prevailed. He spoke to the delegates on the last day of the convention, saying, "Let past differences be banished." And to a reporter he said, "The breach [with Irving Hall] is healed as far as we are concerned."[32]

If there was any actual healing it was short-lived. Along with the presidential race that year, there would be one for mayor (Edward Cooper was retiring after one term). The city's two Democratic party factions—Tammany Hall and Irving Hall—decided to compromise by drawing up a list of twelve candidates each; out of the twenty-four a nominee would be chosen. After the lists had circulated Kelly, in an odd move, announced his support for a man on the Irving Hall list— William R. Grace, the wealthy founder of the shipping firm bearing his name. But Grace also happened to be Roman Catholic and a close friend of both Cardinal McCloskey and Boss Kelly. The Irving

Hall leadership was amazed and perplexed, for Grace was not even a member of their organization. They suspected (probably correctly) that Kelly had conspired to put him on their list so that they could not object to him. (They presumably accepted Grace's presence on the list believing that Kelly would not dare pick him.) No Catholic had ever been elected mayor, and many New Yorkers as well as members of Irving Hall feared that if Grace won he would divert public education funds to parochial schools, a diversion that was not actually possible.

The campaign was a bitter one in which religious bigotry played a distinct factor. Grace barely managed to squeak through with a plurality of 3,045 votes. The rest of the Democratic ticket, however, was defeated. Hancock failed to carry New York State, a loss great enough to hand the presidential election to his Republican opponent, James Garfield. Observers all over the United States—always sensitive to the possible repercussions of political events in the nation's largest state—ascribed Hancock's New York defeat to the divisive effect of Grace's candidacy in New York City. And many blamed Kelly for that. Wrote the *Omaha Herald*, "Mr. John Kelly, pig-headed and obstinate, and so blindly and desperately ambitious of power and place as to be a perfectly reckless and dangerous leader, capped the climax by running a candidate for Mayor who precipitated the very issue which Republicans wanted."[33] One reflection of the widespread indignation was outgoing Mayor Cooper's refusal to reappoint Kelly as comptroller when the Boss's term expired in December 1880.

The electoral setbacks produced serious rumblings among the faithful within Tammany Hall. During a meeting of the Tammany General Committee not long after the election a member objected to a resolution offered in support of the Boss's leadership during the campaign, saying Hancock's defeat was partly caused by poor organization on the part of Tammany. And then there came a startling outburst from another brave, Robert Van Wyck, who many years hence would be mayor of the city. Pointing his finger at Kelly, he shouted, "I tell you that the people of New York are tired of the bossism of John Kelly!"[34] Cries and shouts filled the hall, while Kelly, reported one observer, reacted "as if an earthquake had occurred. He had been so long accustomed to sit still and hear his satellites trumpet the praise of their 'honored leader,' that it was something entirely novel for him to hear his virtue and wisdom impugned. In stolid amazement he looked at Van Wyck, whose voice rang like a clarion . . . and whose words and sentiments provoked applause. . . ."[35]

After much discussion, the resolution backing Kelly passed. But the events that night were a harbinger of troubles to come. When the annual election of Tammany sachems came along in April 1881, a formidable drive to oust Kelly was mounted by members of Irving Hall, who were still on the rolls as Tammanyites. On the appointed day, more than eight hundred braves turned up to vote, more than four times as many as normally took part. But Kelly was ready for them. As recalled years later by an old-time political reporter named Matthew Breen, "The supporters of 'Honest John' Kelly . . . had been provided with receipts [entitling them to vote] beforehand, and the first part of the long line, which stretched down the stairway and into the street, consisted almost entirely of the supporters of Kelly, who received their authorizations to vote without delay. The opposition was kept further back in the line, and the Secretary found it more difficult to find their names in his book than he did those of Mr. Kelly's friends. Some of the opposition were thus prevented from voting until after it was too late. . . . It was announced late that night that John Kelly had won the election."[36] He squeaked through by only fifty votes.

But the rebellion continued. Some of Irving Hall's most prominent members, sensing that their organization had been compromised by the influx of too many arch-Tammanyites, hived off in the early part of 1881 to form a new and much more extensive group, known as the New York County Democracy. Among its leaders were Hewitt, Cooper, and Whitney, and it had Samuel Tilden's blessing. It was more democratically organized than Tammany—lowly party members down in the election districts really did have a voice in choosing the organization's higher-ups—and by the fall of 1881 it could claim more than twenty-six thousand members, compared with an estimated forty-five thousand Tammany adherents in the tight grip of Kelly. It had official clout, too: a state party convention that fall accepted the County Democracy's delegation as the "regular" representative of New York City Democrats, while Tammany's was rejected.

A year later, Kelly's, and Tammany's, fortunes seemed to revive somewhat with the election of Buffalo's Democratic reform mayor, Grover Cleveland, as governor of New York. Along with the County Democracy leaders, Kelly had early spotted Cleveland as a likely winner, and some intensive politicking by the Boss had enabled Tammany's delegation to be seated at the state nominating convention alongside the County Democracy's. Tammany's switch to Cleveland on the second ballot helped put him over the top. After Cleveland's election, Kelly was confident that the Hall would once again be granted its rightful share of state patronage jobs.

Yet this, too, was not to be. Cleveland became a fatal adversary of the Boss. After being in office just a few months, the governor, whose reformist stance led him not only to attack all forms of corruption but to denigrate the role of political parties and machines, made it known that he would steer no patronage toward Tammany Hall. And he proceeded to prove it. Kelly eyed covetously the post of commissioner of immigration because it carried with it control over large sums for the welfare of immigrants, those important Tammany constituents. He was infuriated when Cleveland handed the job to William H. Murtha, who was a member not of Tammany Hall but of Hugh McLaughlin's rival Democratic machine in Brooklyn. Kelly had his Albany legislators bottle up Murtha's nomination in committee, prompting the governor to complain testily that a good man was being denied appointment purely for partisan reasons.

The Murtha nomination went no further, but Kelly had yet to feel the full force of the governor's resolve. In the fall of 1883, the unthinkable (to Kelly) occurred: Cleveland, going beyond simply rejecting Tammany patronage suggestions, specifically requested Kelly to remove someone already in office. It was not just a minor official, either: it was state Senator Thomas F. Grady, leader of Tammany's Albany legislators. Grady, said Cleveland in a private letter to the Boss, "should not be returned to the Senate," as he was obstructing the governor's legislative program.[37] This was too much for Kelly, who decided he must wound the governor as severely as he could. Cleveland had just made a public statement saying it was his policy never to interfere in matters of local political concern. Kelly released to the press Cleveland's Grady letter to show the governor as twofaced. Even though Grady did not get renominated to the Albany legislature, the damage was done. As Arthur Genen has put it, "Why the Tammany boss had released the letter can be understood only in terms of Kelly's vindictive personality. . . . Anyone who attempted to weaken his position [as absolute Boss of Tammany] was viewed as an arch enemy who had to be destroyed."[38]

It was no surprise, then, when Kelly arrived at the Democratic National Convention in Chicago in 1884 and announced his implacable opposition to Cleveland for the presidential nomination, even though the governor was the odds-on favorite. He gave as his reason that Cleveland was "no friend of the workingman," but everyone knew it was because he was no friend of Kelly's. "I will not lift a hand for him," Kelly said. "If he thinks he can be elected without me let him go ahead, but I will never help him." He spread rumors that Cleveland was anti-Catholic and a confirmed drunkard; he charged that Chicago's mayor, a prominent Cleveland backer, had packed the galleries with Cleveland rooters; and he tried unsuccessfully to put together a Stop-Cleveland coalition. That the majority of the delegates were not with him was demonstrated when Thomas Grady— now an ex-senator but a member of the New York delegation—delivered a long speech to the convention attacking Cleveland. When he had finished, a Wisconsin delegate rose on behalf of the governor. Describing the young men of his state, he shouted, "They love Cleveland for his character, but they love him most for the enemies he has made." The declaration brought cheers, and all eyes focused on the Tammany delegation. Kelly did not help himself when he shouted back, with everyone watching him, "On behalf of his enemies, I accept your statement!"[39] After Cleveland was nominated and Kelly was leaving the convention hall, a reporter asked him if he would be supporting the nominee. "Get out of here," growled the Boss. "I don't wish to talk to anybody."[40]

He was true to his word not to help Cleveland—up to a point. He directed all of Tammany's efforts during the early part of the campaign on behalf of his candidate for mayor, Hugh Grant. Grace had proved surprisingly uncooperative on patronage and so was backed only by the County Democracy. Then on October 15, 1884, Cleveland came to New York and met alone with Kelly. There is no record of what transpired or what agreements might have been made, but Tammany Hall immediately swung into line and began electioneering for the Democratic nominee. Even so, many observers thought Cleveland's chances were poor, as the Republican candidate, James G. Blaine, was popular throughout the country, and was even highly regarded by many Tammanyites because he was of Irish descent, with a Catholic mother.

A fluke saved Cleveland. Barely a week before the election, while Blaine was campaigning in New York City, a group of clergymen called on him at the Fifth Avenue Hotel. Their designated spokesman had not shown up and so a Presbyterian minister, the Reverend Samuel Burchard, spoke for them. "We are Republicans," Burchard said to Blaine during his remarks, "and we do not propose to identify ourselves with the party whose antecedents have been rum, Romanism and rebellion." The candidate inexplicably declined to disavow the remark, and with that, observes one chronicler of the event, "Every Democrat and every Catholic in America were gravely offended."[41] The whole campaign turned upside down. Cleveland captured New York and enough other states to eke out a victory.

On election night a gloomy John Kelly sat in Tammany Hall watching the election returns being posted. Not only was Cleveland winning; so was Grace. "We are gone," he said, and he suddenly put his hand to his head. "I am sick—quite ill—am going home."[42]

Kelly never did return. Suffering from a severe bronchial condition and other ailments, he remained at his home, declining slowly, and over the next several months he transacted what Tammany business he could through his deputy, Richard Croker. He died on the first of June, 1886, at the age of sixty-four. As the Tammany historian Gustavus Myers noted, "It was pointed out to his credit that the fortune he left—reputed to be $500,000—was very reasonable for one who so long had held real control of a great city."[43]

Kelly bequeathed a peculiar legacy. In addition to leaving Tammany a much better organized and more efficient machine, under his leadership there were no major scandals involving the Hall, and this erased much of the stigma left by the Tweed Ring catastrophe. By all accounts the Boss himself was incorruptible, but his own limitations—his overweening pride, his spitefulness, his obstinacy—deprived him of the political success that might otherwise have been his and contributed to the disunity that was once again plaguing the Hall. Someone with better self-control and a surer political touch could lift Tammany to heights it had hardly dreamed of—which is precisely what was about to take place.

7

THE MASTER

THE DAY AFTER JOHN KELLY DIED, TAMMANY Hall's Executive Committee began making plans to name a successor. Even as they were doing so, however, Richard Croker walked into Kelly's office in the Wigwam on Fourteenth Street, sat down at the desk, and took over. No one stopped him. He was to direct Tammany's affairs with an iron hand for sixteen years—years in which Tammany would wield a greater and more shocking degree of power over the lives of the people of New York than it ever had in the past or ever would in the future.

That his abrupt and seemingly presumptuous move aroused no apparent opposition within the Hall should have surprised no one. The grim-faced, burly Croker had been Kelly's closest confidant for months, visiting the sick old man every day in his home on the Upper West Side and, so he said, conveying Kelly's instructions back to the membership. (There were those who said the younger man largely ignored what Kelly actually said and executed the Boss's orders—or created them himself—as he saw fit.) Besides, there was something about Croker that persuaded people to fall into line behind him. He exuded authority. As a contemporary observed, he had "a pervasive, intangible quality which words can scarcely describe, that native capacity for, and impulse to, leadership which no other head of Tammany has shown in greater, if as great, degree."[1] Croker's leadership, while overbearing, was not always in the best interests of the city. The writer Mark D. Hirsch has called him "the ablest and most ruthless marauder in [Tammany's] history."[2]

Inevitably Croker, whose sway over the Hall and the city was so pervasive that he came to be known during his time as the Master of Manhattan, is compared with his better-known predecessor, Boss Tweed. In terms of notoriety, there was no contest: Tweed's outright theft of so many millions of dollars put him in a class by himself. But Tweed's excesses were personal; Tammany was virtually eclipsed in the Boss's gargantuan greed. Although Croker was also obsessed with money and acquired great wealth on the job, he did so by manipulating the levers of political power rather than by actual stealing, and his personal success was generally synonymous with that of Tammany. Tweed's image is that of a Rabelaisian monster, chuckling as he rakes in his profits; Croker's is that of a bull raging to get his way. Of the two, Croker was by far the more menacing.

Croker's commanding presence was never so awesomely demonstrated as in the late summer of 1897 when, after a three-year absence from the United States (he had left a deputy in day-to-day charge of the Hall), he returned to New York from his estate in England to find the majority of the Tammany district leaders itching to usurp his power. One of them, Big Tim Sullivan, an imposing pol who ruled the Lower East Side as if it were his own private fiefdom, made no secret of his desire to depose the Boss, and he possessed a sizable following. Croker waited for a few weeks, doubtless to heighten the suspense, then called a meeting of the rebellious Executive Committee. On the appointed afternoon, he arrived at the Wigwam impeccably dressed in a black frock suit and high silk hat, strode through the unfriendly crowd without saying a word and disappeared into his office. A short while later, he made it known that the district leaders could enter. Suddenly meek and dutiful, they filed in to find the Boss puffing on a cigar and glaring at them. He spoke to them quietly for ten minutes or so, then said he had heard that some of them had complaints to make. He would like to know what those complaints were. There was absolute silence. He turned to Sullivan. "Tim Sullivan," he barked, "are *you* dissatisfied?" Sullivan murmured that he was not. "Very well, then," announced the Boss, "there is no dissatisfaction. Now I want you men to go back to your districts and get to work." A critical election was coming up, he pointed out, and there was much to do. Chastened, the leaders dispersed. The insurgency, such as it was, was over. Croker and Tammany won the election and the Boss continued in power for another four years.[3]

Instinctively a brawler, Croker possessed, in the words of a man who knew him, "a strong frame, a deep chest, a short neck and a pair of hard fists. . . . He speaks in monosyllables, commands a vocabulary that appears to be limited to about three hundred words. . . ."[4] Yet this was a man who schooled himself to move easily and effectively among the power brokers of his time. Although he had risen from the rough world of gangs and street fights, he was a study in self-control. "He had learned," said one observer, "to govern by moral force, instead of by the fist. He had discovered the power that is in a look, a word, rather than brutal shoutings. . . ."[5]

Ostensibly Irish, Croker could reasonably claim to be English as well, for he was descended on his father's side from a soldier who had come to Ireland with Oliver Cromwell's invading army in the seventeenth century; his mother's family traced its lineage back to Scotland. The Crokers came to New York from County Cork in 1846 when Richard was three, his father hoping to find work in the new world as a blacksmith or farrier. But his luck proved poor and the family found itself living in a shantytown in what is now Central Park. Finally his father got a job as a veterinarian for a horsecar line, and the family moved to the East Twenties where Richard attended school for a while. At age twelve or thirteen, however, he dropped out to apprentice as a machinist in the Harlem Railroad machine shops, building locomotives. Gangs were rampant in his neighborhood and before long he was a valued member of the vaunted Fourth Avenue Tunnel Gang, which preyed on the teamsters and hackmen who thronged the Harlem line's freight depot. A dogged, relentless fighter, Richard eventually became the gang's leader. Like both Tweed and Kelly before him, he also served as a volunteer fireman.

Because of Croker's impressive thrashing of a professional boxer named Dick Lynch (Croker knocked out all his teeth), he came to the notice of Jimmy "the Famous" O'Brien, the Tammany stalwart who some years hence, in 1871, won notice as the one who delivered the critical evidence to the *New York Times* that betrayed the Tweed Ring. O'Brien thought that Croker would make a fine shoulder-hitter for the Hall. The young Croker was glad to join up. He became best known in those early years, however, as a "repeater" at the polls. In 1865 he succeeded in voting seventeen times for a Democratic candidate in Greenpoint. Three years later, he led a band of 150 toughs to Philadelphia to help swing an election there for a Tammany ally.

By that time he had come to the attention of Boss Tweed, who gave Croker a sinecure as a court attendant for the rascally Tweed

Ring judge, George Barnard. Becoming better known, he also served twice as an alderman, succeeding O'Brien who had moved up to sheriff. On election day, Croker's dependability in mobilizing his men for strong-arm tactics as needed was such that the *New York Times* called him "a rowdy and election bully of well-established fame."[6] In 1870, he was awarded a job in the City Revenue Department and was also appointed a city marshal. He was rising fast.

With the breakup of the Tweed Ring, Croker was faced with a difficult decision. Should he stick with his old friend O'Brien, who having exposed Tweed left Tammany and became one of the leaders of the renegade Apollo Hall movement? Or should he stick with Tammany, which was now under the direction of Honest John Kelly? Figuring that aligning with O'Brien would get him nowhere, he stuck by Kelly. The rough-cut new Tammany chief, who had taken quite a liking to the younger Croker, showed his gratitude by nominating him for city coroner in 1873. Although Mayor William Havemeyer, who held a cordial dislike for Tammany, denounced Kelly for naming a man he said was associated with lawlessness, Croker won his election to the lucrative post, which paid an estimated $15,000 a year in fees.

But the following year he almost lost it all. Despite his newfound prominence, Croker still felt duty bound to help Tammany bull its way to success at the polls. On election day in 1874, as he and his band of toughs were cruising around the East Thirties, they chanced on a rival group headed by none other than Jimmy "the Famous" O'Brien, who happened to be running for Congress against Tammany's Abram S. Hewitt, a millionaire businessman. Insults were traded. Croker called O'Brien a "damned thief" and Jimmy responded, "You damned cur, I picked you out of the gutter, and now you're supporting a rich man like Hewitt against me . . . !"[7] In the ensuing brawl, shots rang out and one of O'Brien's lieutenants, John McKenna, fell mortally wounded. Before he died he said Croker had fired the shot that killed him. Croker was arrested and charged with murder.

At his trial, which Kelly conspicuously attended, making a point of demonstrating his support and even furnishing a capable lawyer for his protégé—Croker denied his guilt, saying he never carried a gun and relied solely on his fists. There was little evidence either way. At the end, the jury split six to six, freeing him. He was never retried. Stories later circulated that a friend of Croker's, George Hickey, had fired the shot and was prepared to step forward and confess if the jury

had found Croker guilty. But the damaging incident cast a cloud over
Croker's future. For a time he was in political limbo. When he went
to City Hall to see the mayor, he told Kelly, "He won't see me.
When I speak to him in the hall, he don't notice me."[8]

Kelly did not desert him. When Croker's term as coroner was up
in 1876, the Boss backed him for another, and when that was concluded he found other work for him, making him virtually his right-
hand man. In 1883, Kelly arranged for the young man's appointment
as fire commissioner. A married man now with a family, Croker kept
quiet, studied the old politician closely, and, more important, learned
where Kelly had made mistakes. When the Boss died in 1886, Croker
was well prepared to take over.

He faced a formidable task. Kelly's misplays had shorn Tammany
of all major local offices. Its rival, the County Democracy, was currently recognized as the "regular" wing of the party. Tammany must
derail the County Democracy and get back into the winning column.
Croker's first move had been crafted even before Kelly's death: in the
1885 local elections he persuaded the Boss to back Hugh Grant, an
attractive and wealthy young Tammanyite, for sheriff. Grant, though
hardly a first-class public servant, had a key advantage: a year or so
earlier New York's Board of Aldermen had been caught in the so-
called boodle scandal: many members had accepted bribes from a
transit mogul, Jacob Sharp, in return for granting him a street railway
franchise. Although some of those board members were Tammany
members, most of the implicated aldermen belonged to the County
Democracy. Alderman Grant, acting on Croker's advice, had voted
against the measure and was thus blameless, but the County Democracy got a black eye. Grant was handily elected sheriff, and Croker
was on his way.

A far greater challenge arose in 1886. The city was to elect a new
mayor, and Tammany desperately needed the City Hall patronage.
The race would be tough: the progressive vote would probably go to
Henry George, a candidate known for his espousal of a radical economic scheme known as the single tax, while the Republicans were
running the dynamic young Theodore Roosevelt, who was known to
have great promise. Croker, now Tammany chief, pulled a fast one.
He persuaded the elderly but widely respected Abram Hewitt, who
had become a power in the County Democracy, to run on a combined Tammany–County Democracy ticket. Hewitt won. Tammany
was on track again.

Two years later, he completed Tammany's resurgence. At the 1888 Democratic National Convention, Croker astonished the assembled delegates by pledging that Tammany Hall would work enthusiastically for the reelection of Grover Cleveland, John Kelly's old nemesis—and the crowd cheered him. All at once, Tammany was back in the good graces of the national party. At home, Croker resolved to dump Hewitt, who though well-meaning and efficient had proved self-righteous and difficult to get along with. Hewitt had awarded scant patronage to Tammany, and he had offended many citizens who were otherwise disposed to admire him, most notably a group of Irish who came asking him to review the St. Patrick's Day parade. Under no circumstances, he said, would he be caught in such an undignified, partisan maneuver. When his visitors protested that they had hoped he would appreciate the honor, he showed them to the door. "Gentlemen, you have my answer," he intoned as they stumbled out. "I shall not review your parade on St. Patrick's Day."[9]

To replace Hewitt, Croker trotted out his friend Hugh Grant, who had avoided making any enemies as sheriff. In the election Grant trounced both Hewitt (running on the County Democracy ticket) and the Republican candidate. Hewitt's loss proved to be the swan song of the County Democracy, which never again posed a threat. The local party was once again unified. "Tammany Hall," the Boss announced on election night, "will be, as it has always been, the only real Democratic organization in the city."[10] Furthermore, Croker had gained total control of City Hall, for Grant was totally under his thumb. (Cleveland had lost the White House, but that hardly bothered Croker: he had made his point.) Soon after taking office, Hugh Grant demonstrated his admiration for the Boss by appointing him city chamberlain, a job that paid a hefty $25,000 a year and put Croker in charge of depositing the city's funds.

With three straight election victories to his credit, Croker basked in the warm glow of success. Tammany was enjoying the good days, too. The city was expanding rapidly, and so there were plenty of construction contracts to pass out and many jobs to award. Croker made his district leaders happy by giving them much more power than Kelly had allowed, in effect returning control of most patronage to them (while holding them strictly accountable for every action). New York was entering the rosy period known as the Gay Nineties, in which the cultivation of pleasure and naughtiness was enshrined. "All New York is in the midst of gaiety and dissipation," observed one writer.

"Splendid carriages, with liveried coachmen and sleek horses, dash up and down the avenues, depositing their perfumed inmates before brilliantly-lighted, high-stooped, brownstone fronts. . . . Dancing and feasting, flirting and gossip bind the hours. . . ."[11] But gambling, prostitution, and widespread corruption were also rife, and in all these less honorable activities Tammany Hall was playing a strong and lucrative role, as would soon be revealed.

One of the signs of the wide-open times was the sudden wealth of Richard Croker. Reputed to have been almost destitute as recently as the early 1880s, when he was still suffering from the obloquy of his murder trial, he now showed signs of having far larger funds at his command than even his substantial chamberlain's salary might produce. After 1890, furthermore, when he resigned the office for health reasons, he ceased drawing down even that official stipend. And Tammany paid him no salary. He was, in effect, without visible means of support. But during these years he was able to move from a simple home in Harlem (then a polite middle-class community) to a large, pretentious dwelling on fashionable East Seventy-fourth Street just off Fifth Avenue that was reportedly worth $80,000. He began to invest heavily in Thoroughbred horse racing, acquiring half-interest (along with upstate political Boss Edward Murphy) in a stock farm in Richfield Springs, New York. He purchased racehorses valued at more than $100,000. In 1893, he bought into the Belle Mead Stock Farm in Tennessee for some $250,000. And he began affecting a luxurious lifestyle that was anything but cheap—traveling by rail he liked to have his own private car, which cost $50 a day. Moreover, this was just the beginning; properties in Florida, England, and Ireland would come later. It has been estimated that he was eventually worth several million dollars.

Where was all the money coming from? Perhaps some of it was being siphoned directly from Tammany, despite his unsalaried position. Graft and bribery schemes were yielding handsome sums these days to the Hall, where Croker's only official position (he was not even a sachem) was chairman of the Finance Committee, an amorphous body that kept no books. Yet the indications are that Croker kept little of the payoff money for himself, feeling that such Tweed-like behavior was too risky; it was better to use the money for the machine's political work or to divide it among his district leaders and other subordinates. Croker's riches instead appear to have derived from a sophisticated use of what he could most efficiently wield—raw political power.

Not long after becoming undisputed Tammany Hall Boss, for example, Croker became a partner of a real estate executive named Peter F. Meyer. Their partnership, Meyer and Croker, soon did exceedingly well: Croker acknowledged at one point that it brought him $25,000 to $30,000 a year. A key source of the firm's prosperity was the money it earned from sales of real estate parcels that happened for one reason or another to be under the control of the city. Such sales were controlled by judges, who would appoint a referee in each case; the referee would then designate an auctioneer, who would handle the sale for a fee. With the judicial system mainly under the control of Tammany Hall, it was no surprise that Tammany's judges invariably appointed referees who were staunch Tammanyites, and these functionaries turned right around and chose Meyer and Croker as auctioneer. The Boss saw nothing wrong in this neat arrangement. It was part of the normal workings of the spoils system, he believed, and if it brought plentiful dividends there should be no objection.

Glimpses into some of the ways Croker accumulated his wealth and how he felt about them were provided from time to time over the next decade by a series of investigations into Tammany Hall that were real eye-openers to New Yorkers. During the famed Mazet Investigation of 1899, for example—a Republican-inspired inquiry that delved into Tammany finances with telling effect—the Boss made some revealing statements. When the Mazet Committee's counsel, Frank Moss, questioned Croker on the linkage between political appointments and lucrative fees, the Boss responded with a remark that startled those in the hearing room.

"So we have it, then," asked Moss, "that you, participating in the selection of judges before election, participate in the emolument that comes away down at the end of their proceeding; namely, judicial sales?"

"Yes, sir," said Croker.

"And it goes into your pocket?"

"I get—that is, a part of my profit. . . . "

"Then," said Moss, "you are working for your own pocket, are you not?"

"All the time," stated Croker, "the same as you."[12] The Boss's bald-faced, defiant admission made headlines in the next day's newspapers and instantly became part of New York political folklore.

But there were many other ways in which a powerful politician could cash in. One was to take advantage of what district leader George Washington Plunkitt, the garrulous bard of Tammany, called honest graft. Big improvements were being made in New York City as it expanded during these years, and a smart politician hearing of some costly project could get in on the ground floor. This may have been what brought about Croker's alleged ownership of stock in an unprepossessing street railway that meandered through some remote sections of the Bronx during these years, informally known as the Huckleberry Railroad. In the early 1890s, stock in the railway was practically given away, but it rapidly appreciated. When the line was eventually taken over by the Metropolitan Traction Company, the shareholders, said one observer, "realized fortunes."[13]

Although Croker admitted participating in such ventures, he steadfastly refused to say what he owned. That was his private affair, he said, and it was nobody else's business. As he announced to Frank Moss during the Mazet hearings, "I have got nothing to hide at all, and if anyone tells me of a nice stock to buy, and I can make a little turn on it, I am going to do it, and I have done so. . . . [But] any questions you ask me about my personal business, I decline to answer."[14]

It is quite possible, of course, that Croker actually paid nothing for his Huckleberry shares, for all the evidence points to his having received, during his stewardship of the Hall, extraordinary amounts of stock utterly free of charge. Such gifts were the happy outgrowth of what was sometimes called the Boss's Wall Street Connection. Enterprising financiers doing business in or with the city were well aware of Croker's political power and often found it prudent to assure his friendship or cooperation by transferring large blocks of securities to his account, if only to avoid trouble. One company that was formed in the 1890s for the purpose of constructing a rapid transit tunnel in New York is said to have given $500,000 worth of stock to Croker. There were undoubtedly many other such gifts, some of which were hinted at—and always denied by the Boss—during the Mazet Investigation and other inquiries that delved into Tammany's workings during the 1890s.

Still another way Croker may have accrued wealth came to light during the first of these inquiries, the Fassett Investigation, which took place during the early months of 1890. The probe had been launched at the behest of a man who plays a somewhat elusive role in the story of Richard Croker: Thomas C. Platt, the Republican Boss of New York State. A slight, wan, cautious figure with parchmentlike skin, Platt began his career as a druggist in Owego, near Binghamton, but from a young age was so diligently and successfully active in

Republican politics that he came to dominate his party's affairs both in New York City and beyond. By the 1890s he was an executive of the U.S. Express Company in downtown New York and was living at the stylish Fifth Avenue Hotel, at Twenty-third Street. He liked to transact his political business on Sunday mornings in the hotel's lobby, on some sofas at the end of the main hall. The gatherings came to be known as Platt's Sunday School Classes and the area was referred to as the Amen Corner because when Platt, after much quiet discussion, announced his decision, those in attendance would murmur "Amen!" as they got up to leave.

But Platt's task was a tricky one: although the state as a whole often went Republican, and his power in Albany and other upstate cities was considerable, New York City was heavily Democratic. If Platt was to keep his city organization alive he must win some patronage for it; this would necessarily have to be gained from Tammany, in return for favors that he might bestow upstate (or in Washington, if a Republican was president). Yet he must not be perceived as a patsy for Tammany. So he was constantly trading jobs and influence, and Croker found it made sense to accommodate him—most of the time. When Platt was crossed, however, he did not take it lightly. It happened that in the late 1880s Hugh Grant, Croker's friend who had become mayor, turned down some polite requests from Platt that he appoint some Republican worthies to city posts. Perhaps Croker was testing his Republican counterpart. But whatever the reason, Platt was incensed. Using his unquestioned authority over the state legislature, which was then controlled by the Republicans, he brought about the 1890 investigation chaired by Senator J. Sloat Fassett that hinted at some of Croker's unusual cash conduits.

Although Platt had seen the inquiry as little more than a slap on Tammany's wrist, it gave the public its first glimpse of just how crude Richard Croker's Tammany could be. The star witness was Croker's wife's brother-in-law, Patrick H. McCann, who was admittedly on far from friendly terms with the Boss after a quarrel over a business venture. McCann testified that in the fall of 1884—a year and a half before taking over as Boss—Croker had shown him a satchel stuffed with $180,000 in bills that were to be used to bribe members of the Board of Aldermen into approving the appointment of Hugh Grant as commissioner of public works; McCann's role was to introduce Croker to an intermediary who would make the necessary contacts. (Grant's successful race for sheriff was to come a year later.) The reason the appointment was deemed so desirable was that if Grant

were named he would designate as the city's cement supplier a contractor near Newburgh who had promised Tammany 10 cents for
every barrel of cement delivered. So great was the amount of cement
needed by the city that the $180,000—Grant was alleged to have put
up $80,000 himself—was considered well targeted. As it happened,
the mayor never appointed Grant to the position, and the money was
returned to its donors.

Croker, who at the moment happened to be at a health spa in
Germany recovering from a stomach ailment, told reporters that Mc-
Cann's story was nonsense. "Imagine me going around town show-
ing McCann a bag full of money and telling him it was boodle.
Rubbish!"[15] The story seemed quite credible, however, leading to
suspicions that Croker might have engineered other payments. Mc-
Cann followed that story up with another that was far more convinc-
ing and damaging to Croker.

After Grant became sheriff, he felt obliged, McCann claimed, to
express his gratitude to Croker by paying him the princely sum of
$25,000, which Grant conferred on successive occasions in an un-
usual way: he handed envelopes containing $5,000 in cash not to the
Boss but to Croker's baby daughter Flossie, Grant's godchild, age
two. As the touching scene unfolded in the Crokers' living room, said
McCann, Flossie would clutch the heavy envelope nervously, then
toddle over and hand it to her mother, who would give it to Croker as
everyone beamed on the youngster. Grant, who in the intervening
years had become mayor, admitted on the stand that he had given the
money but saw nothing wrong with it. "I think," he said, "that if you
will look over the obligation that one accepts when they become a
godfather—of course, I must say that I feel very delicate about discussing such a subject here. . . ."[16] Subsequent to this odd benefac-
tion, however, he had made no other gifts to the child. Toward the
end of the Fassett inquiry, Croker returned from Europe and took the
witness stand. He acknowledged the gifts but said they totaled
$10,000, not $25,000. Asked what he had done with the money, he
said he had combined it with another sum and purchased some real
estate—which, it developed, he had put in his name, not Flossie's.
Grant's beneficence had all the earmarks of a political payoff.

The Fassett Committee also unearthed signs of widespread
Tammany-linked corruption on the Board of Excise, which controlled the licensing of liquor dealers, and in the administration of the
Ludlow Street Jail (Tweed's old haunt), whose inmates, many of
them well-to-do businessmen imprisoned momentarily for debt, paid

the warden and his assistants large sums for weekend privileges and other special favors. But the committee made no attempt to investigate the New York Police Department, widely assumed to be rife with graft and corruption. And it let Croker and his allies off with little more than a rebuke. A few nights after Croker had testified about the gifts to Flossie, he made an appearance in the Wigwam and was greeted with cheers.

In the 1890 mayoral election, Grant was easily reelected. There was no question that the good times were now rolling for Tammany Hall; it could hardly lose an election. Two years later, in 1892, another Croker crony, Tammany Grand Sachem Thomas F. Gilroy, was elected mayor by a margin that elicited wonder throughout the city. Admittedly, the vote in certain districts seemed suspiciously lopsided. On the Lower East Side, for instance, one Bowery election district, headed by Big Tim Sullivan, turned in a vote of 388 to 4 for the Democratic ticket. Through various strong-arm tactics and devious methods, Sullivan had organized his district to perfection. He was once quoted as saying that the best repeaters at the polls were men with whiskers. "When you've voted 'em with their whiskers on," he related, "you take 'em to a barber and scrape off the chin-fringe. Then you vote 'em again with side lilacs and a mustache. Then to a barber again, off comes the sides and you vote 'em a third time with the mustache. If that ain't enough and the box can stand a few more ballots clean off the mustache and vote 'em plain face. That makes every one of 'em good for four votes."[17] But the 1892 result in his district actually disappointed him, as he had pegged it at 389 to 3. "I'll find that feller!" he promised Croker.[18]

By this time the Gay Nineties were in full swing in New York. The center of sporting life, which had originally been located along the Bowery and on side streets near lower Broadway, was now firmly ensconced in the West Twenties and Thirties between Sixth and Eighth avenues. The area was known as the Tenderloin from the widely quoted remark of one of the best known policemen in the city, Captain (later Inspector) Alexander S. Williams, who was called Clubber Williams for his liberal use of the nightstick on suspects. After some years of service in quiet residential districts where the opportunities for graft had been rare, Williams was transferred to the vice-ridden West Side area. "I've had nothin' but chuck steak for a long time," he said, "and now I'm goin' to get a little of the tenderloin."[19] Anyone familiar with the seamy side of New York life understood that the promotion of vice meant hefty cash payments going into the pockets of the police, not to mention those of Tammany Hall district leaders, and that conditions in this nether world were not nice.

Too few New Yorkers were aware of it, however. If they knew about the Tenderloin and similar areas, they preferred to ignore the unsavory details. Moral crusaders could never attract enough attention—not, that is, until a zealous but unprepossessing-looking clergyman, the Reverend Charles H. Parkhurst, took up their cause. Minister of the prosperous Madison Square Presbyterian Church, and active member of the reform-minded Society for the Prevention of Crime, the bewhiskered Parkhurst well understood the connection between Tammany Hall, the police, and organized sin. In 1892, he decided a frontal attack was called for. In his sermon on Sunday, February 14—to which he had taken care to invite a newspaper reporter or two—he inveighed against those responsible for the city's vice.

"There is not a form under which the Devil disguises himself," he thundered, "that so perplexes us in our efforts, or so bewilders us in the devising of our schemes, as the polluted harpies that, under the pretense of governing this city, are feeding day and night on its quivering vitals. They are a lying, perjured, rum-soaked, and libidinous lot."[20] Anyone trying to rescue the city from moral depravity, he said, found himself heavily outgunned by the likes of Tammany Hall. "While we fight iniquity they shield and patronize it; while we try to convert criminals they manufacture them; and they have a hundred dollars invested in manufacturing machinery to our one invested in converting machinery."[21]

Dr. Parkhurst's broadside provoked such an outcry that he was asked to appear before a grand jury and present whatever direct evidence he could muster. He had none, and so the grand jury thanked him and went on to other matters. There was only one thing for him to do: get the evidence himself. He hired a detective, Charles W. Gardner, who agreed to show him the town for six dollars a night and who, in order to conceal the preacher's identity, dressed him the way an out-of-town hick might appear, in black-and-white checked trousers, an old reefer jacket, a red-flannel scarf, and a slouch hat. He also soaped the doctor's hair to straighten it. Then the two men, accompanied by a young volunteer named John Erving whom Gardner similarly disguised, ventured out into the night.

Their first stop was a saloon on Cherry Street, where Parkhurst found it necessary to gulp down a drink of whiskey. "He acted," Gardner recounted later in a book about their exploits, "as if he had swallowed a whole political parade—torchlights and all."[22] Parkhurst was dismayed to see small children coming into the bar to buy pints of whiskey for 10 cents to take home to their mothers and fathers. Then it was on to a series of brothels. In one, the Golden Rule Pleasure Club on West Third Street, Parkhurst was horrified to find not girls but heavily made-up young men who spoke in high falsetto voices. When Gardner explained what they were there for the minister fled the premises. But he would not be deterred. "Show me something worse!" he kept exhorting his guide.

The high—or low—point came on a subsequent night when the group visited the establishment of one Hattie Adams. Five girls were provided the party, each dressed in a Mother Hubbard gown that was immediately doffed. Quite naked, they danced the cancan to the tinny music of a piano played by a man known as the Professor, who had been blindfolded out of respect for his modesty. After that they played leapfrog, Gardner later reporting that "I was the frog and the others jumped over me." Through it all Parkhurst sat impassively in a corner sipping a glass of beer. At one point Hattie tried to loosen him up by pulling his whiskers, but "the Doctor straightened out with such an air of dignity that she did not attempt any further familiarities."[23]

Parkhurst described his explorations in another well-attended sermon a few weeks later, providing names and addresses of the places he visited. The grand jury invited him back and was grateful for his evidence but, despite questioning many policemen, was unable to return any indictments. The police closed a few brothels but business continued much as before. Parkhurst continued his attack in the press, urging reforms in the Police Department. Still no official action was taken. It was 1892, after all, and the Democrats had won handily across the board, even returning Cleveland to the White House after a four-year hiatus. Tammany and the police had no reason to change their ways. But a year later, following a severe economic downturn, the state legislature passed to the control of the Republicans, and Thomas Platt decided the time had come to cash in on Parkhurst's exploits. In one of his Sunday morning sessions in the Amen Corner, he gave the green light to a thorough investigation of the New York Police Department, to commence in March 1894.

Although the inquiry was to be chaired by state Senator Clarence Lexow, its dominant figure was the committee's chief counsel, Irish-born John Goff, a tall, white-bearded former assistant district attorney with deep-set blue eyes and a flair for the dramatic. Though a Demo-

crat, he harbored a cordial dislike for Tammany Hall. Richard Croker
knew about him and readily understood that he was bad news, and
before the Lexow hearings began he sent an emissary to the attorney
offering him $30,000 to turn down the assignment. Goff rejected the
offer. Shortly thereafter, another Tammanyite approached him and
raised the amount to $300,000. Again the answer was no.

Croker took stock of the situation and made the very sensible decision to get out of town lest he become a key victim of the inquiry. A
few weeks after the hearings began he tendered his resignation as
chairman of Tammany's Finance Committee and quietly departed
for England, where by now he had acquired a country estate at Want-
age in Berkshire County, as well as a town house in London. For the
better part of three years, he tended to his racing interests and played
the role of a country squire, communicating only sporadically with
Tammany. The Hall was left in the keeping of a deputy, John C.
Sheehan.

The Lexow hearings, full of surprises and unlikely twists, did not
disappoint the public. One chronicler has called them "the most detailed accounting of municipal malfeasance in history."[24] They con-
clusively proved that New York's Police Department was efficiently
organized for plunder. Not only that, but Tammany Hall and the
department were closely allied for their mutual financial and political
benefit. Goff started at the top with a look at the members of the
Board of Police Commissioners, a supposedly bipartisan body appointed by the mayor whose Republican members were "safe"—not
inimical to Tammany. The board controlled the appointment, promotion, and transfer of all policemen. Commissioner John McClave,
summoned to the stand, found himself unable to explain certain sizable deposits in his bank account that followed his appointing or promoting police officers, and after a few days of Goff's relentless
examination, he came down with what was called brain fever—most
likely a nervous breakdown—and shortly resigned from the board.
Another board member, James J. Martin, admitted that, of all the
appointments, promotions, and transfers he had made as commissioner, some 85 to 90 percent had been recommended by Tammany
district leaders. Not only was appointment to the force predicated on
Tammany membership, it also had its price, generally $300, which
went straight into the pocket of the district leader or someone higher
up.

So lucrative was the appointment racket that district leaders would
force the naming of someone even if it meant that another man doing

a perfectly creditable job had to give way. This was made clear in the case of one Sergeant Schryer, who was sent to a distant precinct to make room for a Tammany favorite. The district leader who got the board to make the transfer, a certain Judge George F. Roesch, was frank about the matter. "I will tell you," he said, "when a man comes to me and wants to get an appointment or transfer, or anything like that, I never stop to consider who is in the place he wants to go to, but my object is to get him there; necessarily, somebody has got to get out of the way, and here it happened to be Sergeant Schryer."[25]

One of the juiciest sources of police graft was prostitution, and Goff produced a seemingly endless array of madams, brothel owners, and plain hard-working prostitutes who testified to the relentless cupidity of patrolmen, wardmen (detectives), and police captains. Charles Priem, who with his wife owned a brothel at 28 Bayard Street (in today's Chinatown), told the committee that in six years he had paid out a total of $4,300 to the police, including $500 each time a new captain took over the precinct and an extra $100 at Christmastime. The police set the amount each house had to pay, generally basing it on the number of girls it employed, and the wardman would come around punctually every month to collect. One madam reported that the wardman requested payment in bills, not coins; if she wanted to pay part of the fee in silver she was asked to fold it within the bills as "he did not want the girls to hear the click" of the coins.[26] If a house did not pay up promptly, a policeman would simply stand in front of the house, which of course frightened customers away. The police also extracted a cut from the earnings of those who supplied liquor and beer to the brothels, as well as from those who delivered food, cigars, and other supplies. A small percentage of the money would be kept by the wardman while another slice was taken by the captain; the rest would be bucked up the line to the inspector and thence to the police commissioners and various Tammany operatives.

The police were so dependent on this income that they would do anything to prevent houses from going out of business. Mrs. Lena Cohen said that when she and her husband tried to close down because the police were taking all their profits, Police Officer Farrell arrested her husband on a trumped-up charge so as to pressure them to stay operating. But sometimes the police advised the brothels to shut down temporarily. Mrs. Augusta Thurow, who kept a "house of ill-repute" on Second Avenue, said that a wardman had told her, "Business is on the bumerina; Parkhurst is on the road, and you have got to lay low for 30 days."[27]

Even though it was in their interest to protect prostitution, the police did frequently make arrests, particularly of streetwalkers (who might be working on their own or might be sent out to bring patrons into a brothel), and here again Tammany Hall profited because it controlled the bail system. Many district leaders specialized in making bail for prostitutes brought into the police station, $5 being the going rate per girl. The leader of the Tenderloin area was believed to bail out twenty to thirty girls a night, clearing at least $100 each evening.

The proceeds from poolrooms rivaled and may have even exceeded those from brothels. The journalist Lincoln Steffens once wrote that he had heard the monthly take from city gambling and poolrooms was $400,000. Outwardly conventional-looking pool and billiard halls were actually centers for horse race betting, and many of them were owned or controlled by Tammany higher-ups. One of the largest and most successful gambling rings in town had been organized by Tammany's Big Tim Sullivan. Another lucrative activity was a confidence game that involved so-called green goods, or counterfeit money. Unsuspecting out-of-towners would be told they could buy, at a discount, currency that had been printed in error or in duplicate. They would be shown the bills and required to put their money down, but then a stack of worthless paper would be substituted on the sly, the victims rarely suspecting. The proceeds from green goods were huge.

That the rewards from such activities could be plentiful was demonstrated when Goff put Clubber Williams on the stand. A tall, bullet-headed man with a long, thick nose and a luxuriant mustache, Williams admitted to having been tried eighteen times by the police commissioners on bribe taking as well as brutality charges, and had been accused of receiving everything from a diamond ring and a gold-headed cane to six pocket handkerchiefs.

"You have become rich upon corruption?" Goff asked him.

"If I was rich, Mr. Goff," Williams replied, "I wouldn't be here answering questions."[28] But on further questioning, he conceded that he owned considerable property in northern Japan (how he acquired such an exotic holding was not divulged) as well as an estate on the shore in Cos Cob, Connecticut, which included a boathouse, a dock, and a fifty-three-foot yacht—expensive items on a policeman's salary.

Yet the Police Department's (and Tammany's) connection to organized vice did not seem to bother, or rather shock, many New Yorkers, who felt that such activity was bound to exist no matter what laws were passed. But there was a dark side to the Lexow hearings that caused people to sit up and take notice.

Many of the police were extraordinarily brutal in dealing with suspects. In recalling the many victims of police brutality that had appeared before it, the Lexow Committee in its final report stated, "The eye of one man, punched out by a patrolman's club, hung from his cheek. Others were brought before the committee, fresh from their punishment covered with blood and bruises, and in some cases battered out of recognition. Witnesses testified to severe assaults upon them while under arrest in station houses, and one witness, a journalist of established reputation, testified that he had been clubbed by an inspector without cause. . . . "[29] One day late in the hearings Goff, for dramatic effect, assembled before the committee some ninety New York policemen, all of whom had been accused of clubbing citizens. One of them had been accused of beating sixteen people, including a fifteen-year-old girl walking on Broadway with her father and whom the policeman had refused to believe was not a prostitute.

Many New Yorkers were also shocked to learn from the hearings that the promoting of police officers largely depended on payoffs and bribes. In revealing this practice, the star witness was Captain Timothy J. Creeden, who was persuaded, only after much agonizing, to tell reluctantly how he had been forced to pay the outlandish sum of $15,000 to achieve captain's rank. An honest cop with a stellar twenty-year record of service, Creeden had taken the examination for promotion from sergeant to captain, had scored 97.82, but had not been promoted. After taking the examination two more times, and ranking among the top candidates but still passed over, he was told by friends that he was wasting his time; he needed to bring "influence to bear" on one of the police commissioners.

This prompted him to call on his Tammany district leader, John W. Reppenhagen, who was said to "represent" Police Commissioner John R. Voorhis. Reppenhagen informed him that the price for a captaincy would be $12,000. A friend of Creeden's agreed to raise the money by getting local businessmen to make contributions as a kind of investment in the officer, assuming that Creeden could never repay the loan on a captain's annual salary of $2,750 but that his illegal earnings would rapidly take care of it. A few days later Reppenhagen told him apologetically that another sergeant had just come up with $12,000 but that Creeden could top him by paying $15,000—which he did. Shortly thereafter, he was summoned to the office of Commissioner Voorhis, who told him that because of his fine record he was being promoted to captain. Voorhis advised him, Creeden said, that there was a rumor that some liquor dealers in his neighborhood had put up money on his behalf; was it true? Creeden, recognizing that the commissioner would have to ask such a question to cover himself, was quick to deny it. Voorhis said he was glad of that. District leader Reppenhagen, questioned by Goff as to the disposition of the money, said that Voorhis had received $5,000, another third had gone to a Tammanyite saloonkeeper named John J. Martin who had helped arrange the deal, and that he had kept the rest. (It happened that before the money was paid over to Reppenhagen, Creeden was informed that he would be sent to the Old Slip precinct, where opportunities for graft were slim; his backers screamed to Tammany Hall, Creeden was reassigned to a more lucrative post, and the transfer was made.)

Creeden's testimony to the Lexow Committee infuriated the Board of Police Commissioners, who voted to suspend him from the force. Goff and the committee, not to be deterred, subpoenaed them and the police superintendent, and the hearing room audience cheered when the officials made their appearance. The board's president, visibly rattled, agreed to reconsider the action, and the next day Creeden was reinstated.

A final link in the elaborate network of control and corruption described at the hearings was the role of the police in helping Tammany control elections. Police officers on duty at the polls who were instructed to report all irregularities, the committee learned, would take care not to notice when repeaters were allowed to vote or when opposition ballots were destroyed. When Republican poll watchers raised objections to the way voting was handled, the Tammany election inspectors would eject them or rough them up—and the police would do nothing to stop it. In fact, said the Lexow Committee in its report, "It may be stated . . . that the police conducted themselves . . . upon the principle that they were there, not as guardians of the public peace to enforce law and order, but for the purpose of acting as agents of Tammany Hall, in securing to the candidates of that organization by means fair or foul the largest possible majorities."[30]

So the circle was complete, and its design was clear. Richard Croker's Tammany Hall, through its district leaders and its captive police board, controlled the police force, who aided, abetted, and profited from organized vice and who helped pass the rewards back to the Hall. The police helped ensure that Tammany remained in power so that the whole glorious system could be kept in place to the benefit of everyone participating in it. The end result was the demoralization of the entire police force. "The policeman who pays for his appointment," said the Lexow report, "commences his career with the commission of a crime, and it is not strange that the demoralization thus engendered should follow him in his further career."[31]

Croker had predicted correctly when he saw that the Lexow hearings would spell trouble. The outcry in New York was loud, almost as loud as it had been thirty years before with the exposure of the Tweed Ring. Again, a phalanx of Republicans and reformers formed a Committee of Seventy, this time to organize a ticket for the 1894 mayoral campaign. The group settled on an independent Republican, William L. Strong, as a Fusion candidate and approached Thomas Platt for his backing. Although Platt distrusted all independents, he realized the hearings had produced an unwelcome ground swell that could not be denied and he gave his assent. Tammany persuaded Hugh Grant to run again, but the Democratic effort was lackluster, and Strong swept to victory by a margin of more than forty-five thousand votes, carrying almost the whole Fusion ticket with him. It was the first truly nonpartisan reform administration the city had ever known. Tammany Hall was out on its ear.

Was the Hall truly finished? Many people thought so. The Strong administration came in with high hopes and great plans. Item one on its agenda was the reorganization of the Police Department. A new Board of Police Commissioners was appointed, but it was no longer allowed to hire or fire policemen: that power was given to a newly powerful chief of police, a position that replaced the former superintendent, who had merely been the operational head of the force. A merit system was instituted for appointments and promotions. One of the new commissioners was thirty-seven-year-old Theodore Roosevelt, who quickly came to dominate the board; another was Frank Moss, who would later serve as counsel for the Mazet Investigation. Many corrupt old-timers like Clubber Williams were retired, and younger corruptionists were shifted from juicy precincts to the boondocks. The city's Street Cleaning Department was taken over by Colonel George E. Waring, Jr., whose zealotry resulted in a cleaner city than anyone could remember. New parks were laid out and new schools built.

How long would the new mood last? Not very long, it turned out. Less than a year into the Strong administration, the city's new police chief complained, "I am willing to play up with T.R., but I cannot help keeping one eye on the signs of the failure of reform and the return of Tammany. Tammany is not a wave; it's the sea itself."[32] In a little more than a year, the Strong administration was rent by dissension and petty feuds; its leaders came to be seen as well-meaning, upper-class gentlemen out of touch with the people. It was not that the populace disliked honest government, but rather that the reformers' idealistic programs often seemed unworkable or extreme. New Yorkers especially resented the closing of the saloons on Sunday—what harm could come from having a few beers on your day off? And politicians of all parties resented Mayor Strong's refusal to heed patronage requests.

But while Tammany Hall's prospects in the next mayoral election, in 1897, seemed to be brightening, both the timing and the circumstances surrounding that election represented a change. Following lengthy studies and much politicking over several decades, New York City, which until now had comprised only Manhattan Island and the Bronx, was authorized by the state in 1897 to expand to take in Brooklyn, Queens, and Staten Island. The new Greater New York would come into being the next year, on the first of January, 1898. That date was picked because the city's elections for the office of mayor were henceforth to occur on off years, the first one to take place in 1897. Thus Mayor Strong, for all his limitations, received an extra year in office.

So it was that Richard Croker, sensing that the time had come for Tammany to recapture its former preeminence, sailed into New York Harbor on September 7, 1897, having been away for more than three years. The press called it his Return from Elba. There was no one to meet him at the dock, but this was as he had wanted it, for he hoped to reenter the city unobtrusively. Despite his prolonged absence, he had never been out of touch with the Hall, and so he knew there was discord and rebellion in the air. Not only did the deputy he had left in charge, John Sheehan, harbor dreams of taking over permanently, but Big Tim Sullivan's threats seemed to be even more dangerous. With a masterful sense of timing and a large helping of bravado, the Boss faced down the rebels and sent them back to work, all in a matter of a few weeks.

What remained was the choice of a candidate for mayor—a selection made especially tricky because the upcoming race, despite Strong's perceived failings, was sure to be difficult. First of all, the city's expansion had caused the political balance to shift. Because Tammany had always been a Manhattan organization, it had opposed the city's consolidation lest its power be diluted; could it now mollify and enlist Brooklyn's Democrats, who had for years been led by their own resourceful boss, Hugh McLaughlin? The Republican chief, Tom Platt, had bet that Tammany would not be able to do so, which ws why he turned out to be one of the principal backers of the unification plan.

Second, the threat represented by the opposition candidates was difficult to assess. The onetime Labor party nominee, single-tax advocate Henry George, was running again and might be just as strong a contender as he had been in 1886. The Citizens' Union and other reform groups had put together a nonpartisan ticket headed by Seth Low, a Republican who had been mayor of Brooklyn and was currently president of Columbia University; he was widely respected and highly capable, though somewhat colorless. As for the Republicans, Boss Platt was faced with a dilemma. Many party associates were urging him to endorse Low. He knew Tammany was vulnerable; but he also had what he later called "the sincerest and the profoundest contempt" for nonpartisanship in local elections.[33] The Strong experience had been enough: he did not wish to make the same mistake twice. So he bypassed Low and dictated the choice of General Benjamin F. Tracy, a law partner of his son's, as the Republican standard-bearer. The assumption was widely held, and probably correctly, that Platt had made a deal with Croker, feeling that it was better to do business with Tammany than to get no business at all from non-partisans.

The question remained: whom would Croker put up? The Master of Manhattan delayed until the very last moment before divulging his choice. When his decision came it dumbfounded everyone, even some of Croker's associates at the Hall, who thought the Boss himself might run. Out of nowhere Croker had picked Judge Robert C. Van Wyck, an unknown with an undistinguished record. He was the perfect machine man, a man who would do as he was told and could be counted on not to second-guess the Boss.

Tammany Hall poured all its resources into electing this nonentity, but the odds seemed to be against it until shortly before election day, when Henry George, the Labor party candidate, suddenly dropped dead. George's son stepped in to take his father's place, but the betting now favored Tammany. At one point during the campaign, the Hall's candidate for district attorney, Asa Bird Gardiner, shouted to his audience during a speech, "To Hell with Reform!" and the crowd cheered him wildly. The phrase became Tammany's slogan. Van Wyck was elected by a wide margin, the first mayor of Greater

New York. On election night, after Van Wyck's triumph had been made known, great crowds paraded and danced in the streets chanting, "Well! Well! Well! Reform has gone to Hell!"[34] As Croker made his way to the Wigwam and, ascending a back stairway, suddenly appeared on the stage of the crowded auditorium, he was greeted with a deafening roar. Tammany was back in charge, and Richard Croker's power was greater than ever.

Just how domineering that power could be was soon demonstrated. As expected, the patronage from the victory was large, and Croker seemed to elevate the business of awarding the spoils into a regal act. Instead of merely summoning job seekers to the Wigwam, he traveled with his top staff and Mayor-elect Van Wyck to a hotel in Lakewood, New Jersey, where he held forth for six weeks in ducal splendor, strolling grandly back and forth in the main lobby, examining applicants, conferring with district leaders and other higher-ups, and slowly deciding on the appointees who would help steer the new administration. He was always careful to make it look as if Van Wyck were in on the discussions and to "suggest" the appointments to him, and the mayor-elect would nod, sagely giving his assent, but there was no question about who was making the decisions. (Away from Croker's presence Van Wyck reputedly exploded in indignation, but he kept his tantrums to himself.) In the evening all present would sit down to dinner wearing—by the Boss's order—formal evening dress, a custom that was foreign to most of the lowly Tammanyites present and caused them acute discomfort. No matter, they were duty bound to obey. The Boss had acquired the habit in England—where, as the humorist George Ade once said, "Their idea of a gentleman is a man who continues to wear evening clothes after he has worn out his underclothes."[35]

The jobs dispensed, Croker moved back to the city and continued his splendid ways. The evening before Van Wyck's inauguration, he threw a magnificent reception at the gaudy Murray Hill Hotel, on Park Avenue at Fortieth Street, and greeted guests wearing a top hat and evening clothes. His residence now (he and his wife were separated) was the newly established Democratic Club, on Fifth Avenue in the Fifties. Those who wished to speak with him inquired of the doorman, "Is he in?" There was no question who "'he" was. In the evening, no one entered the dining room until the Boss did, and after being served (most ordered what he did), no one would start eating before he did.

Although Croker had officially moved back to New York, he went abroad every summer to look after his racing interests and to travel on the Continent. His departures were state occasions, his stateroom filled with floral tributes and champagne and packed with dignitaries. Police boats and pleasure craft escorted his liner down the bay, and on one occasion a police launch fired a twenty-one gun salute as a farewell. The Boss was pleased. "Why, that's the President's salute," he remarked to a companion.[36]

The presidential motif cropped up again during a Jefferson Day banquet in 1899 that perhaps represented the culmination of Croker's grandiosity. For the event, the Boss, acting on behalf of the Democratic Club, engaged no less a spot than the Metropolitan Opera House, whose orchestra seats were removed and replaced with banquet tables. Elaborate kitchens, set up on the sidewalks outside, prepared food for twelve hundred diners who of course wore formal garb. Wives and other admiring hangers-on filled the boxes above the main floor, flowers perfumed the air, and when Croker made his ceremonial entrance the band struck up "Hail to the Chief." All present rose to honor him.

There were people, however, who were shocked at the idolization. The journalist William Allen White voiced their astonishment when he wrote, in 1901, "And all this homage, all this boot-licking, to a mild-mannered, soft-voiced, sad-faced, green-eyed chunk of a man who talks slowly that he may peg in his 'seens' and his 'saws,' his 'dones' and his 'dids' where they belong, who has a loggy wit, who cares neither for books, nor music, nor theatrical performances, nor good wine, nor a dinner, nor the society of his kind! . . . And now he sits on a throne and disposes a sort of jungle justice, while civilization knocks its knees together in stupid, terrified adulation!"[37]

Yet White knew that Croker possessed something else. "The men who shudder at Croker's power," he wrote, "shudder because they fancy it is generated in iniquity, but the truth is that the power to control men is always the sign of some strong quality. No man is all good or all bad, but men follow a leader so long as, in their eyes, his virtues outweigh his vices."[38]

The virtues that people saw in Croker were not hard to understand. In a city undergoing bewildering change, he represented authority and consistency. Tammany Hall, with all its dubious ways, provided a link between the great preponderance of the masses and the otherwise impersonal and often thoughtless city government.

What Tammany offered to the poor and the immigrant was summed up by the Boss himself in an interview that was published in October 1897 in the London *Review of Reviews*. W. T. Stead, the *Reviews* editor, had been on the ship that carried Croker back to New York in the summer of 1897 and had extensive talks with the Boss. He admitted to having straightened out Croker's syntax here and there, but even allowing for that, the Boss's thoughts were not to be dismissed. Only Tammany, Croker said, paid attention to the less fortunate in society. "There is no such organization for taking hold of the untrained friendless man and converting him into a citizen. Who else would do it if we did not? Think of the hundreds of thousands of foreigners dumped into our city. They are too old to go to school. There is not a mugwump [upperclass reformer] who would shake hands with them. They are alone, ignorant strangers, a prey to all manner of anarchical and wild notions. . . . Tammany looks after them for the sake of their vote, grafts them upon the Republic, makes citizens of them in short; and although you may not like our motives or our methods, what other agency is there by which so long a row could have been hoed so quickly or so well? If we go down into the gutter it is because there are men in the gutter, and you have got to go down where they are if you are to do anything with them."[39]

But the reverse side of the picture was all too evident: Tammany's methods could be crude, even cruel, and the Hall's rulers had no interest in bringing about the kinds of reforms that could genuinely help society. Now that Croker was enjoying such extraordinary prestige, he was beginning to abuse his formidable power, and it took an unusual person to stand up to him. A dramatic example of his tendency to excess was recounted years later by Chauncey Depew, who in 1898 had been president of the New York Central Railroad as well as a key figure in New York Republican circles. In that year Theodore Roosevelt was being suggested as a candidate for governor of New York. Depew had been asked to make the nominating speech for him at the Republican State Convention. Roosevelt was anathema to Croker, for he was a mugwump who knew how to operate politically and take the measure of bosses. (Platt was wary of Roosevelt, too, but accepted him because he was a recognized vote getter.) Croker felt that Roosevelt must be stopped, and so he dispatched a high-ranking Democrat to Depew's office who said, "I have a message for you which, personally, I am ashamed to deliver. Mr. Croker has sent me to say to you that if you make that speech nominating Mr. Roosevelt in the Republican Convention, he will resent it on your railroad."

The threat of reprisals against the New York Central was about as bald as could be imagined, and Depew knew what the consequences could be, but he was up to the challenge. "I know Mr. Croker's power," he said to his visitor, "and the injury he can do the road. You can say to him that I am amazed at such a message coming from a man I have always found to be a square fighter, as this is a blow below the belt. I am going to make that speech; but before I make it, I shall resign as president and director of the New York Central Railroad. And when I put Mr. Roosevelt in nomination before the Convention of the State of New York, I will say why I resigned."

Depew's remark found its target. Within an hour the emissary returned to report, "Mr. Croker wishes you to forget that message. His own words were: 'It is withdrawn. I was very badly advised.' "[40] The Boss's arrogance had been called and turned back.

Having failed to derail Roosevelt, Croker proceeded to make another error that resulted in Roosevelt's election to the governorship. Joseph F. Daly, a judge in the state court system and a Tammany appointee, had angered Croker by rejecting a Tammany recommendation for his clerk of court. The Boss refused to renominate him for the 1898 election. Questioned about his decision, Croker was adamant: "Justice Daly was elected by Tammany Hall after he was discovered by Tammany Hall, and Tammany Hall had a right to expect proper consideration at his hands."[41] It was a matter of party discipline, and Daly had disobeyed orders. But to many other people it was something else: a violation of judicial independence. A mass meeting was held at Carnegie Hall at which the key speaker was a former Croker aide, Bourke Cockran, who warned of the dangers of runaway bossism. More important, Roosevelt picked up the issue and made it the centerpiece of his campaign, saying that the voters' choice was between Crokerism and himself. "Croker was a powerful and truculent man," Roosevelt later recalled, "the autocrat of his organization, and of a domineering nature. For his own reasons he insisted upon Tammany's turning down an excellent Democratic judge who was up for reelection. This gave me my chance."[42] On election day Roosevelt narrowly outpolled the Democratic candidate, Augustus Van Wyck, the mayor's brother.

The Democratic defeat had a special significance for Croker: it was the first election he had lost as Boss (he had not been present for the 1894 debacle). His aura of success was shaken.

Also, Croker's Wall Street Connection began to produce problems. He had acquired—whether by purchase or by gift he would

never divulge—stock in the New York Auto-Truck Company, a firm
with tremendous potential now that horse-drawn freight delivery was
yielding to the internal combustion engine. In 1898, the company
wanted to attach its compressed-air pipes to the structures of the
Manhattan Elevated Railroad Company, and in its behalf Croker paid
a call on George Gould, the company's president (and the son of Jay
Gould, the legendary financier). Gould told Croker he would check
with his engineers to see if the structures could carry the load, and
with his lawyers to see if the arrangement was legally proper.

"Oh, hell!" exclaimed Croker. "I want the pipes put on, and I
don't want any circumlocution." Gould asked, "Don't you think it
would be better to give me an opportunity to consult my officials?"
"No," replied Croker, "we want the pipes put on, and we don't want
any fuss about it." "Under the circumstances, Mr. Croker," Gould
was reported as saying, "I will settle the question now, without referring it to my officials. I will say to you now that we will not permit you
to attach your pipes to the elevated structures."[43]

In no time Gould and his associates felt the full weight of Croker's
retribution. The Board of Aldermen, controlled by Tammany Hall,
passed a law requiring Manhattan to place drip pans under its structures at every street crossing. Another law compelled the railroad to
run trains every five minutes day and night, with a $100 penalty for
each violation. Yet another law ordered it to enclose all its stations in
glass. The Health Department declared several hundred points on
the line to be unsafe, another ordinance forbade the company the
right to store its trains on a third track at the end of the line, and the
Parks Department ordered it to remove its tracks immediately from
Battery Park, its terminus.

The severity of these measures puzzled the public. It was only
when the *New York Evening Post* on February 5, 1899, published a
report of the Croker-Gould meeting that the connection became apparent. Croker in a fury denied the *Post* story, but its basic accuracy
can be assumed from the fact that the Boss did not sue the paper for
libel as he could have if the report were untrue. The public outcry
resulted in Auto-Truck greatly reducing its demands, and the draco-
nian measures were never enforced. (A rumor at the time held that
Croker and his associates had owned stock in Manhattan Elevated as
well as in Auto-Truck but had sold their El stock short after Gould's
refusal—figuring to profit when the stock plummeted as a result of
the city's reprisals, which it did.)

While these developments were taking place, the city was reverting to the wide-open ways that had characterized it before the Strong
administration. The symbol of the new laxity—and as such a worthy
successor to Clubber Williams—was the chief of police, William S.
Devery, a tall, bullnecked, red-faced man with a luxuriant mustache
that looked as if it had come direct from the vaudeville stage. Devery
boasted that he had carried his father's dinner pail when the old man
was laying bricks to help build Tammany Hall. He was a cop's cop:
crimes like burglary were to be prosecuted aggressively, but vice was a
fact of life and could never be stopped—and besides, it brought a nice
income. When a minister once came to his station house com-
plaining about prostitutes in the neighborhood, Devery's only response was, "Men that are looking for that sort of thing can find
plenty of it."[44] His favorite advice to other policemen was, "When
you're caught with the goods on, don't say nothin'," and when the
Lexow Committee had put him on the stand to answer questions
about payoffs, he repeatedly stated, "Touchin' on an' appertainin' to
that, there's nothin' doin'."[45]

So blatant had Devery's performance been at the Lexow hearings
that the police commissioners themselves in 1894 decided to try to
upstage the investigation by cleaning house, and they brought
charges against Devery for various kinds of bribe-taking. Devery
ducked out by claiming illness; a friendly police surgeon testified to
his indisposition, and the trial never came off. But the commissioners
demoted him anyway. So it came as quite a surprise when Croker and
Tammany, back in charge in 1898, plucked Devery from his temporary obscurity and made him chief. More than a surprise, in fact:
many saw it as a calculated affront to the defeated forces of reform.

Reform had indeed gone to Hell. The Tenderloin—which of
course had never really shut down—was flourishing as never before.
The liquor laws were ignored. Devery and Big Tim Sullivan were
known to be in control of gambling citywide, along with Frank Farrell, one of the best-known gambling house operators in the country.

But it was at this point that Croker's instinctive fear of what Roosevelt might do was borne out. Soon after taking office in 1899, Roosevelt and his legislative allies in Albany decided to launch yet another
full-scale investigation into Tammany's influence on New York City's
government. This one was to be under the chairmanship of Republican assemblyman Robert Mazet. The committee's chief counsel was
Frank Moss, who had been Goff's assistant during the Lexow hear-

ings and later, with Roosevelt, would be a member of the police board. He was known for his slashing prosecutorial style. His manner may in fact have been too adversarial; the investigation was often quite one-sided, even vindictive. It also tended to become tedious and repetitious, covering much of the ground the Lexow probe had worked five years earlier. But it also yielded a great deal of information, or at least a wealth of allegations, concerning the corporate alliances of the Boss and some of his associates, and this was to prove highly damaging to both Croker and Tammany.

Commencing its investigation in April 1899, the committee began looking into conditions in the Tenderloin by questioning none other than Bill Devery himself, who professed total ignorance of goings-on there even though he visited the area every night. It was his custom, he said, to leave his office in the early evening and head for Eighth Avenue and Twenty-eighth Street, where he would stand on the corner until 1:00 or 2:00 A.M. and talk to people. Did he notice, Moss asked, that right across the sidewalk from him was a saloon that conducted a brisk after-hours business? No, he had never noticed that. Moss: "What do you do on that corner if you do not see?" Devery: "I just stand there to breathe the fresh air." The people who came to talk with him—who Moss implied were critically involved in the gambling business—were, Devery stated, "from the meekest to the highest, no matter who come along I receive them and hear what they have to say."[46] At one point Moss asked him what he thought of the widely held notion that the city was wide open. "The city is certainly wide open," replied the chief. "I never knew it to be closed."[47]

There appeared the same parade of victimized prostitutes as had come before the Lexow investigators, the most convincing being fifteen-year-old Emma Hartig, who testified that there were a great many underage girls working in the house where she had toiled, including one who was thirteen, and that the girls were forced to give their money to pimps and other hangers-on. One of them "throwed a chair at me to make me give up my money. He hurted me."[48] Not only did the police exact their payments on a regular basis, she said, but they often availed themselves of the personnel of the house for free. Moss put Mayor Van Wyck on the stand and asked him what he thought of such matters. "I think there are a few harlots in town," said the mayor, "and there is a lot of liquor sold, as there is all over the State." He was not exercised about the problem and thought Moss was "morbid about conditions of crime."[49]

The tension increased markedly, however, when Richard Croker appeared before the committee. Questioned about his profiting from judicial real estate sales, he made his notorious remark that he was working for his pocket "all the time." He showed his contempt for Moss's tactics: "There is no use playing to the galleries. . . . Give good straight talk and let us get through." He readily answered questions about Tammany Hall but refused point-blank to discuss his personal investments, which he insisted were of no concern to the public, and he angrily denounced the committee for probing his family's finances, especially those of his son Frank, an executive of the Roebling Construction Company, which did business with the city. "This committee has made a set to destroy my two sons in the city," he growled, "and won't allow them to go into business, but I will keep you busy trying to do it." He challenged the committee to probe the law firm where Thomas Platt's son worked: "Go and examine Mr. Platt's family and find out what his boys are in, if you want to be honest. . . . Be fair, bring their books here."[50]

On his stock ownership in such firms as the Auto-Truck Company, he would not give an inch. "Isn't it a fact, Mr. Croker," asked Moss, "that simply because you are the leader of Tammany Hall, and because as such leader you control the city departments, you have been taken into [Auto-Truck] and given a large amount of stock to secure your influence; isn't that a fact?" "No, not at all," replied Croker. "You are away off."[51]

Moss was particularly concerned, for reasons that were not immediately apparent, with the Consolidated Ice Company, a corporation that did business in the city. He asked Croker if he held stock in Consolidated; the Boss at first refused to answer, then acknowledged that he once had but had transferred it to his wife some time back. When John F. Carroll, Croker's deputy at Tammany Hall, came on the stand he too declined to say whether he had any stock in Consolidated. Quite late in the hearings, on October 31, Moss entered into the record a seemingly irrelevant document: a circular put out by the Quincy Gas and Electric Corporation, of Quincy, Illinois, that listed as among its directors Charles W. Morse, president of the Consolidated Ice Company of New York, and John F. Carroll, deputy leader of Tammany Hall. Moss told the committee he simply wanted to show that there was a relationship between the two men. Nothing more, however, was said at the hearings about Consolidated.

The Committee's report, at the conclusion of the hearings, sailed into Croker. Calling him a dictator, it said the city's government was "no longer responsible to the people, but to that dictator. We see the central power, not the man who sits in the Mayor's chair, but the man who stands behind it. We see the same arbitrary power dictating appointments, directing officials, controlling boards. . . . We see incompetence and arrogance in high place. . . . We see the powers of government prostituted to protect criminals, to demoralize the police, to debauch the public conscience and to turn governmental functions into channels for private gain. The proof is conclusive, not that the public treasury has been directly robbed, but that great opportunities have been given by manipulations of public offices to enable favored individuals to work for their own personal benefit."[52] Soon thereafter, the *New York Times* published a detailed report alleging that the city's gambling-house operators were paying more than $3 million a year to a syndicate whose members were not named but which many New Yorkers knew was headed by Police Chief Bill Devery and Big Tim Sullivan.

Three months later, Frank Moss's veiled references to Consolidated Ice and friendly directors were suddenly made clear, and they brought explosive repercussions. The *New York World* had followed up on Moss's leads and found that Consolidated had been superseded by a much larger concern, the American Ice Company, also headed by Charles W. Morse, and that American had bought up every other ice company of consequence in New York City, giving it a virtual monopoly on ice sales in the area. Morse, whom one chronicler described as "an unscrupulous financier of dubious reputation,"[53] had been careful to gain the friendship of New York's most powerful politicians by allegedly handing them large blocks of stock, first in Consolidated and then in American, which would also explain Croker's hesitance about his holdings in Consolidated. In due course, the *World* learned that Mayor Van Wyck was the lucky possessor of stock worth at least $678,000, and his brother Augustus was in to the tune of about a third as much. Tammany's John F. Carroll owned stock worth around $500,000, and Croker and his (estranged) wife held twenty-five hundred shares, whose market value was perhaps $250,000. Even Brooklyn Boss Hugh McLaughlin had been cut in, plus several of his friends—and also Frank Platt, Boss Platt's son. The paper calculated that while Van Wyck's mayoral salary brought him $41.09 a day, his American stock earned $95 a day. Such largesse made Morse a very popular fellow, and Mayor Van Wyck and John Carroll were happy to travel with him all the way to bleak, frigid Maine in April 1900, with all expenses paid and opulent food and lodging provided, for the unlikely pleasure of inspecting his ice-making facilities.

Perhaps more important than these beneficiaries, however, were several other recipients of American stock, New York's dock commissioners, who included not only a key Tammany leader, Charles F. Murphy, but, of all people, Croker's real estate partner, Peter F. Meyer. These men were vital to Morse, as they controlled access to New York's docks and could thus ensure that the ice monopoly was enforced. Sure enough, the World found that many small ice dealers who had refused to sign up with American had been refused rights to unload ice at the piers, and some had seen their equipment demolished by city employees.

The World called the juggernaut the Ice Trust, and on April 4, 1900, it reported the clincher: the Trust had announced that it was doubling the price of ice in the city, from 30 cents per 100 pounds to 60 cents, citing an imminent "shortage" of the substance (the paper later found out the shortage hardly existed). And nothing could be done about it, for the competition had been largely wiped out. The docks were closed to all save American, and the Trust had the government of the country's largest city in its pocket.

The rage and resentment of New Yorkers was massive. No one could do without ice, and the poor especially could not afford the steeper price. The weather was warming up; what would happen in the hot summer? Would food spoilage bring epidemics? The World, taking advantage of a provision in the city charter that required any official to answer charges before a public examination (the provision dated from the time the Tweed frauds were exposed), forced Mayor Van Wyck and the dock commissioners to appear in court before Judge William J. Gaynor. They were evasive; Van Wyck said he had purchased some of his stock and borrowed to pay for the rest, but he produced no documentation and few people believed him. Meanwhile, the American Ice Company, observing the public indignation, announced it was reducing its price from 60 cents to 40 cents, due to "sharp competition," which clearly did not exist. Governor Roosevelt said he was considering exercising his statutory right to remove Van Wyck from office. (In the end he did not carry out the threat.)

The Ice Trust was a terrible black eye for Richard Croker and Tammany Hall. The Boss's handpicked mayor had betrayed his office, and the Tammany higher-ups had enriched themselves through a palpably dirty deal. But the worst aspect was that Croker and his friends had been caught making money at the expense of

their most important constituents, the poor people of the city. This
wasn't "honest graft"; it wasn't educating newcomers for citizenship,
as Crocker had discussed with Stead; it was taking money out of people's pockets. The Hall had always based its appeal on opposition to
the money interests and monopolies—what could it say now? As the
World reported on May 7, noting that a revolt was brewing in Tammany Hall itself, "Many prominent Tammanyites who do not own
stock in the great monopoly wish to know why Tammany Hall adopts
resolutions denouncing the wicked trusts while its leader and deputy
leader are financially and politically interested in the most selfish,
grasping and uncharitable of them all."[54]

The Boss professed to be unconcerned, although he did ease John
Carroll out of the deputy's job. Prudence might have persuaded him
to lie low for a while, as he had successfully done after the Lexow
investigation. Instead, he barged into a larger arena, national politics.

Back in 1896, when he had been absent from the country, Tammany Hall had opposed the Democratic nominee for president, William Jennings Bryan; Bryan lost to William McKinley. Coming up on
the 1900 election, Crocker sensed that Bryan's support remained
strong in New York City and that he therefore must back him this
time, and so he combined with his upstate friend, Senator Edward
Murphy, to force the Democratic state nominating convention to
endorse Bryan. He then moved on to deliver the New York delegation to Bryan at the national convention amid much hoopla.

Not only had he misread the mood of the nation, which was generally not partial to Bryan's free-silver policy, but he found himself personally injected into the campaign by Theodore Roosevelt, who had
been nominated for vice-president to run with McKinley. All over
the United States, Roosevelt taunted Crocker and was applauded for
it. An embarrassing moment for Bryan occurred during a rally in
Madison Square Garden three weeks before the election when, during an attack on monopolies and McKinley prosperity, the candidate
asked the crowd, "They say we are prosperous. Who's we?" Someone in the crowd yelled "Croker!" and the audience roared with
laughter.[55]

The Boss further hurt his cause by some remarks delivered at a
well-publicized press conference a few days before the election.
Claiming that the Republicans could win only by fraud, he said, "I
advise all Democrats to go to the polling places on election night,
count noses, and see that they get counted." He shook his fingers at
the reporters. "If the vote doesn't tally, let them go in, pull out the

fellows in charge, and stand them on their heads. I want you to print this."[56] Police Chief Devery at this point took it upon himself to issue an order that hinted of police bias at the polls, whereupon Roosevelt (who was still governor) informed Croker that he held him personally responsible for seeing that the election went off properly. The voting was uneventful, and although Bryan carried New York City, he lost the state and the nation. Another election had gone against Croker. His foray into national politics had been an error he could not afford.

Van Wyck's mayoralty still had another year to run, but it was discredited by the Mazet hearings and the Ice Trust revelations, and so Croker held out little hope for winning that election, either. At this point the Boss was stung by an open letter sent to Mayor Van Wyck by Episcopal Bishop Henry Potter, who was writing at the behest of a coalition of reformers. In it the bishop enumerated instances of vice and crime promoted by the police with Tammany support and challenged Croker to do something about it. The Boss reacted by naming a high-level Committee of Five ostensibly to find out whether Tammany was indeed culpable. The group was headed by Lewis Nixon, a wealthy and well-respected Tammany hand.

Events were moving too fast now, however, for even as resourceful a man as Richard Croker to cope with them. First, Theodore Roosevelt during his last days as governor issued an order removing New York's district attorney, Tammany's own Asa Bird Gardiner (the man who had yelled "To Hell with reform!"), from office for neglect of duty. Second, the state legislature abolished the office of chief of police, thus ousting Devery. Third, the Boss was facing renewed rebellion from Big Tim Sullivan, who had warned him that Nixon's probers had better stay out of the Bowery or there would be trouble. Croker gave in; the probers did not enter Sullivan's turf. Big Tim was hardly appeased, though. On hearing that Devery had been displaced, he went to Croker and demanded that his friend be somehow reinstated. Once again the Boss surrendered and ordered Van Wyck to name Devery a deputy police commissioner. But Big Tim continued his rebellion.

And the reformist opposition was now gaining strength. A new personality arrived on the scene: Judge William Travers Jerome, who had once been associated with Goff and Moss in the Lexow hearings. He had little respect for Tammany Hall. When Nixon applied to Jerome for a warrant to raid an alleged gambling house on Dey Street, the judge, sensing that Tammany might tip off the house ahead of time, put the warrant in his pocket and went there himself.

He found it operating in full cry, its customers including eight police-men. Jerome arrested a number of those present, set up an im-promptu court on the spot and dispensed justice; among the accused was a man who was reluctant to give his name but who turned out to be Maurice Holahan, the president of the Board of Public Works. Jerome's ploy made good newspaper copy and was followed by fur-ther raids, and presently Nixon's Committee of Five went out of business. Jerome himself became a candidate for district attorney on the new Republican-Fusion ticket.

The ticket was to be headed once again by Seth Low, whom Platt finally decided would have to receive his support. But the sparks of the campaign were provided by Jerome, an incisive, effective speaker who rushed tirelessly about the city arousing audiences to a fever pitch against Tammany Hall. Meanwhile, Big Tim Sullivan chal-lenged Croker head-on. An old ally of Croker's, Patrick "Paddy" Divver, was up for reelection as Tammany district leader on the Lower East Side, and Sullivan put up his friend Tom Foley to oppose Divver in the primary. For weeks the two fought for votes, rushing to beat each other to weddings, funerals, and other events, and freely spending money to win support. When primary day arrived, gangs of Sullivan's toughest troops took over the polling places. Divver's men tried in vain to dislodge them but were beaten up, with the police standing by doing nothing. The result was a foregone conclusion: Foley won by a margin of three to one. "Croker ain't the whole thing!"[57] a triumphant Sullivan told the press. The Boss had been thrown out of the Lower East Side, one of Tammany's key strongholds.

There remained the mayoral election in 1901. Seeking to blunt the reformers' attack, Croker looked for help across the East River in Brooklyn, to Hugh McLaughlin. Together they came up with a can-didate they thought had a chance: Edward M. Shepard, a capable, energetic lawyer who, ironically, had come out for Low four years previously, denouncing Tammany Hall in the process—a transgres-sion now forgiven. Shepard waged a creditable campaign, but the odds were too severe. On election day the turnout was tremendous, and Low won in a landslide.

A morose Croker, holed up at the Wigwam on election night, chewed on his cigar and waited nervously as the returns came in. Of those present, only Big Tim Sullivan was not gloomy. At one point, unable to resist the urge, he went over to Croker and said, "Well, Boss, you see *my* district came through OK." Croker nodded but said nothing. Some time later the Boss broke his silence. "It would appear that Shepard is beaten," he said. "A change is a good thing sometimes; but Tammany Hall will be here when we are all gone."[58]

He was right: it would endure. He resigned—for the last time—his chairmanship of the Tammany Finance Committee and renounced politics. Returning to England, he concentrated on his racing ventures. In 1907, he had the exquisite pleasure of seeing his horse Orby win the Derby, Britain's most prestigious race. (King Edward VII declined, however, to issue Croker the customary winner's invitation to the postrace Derby Dinner.) Croker was now living on a newly purchased estate in Glencairn, Ireland, and spending winters in West Palm Beach, Florida. His wife died in 1914, and some time later, at age seventy-three, he married twenty-three-year-old Beula Benton Edmondson, who was part Cherokee Indian.

Richard Croker finally died at Glencairn in 1922 at the age of seventy-nine. It had been twenty years since the day he had relinquished the reins of Tammany Hall under conditions that led many people, including Croker himself, to believe the institution moribund. But Tammany, as it had so often in the past, refused to play dead. On the contrary, in the intervening years it had risen phoenixlike and gone on to new triumphs under new leadership, on a tack very different from the one Croker had chosen for it.

8

THE SILENT ONE

THE STORY IS TOLD OF CHARLES FRANCIS MURPHY, who succeeded Richard Croker as Boss of Tammany Hall, that during one of the Hall's Fourth of July celebrations a reporter happened to notice that Murphy was not joining in the singing of the national anthem.

"What's the matter with the Boss," the reporter asked a Tammany functionary. "Can't he sing?"

"Sure he can," the man replied. "Why, the chief used to sing with a quartet in his younger days. He can yodel some, take it from me."

"Why didn't he join in 'The Star Spangled Banner' then?"

"Perhaps," said the Tammany hand with a wink, "he didn't want to commit himself."[1]

Charles Francis Murphy spent a lifetime doing his best not to tip his hand. To say he was a man of few words is putting it mildly. As one biographer observed, Murphy's life was "a masterpiece of reticence."[2] In the twenty-two years during which he directed the most powerful and notorious political machine in the United States, he gave virtually no public statements, made no formal speeches, granted no interviews of consequence, and left no records. Croker, Murphy felt, had talked entirely too much; that was not the best way. When responding to questions from the press, from public figures, or even from ordinary citizens he habitually gave one of three answers: "Yes," "No,'" or "I'll look into it." He is not known to have ever written a letter: man-to-man communication, preferably conducted in private, was his preferred mode. He never raised his voice, and an acquaintance recalled that the Boss's voice was so quiet he often could not be heard from more than five feet away. Total silence had much to recommend it, he felt, and he was a master of the art of delayed response. He could outwait anyone.

"Most of the troubles of the world," Murphy reputedly remarked to a protégé, "could be avoided if men opened their minds instead of their mouths."[3] Murphy's mind was always open, and it was a marvel. He was a political strategist of the first order and had a profound understanding of human nature. Occupying the office formerly held by the flamboyant Tweed and the overbearing Croker, this quiet, cautious, bespectacled man ended up achieving far more than either of them had, with all their bluster. He not only was responsible for the election of three mayors of New York, three governors of the state, and two U.S. senators, but he altered the direction of Tammany. For the first time, Tammany used the force of its influence to support beneficial social legislation. Two young men he encouraged, Alfred E. Smith and Robert F. Wagner, became public servants of great national influence and accomplishment. In the words of Tammany historians Alfred Connable and Edward Silverfarb, "Mister Murphy (few addressed him otherwise) gradually became known as the most perceptive and intelligent leader in Tammany history, with an unsurpassed feel for power and its uses, a superb instinct for timing, and a remarkable ability to cut through surface personalities and judge the prospects and motives of the men beneath. As a political chess player, he never met his match."[4] Tweed died in jail, Kelly was barely remembered at his death, and Croker spent the last years of his life in virtual exile. The funeral of the silent, enigmatic Charles Murphy, held in St. Patrick's Cathedral on April 25, 1924, was attended by every top-hatted dignitary in the city and state, and an estimated fifty thousand persons lined nearby streets to pay their respects to a man few people had really known.

What made Murphy's achievements all the more impressive was that the conditions under which Tammany operated were being steadily restricted. New laws were making it more difficult to steal an election: tighter regulations governing the naturalization process cut down the supply of new immigrants ready to blindly vote the party line, rigid sign-in requirements for voters virtually ruled out repeaters, and the introduction of the secret ballot provided protection for those who did not choose to vote as Tammany desired. More and more city jobs were coming under the purview of civil service and so were not subject to patronage.

Perhaps more important than these reforms was the city's recent annexation—in 1898—of Brooklyn, Queens, and Staten Island to create Greater New York. Instead of dominating a whole city, Tammany Hall now directly controlled only one borough, Manhattan. The other boroughs, Brooklyn most notably, had their own party organizations, which Tammany might hope to dominate but which could never be taken for granted. Murphy found himself having to negotiate with all of them; no longer could a Tammany Hall Boss merely dictate his wishes.

All of this took hard work, but Charles Francis Murphy was used to applying himself. Born in 1858 to poor, devout, Irish Catholic immigrant parents who lived in the so-called Gashouse District (named for the giant tanks of the Consolidated Gas Company) in Manhattan's East Twenties, he quit school at fourteen to work in a wire factory and then as a caulker in Roach's shipyard on East Ninth Street, while earning part-time pay helping out in a saloon. In 1875, at the age of seventeen, he landed a job as a horsecar driver on the Twenty-third Street crosstown line. Legend has it that he employed a sly trick to get a stubborn horse to move. He would remove the horse's bridle, quietly replace it, and shout for the animal to move on. Thinking its tack had been removed because it was at the end of its run, the horse invariably went forward. In a way, this was just the kind of cajolery that Murphy would later use on political candidates.

In 1880, with $500 he had saved from his earnings as a driver, Murphy opened a small saloon at Nineteenth Street and Avenue A. Known as Charlie's Place, it offered a glass of beer and a cup of soup for just 5 cents. Murphy himself tended bar, an alert but impassive presence ready to listen patiently—a trait for which he would be well known in the future—to the dock and gas workers who frequented the place. The bar was unusual in two respects: no profanity was allowed, and no women. Charles Murphy was a faithful churchgoer with a strong moral sense, and he knew that the women who hung around bars in those days were all too likely to be prostitutes, whom he wanted none of. Although straitlaced attitudes of this kind were not the ones expected to attract many beer-drinking customers, Murphy's bar prospered, and over the next few years he acquired three more, which brought him a handsome income. One of them, at Twentieth Street and Second Avenue, became the headquarters of the Anawanda Club, a Tammany outpost. Murphy joined the club and became a member of Tammany Hall.

One incident shortly after Murphy joined the Hall brought him to the attention of Tammany higher-ups. A friend of Murphy's, Ed Hagan, the state assemblyman for the Gashouse area, came to him for advice. Tammany had refused to back him for renomination; what should he do? Murphy pondered the situation for a moment, then gave a curt response: "Run independent." With Murphy acting as his campaign manager, Hagan won, defeating the Hall's candidate. It was the only time Murphy ever strayed from party regularity. Hagan was the Tammany district leader and Murphy became his assistant. In 1892, when Hagan died, the thirty-four-year-old Murphy took over the district.

As a leader he again stood out. These were the wide-open 1890s, when Tammany was waxing rich on the kind of graft revealed in the Lexow hearings, but Murphy's district, he decreed, was to be "morally clean." Murphy would have nothing to do with the graft resulting from gambling, prostitution, or illegal saloons. Already he was known for his silence—and for listening. Each night after nine o'clock he would station himself by a lamppost outside the Anawanda Club and hear what anyone wished to tell him.

He was also developing a reputation for personal charity, often bestowed anonymously. After the Blizzard of 1888, for instance, he persuaded the Tammany General Committee to donate $4,000 to a relief fund and, unannounced, provided most of that himself. Many years later, in 1914, when he was already practically a legend as leader of the Hall, he came home from a banquet one freezing night and found a fire raging in a hotel at Eighteenth Street and Third Avenue, a block away from his own house on Seventeenth Street. He instantly began directing relief efforts on behalf of the hundred-odd inadequately clad hotel guests milling around the icy streets, directing them to a nearby restaurant or to his home, ordering police and bystanders to break into nearby stores that could provide clothing (assuring them he would personally pay for the clothing and for damages, which he later did), and even carrying small children himself to shelter. Only when everyone had been provided for did he start home, his evening clothes in disarray and his top hat battered.

When Croker's Tammany Hall got Robert Van Wyck elected mayor in 1897, Murphy's diligence was rewarded with an appointment as one of New York's four dock commissioners. While on the

board, Murphy became a close friend of fellow commissioner J. Sergeant Cram, a Harvard graduate, who was said to have taught him
how to wear a dress suit as well as "how to eat peas with a fork," as
someone put it.[5] For the rest of his life, in addition to being called
Mister Murphy, he was happy to be addressed as "Commissioner."
The Dock post was the only official position he ever held, but it was
highly profitable. The commission, responsible for leasing piers to
commercial concerns, had wide powers and many businesses were
willing to pay liberally for special concessions. Murphy was in fact a
commissioner at the time of the celebrated Ice Trust Scandal in 1900
and had evidently acquired 500 shares of American Ice Company
stock, worth perhaps $50,000. Whether or not he paid for his stock
was never divulged, and in any case, his holding was ignored in the
uproar over Van Wyck's several thousand shares of American.

Such devious ways of making money seemed entirely appropriate
to him. Although he abhorred vice and corruption, he thought there
was nothing wrong with "honest graft," as fellow Tammanyite
George Washington Plunkitt had termed it. In 1901, while still a
dock commissioner, Murphy and his brother, John, organized the
New York Contracting & Trucking Company, whose officers included two political cronies, one of them a Tammany alderman
named James E. Gaffney. Of the company's 100 shares, John Murphy, Gaffney, and the other politico each owned five; the remaining
85 were reported to be held by a party who wished to remain anonymous. It was widely assumed in New York that the anonymous party
was Charles Murphy, and although some years after he became
leader of Tammany Hall he denied that he had any financial interest
in the firm, it is quite possible that he transferred his securities to
someone else prior to the inquiry.

In any event, New York Contracting was a shining example of the
way money could be made if one had the right connections. It leased
a number of piers from the city (courtesy of the commissioner) and
made a 5,000 percent profit on them. When the Pennsylvania Railroad was constructing its station in the West Thirties, it had difficulty
obtaining a franchise from the city to dig the approaches to its tun-
nels; somehow the Board of Aldermen, on which James Gaffney held
great power, was holding it up. Then suddenly the railroad got its
franchise—after awarding the excavation contract to New York Contracting, whose bid had actually been $400,000 higher than that of a
competitor, and whose owners had virtually no experience in the contracting business.

In 1904, using roughly the same tactics, New York Contracting won a contract worth $6 million to construct rail lines in the Bronx for the New York, New Haven, and Hartford railroad. The award, a railroad executive later stated, had been made "to avoid friction with the city," because certain powers in Tammany Hall "had to be taken care of."[6] By 1905, New York Contracting or its associated firms had allegedly won contracts via the city approval process totaling $15 million. (An interesting sidelight of the New Haven affair is that the Board of Aldermen's delay in granting the contract caused so much outcry that the New York State legislature was moved to amend the city's charter so as to take the franchise-awarding power away from the aldermen and give it to the Board of Estimate and Apportionment—which thereby acquired the huge power and influence that it held until it was finally abolished in 1989.)

Whether or not he benefited from New York Contracting's more impressive deals, Charles Murphy was very well off by the end of the Van Wyck administration. When appointed to the Board of Dock Commissioners in 1898, he was said to have been worth $400,000; four years later he was reputedly worth almost $1 million. (His total worth never got much higher than that, however.)

This laconic man was nevertheless still not considered a likely permanent successor to Richard Croker when Croker left the Hall in early 1902 after Van Wyck's defeat. There is reason to believe, in fact, that Croker, departing for England, had not truly intended to sever all his ties to Tammany. On his departure he designated as leader of the Hall Lewis Nixon, the wealthy and proper Tammany dignitary who had previously headed Croker's abortive antivice Committee of Five. Most observers thought Nixon could not last, and they were right. After just four months, on May 14, 1902, Nixon called a meeting of the Tammany Executive Committee and announced his resignation. "I could not retain the leadership of Tammany Hall and at the same time retain my self-respect," he said. A kitchen cabinet of Croker's friends had thwarted him. "Every act of mine has been cabled to England before it became effective . . . and when I rebelled I found that at every turn I would be opposed by this coterie of interferers."[7] In his stead, the committee appointed a triumvirate consisting of a district leader named Daniel F. McMahon, Bronx Borough President Louis F. Haffen (one of the few Tammanyites to survive the election of 1901), and Charles Francis Murphy.

The triumvirate lasted hardly longer than Nixon. Somehow Murphy's willingness to work hard and his aura of authority quickly made the group superfluous: on September 19, 1902, he was declared sole leader. "It was like an eruption of nature," Haffen and McMahon told reporters. "When anything was to be done, Murphy was on the job; no one ever asked for him in vain; he seemed to have no time for himself, but all his time for Tammany."[8]

Murphy soon declared his modus operandi. "I won't do much talking," he said. "I will be at Tammany Hall every day, and spend the hours between 3 and 5 o'clock in the afternoon at work. There is plenty of work to be done, and the less talking the better."[9]

Two things needed to be done as soon as possible, Murphy believed. The first was to eliminate the dissension that had racked Tammany during Croker's final months of command. One potential rival actually posed no threat. Big Tim Sullivan, who had warred with Croker, had no real designs on the top leadership post. He was content to rule his Lower East Side domain in his own inimitable way, and, besides, he and Murphy were good friends—their districts adjoined each other.

A more dangerous challenge, however, was represented by the swaggering former police chief, Bill Devery, who expressed open contempt for Murphy. "It would take a bigger man than what Charlie Murphy is," he said, "to keep Tammany moving." Devery was extraordinarily popular in his own district, partly for the lavish parties he liked to throw featuring free beer and sandwiches and endless entertainments for all comers, and he was well known throughout the city for his effusive but tantalizingly vague testimony in the 1900 Mazet hearings. But to Murphy he symbolized everything that was disgraceful and politically ruinous in Croker's regime, and he had to be sanitized. Examining the Tammany bylaws, Murphy found that a district leader could be drummed out of the Executive Committee if he was found to be "objectionable," and with Big Tim Sullivan's help he persuaded the committee to expel the man. Devery could not believe it, but he never again posed a threat.

Murphy's second imperative was to sever the link between Tammany Hall and commercialized vice. This would not be easy, for the link had lined many a Tammany pocket, but to Murphy it constituted, if nothing else, bad politics—it had lost too many elections. To a meeting of district leaders soon after taking office he announced he would break any leader who was seen to be profiting from red-light houses or similar activities, and he said there was one man present whom he meant to make an example of. He did not name the man, but everyone knew he meant Martin Engel, leader of the Eighth district. Within twenty-four hours Murphy had dispatched Big Florry Sullivan, a cousin of Big Tim's, to the Eighth, and Engel was out. Within a few days the Eighth's red-light houses were shut down. Gambling operations were not affected, but Murphy had made his point, and thereafter Tammany's connections with prostitution were markedly reduced throughout the city.

The soul of efficiency, Murphy soon developed a daily and weekly routine that almost never varied—he wanted people to know where to reach him, as he had during the evenings by the lamppost outside the Anawanda Club. Most mornings and late afternoons he was to be found at the Wigwam on Fourteenth Street, sitting by his rolltop desk and listening to all comers. One night each week he held open house for his district leaders, who would approach him singly and present their problems. He never took notes, but the leaders knew their requests would be tended to. Charles Murphy never forgot a thing.

Each day at noon he repaired via hansom cab (later a Fiat motorcar) to Delmonico's Restaurant uptown, on Forty-fourth Street just off Fifth Avenue, where the atmosphere was different. Delmonico's was an elegant establishment that catered to the city's rich and powerful. Murphy lunched and received visitors in a private room on the second floor to which access was guarded. The Wigwam was for the lowly and the routine; Delmonico's was where Murphy conferred with the more influential members of Tammany, with prominent officeholders and prospective candidates, and with New York's movers and shakers. Visitors, after being approved by Smiling Phil Donohue, a boyhood friend of the Commissioner, would be ushered in to an ornate chamber with scarlet wallpaper, a thick red rug, and a big gilt-framed mirror, to find Murphy seated at a long table in a heavy red plush mahogany armchair. A newspaper at the time of Murphy's death said of the room, "Nearly every important financier in the city is said to have entered it at one time or another," and it was known far and wide as "The Scarlet Room of Mystery."[10]

Although the Commissioner never seemed to stop working, such relaxation as he permitted himself was to be found at his summer home, a fifty-acre estate at Good Ground (today's Hampton Bays) on Long Island. Murphy bought the spread in 1902 for $35,000, and it included a spacious house and a "farm" boasting a few horses and cows. Around it he built a nine-hole golf course on which he pursued the only sport he felt he had time for. In 1902 Murphy also married, for the first time, a widow whom he had known since childhood, and sometimes the Murphys traveled with Mrs. Murphy's daughter to vacation at French Lick Springs, Indiana, where the Commissioner would play golf. When dining with his family in the hotel's main salon, observers noted, he would go through the entire meal without saying a word. The propriety he exuded was formidable. "I would have just as soon thought of telling an off-color story to a lady," said a newspaper reporter, "as I would to Mr. Murphy."[11]

The key measure of a Tammany Boss, of course, was not his working methods or personality but his ability to win elections, still the Hall's main reason for existence. Murphy's overall record during his twenty-two-year tenure was mixed—which should not be surprising in view of the changing political climate in the America of the first part of the twentieth century. After some triumphs at the polls during his first years, he entered a more difficult period in which for a while it almost looked as if he would be swept from power. Only in his last seven or eight years did he achieve the string of successes that were to make him almost a living legend.

His first test went well. In 1902, just two months after he had been granted sole command of Tammany, there was to be a New York gubernatorial election. Murphy picked the city's comptroller, Bird S. Coler, to run against the Republican candidate, Benjamin B. Odell. Coler lost by a narrow margin, but in so doing piled up a 122,000-vote plurality in the city, far larger than anyone had expected.

The mayoralty, however, was everything. In 1903 the incumbent, Republican Seth Low, who had ousted Robert Van Wyck from City Hall, was up for reelection. Low was vulnerable. Although he had governed efficiently and had somewhat reduced the level of corruption that had characterized Van Wyck's time, he was personally unappealing, with an upper-class manner and an artificial-looking smile. In addition, New Yorkers had become impatient with the enforcement of blue laws and with other puritanical policies of the regime. Nevertheless, Murphy knew he could not pluck out of nowhere another pliant nobody like Van Wyck. The candidate must be both capable and respectable. He found his man in George B. McClellan, Jr., the son of the Civil War general, a solid Tammany hand who had served briefly as president of the Board of Aldermen and had represented an East Side district in Congress for several terms. Smart, politically savvy, aristocratic but devoted to his congressional duties, McClellan reluctantly consented to give up his seat and run.

In filling the lesser openings, Murphy pulled a fast one on the opposition. He persuaded two current officeholders, Comptroller Edward M. Grout and Board of Aldermen President Charles F. Fornes, both of them running on the Fusion ticket, to accept Tammany endorsement. The Fusionists cried bloody murder and dropped the two men from their slate. Never mind, the damage had been done, and in the election McClellan (with Grout and Fornes) won handily. On election night, with Murphy and McClellan watching the victory celebration on Broadway, McClellan is reported to have remarked, "Charley, I wonder if they'll be cheering me two years hence." Murphy hesitated for a moment and then replied, "If they're not, it won't be my fault, George. It'll be yours."[12]

The number one question was what kinds of patronage demands Murphy would make on McClellan. It was a delicate matter: Tammany felt it must receive a large share of the spoils, but the new mayor must not appear subservient to the Hall, if indeed he would ever consent to such a role—which McClellan, a proud man, certainly would not. And a successful McClellan administration, even with reduced Tammany patronage, could shine the Hall's tarnished image. At the outset, however, was the possibility of trouble: McClellan insisted on naming his own people to most of the top posts, such as corporation counsel and commissioners of police, street cleaning, and health. "For other offices," McClellan said later, "I accepted the candidates of the organization. Murphy's candidates, while almost all district leaders, seemed to be a very decent lot."[13] As time went on he began to modify that judgment and at length decided most suffered from "painful mediocrity."[14] Murphy sat tight.

McClellan's mayoral record was creditable. There was no resumption of large-scale vice and corruption as the Republicans had predicted. And Murphy, for his part, was beginning to eliminate blackmail and saloon graft as income producers for the Hall. As McClellan's first term drew to a close in 1905, Murphy, though a bit disenchanted with the mayor, was willing to go along with his renomination. Complicating the picture at this point, however, was a strident new figure destined to play a substantial role in the city's politics for the next two decades: the wealthy young newspaper publisher William Randolph Hearst, who had served in Congress and now declared his candidacy for mayor.

Hearst's notorious latter-day reputation as a sensationalistic journalist has obscured his early ties to the progressive movement. Throughout the United States at the turn of the century there was widespread popular indignation against what was described as the repressive manipulations of giant corporations and their ties to political bosses of both major parties. In New York City such sentiments were

voiced by the Municipal Ownership League, whose members campaigned for public ownership of utilities and transit lines, which
would presumably bring lower rates and fares. Hearst, a maverick
Democrat, was the founder of the league. In his newspapers, the
Morning Journal and the *American,* he attacked both McClellan, for
his espousal of private ownership of the city's new subway, and Murphy, for his alleged tie to New York Contracting. Cartoons in his
papers showed Murphy in convict's stripes, and New Yorkers began
calling the campaign "Moiphy voisus Hoist."[15]

Hearst's attacks on Murphy were so pointed that McClellan, put
on the defensive, began promising that if reelected he would act independently of Tammany Hall. Undeterred, Murphy continued to support him, partly because a recent charter amendment had lengthened
the mayor's term of office from two years to four, making the upcoming election a bad one to lose. When McClellan barely eked out a
four thousand-vote plurality over Hearst, many suspected the victory
was fraudulent. Hearst demanded a recount, which failed to alter the
outcome.

The publisher remained a threat, however. Not only were his
newspapers popular and influential, but the Municipal Ownership
League's program was making effective inroads among the city's
poor, whom Tammany liked to think were its mainstay. The following year, 1906, Murphy decided to appease Hearst by backing him as
the Democratic nominee for governor—a move that irritated Mc-
Clellan, who had fastened his own eyes on Albany. With Murphy's
support, Hearst won the nomination but lost the election to the Republican nominee, Charles Evans Hughes. Murphy naturally made
no comment on the outcome, but he must have been pleased, as he
had accomplished three things of considerable importance. First, his
ability to secure the gubernatorial nomination for Hearst showed that
he was close to controlling the Democratic party statewide. Second,
Hearst's loss blunted the threat from the publisher, at least temporarily. Third, and most important, by throwing his support to Hearst
Murphy espoused the basic aims of the Municipal Ownership
League. In retrospect this can be seen as the first step in Murphy's—
and thus Tammany's—move toward backing social reform programs,
a move that would bring Tammany Hall a popularity and respect it
had up to that time rarely achieved. In a losing year, these were no
mean achievements.

Meanwhile, relations with Mayor McClellan were fast deteriorating. Starting his second term, McClellan followed up on his cam-

paign promises by dismissing the Tammany appointees whom he had found wanting and replacing them with persons opposed to the Hall. This was repugnant to Murphy, who felt—justifiably—that the mayor would never have gotten where he was without Tammany support. But worse was to come. The city was just now embarking on a $100 million expansion of its water supply system, reaching out to tap vast areas in the Catskill Mountains. It was a huge project that created a great many jobs. McClellan permitted Tammany to fill none of them.

Finally, acting on reports of inefficiency and wastage in the offices of various borough presidents, McClellan assigned his commissioner of accounts, a young reformer named John Purroy Mitchel, to investigate. Mitchel uncovered massive waste and fraud, and as a result Governor Hughes removed from office both the Manhattan borough president, John Ahearn, who was a close associate of Murphy, and the Bronx borough president, Louis Haffen, the onetime associate of Murphy in the short-lived Tammany triumvirate. (A third borough president, Joseph Bermel of Queens, was not removed but resigned his office on the basis of charges brought by Mitchel. He too was a Tammany appointee.)

These actions hurt. The mayor had wounded Murphy. As a member of Tammany, technically in good standing, McClellan now tried to get the Hall's Executive Committee to oust Murphy as leader. It did not work. Murphy, examining the bylaws, found it was permissible to enlarge the Executive Committee. He thereby named some of his friends to the group, and with the new votes defeated the move.

For the rest of McClellan's administration, there was no contact between Tammany and City Hall. By the 1909 election, Murphy decided he needed a mayoral candidate who stood for integrity and, if possible, for a modicum of at least declared independence from the machine. He got perhaps more than he asked for in his choice for the nomination, state Supreme Court Justice William Jay Gaynor.

Irascible, opinionated, humorous, malicious, the white-bearded, austere Gaynor was one of the most capable and hardworking chief executives the city has ever had. Among New York's mayors, says his biographer, "He towers as a great unorthodox figure, a man of enormous but erratic ability, a vivid and sometimes frightening personality, and with an unyielding sense of public duty."[16] He had come to Brooklyn from upstate as a young lawyer in the 1870s, and, after developing a solid reputation for his successful handling of suits against the city, was elected to the state Supreme Court in 1893. As a judge, Gaynor was efficient and fair, but a terror; lawyers cringed before his withering criticisms of their courtroom behavior. He never made any attempt to be ingratiating. Once while he was mayor, a newspaper reporter tried to get an interview with him (he made a policy of refusing all such requests) by showing up at his summer home in St. James, Long Island. Gaynor looked at the young man's card, gave it back to him and said, "Never heard of you. I suggest you get the hell off my front porch."[17] One would hardly suspect that a cantankerous person of this sort would think to enter politics. But Gaynor, for all his oddities, was ambitious and craved higher office.

One reason Murphy wanted Gaynor was to placate the Boss of Brooklyn's Democratic organization, Patrick McCarren, who detested the Commissioner. In trying to unite the city's Democrats, Murphy had an uneven task. He had never worried about the Bronx, which for years was under the control of his friend Louis Haffen, and both Queens and Richmond (Staten Island) were still so sparsely populated as to be of negligible political importance. But Brooklyn's Democrats guarded their independence zealously. Under McCarren their slogan was The Tiger Shall Not Cross The Bridge. When the Tiger crossed over to pick Gaynor, they were pleased and McCarren himself was pacified; then just before the election McCarren died. His successor, John H. McCooey, "came docilely into the fold with all his cohorts,"[18] as Murphy's biographer Nancy Weiss put it. For the moment, Brooklyn was aboard.

There was nothing docile about William Jay Gaynor, however. During the campaign he paid a visit to the Wigwam, where he said to those assembled to greet him, "So this is Tammany Hall. It is the first time I was ever here. I did not even know where it was. I had to telephone before leaving my home to find out exactly how to get here. But if this is Tammany Hall, where is the tiger—that tiger which they say is going to swallow me up? If there happens to be any swallowing up, it is not at all unlikely that I may be on the outside of the tiger."[19] There was nervous laughter on the platform, though Murphy's reaction is not recorded.

After the election, in which he defeated Hearst, Mayor-elect Gaynor at first seemed pleasantly disposed to cooperate with the Hall. "I fear," he said, "there are a good many people in this town who do not know Charles F. Murphy. Some of them seem to think he has horns and hoofs. I can only say of him what I have seen. He fully realizes that a political organization cannot survive and grow broader on patronage alone, without political ideas and virtue, but must shrivel up and die of worse than dry rot. I would advise some good women and clergymen who are writing to me about Charles F. Murphy . . . to go up and see him. They may be surprised."[20]

Clearly, however, he felt little obligation to do Murphy's bidding, for although Tammany had gotten him elected, the Fusion opposition had swept all the other high-level city offices. When his appointments were announced, none were found to be courtesy of Tammany Hall. Said Murphy, "The new officials are all good men—I guess." Mayor Gaynor, asked what he was prepared to give the Boss, said, "Suppose that we give him a few kind words."[21]

He proceeded to act in a distinctly unkind way toward Tammany. Over the first few months he slashed the city's payroll by about $700,000, eliminating some four hundred politicians, most of them Tammanyites. New York's newspapers, which had been wary of him during the campaign, applauded his efforts (only the Hearst papers remained opposed). There seemed to be few crumbs for Tammany Hall. Said an associate of Murphy's some years later, "I will say this about Mayor Gaynor—he did more to break up the Democratic organization than any other man ever has in this city."[22]

Nine months into his term, Gaynor experienced a tragedy that heightened his ill-humor. Embarking on a transatlantic liner for a vacation in Europe, he was shot at by an embittered Docks Department employee. The bullet entered his neck. He survived but his doctors were unable to remove the bullet, which remained in his throat causing him continued distress; his coughing fits might last half an hour. (In a display of macabre humor he once invited someone to reach down into his throat and feel the bullet.) At a time when the city's problems called for patience and understanding, he became increasingly bitter and vindictive.

A concern that called for special patience was the continuing corruption of the city's police, highlighted by the murder on July 16, 1912, of a big-time gambler named Herman Rosenthal. Gunned down by four hoodlums as he was leaving a restaurant near Times Square, Rosenthal had been a marked man ever since he started relating, in the pages of the World, how he had been double-crossed by Lieutenant Charles Becker, head of the police's antigambling squad. Becker, said Rosenthal, had promised to protect him in return for sizable cash payments, but Becker not only had one of Rosenthal's parlors raided but was unable to prevent Rosenthal's indictment by a grand jury; Becker had, in other words, welshed on their deal. It turned out that Becker—as the World subsequently reported—had arranged for Rosenthal's elimination. It also was discovered that both Mayor Gaynor and his police commissioner, a pleasant young man named Rhinelander Waldo, had received anonymous complaints about Becker but had done nothing about them. There were cries for Waldo's resignation but Gaynor refused to fire him. When a committee of aldermen undertook to investigate the Police Department and invited Gaynor to testify, he defended his commissioner with great spirit and later suggested that "mentally and morally Waldo could carry a whole cart load of [aldermen] in his breeches pocket without knowing that they were there."[23] Commissioner Waldo stayed on.

The entire Becker-Rosenthal affair affected Tammany Hall only slightly: Rosenthal's gambling activities had been partly financed by Tammany's own Big Tim Sullivan. It grieved Murphy, who had been working to disentangle the Hall from police corruption. It was, nevertheless, the last such scandal of Murphy's leadership period. And although he was getting precious little out of Gaynor, things were decidedly looking up for him on the state level. In 1910, when Republican governor Charles Evans Hughes had completed two terms, Murphy successfully backed an upstate Democrat, John A. Dix, for the job and saw him elected. The grateful Dix spent his whole two-year term without denying any request Murphy made of him. Then the Commissioner's string of statewide successes was suddenly and disastrously cut by the incredible saga of William Sulzer.

Casting about for a gubernatorial candidate to succeed Dix—whose mediocrity was all too obvious—Murphy looked for someone with a distinctly liberal cast. For although the Republican nominee, Job E. Hedges, posed no danger, the new Progressive party, founded by former president Theodore Roosevelt, had nominated the well-heeled Oscar S. Straus (his family owned Macy's department store). Straus would appeal to large numbers of Jewish voters normally faithful to Tammany. At length, Murphy settled on Congressman William Sulzer, a hitherto undeviating Tammany politician whose East Side Manhattan district was heavily Jewish. Sulzer was attractive and something of a spellbinder. But he was unpredictable. Murphy would later state that the choice was "the greatest mistake of my life," a judgment no one can gainsay.

Tall and striking, with rugged features and an unruly shock of hair, Sulzer had once been told that he resembled Henry Clay and he thereafter consciously imitated the great Kentuckian, wearing a frock coat and mimicking the man's every gesture. He was vain and self-important. In interviews with reporters, he orated. "Sulzer never sat down at all," recalled one reporter who had merely asked his opinion on some matter. "He strode on long, thin legs, back and forth across a space about four feet wide, spouting words, gesturing with upraised hand or clenched quivering fist. . . ."[24] He professed to be a friend of all humanity; a Washington reporter said of him, "When it comes to preserving our liberties, William is a whole canning factory."[25] His record as a congressman was good, but he had never second-guessed either Richard Croker or (up to this point) Charles Murphy, and few people took him seriously. When Big Tim Sullivan heard that Murphy had picked Sulzer, he said to the Boss, "You can't do that. . . . He doesn't amount to anything. . . . We treat him down on the Bowery as a joke."[26] But Murphy was not dissuaded, and Sulzer was nominated and elected.

Upon being inaugurated in January 1913, and taking possession of the People's House, as he renamed the executive mansion, Sulzer lost no time trying to prove he was free of Tammany control. He solemnly announced that he was now the leader of the Democratic party in the state and would take orders from no one—a statement that must have amused Boss Murphy. Launching full-scale investigations into several state administrative departments, he found evidence of widespread waste and fraud that purportedly implicated Tammany-affiliated contractors. Within a few weeks, he dismissed a number of department heads, including the state highways superintendent. He was also rejecting all of Murphy's suggestions for high-level appointments, and when Murphy asked him to name his onetime business associate, James Gaffney (of New York Contracting and Trucking), as the new highways superintendent, he refused. Murphy said it was a serious matter: "I want you to appoint Gaffney. It is an organization matter and I will appreciate it."[27] The governor would not budge. The stage was set for a confrontation.

If the conflict had been limited to matters of patronage, it might conceivably have been resolved—or ignored, the way Murphy had chosen not to actively dispute either McClellan's or Gaynor's apostasy. For Sulzer was proposing all manner of progressive legislation that Tammany Hall found perfectly acceptable and was even in a position to encourage. But there was no question that Murphy was concerned about the revelations being turned up by investigators probing construction contracts with Tammany-associated firms (would New York Contracting and Trucking be implicated?). Sulzer was a loose cannon that could do plenty of damage. And then the governor proceeded to escalate the dispute by introducing a direct primary bill that would eliminate nominating conventions for all candidates statewide—institutions that were dear to the hearts of Republican as well as Democratic bosses. Murphy's state legislators had already introduced an election reform bill that extended the primary system but stopped short of encompassing top state officials. The bill passed and Sulzer vetoed it. He would accept nothing but his own bill.

Just why he chose such a headlong course is not hard to discern. Although a creature of Tammany Hall throughout his political career, he knew that once he broke with Murphy on any matter as important as patronage Tammany Hall would drop him as a candidate for re-election. It was imperative that he develop his own power base by turning against the machine and appealing directly to the people, while at the same time establishing a route (via the direct primary) whereby he could be renominated without being subject to a Tammany-dominated convention. Besides, who could tell, the path might lead to higher office. He had only to look at the neighboring state of New Jersey, where Woodrow Wilson had defied the state bosses and survived and had gone on to capture the White House. The prospect was a heady one. The trouble was that Sulzer was not Wilson. He was not smart or wise enough, and he was also vulnerable, as Murphy may already have known.

What made the situation appear even stranger was the fact that, despite his bombastic denunciations of Tammany, Sulzer was periodically slipping away from Albany or from major events in the city to confer with Murphy at Delmonico's and work out compromises on certain appointments. When reports of the meetings were made known, even those who might have been prepared to join with him began to wonder about his honesty as well as his ability to pull off his political plan.

The direct-primary impasse continued. Sulzer upped the ante by summoning the chairmen of all the Democratic County Committees to Albany and delivering an ultimatum: all those who failed to rally their state representatives to vote for his bill would be expelled from the party. Such efforts were to no avail, for in May 1913 the legislature repassed the Tammany-endorsed election bill with only minor changes. Sulzer began replacing party regulars throughout the state with his own men.

Some time in May, it seems, Murphy concluded that Sulzer would have to be removed, and the word went out to his people in Albany. When the legislature reconvened on June 16, a committee appointed to look into the operation of the state government suddenly expanded its purview; it was now not only investigating methods used "to influence . . . votes . . . on election or primary legislation" but also the campaign finances of any statewide candidate in the 1912 election. There was no question that the target was Sulzer.

At this point the governor might have averted disaster by coming forth with solid evidence of what he had done in the campaign, perhaps admitting to a few errors of judgment, but all he did was attack the committee. After several weeks the committee announced its judgment: Sulzer had raised far more money for his election campaign than he had stated in his official report to the state, and he had also used these surplus funds to play the stock market. It recommended that he be impeached, and the state assembly so voted.

Sulzer's trial, held before a High Court of Impeachment consisting of the state senate and the judges of the Court of Appeals, began on September 18 and lasted four weeks. His lawyers argued that since the acts for which he was being prosecuted had occurred before he took office as governor, they did not constitute adequate grounds for removing him from that office. It was a telling argument, but the prosecutors countered by insisting that impeachment could be had for any deeds that demonstrated a person's unfitness for office. When Sulzer, who had proclaimed loudly that he would testify in his own defense and reveal all, failed to show up at his trial, his fate was sealed. On October 17 he was found guilty of "wilfully, knowingly and corruptly" falsifying campaign documents (on some other charges he was found not guilty) and was removed from office. It was the only time a governor of the state had ever been impeached, and it has not occurred since.

Murphy may have been justified in moving against the governor in some way or other, and there is no question that Sulzer was guilty of the charges as brought. But the impeachment, an awesome display of political power, shocked the public and there was widespread resentment against Murphy, who was seen as having brought down a popular governor to protect his own suzerainty. As the New York Times expressed it, Murphy had "established himself securely as the Dictator of Democratic policies in the State."[28] Sulzer, in an interview just after his removal, said, "I was impeached not because of the offenses with which I was charged, but because I refused to do Charles F. Murphy's bidding, and because, as the records show, I have relentlessly pursued Mr. Murphy's corrupt henchmen in office."[29] Great numbers of people believed him, and in a way it was true. Murphy himself, in a rare statement to the press (virtually the only one he ever gave), pointed out that Sulzer's failure to testify was tantamount to an admission of guilt, and said that "the only man responsible for the disgrace and downfall of Governor Sulzer is William Sulzer himself."[30] But nothing might have happened if he had not spat in the face of the Boss.

Another election was coming up, this one for the New York mayoralty and for the state legislature, and it proved to be a calamity for Murphy and Tammany Hall. Sulzer sped to New York, filed for election as an assemblyman and began lambasting Tammany from one end of the city to another. The mayor's office was open. William Jay Gaynor, whose health had been deteriorating during the year, was not getting Tammany support for another term. He was nominated by an independent group, but while on the way to vacation in Europe (to rest before campaigning), he died. Murphy had chosen an old friend, Judge Edward McCall, to succeed Gaynor, but the strongest man in the race was the Fusion candidate, John Purroy Mitchel, the onetime prosecutor of Tammany's Ahearn and Haffen and more recently president of the Board of Aldermen. Mitchel was elected with his entire ticket, and throughout the state Democrats who had voted for Sulzer's impeachment were defeated, nine of them in Manhattan alone. Sulzer himself returned to Albany as an assemblyman.

These were bleak days for Charles Murphy, the low point of his career. City Hall was lost, and Albany was no longer friendly territory (a Democratic Lieutenant governor had taken office when Sulzer left, but in 1914 the Republicans elected Charles Whitman as governor). To make matters worse, the Wilson administration in Washington was decidedly hostile toward Tammany and for a while attempted to organize a rival Democratic organization in the city. All at once there was talk in Tammany itself of Murphy's retirement. It did not help when some hostile words were received from the crusty former Boss, Richard Croker, who wrote from Ireland: "The Hall will never win under Murphy's management. I hope some good man will get in and drive all them grafters-contractors out."[31] Murphy's response was in character: "I'm the leader of Tammany Hall and I'm going to remain the leader of Tammany Hall."[32]

It would have been hard to believe, given these circumstances, that within just a few years all this would be reversed and that Murphy's days of greatest prestige and power were still to come.

For all the time that he had been grappling with the likes of Hearst, Gaynor, and Sulzer he had been quietly encouraging what for New

York City was a new breed of politician: young, reform-minded but politically astute leaders who believed that Tammany Hall's future lay in its acceptance and espousal of forward-looking social legislation— programs that could help people in a way that Tammany with its ancient benefactions never had even during its balmiest days. Their intent meshed with the nationwide Progressive movement that worked in support of a number of issues, including removing "corrupt special influence" from the economy, changing government to allow more direct popular participation, and expanding the role of government to meet new social needs. These issues were now promoted in particular by two bright young Murphy protégés: Alfred E. Smith and Robert F. Wagner.

The Boss had plenty of conservative friends, most notably businessmen, such as traction magnate Thomas Fortune Ryan, who were anxious to ensure that Tammany would help protect their interests. But as the arguments advanced by Hearst and the reform legislation pushed by Governor Charles Evans Hughes began to find acceptance among the electorate, Murphy turned increasingly to the younger Tammanyites.

Al Smith (as he would become nationally known), a wisecracking Irish Catholic from the Lower East Side, had been elected to the state assembly in 1904, at the age of twenty-nine. There he had befriended the young Robert F. Wagner, an assemblyman from Manhattan's German-dominated Yorkville section on the Upper East Side—and a Protestant. Both were quick learners and politically adept, and both were looked upon favorably by Murphy. When the Democrats took control of the state legislature in the 1910 election, which brought John Dix in as governor, Murphy bypassed older Tammany legislators to arrange for the naming of Smith as speaker of the assembly and Wagner, now a state senator, as majority leader of that body.

Up to this time, neither Smith nor Wagner, nor for that matter any of the other Tammany legislators, had been especially partial to reform legislation. What changed their outlook was the ghastly fire at the Triangle Shirtwaist Company in New York on March 25, 1911, which took 146 lives (most of them young working women) and revealed the gross inadequacy of existing fire safety laws. Responding to public outrage, the legislature appointed a Factory Investigating Commission with Wagner as chairman and Smith as vice-chair. But already in 1911, before recommendations from the commission were made, Smith and Wagner—by now conferring regularly with Murphy at Delmonico's or sometimes at Good

Ground out on Long Island—had spearheaded the enactment of
the first factory legislation.

Murphy's involvement in all of this is hard to pin down, but something of his role can be glimpsed from the recollections of Frances
Perkins, at that time a young social worker and much later, in the
1930s, secretary of labor in Franklin D. Roosevelt's New Deal administration. She had called on Murphy at the Wigwam in 1911 to
urge the passage of certain factory safety bills and found the Boss
sitting at his rolltop desk. "Mr. Murphy, solemn dignity itself," she
said, "received me in a reserved but courteous way. He listened to my
story and arguments. Then, leaning forward in his chair, he said quietly, 'You are the young lady, aren't you, who managed to get the
fifty-four hour bill passed?' I admitted I was. 'Well, young lady, I was
opposed to that bill.' 'Yes, I so gathered, Mr. Murphy.' 'It is my
observation,' he went on, 'that that bill made us many votes. I will tell
the boys to give all the help they can to this new bill. Good-by.' "[33] A
coda to this observation was added by Edward J. Flynn, in later years
a prominent Democratic politician from the Bronx. "You have to
remember," he said, "that none of the progressive legislation in Albany could have been passed unless . . . [Charles Murphy] urged it
and permitted it to be passed."[34]

The year 1913, however, saw the most impressive advances in this
regard, despite the conflict between Murphy and Sulzer. Work-place
sanitary regulations were upgraded, work hours for women limited,
fire alarms mandated, insurance requirements tightened, widows'
pensions instituted, and scholarships for the underprivileged authorized, among many other measures; a statewide referendum on
woman suffrage was scheduled; the Federal Income Tax amendment
was ratified, as was the amendment authorizing the direct election of
U.S. senators; the state's Public Utility Commission was given
broader powers; the New York Stock Exchange was incorporated and
a number of regulations were adopted that cut down the opportunities for speculators on Wall Street. It was an extraordinary year. As
Frances Perkins later wrote, "The extent to which this legislation in
New York marked a change in American political attitudes and policies can scarcely be overrated. It was, I am convinced, a turning
point."[35] A number of historians have said that the new state laws
were a precursor of Roosevelt's New Deal in the 1930s.

In 1914, Murphy astonished everyone by coming out for the one
thing that had purportedly been the crux of his fight with Sulzer:
direct primaries for all state offices. As usual there is nothing on rec-

ord to explain his about-face, but one can guess that he had come to the conclusion that the change was inevitable—so why not work for it and have the Democratic party get the credit? He may also have decided that primaries would require party machines perhaps even more than state conventions had, for only a good organization could produce the necessary qualifying petitions and other support that any bona fide candidate would require.

A subtle but large-scale shift was taking place. The wave of social legislation produced during these years by New York's Democrats (with Tammany backing) was marking the Democratic party as the party of reform, of liberal advances that would help the working person and many others. It had never been so before, but it has been so ever since.

Having seen how well Al Smith and Bob Wagner had performed in the legislature, Murphy was eager to move them along—Smith in particular, as he seemed to have more popular appeal. In 1915, he persuaded Smith to run for sheriff of New York County, a post that some observers thought unworthy of the young man's political talents—but the Boss wanted to give Smith a broader political base than he had commanded as an assemblyman. Smith won—Tammany's first step back from the calamities of 1913 and 1914.

Two years later the Fusion mayor, John Purroy Mitchel, was up for reelection. Both Smith and Wagner expressed strong interest in the post. So also did the now-familiar figure William Randolph Hearst. Murphy played his usual waiting game, pondering the question of who would most likely defeat Mitchel. At length, he decided that Hearst, with his powerful newspapers, would have to be placated, though he did not relish the prospect of Hearst as a Tammany candidate. He persuaded Wagner to stand aside (he would have him named a judge of the state Supreme Court in 1919, and Wagner would later become a U.S. senator), asked Smith to run for president of the Board of Aldermen, and once again went across the river to the Brooklyn organization for his mayoral candidate: a well-meaning but somewhat naive judge, the amiable, red-haired John F. Hylan, who happened to be a good friend of Hearst. According to one story, Murphy met with "Uncle John" McCooey, Brooklyn's Democratic Boss, and asked him if he thought Hylan was a man who could be trusted, someone the party could "do business with." "He certainly is," said McCooey. "Do you want to meet him?" "No," replied Murphy, "I want you to ram him down my throat."[36] So Hylan was put forward as a candidate whom Murphy had only "reluctantly" accepted, Hearst withdrew from the race, and the Democrats, buoyed by Smith on the ticket, made a clean sweep of the election. Tammany Hall was once again in possession of City Hall.

With Republican governor Whitman's second term ending in 1918 (he had been reelected in 1916), there was a good chance to retake the state house as well. Al Smith was Murphy's most likely choice, but the Boss hesitated—or appeared to—because Hearst was once again in the running and because Smith's Catholicism might prove a hindrance in a statewide race. Even as the state nominating convention was getting under way, Murphy had not made public his decision. Among those reportedly importuning him in favor of Smith was a political reporter named Edward Staats Luther. This prompted Murphy, in a rare display of humor, to call out to a subordinate, "Come in here and listen to a man named Luther trying to convince a man named Murphy that a Catholic can be elected Governor of New York State!"[37] The Boss decided the gamble was worth it, and Smith went on to victory.

Charles Murphy was now in a stronger position than ever before, and without any internal challenges to his leadership of the Hall, perhaps more strongly entrenched than any Tammany Hall leader had ever been in the organization's history. Mayor Hylan, whom the *New York Times* described as a man of "marvelous mental density,"[38] was perfectly happy to let Tammany take care of most political appointments, and so the patronage was bounteous. Al Smith in Albany was a new kind of ally, a Tammany insider enjoying Murphy's full confidence, and strong enough to be able to act almost independently of the Hall. (He was unusually popular even among Republicans and independent voters.) Murphy had been careful to spell out for him what he thought should be their relationship. "I shall be asking you for things, Al," he said during a postelection conversation at Good Ground, "but I want to say this to you: You understand these things much better than I do. If I ever ask you to do anything which you think would impair your record as a great governor, just tell me so and that will be the end of it."[39] A successful Governor Smith, in other words, should be reward enough for Tammany.

Smith proceeded to make his own appointments purely on the basis of competence, surrounding himself with a highly skilled, devoted circle of advisers that included the young Robert Moses (a Republican) and the social worker Belle Moskowitz, who helped make his administration one of the most enlightened in state history. Murphy beamed in approval.

At the same time, Murphy found himself in the odd position of trying to withdraw from an "honest graft" business venture because it was making too much money. In 1918, with the United States at war, a businessman named Louis N. Hartog, who was engaged in selling malt dextrine (a beer ingredient) to the British government, approached Tammany district leader James H. Hines and asked him whether he knew anyone with enough political clout to persuade the Corn Products Refining Company to sell him glucose, which he needed to make malt dextrine. Hines said Murphy was the man, and a deal was arranged whereby Murphy would invest $175,000 in Hartog's firm in return for making the necessary calls. The arrangement was extremely profitable, netting Murphy an estimated $5,000 a day—too high, he decided. He told Hartog he wanted to pull out and get his $175,000 back. "I am going out of the business," he said, "because I can't afford to stay in this business—the head of Tammany Hall profiteering on foodstuffs, especially war time."[40] Hartog refused and sued the Boss for breach of contract; Murphy countersued to get his money back; the dispute was eventually settled out of court. But there was one minor twist. A grand jury in 1920 voted to indict Murphy and various Corn Products Refining officials for conspiracy to hide earnings from the Hartog transaction and thus evade taxes. A year later a state Supreme Court judge dismissed the indictment saying the grounds were insufficient. The judge was Robert F. Wagner.

Not only was Murphy riding high on the local and state level; his influence was being felt on the national scene as well. At the 1920 Democratic National Convention, he was instrumental in forcing the nomination of Governor James Cox of Ohio for the presidency—and praised for it. The *New York Times* observed, "Tammany has emerged from the . . . Convention of 1920 with greater honor and credit than has been its portion at any other convention within the memory of the present generation in politics."[41]

Cox lost, of course, to Warren G. Harding, and in the Democratic debacle (Cox failed even to carry New York City) Al Smith failed in his reelection bid for the governorship. The setback for him as well as for Murphy was only temporary, however. The following year Red Mike Hylan—as he was popularly known—won a second term (Murphy had been dissatisfied with him but decided against abandoning him for fear of alienating both McCooey and Hearst), and in 1922 Smith became governor once again, though his return to office was anything but a shoo-in. Hearst had never forgiven Smith for besting him in 1918 and was back as a full-fledged candidate, with

McGooey's support. If he could not be governor he would settle for U.S. senator. Murphy, who disliked him heartily, hesitated to reject him outright for either office for fear of splitting the party.

So the Boss again played his classic waiting game. Reporters pursuing him for a statement were given a wonderfully vague reply: "You never can tell." By the time the state convention opened, Murphy still had not given his decision. When groups of delegates called upon him in his hotel room he simply asked them to check with Smith. The former Governor adamantly rejected any sort of a deal. "Nothing doing," he said. "Say, don't you think I have any self-respect? You can tell Murphy I won't run with Hearst on the ticket and that goes."[42] Naturally they did not have to tell Murphy; he knew it all along, for the whole thing had been arranged in advance between Smith and the Boss. Finally, Hearst caved in and agreed on a compromise candidate for the Senate, Royal Copeland, who, with Smith, won in November.

By now Murphy was something of an elder statesman on the political scene. Meeting with him periodically was his "war board," a group of his protégés who periodically gathered at Delmonico's or out on the Island to discuss both political and legislative strategy. In addition to Al Smith and Bob Wagner there was Jeremiah Mahoney, a law partner of Wagner and later also a judge; Surrogate James A. Foley, who had married the Boss's daughter; Jimmy Walker, majority leader of the state senate and later mayor of New York; and various other ranking Tammanyites close to Murphy. As Mahoney remarked, "We just thought out the problems."[43] The answers they came up with set the state's Democratic party on the progressive course it was to follow for the next generation. It is hard to imagine a William Tweed or Richard Croker playing such a role.

And the Boss kept working his wiles in mysterious ways. Ed Flynn recalled that when Arthur Murphy (no relation to Charles), the party leader in the Bronx, died in 1922, there was no agreement in the Bronx County Executive Committee on a successor. Flynn wanted the job, but there were those on the committee who opposed him and they had enough votes to block his election. Meetings went on endlessly with no decision. Flynn was getting "more and more angry and uncomfortable." Finally, unable to stand it any longer, he got in his car and drove down to the Wigwam on Fourteenth Street to see Murphy—who of course technically had no control over events in the Bronx. As Flynn blurted out his despair and said he was ready to call a meeting of his supporters and get himself declared leader no matter what, Murphy listened imperturbably. When Flynn had finished, the Boss looked at him in a kindly way and said simply, "There will be a meeting of the Committee tomorrow, and you will be elected chairman." And that is exactly what happened. Flynn never found out how he did it.[44]

After more than twenty years as head of Tammany Hall, Murphy harbored one last ambition: to see Alfred E. Smith nominated for the presidency of the United States. As the two men planned it, 1924 was to be the year. Planning was well advanced in preparation for the Democratic National Convention, which was to be held in late June in New York City. On the morning of April 24, however, Murphy collapsed in his bathroom at home, and at 9:05 A.M., he died. He was sixty-five.

Tammany Hall was at its apogee. Murphy had put it there. He had taken over a virtually moribund institution that had been repeatedly rebuked for its corrupt ways and condemned for exploiting those whom it purported to help, and he had singlehandedly changed it into an extraordinarily successful and responsive organization dedicated to the betterment of society. But his loss was fatal to Tammany, for there was no one of his stature, skill, and perception to take over in his stead. The ancient establishment would never be the same again.

CHAPTER

9

THE DECLINE

ON THE EVENING OF DECEMBER 7, 1929, A BI-
zarre incident with unexpected political repercussions took place. At
the Roman Gardens, a restaurant on Southern Boulevard in the
Bronx, a ceremonial fund-raising dinner was being held in honor of
Magistrate Albert H. Vitale, a city judge who was also the leader of
the Tepecano Democratic Club, the local Tammany Hall organization. The popular Vitale had been a judge for nine years and active in
Tammany politics for more than two decades. There was speculation
that he might be available for higher office. He had, after all, worked
hard to turn out a big vote for the successful reelection bid earlier that
fall of Tammany's own mayor of New York, Jimmy Walker. Among
the well-heeled guests at the dinner was Ciro Terranova, a Mafia
operative known as the Artichoke King for his control of the artichoke
trade, and a familiar figure to law enforcement agencies as a racketeer
of some stature; six other guests also had police records. It was a
congenial crowd.

Suddenly at 1:30 A.M., as Vitale was delivering a speech, six
masked gunmen burst into the hall, ordered everyone to freeze, and
relieved them of an estimated $2,000 in cash and $2,500 in jewelry.
A veteran city police detective who was present surrendered his revolver without attempting to use it, as did two armed court attendants. Magistrate Vitale managed to save his diamond ring only by

232

slipping it off and dropping it to the carpet, but the invaders got $40 from him. Then they fled.

The rude proceedings broke up the dinner, but no one called the police. Still odder things now occurred, however. The embarrassed Vitale hurried to the Tepecano clubhouse and made a few phone calls. Two and a half hours later he phoned the police detective who had been at the dinner and asked him to stop by. There the detective found on Vitale's desk his own revolver and the other two guns plus all the missing cash and jewelry. Asked how the loot had been retrieved, Vitale deigned not to say, and as to who the gunmen were he could only guess that the raid had been staged by "the boys from downtown, around Kenmare Street."[1] That meant they had been sent by Albert Marinelli, a Tammany potentate with links to organized crime. It later became known that the leader of the invading banditti was Trigger Mike Coppola, a torpedo from the Unione Siciliane who was an expert in all forms of wholesale murder.

Just why and how all this took place has never been disclosed, but when the public finally learned of the unlikely stickup, it demanded answers. Why was a judge consorting with known hoodlums? Why had the detective and the other two officers yielded their guns without so much as a protest? Why did no one call the police —not even the detective himself? How could Vitale get the guns, jewelry, and money back merely by making a few calls? Was it an inside job, and if so, how was the judge implicated? Reacting to the storm, the city's bar association demanded that Vitale be removed, citing an allegation made by Republican congressman Fiorello H. La Guardia that Vitale was in hock to the celebrated gambler Arnold Rothstein for a loan of $19,600; the loan pointed to ties between the courts and the underworld. Vitale was tried by the Appellate Division of the Supreme Court and, after failing to explain how during the past four years he had accumulated $165,000 in his bank account when his judicial salary for the period totaled only $48,000, was dismissed from the bench. But the Vitale case and other revelations at this time led New York's governor Franklin D. Roosevelt to order the first of three investigations that took place between 1930 and 1932. Conducted by former judge Samuel Seabury, the probes not only shook New York politics (among other things they demolished Jimmy Walker and ushered in the mayoralty of La Guardia) but dealt a body blow to Tammany Hall from which, in the long run, it never recovered.

Just a month before the Vitale dinner, Tammany seemed to all intents and purposes on top of the world. The Democrats ruled New York, and the Hall was calling the Democratic tune. The debonair, wisecracking Jimmy Walker had breezed to a new four-year mayoral term, and Tammany's machine appeared invincible. Times were good; who really cared if a city magistrate had been in cahoots with a gambler? Even when Arnold Rothstein was gunned down in the fall of 1928 and the police were unable to find the killers, few people saw anything amiss. But in October 1929, a mere six weeks before the Tepecano escapade, a quite different occurrence, one of dread proportions, had taken place: the stock market crash. Henceforth, with the onset of bad times, people would no longer feel they could afford to joke about politicians who stole. Charges of malfeasance in office would be listened to and taken seriously, and Tammany would reap the whirlwind.

The good times had concealed a glaring weakness in Tammany Hall: the death of Charles F. Murphy had left a vacuum that seemingly could not be filled, and when the depression arrived the Hall's inept leadership was unable to cope. Jimmy Walker had remarked at the time of Murphy's passing, "The brains of Tammany Hall lie in Calvary Cemetery."[2] He could not know, of course, that he would be one of the most dramatic casualties of the loss. And coping was much more difficult now than it had ever been in the past, for Tammany's power base was dwindling. The Hall had risen to supreme power largely as the benefactor of immigrant peoples, but immigration restrictions following World War I had reduced the inflow to a trickle, and so vastly fewer newcomers were now dependent on the machine. On top of this, Tammany's own bailiwick, Manhattan (otherwise known as New York County), was losing population to the other boroughs, Brooklyn in particular. At the turn of the century, fully half the city's population had resided on Manhattan Island, but by 1930 only a quarter of New Yorkers were Manhattanites, and the percentage kept dropping further, weakening Tammany's ability to lead. Finally, as Tammany's power declined, it found itself relying more and more on payoffs from organized crime, and when such arrangements became known the Hall was further discredited.

Just how much the Hall missed Charles Murphy was evident at the 1924 Democratic National Convention, held in New York's Madison Square Garden (then on Twenty-Sixth Street) in July of that year, just two months after the Boss's passing. Murphy's protégé, New York governor Alfred E. Smith, was one of the key contenders for the nomination and, with the galleries cheering him on, seemed to have a good shot at it. But he faced strong opposition from prohibitionists and anti-Catholics. In Murphy's absence, the governor had decided to direct his own campaign, a fatal error. When the convention deadlocked, Smith could not bring himself to compromise. But compromising, many observers felt, would have been Murphy's instinctive course and would have curtailed the ruinous balloting (103 were cast), allaying the bitterness that doomed the party's efforts that year. (The eventual nominee, John W. Davis, lost heavily to Coolidge.) Some believed the repercussions marred Smith's own presidential campaign four years later.

Barely a week after the convention adjourned, Tammany picked a new leader. The Executive Committee's first choice had been Murphy's son-in-law, Surrogate James A. Foley, a highly respected and intelligent public servant. But Foley declined the offer, and so with Al Smith's blessing, the mantle fell on a judge of the court of general sessions, George W. Olvany. Tall, blue-eyed with a high-bridged nose and a rugged build (the first sachem who actually looked like a brave, someone said), Olvany had been chairman of Tammany's Law Committee and as such had been close to Murphy. He was the first Tammany Boss in history to have received a college education. Though utterly humorless, he bore a clean reputation. The story goes that one day when he was seated as a member of the Board of Aldermen in the early 1900s a youngster had poked his head into the chamber and yelled, "Alderman, your saloon is on fire!" Olvany was the only alderman who did not get up and leave.[3]

Upon assuming the leadership of Tammany, Olvany announced he was retiring from the bench and would rejoin his old law firm, Olvany, Eisner and Donnelly. He professed a rigid moral stance. "When I resume my practice," he announced, "I shall scrupulously comply with the ethics of the profession regarding the clients by whom I am retained and in the legal business which I accept."[4] Pressed by reporters to speculate how his political eminence might possibly help his law practice, he grinned and said, "Well, it won't hurt any."[5] Indeed, it would not, as the Seabury investigation was to show several years hence.

Not long after Olvany's accession, New York's Democrats faced the difficulty of agreeing on a mayoral candidate for the 1925 election. The City Hall incumbent, Mayor John F. Hylan, had already served two terms and, though popular and hardworking, had shown himself to be simply not up to the job. Al Smith, who was still governor, scorned Hylan and resented the mayor's alliance with publisher William Randolph Hearst, whom Smith despised. Hylan, however, refused to step aside, and he had the strong backing of Brooklyn's boss John McCooey and a number of leaders from Queens and Staten Island.

Olvany, eager to do Smith's bidding, got together with the Bronx County leader, Ed Flynn, to find a better candidate. After some time they settled on state Senator James J. Walker, who was attractive and smart and had done well as Senate majority leader. Smith had reservations about Walker, whom he had observed over many years in Albany and considered unsteady, and whose wandering eye the governor (a devout Catholic and solid family man) disapproved of. But after much arguing, Smith reluctantly went along with the Olvany-Flynn choice. The two bosses had picked a winner. Walker defeated Hylan in the primary and went on to take the election handily.

Although he was one of the brightest and most beguiling men ever elected mayor, Jimmy Walker (no one ever called him James) was fundamentally flawed. The son of a Tammany leader from Greenwich Village, he had wanted to be a songwriter and had even produced one great success, a ballad called "Will You Love Me in December as You Do in May?" But his father felt Tin Pan Alley was unworthy of the son's talents, and to please him Jimmy agreed to study law and go into politics. A slight, slim figure with a ready smile and a taste for elegant clothing, he possessed a loud speaking voice and proved a strong vote getter when he successfully ran for the state assembly in 1910. Charles Murphy thought him promising and moved him up to the state senate, where he won notice as the sponsor of bills to legalize boxing in New York State and to permit Sunday baseball games. He was one of Murphy's boys, a comer.

But even in the legislature he was acquiring a reputation for high living and for spending less than full-time on the job. His agile, acquisitive mind and quick wit carried him along. Walker's extraordinary ability to master a wealth of facts on a moment's notice was described by the journalist Warren Moscow, who observed him close hand after Jimmy became mayor. "In City Hall," Moscow recalled, "a problem could hang fire for months, finally reaching the last deadline for settlement. Walker would start out of his private office, annexing an aide or expert on the problem as he went through the door. The briefing lasted as long as it took the two of them to mount the single flight of stairs to the Board of Estimate Chamber, with Walker digesting every morsel that could be crammed in en route. By the time he took his seat, he had the solution that would be city policy. After he uttered it, he never gave it another thought. . . . It is astounding, in retrospect just as it was at the time, how much he could get done that way, how much city progress followed his waves of the magic wand."[6]

Robert Moses, who served on Al Smith's staff (and later achieved a name for himself building highways and parks for New York City), once observed that Walker was "incapable of sustained effort . . . if [he] is given a two-page memo he reads the first page, and then his attention wanders."[7] He seemed to take nothing seriously. He "didn't give a damn about money," wrote Moscow, "who gave it to him, who got it, or where it came from, as long as he or a friend had it to spread around for a good trip, a good party, a not-so-good girl."[8] It was virtually impossible to dislike him, as Ed Flynn recalled: "When, as frequently happened in my relations with him, he would do something that annoyed me, I found that his manner was so boyishly disarming that my resentment usually evaporated."[9] Just as he had no enemies, Walker found it difficult not to trust his presumed friends, some of whom harbored motives that were not completely innocent. In the long run they did him in.

"The people," says the historian Charles Garrett, "had chosen a musical-comedy mayor to head one of the greatest corporations in the world. The interesting fact is that relatively few cared during his first four years. If Walker neglected his responsibilities as Mayor, it was not an age of caring about civic responsibilities. It was a zany, materialistic age in which people wanted to be let alone to grow rich quickly and to have fun."[10] New Yorkers loved their nightclubbing mayor and happily quoted his wisecracks, as when he defended his naming of ex-Mayor Hylan to be judge of the children's court in Queens by saying, "The appointment . . . means the children can now be tried by their peer."[11] They loved the incessant ticker-tape parades led by Hizzoner welcoming everyone from Charles Lindbergh to Queen Marie of Romania. The first Walker administration was also not without accomplishment, producing the first citywide sanitation system, the city's first Hospitals Department, new docks for superliners, and a multitude of new highways.

And Tammany prospered apace. If the Hall's true power was ebbing during these years, no one detected it. Walker went along with every request from the sachems, and with prosperity reigning in the United States and the Democrats in charge in New York there were plenty of patronage jobs to go around. Money flowed into Tammany pockets from every sort of scheme, large and small, much of it surely endemic to any large city but some newly devised now that the staid and strict Murphy was no longer in command of the Wigwam (Olvany had talked about propriety but ran the Hall with a loose rein). Police extracted money from storekeepers, prostitutes, and gamblers; rackets flourished in the fish and poultry markets and on the docks; licensing fees for various trades were illegally hiked with Tammanyites acting as middlemen. No one seemed to mind.

A subtle shift occurred in local Democratic power in 1928 after Al Smith, in his second try for the presidency, took the Democratic nomination but lost the general election to Herbert Hoover. Smith was concerned about finding a strong candidate to succeed him as governor of New York. He and his associates were delighted at being able to persuade Franklin D. Roosevelt to run. Roosevelt, out of public office since 1920 and still recovering from polio, had felt he was not ready to return to politics, but he finally agreed to Smith's blandishments and was nominated. Then came the surprise. Although Smith failed to carry New York State in his presidential bid, Roosevelt won the race for governor. Tammany's shining star was suddenly out of power, and a dynamic new executive moved into Albany's executive mansion. The implications were not good for Tammany. Roosevelt, though a good Democrat, was distinctly unfriendly to the Hall, and if trouble were to come—as it soon did—he could not be counted on to be sympathetic to Tammany's case.

One side effect of the power shift was a sudden and unfortunate break in the friendship between Smith and Roosevelt. Since Smith had so much experience in running New York State and was so highly regarded, and since he had been responsible for Roosevelt's making the gubernatorial run, he assumed his successor would call upon him for advice. It did not happen. Roosevelt understandably wanted to run his own show and not be obligated to his predecessor. The balance had tipped. Confused and embittered, the Happy Warrior never forgave Roosevelt.

Compounding the difficulty, Roosevelt refused to reappoint Robert Moses, who had been Smith's secretary of state and whom Smith felt would be especially valuable in providing continuity between the two administrations. Instead Roosevelt chose Edward J. Flynn, who as Democratic leader of the Bronx symbolized Tammany's ebbing influence in the city itself.

Another shift occurred in March 1929, with George Olvany's resignation. "Because of ill health and on the advice of my physicians,"

his statement read, "I resign as leader of Tammany Hall." Observers
were puzzled: he seemed the picture of health (indeed he lived until
1952). Whether he had premonitions of trouble lying ahead and
pulled out of his own accord or whether the Tammany sachems saw
the same trouble and forced him out is not known, but two years later
the Seabury inquiry provided an explanation. Ever since Olvany had
become leader his law firm had been representing clients before the
city's Board of Standards and Appeals, whose members were all appointed by the mayor with Tammany approval and whose chairman
was a close friend of George's. The board ruled on all zoning questions—on who could build what in which location. Up to the time of
the Seabury investigation, Olvany's firm earned some $5 million in
fees for handling such cases.

Olvany knew it would be improper, of course, for the firm to handle these matters directly. So another firm would ostensibly represent
his client before the board—and would split the fee with Olvany,
Eisner and Donnelly, being careful to pay in cash. In responding to
Seabury's questions in 1931, Olvany intoned, "We avoided city matter as much as we possibly could. . . . We could have had all the
business we wanted, but I refused to allow this business to come into
the office."[12] In truth, he had refused nothing of the kind. The eminent New York builder Fred F. French, for example, had paid a total
of $75,000 in fees to a third-party lawyer for obtaining variances for
the construction of the large Tudor City project on East Forty-second
Street, but most of this the lawyer dutifully turned over to Olvany's
firm in hefty cash payments.

Finding a replacement for Olvany was not easy, but after several
weeks the mantle was given to fifty-five-year-old John F. Curry, a
veteran but plodding district leader from the Upper West Side. He
had beaten out a far abler man, Eddy Ahearn of the Lower East Side,
the preferred candidate of Al Smith, but Smith's influence was on the
wane. Also disappearing was the idea of a "New Tammany" as envisioned by Charles Murphy—a liberal-minded, scandal-free institution
favoring progressive legislation. Curry left no doubt where he stood.
"It is fiction, this 'New Tammany,'" he said. "I will carry out the
politics in which I grew up."[13] It would be business in the old style at
the Wigwam.

Born in Ireland, Curry had come to the United States with his
parent when he was still an infant. At thirteen he left school to work
for Western Union, and later founded his own insurance concern. He
had come up through Tammany's ranks in the traditional way. For-

merly a star athlete, he was still trim, with close-clipped white hair
and a neat mustache; he did not drink and smoked only three cigars a
day. Although he looked and acted the complete political boss, he had
one major drawback. He was not smart enough for the job. His tenure
was marked by a succession of bad judgments that grievously hurt the
Hall.

The stupidities would come later. For the moment all was serene,
and to mark a year that may be considered the apogee in the fortunes
of America's oldest political machine, Tammany dedicated a new
clubhouse on July 4, 1929. The famed building on Fourteenth Street
that had known Tweed, Kelly, Croker, and Murphy was now deemed
woefully deficient. Olvany decided on the move before his resignation. The new and larger structure, just three blocks uptown at Seventeenth Street overlooking Union Square, cost almost $1 million
and boasted an imposing colonial-style portico including a liberty-cap
medallion. There were offices for the Tammany Society and also for
the New York County Democratic Committee (the Hall's official
name), as well as several assembly rooms. The whole effect was one
of well-heeled solidity, and few people could doubt that Tammany
would be there for generations to come.

In further testimony to Tammany confidence and the Hall's desire
to continue the corrupt ways that had become so profitable throughout the 1920s, Mayor Walker in early 1929 named a new police
commissioner, Grover Whalen. Walker's first commissioner, George
McLaughlin, had alienated Tammany by reinstating the Police Department's Confidential Squad, a unit that had been formed by former mayor John Purroy Mitchel in 1914 to ferret out police
corruption but that had been dissolved by Mitchel's successor, John
Hylan. Walker was apprehensive that Tammany might object to Mc-
Laughlin's move but decided to go along with it, and the commissioner appointed as head of the unit Lewis J. Valentine, a rigidly
incorruptible and fearless officer who with his cohorts immediately
began raiding Tammany political clubs that were being used as gambling hangouts; Tammany complained to the mayor but for the moment Walker hedged. McLaughlin was soon succeeded by Joseph
Warren, a friend of the mayor's. Walker told Warren he'd like to see
the squad abandoned. But Warren not only kept it but promoted
Valentine to deputy chief inspector. The raids continued. Then in
1928 came the Rothstein murder. Warren's health broke under the
strain of trying to solve the crime, and in his place Walker appointed
Whalen, the suave, dapper department store executive who had ear-

lier served as New York's official welcomer and parade impresario. This time there was no dillydallying. Whalen abolished the Confidential Squad, demoted Valentine all the way back to captain and transferred him to a precinct in Long Island City, the equivalent of Siberia. It was clear the mayor would no longer stand for anything unduly aggravating to Tammany.

Jimmy Walker's lifestyle was more abandoned than ever. He rarely got to City Hall before noon and was frequently away from the job on trips paid for by wealthy friends. Although technically still married to his wife of seventeen years, he had acquired a steady girlfriend, an attractive young actress named Betty Compton. The mayor's behavior was beginning to annoy some people. Governor Roosevelt was irked that when he came down from Albany Walker always seemed too busy to see him. Al Smith's scorn was more pointed: as a devout churchgoer he was offended by Walker's carryings-on and considered them political poison. Confronting Jimmy, he advised him not to run for reelection in the fall of 1929. "The wind is getting stronger and stronger," he warned, "and you'll be blown sky-high."[14] Walker decided to defy him and run.

His opponent was the fiery, unorthodox, hardworking congressman from East Harlem, Fiorello H. La Guardia, nominally a Republican but a determined fighter for progressive causes. During the campaign, La Guardia charged the Walker administration with graft and corruption and cited Vitale's loan of $19,600 from Arnold Rothstein. Walker ridiculed the charges and hardly campaigned at all. One night during the campaign he dropped in at the new Wigwam and said, "I am the candidate of Tammany Hall and if elected I will be a Tammany Hall Mayor. I never was a charlatan or a faker and I won't be one in politics. Tammany Hall is assisting me and when re-elected I will take my leadership and advice from John F. Curry."[15] Walker defeated La Guardia by a two-to-one margin.

Just before the election, the New York Stock Exchange experienced its tumultuous drop, with historic consequences. A month afterward came the Vitale dinner. The ground was beginning to shift.

Spurred by the Vitale affair, the U.S. district attorney in New York, Charles Tuttle, began investigating certain income tax returns and discovered that, for example, a veterinarian named William F. Doyle had taken up representing people before the Board of Standards and Appeals and had somehow managed to bank more than $1 million over a nine-year period; a Brooklyn judge, Bernard Vause, had been paid a fee as high as $190,000 for acquiring pier leases for a shipping concern; and a city magistrate, George Ewald, had paid a Tammany leader $10,000 for his appointment to the bench to succeed Judge Vitale. Tuttle turned all these cases over to the New York district attorney, an aging Tammany appointee named Thomas C. T. Crain, and although Vause was tried and convicted, the others went free. Something fishy was going on.

Contributing to the sense of uneasiness was another strange affair that to this day has never been solved. One afternoon in August 1930, state Supreme Court Justice Joseph F. Crater bid some friends good-bye in front of a restaurant on West Forty-fifth Street in Manhattan, stepped into a taxi and was never seen again. Investigation revealed that the otherwise proper jurist, who had served as president of a Tammany Hall club on the Upper West Side, had been involved in shady real estate deals and also had secretly been keeping a mistress in a midtown hotel. But was he rubbed out or did he commit suicide, and if the latter, where was the body? No one has ever found out.

None of this seemed to bother Jimmy Walker. One evening at about the time of Crater's disappearance, Walker and Betty Compton were caught in a gambling raid at the Montauk Island Club on eastern Long Island. He had not been gambling but Betty was playing for high stakes. When the Suffolk County police stormed in, Walker ducked into the kitchen and, donning an apron, tried to look like a waiter, but Betty was taken to the police station and released. New York's tabloids loved it.

Meanwhile, reform groups and leaders of the New York Bar were urging Governor Roosevelt to authorize a full-scale investigation into the magistrates' courts. On August 21, 1930—though concerned about the effect it might have on his own reelection bid that fall—he ordered the inquiry. To conduct it he chose one of the most widely respected personages in New York City, the austere and imposing fifty-seven-year-old Samuel Seabury.

A direct descendant of the Samuel Seabury who was the first Protestant Episcopal bishop in the United States after the American Revolution, he exuded propriety (people called him "the bishop," though not to his face). Seabury exhibited both an awesome intelligence and a dedication to public service from an early age. Graduating from law school at twenty, he had been elected a city court judge at twenty-eight and soon acquired a reputation for both severity and fairness. (He once threw New York's crusading district attorney William Travers Jerome out of his courtroom for making an inappropriate remark.) He went on to become a state Supreme Court judge and then, in

1914, a member of the state Court of Appeals. In 1916, persuaded to run for governor on the Democratic ticket, he lost and, having resigned from the bench, entered private practice—which proved quite lucrative. Although his 1916 electoral loss (to Charles Whitman) may have been inevitable given the politics of the time, Seabury blamed his defeat on Tammany's lack of enthusiasm for his candidacy and nursed a desire for revenge. Roosevelt's call gave him his chance.

Seabury's investigative technique, which was developed by his chief counsel, a brilliant lawyer named Isidore Kresel, was revolutionary at the time, though it has since become standard. Instead of relying on confessions, the staff gathered mountains of facts: bank accounts, income tax returns, leases, title records, brokerage accounts, and the like. When confronted with such evidence, a witness could not duck the truth. The results were devastating.

The public hearings started off on a sensational note with the revelation of a vast ring set up to extort women. The combine preyed on prostitutes as well as innocent women who were framed on prostitution charges. The network included policemen, bail bondsmen, lawyers, and even an assistant district attorney. Women would be arrested on trumped-up charges and forced to pay exorbitant bail (of which all members of the ring took a cut). The case would then somehow be dismissed and the accused discharged. A star witness was a $150-a-week agent provocateur named Chile Mapocha Acuna, who specialized in gaining entrance to a woman's room, planting marked money on her, and removing his clothes just as the vice squad broke in. So lurid were his tales that they inspired a popular song called "Chile Acuna, the human spittoona." Less humorous was the testimony of a woman who had simply been in her apartment talking with a man about a real estate deal while waiting for her husband to arrive for dinner. The police broke in, roughed up the man, and carted the woman off; she was tried and convicted on prostitution charges based on the evidence of one "Joseph Clark," who was not at the trial and whose given address would have located him in the middle of the Hudson River. She spent many weeks in jail before her conviction was reversed.

The most notable magistrate involved in such doings was Jean Norris, the city's first woman judge—who had been recommended by Charles Murphy himself. Known for harsh sentencing, Judge Norris was found to have disregarded the rights of defendants, to have altered court records to protect herself from judicial review, and to have been deriving income from a bonding company whose profitability was affected by her rulings. As a result of her testimony, she was removed from the bench by the state court's appellate division, which had jurisdiction over the lower courts. Also removed was a Bronx magistrate named Jesse Silbermann, whose only qualification for judicial duty was that he was a faithful Tammany worker.

As the inquiry proceeded, magistrates began resigning; one did so for what he termed health reasons—he had arthritis in one finger. For the first time Mayor Walker registered alarm. Shown a list of the magistrates he had appointed and the excesses they had committed, he expressed amazement. "That thief! That thug! . . . God knows they can never accuse me of not being loyal to the organization. Lord, what a gang."[16] His outrage did not prevent him, however, from going off for a vacation break at the estate of Tammany lawyer Samuel Untermyer in Palm Springs, California, where he displayed his usual wit. When an Indian chief from a reservation in the vicinity asked him if he would like a free thermal mud bath he shot back, "Thank you, no. I've been in one constantly for the past 18 months."[17]

Even as the magistrates' inquiry was under way, New Yorkers were shocked to learn that a key witness, Vivian Gordon, who was to have testified about her improper arrest by the vice squad back in 1923, was found strangled in Van Cortlandt Park in the Bronx. The slaying reminded people that many previously identified miscreants had not been brought to justice, and it led to Roosevelt's authorizing a second investigation, this one to examine charges against District Attorney Crain for allowing Doyle, Ewald, and others to escape punishment. Seabury would be in charge of this one as well.

Crain had been a state Supreme Court judge with a good record before consenting to Tammany's request that he run for district attorney. At age sixty-nine he was alert but plainly not as energetic as he might be. Seabury's staff found that he had begun inquiries into racketeering in the Fulton Fish Market as well as in the millinery industry, but had not obtained any convictions. The Rothstein murder remained unsolved, and Crain had failed to prosecute many other cases. Clearly, he was not doing his job, although he could not be accused of any wrongdoing. After pondering the evidence, Seabury concluded he had insufficient grounds for removing him, and he so reported to Roosevelt, who thereupon dismissed the charges.

But Seabury's job was hardly finished; indeed, the most important phase was about to begin. In the spring of 1931, the Republican-led state legislature voted to conduct a full-scale investigation of the city's affairs, and the governor, although he had previously been wary of such a move, now gave his approval and authorized a budget of $250,000 to pay for it. Again, the inquiry would be led by Seabury, who by this time had acquired quite a work load. In the magistrates' inquiry, his title had been referee; in the Crain matter, he had been called commissioner; this time, the panel of state legislators would be chaired by Republican state senator Samuel H. Hofstadter of New York City, and Seabury's title would be counsel. For a while, the indefatigable ex-judge was supervising three inquiries at once, and although his title and role differed from one to the other, the three are collectively known as the Seabury investigations.

This third and last inquiry was a massive undertaking and has been called "the most far-reaching investigation in the New York history."[18] It lasted well over a year. More than two thousand persons were examined in private, 175 of them later testifying in public sessions; the private testimony filled forty-seven thousand pages, the public another five thousand. When the original appropriation ran out, the state legislature voted another $250,000, for a total cost of half a million dollars. As one historian has said, "No other single investigation during this period did so much to show the citizens the pervasiveness of corruption and looseness in the city government extending from the smallest politician to the Mayor himself."[19] And at virtually every turn the heavy hand of Tammany was readily observed.

The first major witness was the eminent but elusive horse doctor, William F. Doyle, who had escaped Crain's clutches. A Tammany member in good standing, Doyle had once been chief veterinarian of the Fire Department, but Mayor Hylan, opting to ignore the man's acknowledged expertise, had made him chief of the Bureau of Fire Prevention. This turned out to be a mistake when, a few years later, Doyle was indicted for failing to inspect a building that subsequently went up in flames. Nothing daunted, he found his true calling representing builders, contractors, and landlords before the Board of Standards and Appeals (which required no law degree or any other certification of those petitioning it). As one observer noted, he "had quit doctoring horses and was earning $300,000 a year by doctoring the map of New York."[20] Among his many achievements over an eight-year period were winning 244 permits for garages previously forbidden and 52 permits for gas stations previously turned down by the Fire Department.

Doyle proved a recalcitrant witness, refusing to answer questions about whether he had split his fees with anyone or bribed any politician. He said that answering would incriminate him. As his silence persisted, the committee voted (along party lines) to cite him for contempt. He was sentenced to thirty days in jail. At this point Tammany's John Curry stepped in, locating a sympathetic judge who happened to be vacationing way up in Lake Placid, New York, but who was glad to be able to do Curry a favor by granting a stay of the order jailing Doyle.

This was not a smart move on Curry's part. It infuriated Seabury, prompting him to summon Curry himself to the hearings. On the witness stand, the Boss said, "I wanted to have the powers of the committee tested." Pressed to amplify, he finally blurted out, "This is a crucification, if it can be had, of the Democratic party of the City of New York."[21] Seabury pursued him no further, but in his eventual report to the committee he heaped scorn on the Tammany leader. "The truth of the matter was," he wrote, "that the political organization with which Doyle had had his relations was taking up the cudgels when an exposure of those relations was threatened and particularly when there was danger that continued incarceration might weaken Doyle's resistance to disclosure."[22]

Doyle's hesitancy in discussing his work before the Board of Standards and Appeals was followed by testimony from George Olvany, who had also done well in connection with the board. Olvany insisted that although the board's chairman, William E. Walsh, was a close friend of his and would often stop off at Tammany Hall on his way home from work for a chat, their discussions were always on a high ethical plane. Seabury was intrigued. "Have we got it this way," he asked, "that the only occasions in which you ventured to interject your personality into the situation . . . [were] where you acted . . . to help someone that needed help?" Olvany nodded. "As a good Samaritan," he replied.[23]

A chief focus of the inquiry was the illegal use of political clubs around the city as gambling dens, and a notable witness was Thomas M. Farley, a high Tammany potentate. A glowering, 250-pound man who had only an inch and half of brow between the top of his nose and his hairline, he was not only leader of the Fourteenth Assembly District on the Upper East Side and proprietor of the Thomas M. Farley Association on East Sixty-second Street but sheriff of New York County. Farley's clubhouse had been raided several times by Inspector Valentine's Confidential Squad, but each time it managed to escaped being padlocked. The sheriff stoutly denied that any gambling took place on his premises and said he assumed that the two associates of Arnold Rothstein who frequented the place were there for simple "recreational activities." The bars on the clubhouse windows, he said, were "to prevent the kids in the neighborhood from pilfering," and he insisted that the large number of men who were found at the club at 2 A.M. in the morning were busily packing baseball bats, rubber balls, and skipping ropes for the club's annual picnic the next day.[24]

Boring in, Seabury asked Farley how it came to pass that he managed to put $396,000 in the bank over a seven-year period when his salary for the time added up to only $87,000. Farley said it was "monies that I had saved." Seabury: "Where did you keep these monies that you had saved?" Farley: "In a big box in a big safe." Seabury: "And, Sheriff, was this big box that was safely kept in the big safe a tin box or a wooden box?" Farley: "A tin box." Seabury: "Kind of a magic box, wasn't it, Sheriff?" Farley: "It was a wonderful box."[25] The phrase, reported in all the newspapers, delighted New Yorkers so much that the sheriff was thenceforth known for all time as Tin-Box Farley. Just as George Washington Plunkitt had been forever associated with the idea of honest graft, so did Farley become the everlasting symbol of the unscrupulous politician pursuing illegal gains.

But Farley also differed from Plunkitt in that, unlike his predecessor, he got punished for his excesses. So preposterous was his story of the tin box that Seabury referred the case to Governor Roosevelt, who summoned Farley to Albany for a hearing. After questioning him about the box and also about some $15,000 in interest that the sheriff was accused of stealing from a fund he supervised, Roosevelt ordered him removed from office. As his rationale for doing so the governor wrote, "As a matter of sound general public policy . . . where a public official is under inquiry or investigation, especially an elected public official, and it appears that his scale of living, or the total of his bank deposits, far exceeds the public salary which he is known to receive, he . . . owes a positive public duty to the community to give a reasonable or creditable explanation of the sources of the deposits, or the source which enables him to maintain a scale of living beyond the amount of his salary."[26] The ruling was widely interpreted as bad news for Mayor Walker, who was known to be under investigation by the Seabury staff for his own sources of income. It was similarly an unwelcome turn for Tammany Hall, many of whose higher-ups might be vulnerable to the same judgment. And it set a precedent that still holds today concerning both elected and appointed public officials: if you cannot explain where the money came from, it will be assumed you got it illegally.

Luckily for First Deputy City Clerk James J. McCormick, he had a ready explanation of the way he had amassed some $385,000 over a six-year period when his salary was only $8,500 a year. McCormick performed marriage ceremonies at the Municipal Building, and although the official fee was only $2.00 he was happy to receive something extra, a gesture that he encouraged by leaving a desk drawer open that was overflowing with bills of various sizes. When a bridegroom took the hint and added to the pile the clerk would say "God bless you" to the couple. If the newlyweds failed to take the hint he would gesture toward the drawer and ask, "How about it?" If they then refused, all they got from him aside from the brief ceremony was a scathing "Cheap skate!"[27]

Perhaps the most delightful, if unconvincing, testimony provided to the committee was that of the Honorable James A. McQuade, register of Kings County. McQuade was proud of the fine "library" in his political clubhouse, but Seabury pointed out that the police who had raided the premises found no books; they did find a number of men gambling. Well, said the register, the members were able to "sit there and study or do whatever they wanted to do." Seabury pointed out that the only publication present seemed to be *Armstrong's Scratch Sheet*, and that the only literary notes visible were slips of paper bearing such jottings as "Phillips, first entry and contract 0-2-0, parlay, Faithful Friend and Sir Murice."[28] McQuade cheerfully insisted the men were conducting a social gathering.

When Seabury asked McQuade how he could have deposited $520,000 in his bank account in six years when his salary would have produced no more than $50,000, the witness gave him a long-winded explanation of how he had borrowed to support his far-flung family. When the family business had failed, he said, "the 34 McQuades were placed on my back, I being the only breadwinner, so to speak, and after that it was necessary to keep life in their body, sustenance, to go out and borrow money. . . . I felt it my duty, being that they were my flesh and blood, part and parcel of me, to help them. I am getting along in fairly good shape, when my mother, Lord have mercy on her, in 1925 dropped dead. I am going along nicely, when my brother, Lord have mercy on him, in 1926 or 1927 dropped dead. . . . Two other brothers, who have been very sick, and are sick, so much so that when your committee notified me, I was waiting for one of them to die. . . . The extra money that you see in this year or any year from that year on has been money that I borrowed—not ashamed of it."[29]

Seabury asked him if he would tell the committee whom he had borrowed money from. "Oh, Judge," he replied, "offhand I could not." But he said that he might borrow $1,000 from a man, and when the man demanded his money back McQuade would have to borrow another $1,000 to pay him, and so on, "where in reality there would be possibly ten thousand dollars deposited for the thousand dollars that was actually working." Exasperated, and unable to make sense of the tale, Seabury finally excused the witness. Leaving the hearing room, McQuade grinned and asked reporters, "How did my story go over?"[30] A day or so later a *New York Sun* reporter tracked down some of the "34 starving McQuades" and found that many of them were doing nicely on the city payroll and several were prosperous real estate owners in Queens. None of this mattered to Brooklyn boss John McCooey, who decided that McQuade deserved a reward. He accordingly nominated him for sheriff of Kings County, and in the 1931 election McQuade was easily voted in.

Leases, permits, and franchises had implicated George Olvany; now, as the investigation continued, they involved the mayor himself. When a citywide bus franchise had been granted in 1927 to the Equitable Coach Company, reporters had noticed that although Equitable had shaky financing and owned no buses, its cause had been aggressively pushed by the mayor—despite the fact that another firm, with an established reputation, had bid lower. What had not been known at the time, but was uncovered by the Seabury staff, was that a day or two after signing the franchise Walker had sailed for Europe holding a $10,000 letter of credit arranged and paid for by Equitable. Although Equitable's franchise was canceled two years later when its financing collapsed, the question remained: had the mayor sold his influence?

Then there was the gift to the mayor of $26,000 worth of bonds from J. A. Sisto, an investment banker whose firm owned a large interest in the Checker Cab Company, which did business in the city. Sisto said the bonds represented Walker's profit in a securities transaction, but it concerned stock that the mayor had not paid for with any of his own money. Whatever the ostensible reason, soon after the bonds were handed to the mayor a Taxi Control Board was set up that greatly benefited Checker and similar firms. What was really going on? And what about the newspaper publisher Paul Block, who said he simply admired the mayor and thought His Honor wasn't adequately paid for all his hard work, and who therefore set up a joint brokerage account for "P.B. and J.J.W.," which earned Walker $246,693 over a two-year period? Walker had not put a cent into it. Was Block doing this because he held stock in a company that was hoping to sell tiles to the city's subway system?

Most perplexing was the matter of Russell T. Sherwood. A book-keeper in Walker's old law office, Sherwood had become Walker's financial agent, handling the mayor's checkbook and securities trans-actions after he was elected mayor. The investigators learned that Sherwood opened a secret account in a reputable downtown broker-age firm in March 1927. By August 1931 he had deposited nearly $1 million in the account and in various banks for Walker. At least $750,000 of this had been in the form of cash. The investigators had one big problem, however: Sherwood had skipped town. Process servers traced him to Atlantic City, then Chicago, and finally to Mex-ico City, where he spurned the committee's subpoena. Because the extradition treaty between Mexico and the United States did not cover recalcitrant witnesses, he could not be made to return and tes-tify. Any explanation would have to come from Walker himself.

At length, on May 25 and 26, 1932, Walker appeared before the committee. As nattily dressed as ever, he was cheered upon arrival outside the courthouse ("Atta boy, Jimmy!") by a crowd estimated at more than five thousand; the courtroom was packed with his admir-ers, who applauded every time he got off a good line. He was in fine form, jaunty, quick on the uptake. Seabury had been cautioned to avoid looking directly at the mayor, who was described as having "an uncanny ability to stare you down,"[31] and so when he began his ex-amination of the mayor at 11 A.M. he leaned against a railing near the witness stand and gazed toward the committee members. He began by asking Walker about the Equitable Coach franchise.

The mayor professed no regrets at having awarded the franchise to Equitable. It had been the best company, he said. If another company had offered more, that did not mean a thing. "Why, the best offer the city ever had for bus operation came from a company located on Long Island; upon investigation, it turned out that they were in the hay and feed business."[32] The audience laughed and committee chairman Hofstadter banged his gavel to restore order. At one point Walker accused Seabury of making a misstatement and Seabury re-sponded by saying, "Apparently you are making a speech, Mr. Mayor." The witness shot back, "Well, they're not so bad. Did you ever listen to one of them?" Again there was a roar of delight.[33]

When Seabury tried to pin him down on the franchise award and recited a list of events that led up to the Board of Estimate's vote, the mayor waved his glasses and said with irritation, "Don't please testify for me, and ask me to meet your questions as you frame them."[34]

Asked about the $10,000 letter of credit from Equitable, the mayor pleaded innocence. He knew nothing about how or why the letter was drawn up, and when Seabury pointed out the coincidence of the franchise award and Walker's trip he became indignant. "If you are trying to write a scenario," he said, "why not make it complete and say that I ran off to Europe with a huge treasure stolen from the city and hid it there?"[35]

He saw nothing improper in his relationship with the publisher Paul Block. The man's life has been "characterized by generosity," he said. He was vague about the financial details: "I haven't seen a checkbook of my own or a stub or canceled voucher in six years."[36] As for J. A. Sisto, the man was nothing more than a chance acquaintance who had given Walker an opportunity to invest in a good thing. The fact that the mayor had not contributed a cent to the stock purchase was of no significance.

The matter of Russell T. Sherwood occupied much of the mayor's second day on the stand. Walker denied the allegation that Sherwood was his financial agent; the man merely did favors for him, he said. He knew nothing about a joint safe-deposit box or brokerage account, and he had no information about the source of the $1 million in the account. "I think the question is very general," he said. "I don't know anything about his private affairs because he never told me and I never inquired."[37] If Sherwood chose not to return from Mexico City, that was his business. The mayor said he saw no reason why he should have tried to persuade Sherwood to return.

As Walker left the courtroom at the end of the second day a group of women showered him with roses, and the crowd outside cheered him—though not as loudly as it had the first day. He had survived; indeed, he had not been trapped into saying anything that would incriminate him. There was suspicion that he had been bribed, but no proof. Curry and the sachems of Tammany Hall were relieved. The mayor's popularity seemed unaffected. Even if he were now to be removed from office in accordance with the precedent-setting rule that Roosevelt had enunciated in the Farley case, they could run him again and probably win.

Seabury pressed ahead. On June 8 he sent Roosevelt a statement of charges against Walker, claiming that they rendered him "unfit to continue in the office of Mayor." The Governor relayed them to Walker and asked for a response. The mayor simply denied any wrongdoing. Roosevelt scheduled a hearing in Albany for August. In the intervening weeks, however, the governor's own position changed dramatically. He became the Democratic nominee for president—and this would affect both Walker and Tammany Hall.

Roosevelt's successful record as governor of the most populous state in the union had made him the odds-on favorite for the nomination, except for one stumbling block—Al Smith. The former governor had renounced any intention of again becoming a presidential candidate, and as late as a year prior to the 1932 nominating convention, he told Edward J. Flynn, the Boss of the Bronx, that he had no objection to Flynn's working for FDR's nomination. Then in 1932 he suddenly declared his availability. Part of his change of heart was probably due to his lingering resentment over Roosevelt's having ignored his offer to act as adviser, but, in addition, he thought—as did many others at the time—that FDR was a lightweight. Roosevelt, for his part, thought that Smith, despite his fine record as governor, did not have the mental capacity to be president in a time of severe economic crisis.

With the convention approaching, Tammany Hall, its eye blackened by the Seabury probes that Roosevelt initiated, eagerly embraced Smith, its old comrade and sachem. Curry, demonstrating his petulance, lined up every other big-city machine in the country behind Smith: Jersey City's Frank Hague, Chicago's Kelly-Nash organization, and Kansas City's Pendergast machine, among others. It was not enough. After a few ballots the Roosevelt forces concluded a deal that brought the California and the Texas delegations into their column, and took the nomination. Still, Curry refused to make the nomination unanimous. As the convention erupted in a victory celebration, the Tammany delegates from New York sat in glum silence.

Curry's obduracy boded ill for Tammany's treatment in a future Roosevelt administration—it was his first major blunder as Boss. The second occurred a couple of months later when New York's Democrats met in convention to choose a gubernatorial nominee to succeed Roosevelt. The logical choice was Herbert Lehman, who had been lieutenant governor under Roosevelt and, before that, a valued adviser to Al Smith, both of whom backed him enthusiastically. John Curry did not. Lehman, he thought, must share some of the blame for the Seabury investigations and the Hall's "crucification," and anyway, Lehman was too independent for the Boss's taste—he preferred governors who were more compliant. His stand angered Roosevelt; Smith was furious. Cornering Curry in his hotel room, Smith told the Boss that if Lehman was not nominated, "I'll come down to New York and run for mayor and take the town away from you." "On what ticket?" asked Curry. "Hell, on the Chinese laundry ticket," said Smith.[38]

At the last moment, as the convention was getting under way, Curry tried to pull a fast one. That dependable Tammanyite Robert Wagner, who had been elected to the U.S. Senate in 1926, was due for renomination. Knowing him to be more malleable than Lehman, Curry, together with Brooklyn's McCooey and some upstate political leaders, tried to persuade him to run for governor. Lehman could get the Senate nomination. Roosevelt and Flynn got wind of the scheme and informed Lehman, who was persuaded by his advisers to scotch the move himself. He marched into a meeting the bosses were holding with Wagner and told them he would not knuckle under. If his name were to be put in nomination for the Senate, he said, he would decline. His name would be entered for governor—and the bosses knew Roosevelt would be the man to enter it. That said, Lehman stormed out. A couple of hours later a morose Curry telephoned him and said, "You win."[39] But the Tammany Boss's acquiescence merely solidified Lehman's enmity toward him.

By the time this had taken place, the fate of Jimmy Walker had been unexpectedly resolved. His hearing before Roosevelt (by now the nominee, but not yet campaigning) began on August 11 and lasted two grueling weeks. The governor had faced a dilemma: he must not be soft on Tammany corruption, but if he removed the popular mayor he might offend New York's voters, whose support he badly needed in November. He conducted the hearing (which took place in his executive chamber) with severity and dispatch, surprising many of those present with his skill and his detailed knowledge of the law. Walker was a far more subdued witness than he had been before Seabury. As the columnist Franklin P. Adams quipped, "The old gay Mayor, he ain't what he used to be."[40]

After two weeks the hearing was temporarily adjourned because of the death of the mayor's brother. Back in New York, Walker was summoned to a meeting of Tammany leaders. Most of them thought he should continue to fight the charges and, if removed, run again. But Al Smith, the last to speak, told him, "Jim, you're through. The public don't want you. You must resign for the good of the party." Later that evening—it was September 1—Walker sent a short message to the city clerk: "I hereby resign as Mayor of the City of New York, the same to take effect immediately."[41] A week later he sailed for Europe. Governor Roosevelt heaved a huge sigh of relief—a great burden had been lifted from his shoulders.

At first Walker planned to return and run again to fill the vacancy caused by his resignation. That he did not was due largely to a pointed—and unprecedented—hint from the Catholic Church, delivered at the funeral of a prominent and longtime Tammany district leader. New York's cardinal Patrick Hayes directed one of his key assistants to deliver the eulogy, in which he went out of his way to praise the departed for leading an upright moral life. The man had never been unfaithful to his wife, it was noted, and had never taken a gratuity for a favor. Curry and McCooey were both present and they got the message. They would no longer support Jimmy. His public life was finished.

Curry now made his third major blunder. A special election would be held in November to choose an interim mayor who would serve for a year. An ideal Democratic candidate was at hand: Joseph V. McKee, who had been president of the Board of Aldermen during Walker's entire tenure and had moved up to Acting Mayor on Walker's resignation. McKee was handsome, hardworking, and a model citizen. He also wanted the job. But to Curry he would not do, for he was from the Bronx and was a protégé of the now scorned Ed Flynn, adviser to the detested Roosevelt. If McKee were elected, Curry theorized, Flynn would call the tune in city politics. So Tammany Hall and its allies in the other boroughs instead chose Manhattan Surrogate John P. O'Brien to run for mayor.

He was at best mediocre. A tall, hulking figure with a massive jaw and what seemed to be no neck, he had plodded his way up the Tammany ladder with no distinction. True, he was the exact opposite of Walker, dull, diligent, and a good family man, and thus represented a change. But otherwise there was little to recommend him. And he had an unfortunate way of saying the wrong thing, as when he tried to win favor from a Jewish audience by praising "that scientist of scientists, Albert Weinstein."[42] His detractors began calling him "the wild bull of the china shop."[43] In the November election—the one that also elected Roosevelt (and Lehman)—he won narrowly, taking just 51 percent of the vote against a weak Republican candidate. But the big surprise was that McKee, who was not on the ballot, received an astonishing and unprecedented 252,000 write-in votes from all over the city. New Yorkers were plainly offended by the O'Brien candidacy.

He proceeded to fulfill his lack of promise. Right off the bat he proved his dependence on the Hall. Asked who his police commissioner would be, he replied, "I don't know. They haven't told me yet."[44] His administration was undistinguished, and he continued to make unfortunate remarks: once he told an audience in Harlem, "I may be white but my heart is as black as yours."[45] In good times nobody might have cared, but this was the depth of the Depression.

Curry decided to stay with him anyway for the regular mayoral election in November 1933. The Republicans and independents of the city, seeing an unusual opportunity, finally settled on a Fusion candidate: Fiorello La Guardia, now more appealing than he had been in 1929—his old accusations proving well founded. The contest looked like a simple two-man affair until September, when McKee suddenly announced his candidacy on behalf of what was called the Recovery party, a hastily constituted group organized by the Bronx's Ed Flynn with President Roosevelt's blessing.

Until quite late in the game the race seemed too tight to call. Then McKee made the mistake of calling La Guardia a Communist. The Fusion candidate responded immediately by producing a magazine article that McKee had written some twenty years previously in which he said some uncomplimentary things about the Jews. McKee's candidacy nosedived. In the election itself, Tammany resorted to every dubious tactic it could think of and managed to elect a Manhattan borough president and a district attorney, but at the top of the ticket La Guardia pulled out a victory over O'Brien to become the city's next mayor.

O'Brien's defeat marked the end for Curry. The Democrat in the White House was no friend of the Hall's. Neither was the Democratic governor of the state. And the new mayor, although a liberal who believed in everything that Al Smith had stood for, had nothing but contempt for Tammany. The Wigwam would get no patronage from any of the three. True, some jobs might be handed out by Ed Flynn of the Bronx, whose reputation was unscarred by McKee's loss and who remained close to the president, but Tammany would get no credit for them. It might be a long time before the situation got any better. It was time for some new leadership. Curry, stubborn as ever, refused to quit, but on April 21, 1934, the Tammany Executive Committee voted him out of office.

It was not easy to pick a new leader, for the Executive Committee was split between the partisans of Eddy Ahearn, the Lower East Side leader who had lost to Curry in 1929, and those obeying the orders of

a powerful leader from the West Side, Jimmy Hines. Just when the
popular Ahearn seemed to be ahead, he came down with acute ap-
pendicitis and withdrew, throwing his support to a compromise candidate, forty-one-year-old James J. Dooling, who was thereupon
elected. Well-to-do, handsome, and personable, Dooling seemed to
have great promise. Yet under the circumstances there was precious
little that he could do.

For Mayor La Guardia was doing his best to chip away at the
remaining sources of Tammany power. Not only was he making his
top appointments on the basis of merit rather than political muscle,
he was also reducing the number of municipal jobs that were exempt
from civil service rules. In 1933 barely more than half of all city
employees had been required to take competitive exams to qualify for
jobs; by 1939 almost three quarters had to. The exams themselves
had been carelessly administered, with Tammany applicants secretly
favored; La Guardia had procedures tightened and made much fairer.

A new crackdown on police corruption was under way, too. Lewis
Valentine, who in his career had twice been demoted for his zeal,
found his savior in the new mayor, who brought him back from outer-
borough exile, made him chief inspector, and revived the Confidential Squad. Late in 1934, La Guardia went the final step and made
him police commissioner. The mayor and Valentine waged a relentless war on gambling of all sorts, banning slot machines from the city
(La Guardia smashing many of them personally, on camera, with a
sledge hammer) and attempting to eradicate pinball machines. Racketeering in the city's food markets was greatly reduced, at least for the
time being.

Tammany's adversary in Washington, Franklin Roosevelt, was also
doing damage. La Guardia's crackdowns hurt the Hall, but Roosevelt's New Deal programs, expanding on federal welfare, had tremendous impact on Tammany. Unemployment insurance legislation and
public works programs undercut the Hall's appeal to the poor. Tammany's own Senator Robert Wagner played a strong role in the enactment of new labor laws and the Social Security system. Given such
new legislation, the Hall's fabled bushels of coal and turkeys at Christmas seemed pale stuff. No longer did the poor have to look to the
local district leader in time of need.

Dooling's effectiveness was also weakened by opposition from
Tammany's old guard, who were still smarting from Curry's dismissal,
and by the advent of a new power in the rival Brooklyn organization,
Frank V. Kelly, who had succeeded the aged John McCooey. Dool-

ing's three uneventful years ended with his sudden death in July 1937. His successor was Christopher Sullivan, the popular, venerable dean of a once-potent Lower East Side machine—Big Tim Sullivan, the man who had defied Boss Croker, was his cousin.

Christy Sullivan had represented his district in Congress since 1917 with little to show for it. (When his selection as the new Tammany head was announced, a New York press service reportedly asked its Washington correspondent for 250 words on his congressional record and was told, "Impossible. Sullivan has no Congressional record."[46]) Christy had not really wanted the job and during his five-year tenure as "Boss" he was content merely to go through the motions and make few decisions on his own. In reality, however, there was no Boss of Tammany Hall now. Such power—insofar as there was power—was exercised by two figures behind the scenes, the young and crafty Bert Stand, the Hall's secretary, and Clarence H. Neal, leader of the Twentieth Assembly District and a former associate of Eddy Ahearn. But little actually happened during Christy's tenure.

The real power and influence over the Hall, and increasingly, over city politics, was coming now from an outside source: organized crime. The linkage between the Hall and organized crime that was revealed at Albert Vitale's celebrated 1929 dinner was stronger now than ever before. The reason was simple: Tammany Hall was poor and growing still poorer, while the mobsters (despite La Guardia's crackdowns) were wealthier than ever. Recognizing the value of protection, the gang leaders required—even demanded—Tammany's aid. By now they were virtually calling the shots, and Tammany could hardly refuse to listen, for it desperately needed the money. The 1931 designation of Albert Marinelli (who had figured in the Vitale episode) as a Tammany district leader, for example, had been made at the express order of the narcotics peddler Charles Luciana, better known as Lucky Luciano.

One Tammany operative who seemed potent enough to hold his own against the mob was Jimmy Hines, the former blacksmith who was the undisputed and highly popular leader of the Eleventh Assembly District that controlled much of the Upper West Side and Harlem. During the 1920s Hines had become the principal protector of liquor and gambling operations throughout most of western Manhattan, including the Times Square area. When Manhattan's feeble district attorney, Thomas Crain, finally ended his term of office in 1933 it was Hines who picked his successor, William C. Dodge, whose election that year was one of Tammany's few achievements. In the 1930s Hines was receiving large amounts of protection money from Arthur (Dutch Schultz) Flegenheimer, who controlled New York's numbers racket. But the law finally caught up with Hines in the person of Thomas E. Dewey, an aggressive young lawyer who had been appointed a special rackets prosecutor by Governor Lehman in 1935 and who two years later took over the district attorney's office. Dewey got Hines indicted for protecting Schultz, convicted him, and sent him to prison. The conviction, and that of Luciano, would later help propel Dewey into the New York governor's mansion and almost into the White House.

A much closer relationship between Tammany and the underworld was revealed to New Yorkers a few years later, in 1943, when the then district attorney, Frank Hogan (Dewey's successor in the post) released to the public the text of a wiretapped phone message. One of the participants had said, "When I tell you something is in the bag, you can rest assured." The other had replied, "Right now I want to assure you of my loyalty for all you have done. It's undying."[47] The first man, Hogan stated, was Frank Costello, a onetime bootlegger who had moved into the slot machine business to become one of the most powerful mobsters in the New York area. The second man was Magistrate Thomas A. Aurelio, a Tammanyite currently running for the state Supreme Court on both the Democratic and Republican tickets. The revelation almost destroyed Aurelio: he barely parried efforts to remove him from the ballot, and even to disbar him, then won election and established a fine record in his new role. But more would be heard from Costello, who throughout the late 1930s had maneuvered himself virtually to the center of the Hall itself. For when Christy Sullivan, who had managed to lose several key local elections (including those which brought La Guardia his second and third City Hall terms), was voted out of office in 1942, the Executive Committee that chose his successor, Michael J. Kennedy, had as its guest that day none other than Frank Costello. Kennedy indeed had been Costello's man—the gangster freely admitted it. Now the mob was sitting with the sachems. In some Democratic quarters Costello was referred to as "the boss."[48] And Costello had his own protégé: a rising Greenwich Village Tammanyite named Carmine De Sapio, from whom more would be heard later.

In Tammany's musical chairs game Michael Kennedy lasted less than two years, being forced to resign after the Aurelio affair broke. By the time of his departure, the Hall had undergone what was almost a final ignominy. It lost its handsome new clubhouse on Seventeenth Street, which it had inhabited for little more than a decade. The organization could no longer afford such digs. Accordingly, the building was sold to a local of the International Ladies Garment Workers Union in 1943, and Tammany moved out. A collection of Tammany Society memorabilia was shipped off to a warehouse in the Bronx, the sachems took up residence in the National Democratic Club on Madison Avenue at Thirty-seventh Street, and the New York County Democratic Committee was relocated to an office building a few blocks away.

The Tiger had fallen a long way. It had no real home and seemed unable to produce a strong leader. To all intents and purposes it was tired, rudderless, and broke.

But did this mean that the ancient society with its storied political arm had at last come to the end of its days? Many New Yorkers assumed so. Once again the obituaries were premature. Tammany would rise yet again, to enjoy one final season of glory.

10

THE TWILIGHT

FOR TAMMANY, BEING FORCED TO LEAVE THE Wigwam on Seventeenth Street was devastating for two reasons. The loss was first of all psychological. The imposing structure had symbolized the organization's formidable power: like its predecessor on Fourteenth Street, it had been truly a grand establishment. Tammany's Wigwams were places where outsized and outlandish figures held sway and where momentous events took place. The same could never be said of a set of nondescript rooms in a midtown office building. But second, and more important, the building's loss, together with the resulting separation of the Tammany Society from the New York County Democratic Committee, effectively wiped out the Society's single most potent weapon that had helped it to endure for so long: its right to lock the clubhouse doors to any political group of which the sachems disapproved. Because the Society-owned building and the Democratic County Committee had for so long been synonymous, the Society had zealously preserved this right to great effect. With that right gone, so was its power. No longer did the Tammany sachems have the means to decree who was "regular" and who was not. Technically speaking, the Democratic County Committee was no longer synonymous with Tammany Hall, for the Society's control over it was extinct.

Yet Tammany had rebounded in the past. Was there a chance that it could do so again? Could a strong new leader emerge who would restore the Hall's shattered image? Given the new political realities in New York, this seemed unlikely indeed. Tammany's traditional well-springs of power—its control over patronage, its ability to command the loyalty of immigrant groups whom it had befriended and helped, its skill at manipulating elections—were all virtually defunct. Throughout the remainder of the 1940s, no strong leader did emerge. But for a while in the 1950s, it looked as if one had. The canny and austere Carmine De Sapio thought he saw a way to revitalize Tammany. However, the organization would have to be modernized and reshaped, and he set out to do this. The scheme came remarkably close to working. And so strong was the memory and myth of the old-time Hall that De Sapio was called the Boss, even though such a creature could no longer exist. While Tammany Hall no longer really existed as a political reality, people seemed to need to keep it alive in their imaginations to praise or revile it. Ironically, it was the weight of this imagined Tammany, its remembered past, that finally destroyed De Sapio.

Carmine De Sapio's rise in politics was remarkable partly because it meant reversing Tammany Hall's eclipse and also because he had to overcome the long-standing antipathy of the Irish-dominated Democratic organization toward Italians. Only one Italian-American, Albert Marinelli in the early 1930s, had ever become a district leader and member of the Tammany Executive Committee, and that was only because the gangster Lucky Luciano had threatened force to get him installed. To rise above the prejudice required energy, patience, and imagination, and De Sapio was well endowed with all three.

He was born in New York's West Village in 1908 to Sicilian immigrants; his father operated a prosperous trucking business out of a shed next to the family home at Varick and Grand streets. Young Carmine was always a hard worker. In addition to helping his father after school hours he also ran errands for the Huron Club, the Tammany headquarters for the First Assembly District in the southwestern corner of the city.

Needy families in the district got used to seeing the dark, quiet, handsome youth delivering buckets of coal and turkeys to them in the winter and ice in the summer. Early on, Carmine adopted a special technique: he always thanked people for allowing him to make a delivery, implying that they were doing him (and Tammany) a favor by accepting the handouts. Put in charge of rambunctious children on a Huron Club outing, he would thank their mothers for the chance to get to know the youngsters. His courtly air became central to his personality and later, when he was county leader, earned him the sobriquet "the Bishop."

At age fifteen Carmine contracted iritis, a rheumatic ailment that permanently impaired his eyes and required him to undergo continual treatment and to wear dark glasses, which gave him a misleadingly devious and sinister look. Up till then, he had intended to go to law school, but the iritis made reading painful, and so law school was out; his eyes could not take the strain. Instead, Carmine helped his family in its new business (managing a bungalow colony in the Rockaways), and concentrated on politics. There he showed great promise. By 1937, now an impressive six feet tall and married, he had such a following that he was ready to run for district leader.

He faced a formidable opponent. The current district leader was Daniel E. Finn, Jr., sheriff of New York County and the grandson of Battery Dan Finn, a popular Tammany leader at the turn of the century. But young Dan, a short, personable man, was vulnerable because he spent little time among his neighbors. He left the bothersome details to Carmine. So, Carmine figured, since he was tending to district business and doing people favors on behalf of Finn, why shouldn't he get the credit?

Carmine began by creating a rival club, the Tamawa Club, which many of his friends and followers from the Huron Club joined. In 1937, he ran for district leader and lost heavily in the fall election. That did not matter; it was just a trial run. In 1939, now age thirty and still more popular, he tried again. The campaign was a bitter one, as this time Finn knew Carmine was stronger. The election returns showed Finn the winner, but Carmine's forces claimed the outcome was fraudulent and appealed to the courts, which ordered a new election. This time De Sapio won by just fifty-one votes.

By Tammany custom, duly elected district leaders made up the Hall's Executive Committee. But Tammany's county leader at this time, Christy Sullivan, refused to recognize De Sapio, invoking the ruling handed down decades previously by Charles Murphy when he had banned Big Bill Devery from the Committee on the grounds that he was "objectionable." Al Marinelli had been accepted, as no one wanted trouble from Luciano, but Sullivan wanted no more Italians. Finn essentially stayed on as district leader and remained on the Executive Committee. It was as if the election had never taken place.

De Sapio and his followers refused to bow down—picketing Tammany Hall and also Sheriff Finn's office, waving placards that called on Finn to "step down. You were defeated at the polls. The people don't want you."[1] Finn and Sullivan did not budge. In 1941, De Sapio made another run. He was outvoted again and once more claimed fraud, but this time lacked evidence on which to appeal.

By 1943, however, the scene had changed. Christy Sullivan had been forced out of the Tammany leadership and supplanted by Michael Kennedy, who had been backed by Frank Costello, New York's prime underworld figure. Furthermore, the office of sheriff had been abolished and so Finn lost not only his job but his patronage rights. He duly retired from politics, closing down the Huron Club. De Sapio easily won that year's district election, joined the Executive Committee, and saw his Tamawa Club recognized as Tammany's official outpost.

The Tammany leadership that De Sapio now joined was very much under the influence of Costello and other Italian-American members of the underworld who befriended the machine for business purposes: they needed political protection and Tammany Hall, strapped for cash, felt obliged to supply it to the extent possible. It is not known how close De Sapio and Costello were; both men were quoted years later as saying they were mere acquaintances. It is accepted, however, that in every instance in which Costello made his desires known to the Hall, Carmine voted to go along. Over the next few years De Sapio was clearly on the rise as fellow Tammanyites increasingly noted his ability and good sense.

Another figure coming into prominence at this time, whose career seems to have also been linked to the underworld in ways that have never been satisfactorily explained, was William O'Dwyer. Charming and gregarious, O'Dwyer was hardly the typical Irish-American politico; he was not even a member of Tammany Hall and was actually antagonistic toward it. Born in Ireland of well-educated parents, he was a cultivated man who not only could quote from Dante and Byron but had briefly trained for the priesthood at the University of Salamanca in Spain. Deciding not to take the cloth, he came to the United States in 1910 at the age of twenty with $25.35 in his pocket. After working at a succession of lowly jobs —coal-passer, plasterer, hod-carrier, bartender—he became a policeman, and began attending law school. By 1932 he was appointed a city magistrate in his home borough, Brooklyn. Before long he became a county court judge and finally district attorney of Brooklyn, a post in which he won citywide fame as the prosecutor of a mob ring that the press had dubbed Murder, Inc. In 1941, he ran for mayor (backed, with some reluctance, by Tammany Hall, which was not sure it could trust him) against the imcomparable Fiorello La Guardia, and lost. But clearly he was a comer.

Already, however, there were suspicions that not all was on the up-and-up with Bill-O, as he had come to be called. In the Murder, Inc. investigation, the top quarry had been gangland boss Albert Anastasia, but to convict him the prosecution needed the testimony of Abe "Kid Twist" Reles, a hoodlum who had been taken into custody. Some-how, while Reles was being held at a Coney Island hotel he either jumped or was pushed out the window to his death, inviting specula-tion that someone had been persuaded to get rid of him so as to protect Anastasia. Similarly, an investigation into Brooklyn waterfront rackets, though highly promising, was for some reason or other shelved by O'Dwyer. Possibly implicated in these affairs was O'Dwyer's chief clerk, James J. Moran, a large, bland, and cryptic figure who had been Bill-O's secretary when he was a judge and would be a key associate through the remainder of O'Dwyer's politi-cal career. Years later, Moran would admit casually destroying much of the evidence in the Anastasia case. Was he O'Dwyer's conduit to the underworld, making it possible for Bill-O to get credit for fighting the mob while sparing the top suspects? There has never been a clear answer.

Although O'Dwyer joined the army in World War II, he clearly was keeping his eye on the 1945 mayoral election. In 1942, it was later alleged, he met with Frank Costello at the gang leader's apart-ment on Central Park West to smooth his path to the nomination. O'Dwyer was to insist later that his visit was for the purpose of asking Costello about possible mob involvement at Wright Field, an air in-stallation in Ohio. It just happened, however, that the other guests included Tammany leader Michael Kennedy, Tammany secretary Bert Stand, and a prominent gangland figure named Irving Sherman who was associated with Costello in a number of shady ventures. Few observers believed the purpose of the visit was anything but political.

Whatever actually occurred, O'Dwyer had no trouble gaining the nomination after leaving the army in 1945. But even then his choice of running mates revealed, to those on the inside at least, an instability as well as a reluctance to offend highly placed mobsters that would mark his entire mayoralty. For on the ticket, running for president of the City Council, was a complete unknown, Vincent Impellitteri, who was nothing more than a secretary to a state Supreme Court judge. When Tammany Hall's Bert Stand was asked by reporters to explain the choice, he made up a story: needing a Manhattan Italian to balance the ticket, Tammany hands had simply hunted through the Little Green Book, or city directory, until they found a likely name. This was good for a laugh, but the truth was later revealed to be otherwise. A Bronx Italian, Lawrence Gerosa, had initially been chosen to run for comptroller, and the Jewish Irwin Davidson, from Manhattan, for city council president. But O'Dwyer got a phone call from Washington from Congressman Vito Marcantonio of East Harlem, a onetime protégé of Mayor La Guardia's who controlled the city's American Labor party. Marcantonio, it was subsequently reported, was a close friend of Thomas Luchese, a rising gangland operator also known as Three Finger Brown, and Luchese had other ideas about who should be running. He was communicating them through Marcantonio. "Bill-O," Marcantonio said on the phone, "you've got to rearrange the ticket. I've got my own ginzo [Italian slang for one of their own] from Manhattan, Vince Impellitteri."[2] O'Dwyer did as he was told. Gerosa and Davidson were off the ticket; Impellitteri and Lazarus Joseph from the Bronx were on. The remade ticket coasted to victory in the general election. Some years hence, Impellitteri would present quite a problem for Carmine De Sapio.

The return of the Democrats to City Hall was greeted with joy and high optimism by De Sapio and his associates on the Tammany Executive Committee. Perhaps everything would be rosy again for Tammany. It must be recognized, however, that a signal change had by this time taken place: the Committee was no longer the automatic fiefdom of the Tammany Society. Because the Seventeenth Street clubhouse had been sold and both the Society and the Executive Committee had moved—separately—uptown, the ancient link between the two institutions had been severed. The Committee, in effect, was on its own, subject to the will of many party workers aside from the remaining members of the Society. Because legends die hard, most New Yorkers still thought the hoary Tammany of old was still in control. It was not; only the mystique was left. Strictly speaking the Committee was now a semifiction.

In any case, the Committee's optimism following the 1945 election was short-lived. For Mayor O'Dwyer, after initially approving all the patronage requests of the city's five county leaders, soon shifted his tactics and began berating the Tammany leadership. In 1947, he arranged the ouster of the then county leader Edward Loughlin (who had succeeded Michael Kennedy) and installed his own man, Frank Sampson, with orders to rid Tammany of its underworld connections. Significantly, he privately warned Frank Costello of Sampson's mission. Sampson himself was cordially disliked by the party's rank and file, many of whom he dismissed from their patronage posts, and he was generally ignored by most of the Executive Committee, who set up a four-man subcommittee (which included De Sapio) to operate in defiance of him.

In this leadership vacuum, in fact, Carmine De Sapio was rapidly gaining stature. By the late 1940s there were several other Italians on the Committee and he was their unquestioned leader. Late in 1946 the Committee members demonstrated their confidence in him by appointing him to the citywide Board of Elections. The job not only paid well but enhanced his prestige: henceforth any district leader in Manhattan who had election problems would have to come to Carmine for advice.

As for Frank Sampson, he lasted little more than a year as county leader. There was no question by this time that De Sapio was the ablest candidate to succeed him. The Italian bloc on the Executive Committee, however, did not feel strong enough yet (despite their backing from Costello) to force his selection. So a compromise was worked out and the leadership went to Hugo E. Rogers, who was the Manhattan borough president.

It was beginning to look as if no one could hold on to the post of county leader for any time at all. Rogers hung on for an even shorter period than Sampson. In a special congressional election on Manhattan's West Side in the spring of 1949, Rogers ran a relative unknown against the glamorous candidacy of Franklin D. Roosevelt, Jr., the late president's son, who had the backing of the Liberal party. Roosevelt trounced Roger's man handily. Emboldened, the Italian bloc made its move. On July 20, 1949, it voted out Rogers and elected De Sapio as county leader. Significantly, the Irish members of the Executive Committee, although not coming out against Carmine, abstained from the vote. But there was no question about the larger meaning of the event. The torch in what remained of Tammany Hall had been passed from the Irish to the Italians.

Because of Frank Costello's known involvement in previous Tammany affairs and because of his friendship with Carmine De Sapio, there was widespread speculation among political insiders on the extent of the powerful mobster's influence over De Sapio. Warren Moscow, an experienced political reporter and the biographer of De Sapio, has argued that Costello could well have felt it was in his best interests, as well as in those of the Italian community as a whole, for him to keep hands off. By the late 1940s, the gangster was rich and aging and beginning to seek respectability. There is no knowing what might have passed between the two men, but according to Moscow, it makes sense to assume that Costello would have in effect said to Carmine, "You're a nice young guy with a future. I'm going to tell the boys to put you in as leader. Let the rackets take care of themselves. Keep your own nose clean. The Italians in politics have been smeared by all these investigations. You can restore the Italian name in politics by running a good clean show. You'll get no interference from me, and if you need any help in keeping the boys in line, let me know."[3]

One reason this rings true is that Costello's influence from that time on appears to have diminished greatly: there is no indication whatsoever of his giving orders from behind the scenes as he had done previously. De Sapio ran his own show without interference. It is worth noting also that Carmine did "keep his nose clean." In all the years during which his influence was so vast there was never any allegation of wrongdoing or illicit personal gain. He lived unostentatiously. To be sure, he never seemed to lack for cash despite his habit of picking up the check at any gathering. A man who served on the Executive Committee with him remembers that De Sapio gave every member expensive silver cuff links one Christmas. "I would not have thought he could afford them," the man says. "But money seemed available—that's the way it is in that world."[4]

De Sapio's accession to the leadership occurred while the 1949 mayoralty campaign, one of the strangest in recent New York history, was already under way. Coming into 1949 Mayor O'Dwyer appeared to be assured of an easy victory that fall. He was popular, seemed to like the job, and was able to take credit for many accomplishments in office. Yet he announced that he would not be a candidate for reelection in the fall. No one took this seriously: the mayor, it was said, must be inviting a draft. Not so, he insisted, and he repeated his refusal.

There were those who were aware that back in 1945, before his first mayoral campaign, O'Dwyer had secretly inquired into the chances of being named to the state Supreme Court instead of becoming a candidate for mayor. Now, four years later, he seemed once again to be veiling his feelings. As Warren Moscow observed, "O'Dwyer liked the power that went with the mayoralty, yet he acted as though he feared the spotlight would search out some vulnerable point in his own past."[5] If the vulnerability had to do with Abe Reles or O'Dwyer's possible dealings with Costello, that seemed to be old news. What was going on?

In a memoir published after his death, O'Dwyer attributed his decision to his poor health, which he said was thought to be caused by a thyroid condition that made him nervous and irritable. But he also admitted that he knew in early 1949 that the Brooklyn district attorney was investigating bookmaking in that borough, an inquiry that would lead to the sensational Harry Gross revelations the following year, revelations that might seem to implicate the mayor. He conceded that this might have contributed to his nervousness and ill health.

While most of New York's Democratic county leaders began looking for substitute candidates, Edward Flynn of the Bronx had an idea. If O'Dwyer could be persuaded to run but with the understanding that he would have to serve only a few months of his second term, a new election would then have to be held in 1950 to elect his successor, and this might help the Democrats. For 1950 would be a gubernatorial election year, and the two races—for mayor and for governor—occurring in tandem should bring out a much larger vote, benefiting his party. Flynn, New York's senior county leader and still highly influential in Washington, asked President Harry S. Truman to go along with the notion by promising to appoint O'Dwyer ambassador to Mexico in the summer of 1950. Truman, who did not like O'Dwyer, nevertheless consented to Flynn's plea. The deal was done—with, as it happened, fearful repercussions for De Sapio the next year. But for now, with his future taken care of, O'Dwyer announced that he would run for a second term after all. His acceptance statement was a bit odd, considering the mayor's alleged past dealings with the underworld: he was running, he said, to prevent "the sinister [that is, crime-connected] elements" of Tammany Hall from gaining control of the city.[6]

His assent came just as De Sapio was taking over the Tammany Executive Committee. De Sapio's first major task, in turn, was to find a candidate for Manhattan borough president to succeed Hugo Rogers, who was departing in the wake of his unfortunate tour of duty as county leader. The man De Sapio came up with would loom large in the new Boss's career: Robert F. Wagner, Jr., the son of New York's senior senator. Wagner had literally grown up in the world of politics and had already, at age thirty-nine, established a creditable record of public service. He had been a state assemblyman, a member of the city's Tax Commission, commissioner of the Department of Housing and Buildings and, most recently, chairman of the City Planning Commission. He was attractive and articulate and a seasoned politico.

Because Wagner was very much his own man and unlikely to take orders from a County Executive Committee that was still dominated by old Tammany hands, De Sapio engineered a deal to placate his right wing. He persuaded the Liberal party to announce that it might nominate the young man, but only if the Tammany committee did. The Committee, faced with the possibility that the Liberals might otherwise endorse an opposition candidate, fell into line. Wagner, in turn, announced that he was accepting the Tammany designation "with the understanding that when elected I shall have a free hand in organizing the office of borough president and in discharging the duties of that office."[7] He would run his own show, and the Tammany organization might or might not have a hand in the patronage rewards. De Sapio's acceptance of Wagner's statement reprised Charles Murphy's professed attitude toward Governor Al Smith three decades earlier: a public servant's good record in office was the best politics and outweighed all other considerations, even patronage requests.

In any event, the O'Dwyer ticket breezed to victory in November. The odd streak in O'Dwyer's makeup surfaced again during the following month, however. Confined to a hospital bed with a virus attack, he abruptly filed retirement papers with the city's Retirement Board, a move that technically meant he was resigning from office. By chance his close aid, Jim Moran (who had been serving throughout the O'Dwyer administration as first deputy fire commissioner), learned of what Bill-O had done; he raced downtown to the board office, retrieved the papers before they could be processed, brought them to the hospital and burned them in the mayor's presence. The public might never have learned of the affair if the blaze had not set fire to the curtains in the hospital room, which brought the Fire Department and, soon after, the press.

Chastised, O'Dwyer was sworn in for his new term on January 1, 1950. And right on schedule the following August, President Truman announced that O'Dwyer would go to Mexico City as ambassador. With O'Dwyer's departure the president of the City Council, Vincent Impellitteri, moved up to become acting mayor.

For the moment, no one took Impellitteri seriously; he was expected to serve only until a new mayor could be elected in the fall. The Democrats had a ticket ready, their mayoral candidate being Ferdinand Pecora, a respected judge and former prosecutor. But Impellitteri upset the applecart by deciding to run for mayor himself, backed by what he called the Experience party—a triumph of bragga-

docio in view of his own nondescript record as City Council president. Many political insiders scoffed, but "Impy," as he came to be
called, fooled them. Running against "the bosses," he won.

It was a disaster for the Democrats: all of their candidates lost
except for Herbert Lehman, who since leaving the governor's office
had been serving in the U.S. Senate. He was just barely reelected. Ed
Flynn's image was tarnished. Not only had he contrived O'Dwyer's
departure, which led to the entire fiasco, but he had also been instrumental in picking Pecora, who proved a poor campaigner. But De
Sapio suffered more: it was the first election in which he had fully
participated as county leader, and he had nothing to show for it. His
job was on the line. To make things even worse, Impellitteri appointed Frank Sampson, no admirer of Carmine, as his patronage
chief, which meant that De Sapio and his Executive Committee regulars would get no patronage from City Hall.

But by being tough and by not standing still Carmine survived. A
number of district leaders had defected to "Impy" during the campaign: they would have to be removed. He got rid of some by encouraging their subordinates to vote them out of office. Others he
mousetrapped by merging or realigning districts, thus either wiping
out the offender's job or bringing about a primary battle that would
defeat him. "Sometimes I had to get a little rough," he recalled some
years later.[8] He visited clubhouses throughout Manhattan to rally his
partisans. He met with political reform groups to ask for their help.
He worked long hours; no one ever saw him relax. Gradually, his
potential opposition within the Executive Committee was either
eliminated or neutralized. Having no obvious rivals also helped him.
If Carmine should depart, there was no one else to take over.

And he did have a few resources at his command. Although there
was no patronage from the city, De Sapio could still dispense jobs at
the county level (through the borough president's office), in the judicial system, or in the state legislature. He used these to win more
friends. Not long after Impellitteri became mayor, he tried to remove
De Sapio from the Board of Elections. The Executive Committee
rejected the attempt and continued Carmine on the board.

While saving himself, he now came to the conclusion that he must
also save what was left of Tammany Hall. "I felt something drastic
had to be done," he remarked some years later, "to disprove the
public impression of me and my organization. Unless we put our
house in order, the Democratic Party in New York would have no
value as a party at all. I watched very carefully for the right places to

push for or against the right program. Either we were gonna get the confidence of the people or perish."[9]

He proceeded to reform the old-time system of selling judicial nominations. The sale of judgeships had long been a Tammany custom and prerogative. Although no elective judges who had attained their appointments by this method had ever been shown to have been anything other than properly impartial (some appointive judges had been less upright), the payments demanded were as high as $75,000, an invitation to corruption for any but the wealthiest candidates. (Tammany legend had it that once when a district leader tried to get a judge to "fix" a case, saying His Honor owed it to the organization, the judge replied, "I don't owe anybody a damn thing. I paid cash on the barrelhead."[10]) De Sapio cut the figure to the equivalent of one year's salary, which at the time was rarely more than $25,000, and used the money to defray campaign expenses. The judiciary was grateful.

He also came out in favor of social legislation to an extent that had not been seen since the days of Charles Murphy and Al Smith. He backed President Truman's Fair Employment Practices legislation and endorsed such items as continued rent control, compulsory automobile insurance, and voting for eighteen-year-olds.

In the spring of 1951, while De Sapio was working on reforms of this nature, the public was treated to a political sideshow. A U.S. Senate committee chaired by Senator Estes Kefauver of Tennessee was investigating organized crime. Although the Kefauver hearings, publicly staged in the city, did not injure De Sapio directly, they were intensely annoying because they reinforced the public's impression that what was left of Tammany was in league with the underworld. The committee's star witness was Frank Costello, who admitted that he knew a great many Democratic district leaders and was accustomed to doing favors for them. He freely acknowledged his friendship with Carmine De Sapio. (By previous agreement with the investigators, Costello's face was not to be photographed by the television cameras, and so the cameramen focused on his hands, whose twitching fascinated viewers.) Former Mayor O'Dwyer was summoned from Mexico to testify and proved an evasive witness, replying inconclusively to questions about the Abe Reles affair, the Anastasia case, and Costello's notorious 1942 cocktail party.

At the very end of the hearings, the investigators produced a surprise witness—John P. Crane, president of the Uniformed Fireman's Association. Crane said that between 1946 and 1949 he had given

James Moran, O'Dwyer's deputy fire commissioner, a total of $55,000 to help secure the passage of legislation befitting firemen, and that he had once given the mayor himself an envelope containing $10,000 in cash right on the porch of the mayor's official residence, Gracie Mansion. The $10,000 exchange was later proved to be false, but the charges against Moran stuck. Moran was convicted of extortion and income tax evasion and went to prison.

In its final report, the Kefauver Committee stated that "Costello's influence continues . . . strong in the councils of the Democratic Party of New York County,"[11] a charge that prompted De Sapio to fight back. He challenged the New York City Bar Association to cite a single instance in which a judge nominated during Carmine's county leadership owed his nomination to Costello. The Bar Association did not respond, an admission that the committee's claim was unfounded. Costello's influence was indeed very much on the wane.

Meanwhile, De Sapio was gearing up for the 1953 mayoral election. Mayor Impellitteri had proved to be a lightweight, just as De Sapio had known all along: he consistently ducked out of making decisions and seemed to coast through every day. Early in 1953, De Sapio mailed out forty-one thousand postcards to registered voters in the city asking whether they wanted the mayor to continue in office, and got a four-to-one negative response. The county leaders of Brooklyn, Queens, and Staten Island chose to stick with the mayor anyway, having fared well during his administration, but De Sapio clearly favored Robert Wagner, who had made a good record as borough president. Ed Flynn of the Bronx agreed with De Sapio. Flynn, incidentally, had acquired both a fondness and a respect for his Manhattan counterpart. "Carmine De Sapio," he said, "is the first Tammany man since Murphy who I can sit down with and not have to talk out of the side of my mouth."[12]

Despite the opposition facing him, Impellitteri refused to pull out of the race. But Wagner beat him handily in the primary and went on to defeat a weak Republican candidate in November.

The win established De Sapio as the unquestioned political leader in New York City. Ed Flynn had died during the summer, and so there was no else approaching Carmine's stature. De Sapio now moved to consolidate his power by pressing for the replacement of the Brooklyn and Queens leaders who had backed Impellitteri; the new leaders could be counted on to side with De Sapio. Beyond that, twelve district leaders in Manhattan who had gone over to Impellitteri had been ousted in the election and supplanted by pro-Wagner (and thus pro-De Sapio) men. Carmine's control of the Executive Committee was thus stronger than ever. For the first time since at least John Curry's day, what was left of Tammany Hall had a Boss who exercised authority almost without question. De Sapio was also chosen New York's national Democratic committeeman at this point, to succeed Flynn.

Relations with Mayor Wagner were cordial, too. De Sapio took it upon himself to marshal support for the mayor's favored legislation in the City Council and in the state legislature. The two men had no problem with patronage questions: De Sapio would submit a list of names for a certain post and Wagner might pick his appointee from it or he might not. De Sapio would abide by the mayor's decision. "I must say," Wagner recalled many years later, "he was always very cooperative."[13]

Of all the advances brought about by De Sapio at this time, however, perhaps the most significant were those affecting the party itself. A new state law canceled the right of a party to expand the size of any county committee; De Sapio went further and reduced the Manhattan committee's size from an unwieldy 11,762 members to a far more manageable 3,471. He ruled that henceforth district leaders would be chosen by the direct vote of enrolled party members in the area rather than by members of the county committee. And he further stated, "Any man who can't carry his own assembly district with his name on the ballot should not be the leader."[14] It was an eminently sensible reform; it would, for example, have prevented Danny Finn from continuing as a member of the Executive Committee after De Sapio outpolled him back in 1939. At this stage, no one could have guessed that one day this new rule would be turned on De Sapio himself.

With New York City securely under his control, Carmine set his sights on the governor's mansion in Albany, whose next occupant would be chosen in 1954; Thomas E. Dewey was retiring after three terms as governor. The early Democratic favorite seemed to be Franklin D. Roosevelt, Jr., who had been a popular congressman. But De Sapio considered him politically unreliable and decided to offer the candidacy instead to Averell Harriman, the wealthy onetime investment banker, secretary of commerce, U.S. ambassador, and expert on international affairs. Harriman had eyed the governorship for some time as a presumed stepping-stone to a presidential candidacy, and he gave his consent; Roosevelt was persuaded to run for attorney general. In the election, Harriman won, if just barely, while Roosevelt lost.

Once again, De Sapio's judgment proved correct. A grateful Harriman made him his secretary of state, a ministerial office designed to enable its occupant to be the governor's chief political adviser. On the face of it, De Sapio, in control of the Democratic party apparatus in both the city and the state, seemed now to exercise greater political power and enjoy greater prestige than any Tammany Boss or New York County leader since the days of Charles Murphy. Perhaps more—for Murphy had never been named secretary of state.

While scaling these heights, De Sapio had been working on his image, largely under the direction of a brash public relations operative and speech writer named Sydney Baron. He had abandoned the flashy jackets and slacks of his early career and taken to wearing dark, conservatively tailored, bankerlike suits, elegant but subdued neckties, and starched collars. He made endless public appearances, moving with ease at state occasions and attending high-level dinner parties. He received the praise of such worthy organizations as the Federation of Jewish Philanthropies and the American Legion. And he not only made himself widely available as a speaker at Ivy League colleges, urging more public participation in party politics, but even wrote (or had Baron write) articles for such prestigious publications as the Harvard Law School *Record*. This kind of thing would never have been attempted by Tammany bosses of old, especially the revered Murphy. Some party workers complained that the only chance they had of seeing De Sapio was on television. Others told him he was making a mistake in going public. "Why the hell don't you stick to your knitting, which is politics," said the new Bronx County leader, Charles Buckley, "and keep your mug out of the newspapers? Stay away from those lecture platforms, too. You don't need them."[15]

Buckley may have been right. De Sapio seemed to be doing very well, but his power base was thin. His sudden success had been based on two fortunate candidacies, those of Wagner and Harriman; a couple of unfortunate ones could hurt him badly. Without extensive patronage to command or welfare services to hand out, he had no firm hold over the party organization or over any sizable bloc of constituents, and so he could not "deliver the vote" in a crucial situation. Ironically, the one bloc he might have swung was that of Italian-Americans; but their great hero had been Fiorello La Guardia, and he had preached political independence. Many party old-timers were dubious about De Sapio's newfangled ideas. "Carmine has all the marbles," said one who chose to remain anonymous, "so we play it his way—but just let him slip once and the long knives will be ready."[16]

An odd incident occurred in July 1957 that could have done him grave damage, but did not. One morning De Sapio took a taxi from his apartment house on lower Fifth Avenue to the Hotel Biltmore in midtown, where he maintained his office as national committeeman. After he had exited the driver found on the rear seat an envelope containing $11,200 in faded $50 and $100 bills. The cabbie turned the money in to a nearby police station, saying his passenger had been a tall man wearing dark glasses. Upon seeing the story in the papers, De Sapio said he had been the passenger but denied knowing anything about any envelope. The mystery was never solved; no one ever appeared to claim the envelope, nor could it be connected to De Sapio, and after a year the money was turned over to the driver. Most people in the political world assumed that De Sapio was its owner but that he was not about to admit it. If it had represented some unlawful payment and De Sapio had been tied to it, he could have been ruined—a particularly surprising denouement in view of his unblemished record for financial probity.

But a far greater threat to De Sapio, and to the long-term possibility of any real revival of Tammany Hall, was beginning to come now from an entirely different direction. This was the so-called Reform movement, which originated in the late 1940s when large numbers of idealistic young men and women—many of the men lawyers and World War II veterans—tried to take part in local New York politics only to find their way barred by the old hands. The regular Democratic clubs had become so ingrown and so unaccustomed to new blood that they rejected the influx. "Save your five dollars, kid," one applicant for membership was told by a Tammany worker. "We'll get in touch with you if we need you."[17]

A number of these form-minded activists banded together to found the Lexington Democratic Club, which set itself against the local "Tammany" organization. By 1953 there were a number of such clubs. They began winning local party elections, and actually placed two of their group, Jean Baltzell and Alice Sachs, on the New York County Democratic Executive Committee.

There had been reform movements before, generally short-lived, but this one was different. The city's previous reform efforts, like those that elected Seth Low as mayor in 1901 or John Purroy Mitchel in 1913, were based on the Fusion idea, the joining of Republicans, independents, and other opponents of the Tammany Hall machine in a broad coalition to throw out the allegedly crooked incumbents and bring back truly representative, progressive government to the city. Such administrations never lasted longer than a single term (until the arrival of Fiorello La Guardia, the exception to every rule) because their programs, in the end, were often unpopular or because once they achieved what they had set out to do they had no further ideas. These new reformers, however, did not want to become an opposition party dedicated to throwing out the malefactors; they aimed to work within the Democratic party itself and change the entire system. They would throw the malefactors out of *their* party and remake it with new rules and procedures.

The trouble with the regular organization, they said, was that it was unresponsive and undemocratic. Ideas and programs were imposed from above and rigidly carried out by the troops below. The flow, they insisted, should be the other way around—from the bottom up. Ideas and programs should be thrashed out at the local level (they carried on endless debates) and filter up, not down. This would prevent party hacks from stifling progressive proposals and make for a far more energetic and successful party organization. The hero of most of the Lexington Club members and their ilk was Adlai Stevenson, whom they saw as a man of integrity who represented their liberal approach, and they labored hard for him in his losing 1952 presidential candidacy.

As the Reform movement gathered steam, Carmine De Sapio professed to welcome it. When two of the reformers, lawyer Lloyd Garrison and newspaper publisher Dorothy Schiff, were elected to the Democratic State Committee he said, "I look forward to their serving on the . . . committee as true Democrats who will encourage the progressive policies of the party and will keep on fostering a real people's program."[18] And why would he not welcome them? He too had once been an insurgent, and he too desired to reform the party.

But there was a catch. For all his forward-looking ideas, De Sapio was still a political boss schooled in the ancient way of ordaining from above. If the time were to come when De Sapio and the new reformers differed over some basic point, and the reformers were strong enough, there could well be an explosion. Already in 1956 De Sapio had annoyed them by going into the Democratic National Convention committed to Harriman rather than Stevenson; he had not even asked their opinion. He had not, as a matter of fact, cleared his decision with Mayor Wagner or Senator Herbert Lehman either, and both of those men began to wonder if he was getting a bit high-handed. Recalled Wagner many years later, "He was bright. He was articulate. But he was assuming a little too much, and I didn't like that."[19]

Beyond the threat offered by the Reform movement, furthermore, lay some basic shifts taking place in American politics. The percentage of the voting population was declining, but those who did vote tended, at least in New York City, to be better educated and more affluent—and more critical of traditional party programs and slogans. They were living in high rises instead of small houses or tenements, and so the traditional party worker found it much harder to reach them, if he even wanted to. Television threatened to make the old-time political rally obsolete and to replace the traditional ways in which parties communciated with voters. Finally, political parties themselves were becoming less sacrosanct; increasingly the important power in a community lay with such alternative groups as labor unions, churches, civic organizations, and neighborhood activists. The political machines were in danger of being bypassed.

One grizzled political organization that disappeared at this time was the 165-year-old Society of St. Tammany, or Columbian Order, which had never recovered from the abandonment of its clubhouse. Into the 1950s, the Society continued to hold its annual dinners, but its membership was declining, and toward the end of the decade it dropped out of sight.

Political success, nevertheless, seemed to continue to shine on Carmine De Sapio. In 1957 Robert Wagner, having completed a praiseworthy first term, was handily reelected, this time with all five county Democratic organizations pulling hard for him. De Sapio looked forward to the 1958 elections with high hopes of reelecting Governor Harriman, who would then be well positioned for a run for the presidency two years later. It was at the state nominating convention in 1958, however, that De Sapio committed the error that began his downfall.

The problem that caused so many tempers to flare was not Harriman's candidacy—that was a foregone conclusion—but the choice of a candidate for the U.S. Senate to run on the same ticket. Harriman and De Sapio agreed that the candidate should probably be a Roman Catholic, but they agreed on little else. Robert Wagner was considered by most observers to be the ideal candidate, for he was popular (and Catholic) and had often expressed a desire to follow in his father's footsteps on Capitol Hill; but Wagner said he did not wish to run, as he had pledged in his 1957 reelection race to serve out his full second term. There was another factor, too, Harriman himself. Although a skilled negotiator on the international scene, he was inept at state and local politics. He had told Wagner early in the year that in view of current allegations of corruption in New York he thought the mayor should *not* be a senatorial candidate. Although Wagner replied that he was not interested anyway, he was irritated by Harriman's telling him what to do.

The governor's choice was Thomas E. Murray, Jr., a former member of the Atomic Energy Commission and a prominent Catholic layman. But De Sapio, after meeting Murray and watching him field questions at a meeting of county leaders, was convinced he would be an extremely weak candidate, and the other county leaders agreed with him. De Sapio's candidate was New York district attorney Frank Hogan, whose reputation was unblemished. But to avoid a break with Harriman, De Sapio maintained publicly that he had not made up his mind. And he did not even tell the governor where he stood.

The Reform wing of the party, in turn, had its own candidate, former U.S. Air Force secretary Thomas K. Finletter. There were two problems with Finletter: he was not a Catholic, and he and Harriman detested each other. So the governor was firm against him. But the reformers insisted he was the best man, and they could not stomach Murray, whose tactics on the Atomic Energy Commission had offended many of them when the commission was investigating one of their heroes, atomic physicist J. Robert Oppenheimer. Hogan they appeared not to take seriously, for De Sapio seemed not to be pushing him.

Soon after the convention opened in Buffalo and as negotiations proceeded behind closed doors on the difficult senatorial question, Harriman made a tactical error: he allowed himself to be nominated before an agreement had been reached on the Senate candidate. Now he had no bargaining power, for he could not say he would refuse to run without Murray. De Sapio was still silent. When the time came, his plan was to have one of the other county leaders declare for Hogan so that Carmine could simply join in and not appear to be dictating the choice.

But the standoff continued as the convention delegates waited. Wagner had repeatedly said he would not run. Now, in a meeting of Harriman, Wagner, De Sapio, and state Democratic chairman Michael J. Prendergast, Harriman finally turned to Wagner and asked him for the sake of party unity to consent to run. The request coming from someone else would have been impossible to resist, for despite any pledges he had made, Wagner was a loyal Democrat. But his pride had been injured. He reportedly stated to the governor, "You didn't want me on the ticket three months ago. I don't see how you need me now."[20] He had slammed the door for the last time.

Harriman played his last card on behalf of Murray. Turning to De Sapio, he said "You are my secretary of state, my appointee. I want you to be with me." De Sapio replied, "I can't." Somehow he had maneuvered himself into a position where he could not give in. It was a terrible mistake.

Unable to patch up their quarrel, the quadrumvirate announced that the decision would be made on the convention floor. There De Sapio had all the weapons he needed, and a steamroller for Hogan got under way. A demonstration for Finletter planned by reformer delegates could not even get started; someone told the band to stop playing. Hogan won on the first ballot, 772 votes to Murray's 304, with Finletter getting only 66.

It may be argued that the agony had all been for naught, for the Democrats had not reckoned with the soon-to-be-nominated Republican gubernatorial candidate, Nelson Rockefeller, who proved a whirlwind campaigner with infinite financial resources. He easily triumphed over Harriman and even pulled his senatorial candidate, Kenneth Keating, to victory with him, burying Hogan. But the bitterness from the Buffalo convention had begun to have an impact long before the election itself, and when the Democrats went down in defeat there was widespread anger among party members of every stripe. In retrospect the blame for the fiasco can be split three ways: first to Harriman, who was clumsy and inflexible; then to Wagner, who was unnecessarily vindictive against the governor; and lastly to De Sapio, who played it cute for too long on the Hogan nomination and then, in the crunch, refused to yield to the governor to whom, in theory, he owed allegiance. But to the leaders of the Reform movement there was only one culprit. De Sapio had stifled their candidate and rammed Hogan down the delegates' throats. It was a display, they felt, of raw, naked machine power by a Tammany Boss. They resolved to go to war against him. Up to this time they had been a straggling, unfocused movement. Now they were an army.

They soon had a leader, if an unlikely one. He was the aging Herbert Lehman, now retired from the U.S. Senate, who directed his fury at De Sapio for just one reason: Carmine had defied Harriman. As a former governor, Lehman felt that such insubordination was an affront. It must not be tolerated. But if the system could produce such a man, then the system must change. Associated with Lehman were

Finletter and Eleanor Roosevelt, the widow of the former president, but Lehman was clearly in charge. In January 1959, he announced the formation of the Committee for Democratic Voters, dedicated to advancing the cause of party reform and to preventing "the urge for personal power by political professionals." Reporters asked Lehman if he would try to unseat De Sapio. The old man was blunt: "Yes, certainly."[21]

De Sapio professed to be unconcerned. He would only say, "I sincerely regret that Senator Lehman has seen fit to engage in personalities. The Democratic Party . . . is above that. No one individual is more important than his party."[22] But Lehman's cause was well financed, largely by wealthy admirers of Stevenson, and it soon drew blood. In the primary elections held in September 1959, Reform movement insurgents captured several new assembly districts, giving them a much larger voice in the County Executive Committee, and De Sapio himself barely survived a challenge to his own district leadership in lower Manhattan when he beat out a politically inexperienced newcomer by fewer than six hundred votes out of more than nine thousand cast.

His narrow escape in his own territory pointed up his vulnerability to the rule he had himself voiced, namely that no man should be on the Executive Committee if he could not carry his own district. At the very least, he had been discredited. He might have been able at this point to turn his district post over to a lieutenant and find some other way to retain his county leadership, but he was too proud to resort to such tactics while under fire. It was also too late anyway to retreat, he felt. Perhaps events in 1960, a presidential election year, would bring a change for the better.

But 1960 did him further damage. His earlier plan, to back Harriman for the Democratic nomination, was of course obsolete now. Without a candidate of his own, he could do either of two things. He could get behind the supposed winner well in advance of the convention in order to be in the good graces of the nominee in case he should win the election; or he could withhold New York's support until the critical moment when it could put the eventual nominee over the top. He chose the second course. It was an error. He was completely bypassed by the forces working for John F. Kennedy, who won the allegiance of several county leaders in the state—including Charles Buckley of the Bronx—and ended up virtually taking control of the state delegation long before the convention. De Sapio was left high and dry.

A needless incident toward the end of the campaign brought further unfortunate repercussions. A few days before the election Kennedy was scheduled to speak at a large rally in New York's Columbus Circle. To show that he had broad backing for his campaign he wanted to have both Herbert Lehman and Eleanor Roosevelt conspicuously present. Both agreed to come but only if they were allowed to speak, and not simply be present as window dressing. State chairman Prendergast declined to permit them to speak. Learning of this, Kennedy telephoned De Sapio, who told him he would take care of it. On the appointed day, Kennedy learned from a furious Herbert Lehman that Prendergast had refused to budge. "You weren't double-crossed," Kennedy told Lehman. "I was. And I'll get the dirty son of a bitch bastard who did it if it's the last thing I do."[23] Soon after the rally, he sent an aide to De Sapio to demand that Prendergast be dismissed. De Sapio refused, which was surely an honorable response but did not win him any friends in the Kennedy camp.

A more threatening break was also approaching between De Sapio and his onetime staunch ally and protégé, Mayor Wagner, a possible candidate for election to a third mayoral term in 1961. During the 1960 campaign, a reform candidate for Congress on Manhattan's West Side, William Fitts Ryan, had fought his opponent in the primary, Congressman Ludwig Teller, simply by having his workers paste a sticker on Teller's posters labeling him De Sapio's Candidate. On the basis of this tactic alone, Ryan won the primary. A few months later, as Wagner was meeting with some of his aides to discuss the possibility of his running again, he suddenly was heard to remark, "After what happened to Lou Teller, what I want to know is how anyone can win if he has De Sapio's support."[24] It seemed the mayor was wondering whether, in order to survive, he would have to turn against the man who had gotten him his job so many years back.

Soon thereafter he made his break, severing relations with De Sapio and taking on the Liberal party leader, Alex Rose, as his political agent. When the need arose to designate a new Manhattan borough president, Wagner went head-to-head with Carmine and imposed his own choice over De Sapio's objections. He followed this up with a statement urging De Sapio to resign for the sake of party harmony. De Sapio declined. In June Wagner announced that he would run for a third term.

De Sapio had been making soundings and was convinced that without the support of the party apparatus Wagner could not win. He and the other county leaders thereupon put together a slate headed by

New York state comptroller Arthur Levitt for mayor. But Wagner had his own information, given him by polling expert Louis Harris, who said that if the mayor ran on an antimachine, antiboss platform he would prevail. During the primary campaign Wagner ignored Levitt and kept up a steady attack on De Sapio. It was a machine man fighting the machine, no less.

Many members of the Reform movement had been less than enthusiastic about Robert Wagner's record as mayor and were unsure about whether to endorse him. Lehman put them straight. They should get behind the mayor, he said, for there might never again be as good a chance to destroy Tammany Hall once and for all, while if they opposed Wagner their cause might be irrevocably compromised. Obediently, the reformers fell into line. Meanwhile Lehman, Mrs. Roosevelt, and Thomas Finletter persuaded James Lanigan, an experienced former aide to Adlai Stevenson, to run against De Sapio for the leadership of the downtown district that was the county leader's home base.

The primary election in September 1961 came like a thunderclap. Wagner defeated Levitt by almost a two-to-one margin and brought the rest of his ticket with him. Reform candidates won fourteen of the sixteen district contests. And in the lower Manhattan race Lanigan beat De Sapio by 6,165 votes to 4,745. De Sapio was no longer even a county committeeman.

As the vote coming in showed that he had lost, De Sapio addressed his followers at the Tamawa Club. "You and I have not lost this contest with any degree of shame," he said. "It may be disappointing to you because this is the first contest we've lost since 1939. But I don't concede that this is a defeat on any level except for a personality. I'm not indispensable or immortal. If I've let you down, I'm sorry."[25] He was no longer district leader and therefore not the county leader either. He was out. Many of those present were in tears.

If any one moment could be identified as the final glimmering of Tammany Hall, that was it. The party was over. Two years later, De Sapio ran again for district leader but lost again. The last Tammany Boss was through, and in terms of power and influence he had no real successors. Current laws and restrictions made it extremely unlikely that a political machine could ever again flourish in the Tammany Hall fashion—headed by a Boss who had no other visible means of support. And Manhattan, or New York County, was no longer paramount within the city. With De Sapio went the last vestiges of a system that had survived, for better or for worse, for more than a century and a half, the longest running political show in America.

Much of that long-running show had been evil, for Tammany, largely because of the likes of Tweed and Croker, had justifiably come to personify the worst kind of urban political corruption in the United States. But the Hall must also be seen as an integral part of America's political coming of age. Elections in the old days were crooked because no one knew how to regulate them; in time, the electorate learned. Honest graft had once seemed almost proper, but then conflict-of-interest laws banished it. And for every Tammany district leader like Big Tim Sullivan exploiting the poor, there was a John Kelly or a Charles Francis Murphy looking for ways to connect the machine to better public service. As party politics grew and changed in Tammany's century and a half, the Hall adapted itself, for better or for worse. Finally history caught up with the Hall and made it obsolete.

Part of the historical shift was represented by the decline of political parties in the United States, and with that decline came the disappearance of the close connection between the local politician and the individual. In the 1960s a Tammany veteran, looking back on his early days, wrote, "The 'modern' captain of the soaring 'sixties no longer remained close to his constituents. It was, and is, a far cry from the days when I climbed six flights of stairs to see voters in squalid tenements. . . . Now, staircases have become obsolete in the soaring structures whose elevators haul tenants up and down."[26] No one was ringing doorbells anymore, and the idea of politics as a personal calling had virtually disappeared.

When Tammany Hall finally perished, much that was bad went with it. But something was lost, too, and it will be missed.

NOTES

PREFACE

1. M. R. Werner, *Tammany Hall*, viii.
2. Lothrop Stoddard, *Master of Manhattan: The Life of Richard Croker*, 125.

Chapter 1
THE FOUNDING

1. Edwin P. Kilroe, Abraham Kaplan, and Joseph Johnson, "The Story of Tammany," *Tammany, A Patriotic History, 1786–1924*, 10.
2. Ibid., 15.
3. Edwin P. Kilroe, *Saint Tammany and the Origin of the Society of Tammany, or Columbian Order in the City of New York*, 48.
4. Ibid., 142.
5. Alfred Young, *The Democratic Republicans of New York: Their Origins, 1763–1797*, 202.
6. M. R. Werner, *Tammany Hall*, 12.
7. Edwin P. Kilroe, *Saint Tammany*, 176.
8. Ibid., 136.
9. Gustavus Myers, *The History of Tammany Hall*, 8.
10. Moisei Ostrogorski, *Democracy and the Organization of Political Parties*, 154.
11. Peter Paulson, "The Tammany Society and the Jeffersonian Movement in New York City, 1795–1800," *New York History* 34 (1953), 77.

12. Jerome Mushkat, "Matthew Livingston Davis and the Political Legacy of Aaron Burr," *New-York Historical Society Quarterly*, LIX (April 1975), 123.
13. Milton Lomask, *Aaron Burr: The Years from Princeton to Vice President, 1756–1805*, 239.
14. Ibid., 241.
15. Ibid., 242.
16. Ibid., 244.
17. Mordecai Myers, *Reminiscences, 1780 to 1814*, 11.
18. Myers, *History of Tammany Hall*, 15.
19. Dorothie Bobbé, *De Witt Clinton*, 88.
20. Myers, *History of Tammany Hall*, 20.
21. Mushkat, "Matthew Livingston Davis and the Political Legacy of Aaron Burr," 136.
22. Myers, *History of Tammany Hall*, 31.

Chapter 2
GROWING PAINS

1. Gustavus Myers, *History of Tammany Hall*, 46.
2. Leo Hershkowitz, "The Loco-Foco Party of New York: Its Origins and Career, 1835–1837," *New-York Historical Society Quarterly* 46 (July 1962), 328.
3. De Witt Clinton, "The Martling-man; or, Says I to Myself, How is This?" 4–5.
4. Alfred Connable and Edward Silverfarb, *Tigers of Tammany: Nine Men Who Ran New York*, 82.
5. Robert V. Remini, *Martin Van Buren and the Making of the Democratic Party*, 11.
6. M. R. Werner, *Tammany Hall*, 32.
7. Myers, *History of Tammany Hall*, 76.
8. Robert Ernst, *Immigrant Life in New York City 1825–1863*, 162.
9. Denis T. Lynch, *An Epoch and a Man: Martin Van Buren and His Times*, 325.
10. Jerome Mushkat, *Tammany: The Evolution of a Political Machine 1789–1865*, 121.
11. Myers, *History of Tammany Hall*, 79.
12. Amy Bridges, *A City in the Republic: Antebellum New York and the Origins of Machine Politics*, 23.
13. Myers, *History of Tammany Hall*, 89.
14. Connable and Silverfarb, *Tigers of Tammany*, 97.
15. Ibid., 97–98.
16. Myers, *History of Tammany Hall*, 91.

17. Joel Tyler Headley, *The Great Riots of New York, 1712 to 1873*, 69.
18. Bridges, *A City in the Republic*, 80.
19. Myers, *History of Tammany Hall*, 124.

Chapter 3
FERNANDO

1. Leonard Chalmers, "Fernando Wood and Tammany Hall: The First Phase," *New-York Historical Society Quarterly* 52 (October 1968), 380.
2. Ibid., 380.
3. Jerome Mushkat, *Fernando Wood: A Political Biography*, 41.
4. Alfred Connable and Edward Silverfarb, *Tigers of Tammany*, 111.
5. Quoted in M.R. Werner, *Tammany Hall*, 45.
6. Quoted in Edward K. Spann, *The New Metropolis: New York City, 1840–1857*, 348.
7. Werner, *Tammany Hall*, 75.
8. Gustavus Myers, *History of Tammany Hall*, 140.
9. Denis T. Lynch, *"Boss" Tweed*, 73.
10. Connable and Silverfarb, *Tigers of Tammany*, 118.
11. Mushkat, *Fernando Wood*, 41.
12. Werner, *Tammany Hall*, 85.
13. Mushkat, *Fernando Wood*, 25.
14. Ibid., 37.
15. Lynch, *"Boss" Tweed*, 126.
16. Werner, *Tammany Hall*, 79.
17. James F. Richardson, "Mayor Fernando Wood and the New York Police Force," *New-York Historical Society Quarterly* 50 (January 1966), 11.
18. Mushkat, *Fernando Wood*, 47.
19. Chalmers, "Fernando Wood and Tammany Hall," 389.
20. Myers, *History of Tammany Hall*, 177.
21. Robert Ernst, *Immigrant Life in New York City 1825–1863*, 170.
22. Mushkat, *Fernando Wood*, 56.
23. Spann, *The New Metropolis*, 384.
24. Ibid., 387.
25. Lynch, *"Boss" Tweed*, 188.
26. Spann, *The New Metropolis*, 393.
27. Ibid., 390.
28. Mushkat, *Fernando Wood*, 75.
29. Spann, *New Metropolis*, 395.
30. Ibid., 395.
31. Mushkat, *Fernando Wood*, 82.

32. Ibid., 83.
33. Leonard Chalmers, "Tammany Hall, Fernando Wood, and the Struggle to Control New York City, 1857–1859," *New-York Historical Society Quarterly* 53 (January 1969), 20.
34. Ibid., 23.
35. Amy Bridges, *A City in the Republic*, 147.
36. Werner, *Tammany Hall*, 93.
37. Mushkat, *Fernando Wood*, 113.

Chapter 4
THE RING

1. M. R. Werner, *Tammany Hall*, 108.
2. James Parton, "The Government of New York City," *North American Review* (October 1866), 439.
3. Leo Hershkowitz, *Tweed's New York: Another Look*, 5.
4. Ibid., 12.
5. Alexander B. Callow, *The Tweed Ring*, 14.
6. Gustavus Myers, *The History of Tammany Hall*, 212.
7. Callow, *Tweed Ring*, 16.
8. Croswell Bowen, *The Elegant Oakey*, 41.
9. Callow, *Tweed Ring*, 40.
10. Werner, *Tammany Hall*, 124.
11. Ibid., 107.
12. Ibid., 110.
13. Denis T. Lynch, *"Boss" Tweed*, 239.
14. Werner, *Tammany Hall*, 111.
15. Callow, *Tweed Ring*, 22.
16. Matthew Breen, *Thirty Years of New York Politics Up-to-Date*, 155.
17. Quoted in David McCullough, *The Great Bridge*, 127.
18. Breen, *Thirty Years of New York Politics*, 129.
19. Werner, *Tammany Hall*, 112.
20. Bowen, *Elegant Oakey*, 4.
21. Ibid., 32.
22. Ibid., 53.
23. Callow, *Tweed Ring*, 35.
24. Werner, *Tammany Hall*, 123.
25. Breen, *Thirty Years of New York Politics*, 122.
26. Ibid., 120.
27. McCullough, *Great Bridge*, 131.
28. Werner, *Tammany Hall*, 135.
29. Callow, *Tweed Ring*, 213.
30. Lynch *"Boss" Tweed*, 295.
31. Werner, *Tammany Hall*, 120–21.
32. Ibid., 175.

33. Callow, *Tweed Ring*, 202.
34. John W. Pratt, "Boss Tweed's Public Welfare Program," *New-York Historical Society Quarterly* 45 (October 1961), 407.
35. Ibid., 407.
36. Lynch *"Boss" Tweed*, 331.
37. Ibid., 327.
38. Callow, *Tweed Ring*, 168.
39. George Templeton Strong, *Diary*, Vol. 4, 264.
40. Callow, *Tweed Ring*, 241.
41. Werner, *Tammany Hall*, 173.
42. Ibid., 196.
43. Hershkowitz, *Tweed's New York*, 123.
44. Werner, *Tammany Hall*, 194.
45. Callow, *Tweed Ring*, 252.
46. Werner, *Tammany Hall*, 190.
47. Ibid., 191.
48. Ibid., 193.

Chapter 5
THE COLLAPSE

1. Board of Aldermen of New York City, *Report of the Special Committee of the Board of Aldermen Appointed to Investigate the "Ring" Frauds, Together with the Testimony Elicited During the Investigation*, (January 4, 1878), Document No. 8, 555.
2. Meyer Berger, *The Story of the New York Times*, 35. Copyright © 1951 by Meyer Berger, copyright renewed © 1979 by Mae G. Berger. Reprinted by permission of Simon and Schuster, Inc.
3. Alexander B. Callow, *Tweed Ring*, 254.
4. Gustavus Myers, *The History of Tammany Hall*, 237.
5. Denis T. Lynch, *"Boss" Tweed*, 358.
6. Berger, *The Story of the New York Times*, 42.
7. Ibid., 44.
8. Ibid., 48.
9. Ibid., 46.
10. Ibid., 48.
11. Matthew Breen, *Thirty Years of New York Politics Up-to-Date*, 336.
12. Lynch, *"Boss" Tweed*, 364.
13. Callow, *Tweed Ring*, 269.
14. M. R. Werner, *Tammany Hall*, 217.
15. Lynch, *"Boss" Tweed*, 371.
16. Callow, *Tweed Ring*, 268.
17. Leo Hershkowitz, *Tweed's New York*, 184.
18. Breen, *Thirty Years*, 359.
19. Werner, *Tammany Hall*, 228.

20. Ibid., 224.
21. Ibid., 225.
22. John Foord, *The Life and Public Services of Andrew Haswell Green*, 96.
23. Breen, *Thirty Years*, 365.
24. Foord, *Andrew Haswell Green*, 103.
25. Alexander C. Flick, *Samuel Jones Tilden: A Study in Political Sagacity*, 222.
26. Foord, *Andrew Haswell Green*, 116.
27. Ibid., 116.
28. Lynch, *"Boss" Tweed*, 377.
29. Hershkowitz, *Tweed's New York*, 189, and Callow, *Tweed Ring*, 274.
30. Lynch, *"Boss" Tweed*, 386, and John D. Townsend, *New York in Bondage*, 96.
31. Callow, *Tweed Ring*, 283.
32. Ibid., 283.
33. Board of Aldermen, *Report*, 30.
34. Ibid., 699–711.
35. Callow, *Tweed Ring*, 285–86.
36. Hershkowitz, *Tweed's New York*, 215.
37. Werner, *Tammany Hall*, 239.
38. Ibid., 240.
39. Ibid., 241.
40. Hershkowitz, *Tweed's New York*, 284.
41. Werner, *Tammany Hall*, 252.
42. Board of Aldermen, *Report*, 123.
43. Ibid., 367.
44. Flick, *Tilden*, 229.
45. Werner, *Tammany Hall*, 262–63.

Chapter 6
HONEST JOHN

1. Alfred Connable and Edward Silverfarb, *Tigers of Tammany*, 175.
2. Arthur Genen, *John Kelly, New York's First Irish Boss*, 1971.
3. J. Fairfax McLaughlin, *The Life and Times of John Kelly*, 1885.
4. Genen, *John Kelly*, 24.
5. Ibid., 30.
6. Ibid., 30.
7. M. R. Werner, *Tammany Hall*, 281.
8. Howard Furer, *William Frederick Havemeyer: A Political Biography*, 335.
9. Quoted in Genen, *John Kelly*, 48.
10. Werner, *Tammany Hall*, 293.

11. William L. Riordon, *Plunkitt of Tammany Hall: A Series of Very Plain Talks on Very Practical Politics*, 32.
12. Ibid., 29.
13. Ibid., 3.
14. Ibid., 28.
15. Ibid., 93.
16. Quoted in Werner, *Tammany Hall*, 297.
17. Riordon, *Plunkitt*, 17.
18. Genen, *John Kelly*, 61.
19. Ibid., 71–73.
20. Werner, *Tammany Hall*, 286.
21. Ibid., 289–90.
22. Genen, *John Kelly*, 104.
23. Flick, *Tilden*, 262.
24. Ibid., 262.
25. Genen, *John Kelly*, 101.
26. Ibid., 142.
27. Seymour J. Mandelbaum, *Boss Tweed's New York*, 138.
28. Genen, *John Kelly*, 170.
29. Mark D. Hirsch, *William C. Whitney: Modern Warwick*, 150.
30. Genen, *John Kelly*, 205.
31. Ibid., 223.
32. Ibid., 237.
33. Ibid., 249.
34. Ibid., 251.
35. Matthew P. Breen, *Thirty Years of New York Politics Up-to-Date*, 624.
36. Ibid., 670–71.
37. Connable and Silverfarb, *Tigers of Tammany*, 194.
38. Genen, *John Kelly*, 301.
39. Hirsch, *William C. Whitney*, 234.
40. Genen, *John Kelly*, 312.
41. Connable and Silverfarb, *Tigers of Tammany*, 196.
42. Genen, *John Kelly*, 315.
43. Gustavus Myers, *History of Tammany Hall*, 266.

Chapter 7
THE MASTER

1. E. J. Edwards, "Richard Croker as 'Boss' of Tammany," *McClure's Magazine* (November 1895).
2. Mark D. Hirsch, *William C. Whitney*, 357.
3. Lothrop Stoddard, *Master of Manhattan*, 175–77.
4. Otto Kempner, *Boss Tweed's Career*, 5–6.
5. Edwards, "Richard Croker."

6. Stoddard, *Life of Richard Croker*, 46.
7. Ibid., 54.
8. Alfred Connable and Edward Silverfarb, *Tigers of Tammany*, 202.
9. M. R. Werner, *Tammany Hall*, 313.
10. Connable and Silverfarb, *Tigers of Tammany*, 206.
11. Stoddard, *Life of Richard Croker*, 131–32.
12. Ibid., 125.
13. Harry Wilson Walker, "The Trail of the Tammany Tiger," *Saturday Evening Post* 186 (March 7, 1914).
14. Werner, *Tammany Hall*, 341.
15. Stoddard, *Life of Richard Croker*, 116.
16. Werner, *Tammany Hall*, 322.
17. Ibid., 439.
18. Stoddard, *Life of Richard Croker*, 232.
19. Ibid., 133.
20. M. R. Werner, *It Happened in New York*, 36.
21. Werner, *Tammany Hall*, 348.
22. Stoddard, *Life of Richard Croker*, 137.
23. Werner, *Tammany Hall*, 354.
24. Connable and Silverfarb, *Tigers of Tammany*, 213.
25. Werner, *Tammany Hall*, 358.
26. Lexow Investigation, 1045.
27. Ibid., 1078.
28. Werner, *It Happened in New York*, 109.
29. Lexow Investigation, 31.
30. Ibid., 16.
31. Ibid., 49.
32. Connable and Silverfarb, *Tigers of Tammany*, 215.
33. Harold F. Gosnell, *Boss Platt and His New York Machine*, 233.
34. Stoddard, *Life of Richard Croker*, 185.
35. Werner, *Tammany Hall*, 458.
36. Stoddard, *Life of Richard Croker*, 194.
37. Werner, *Tammany Hall*, 461.
38. William Allen White, "Croker," *McClure's Magazine*, XVI (February 1901).
39. Werner, *Tammany Hall*, 449–50.
40. Stoddard, *Life of Richard Croker*, 200.
41. Ibid., 203.
42. Ibid., 204.
43. Werner, *Tammany Hall*, 344.
44. Ibid., 404.
45. Alfred Hodder, *A Fight for the City*, 3–5.
46. Mazet Investigation, 138–43.
47. Ibid., 169.

48. Werner, *Tammany Hall*, 377.
49. Ibid., 403–4.
50. Mazet Investigation, 451.
51. Ibid., 472.
52. Ibid., 6.
53. Stoddard, *Life of Richard Croker*, 214.
54. *New York World*, May 7, 1900.
55. Connable and Silverfarb, *Tigers of Tammany*, 221.
56. Stoddard, *Life of Richard Croker*, 225.
57. Ibid., 246.
58. Ibid., 255.

Chapter 8
THE SILENT ONE

1. Nancy Joan Weiss, *Charles Francis Murphy, 1858–1924: Respectability and Responsibility in Tammany Politics*, 98.
2. Dictionary of American Biography.
3. Alfred Connable and Edward Silverfarb, *Tigers of Tammany*, 260.
4. Ibid., 232.
5. Weiss, *Charles Francis Murphy*, 22.
6. Gustavus Myers, *The History of Tammany Hall*, 314.
7. M. R. Werner, *Tammany Hall*, 482–83.
8. Weiss, *Charles Francis Murphy*, 27.
9. Ibid., 27.
10. Werner, *Tammany Hall*, 486.
11. J. Joseph Huthmacher, *Senator Robert F. Wagner and the Rise of Urban Liberalism*, 24.
12. Harold C. Syrett, ed., *The Gentleman and the Tiger: The Autobiography of George B. McClellan, Jr.*, 23.
13. Weiss, *Charles Francis Murphy*, 40.
14. Ibid., 41.
15. Connable and Silverfarb, *Tigers of Tammany*, 242.
16. Mortimer Smith, *William Jay Gaynor, Mayor of New York*, ix.
17. Ibid., x.
18. Weiss, *Charles Francis Murphy*, 44.
19. Smith, *William Jay Gaynor*, 73.
20. Ibid., 79.
21. Ibid., 83.
22. Ibid., 85.
23. Ibid., 136.
24. Jacob A. Friedman, *The Impeachment of Governor William Sulzer*, 20.
25. Ibid., 21.

26. Thomas M. Henderson, *Tammany Hall and the New Immigrants: The Progressive Years*, 115.
27. Connable and Silverfarb, *Tigers of Tammany*, 253.
28. J. Joseph Huthmacher, "Charles Evans Hughes and Charles Francis Murphy: The Metamorphosis of Progressivism," *New York History* XLVI (January 1965), 30.
29. Friedman, *Governor William Sulzer*, 248.
30. Ibid., 256.
31. Werner, *Tammany Hall*, 556.
32. Weiss, *Charles Francis Murphy*, 64.
33. Ibid., 87–88.
34. Quoted in Weiss, *Charles Francis Murphy*, 87.
35. Huthmacher, "Charles Evans Hughes and Charles Francis Murphy," 32.
36. Connable and Silverfarb, *Tigers of Tammany*, 260.
37. Ibid., 262.
38. Ibid., 261.
39. Weiss, *Charles Francis Murphy*, 77.
40. Ibid., 62.
41. Ibid., 72.
42. Connable and Silverfarb, *Tigers of Tammany*, 256–66.
43. Weiss, *Charles Francis Murphy*, 79.
44. Edward J. Flynn, *You're the Boss*, 33.

Chapter 9
THE DECLINE

1. Craig Thompson and Allen Raymond, *Gang Rule in New York: The Story of a Lawless Era*, 203.
2. Alfred Connable and Edward Silverfarb, *Tigers of Tammany*, 269.
3. Herbert Mitgang, *The Man Who Rode the Tiger: The Life and Times of Judge Samuel Seabury*, 162.
4. Harold Zink, *City Bosses in the United States*, 171.
5. Mitgang, *Judge Samuel Seabury*, 163.
6. Warren Moscow, *What Have You Done For Me Lately?*, 22–23.
7. George Walsh, *Gentleman Jimmy Walker: Mayor of the Jazz Age*, 40.
8. Moscow, *What Have You Done For Me Lately*, 151.
9. Edward J. Flynn, *You're the Boss*, 52
10. Charles Garrett, *The La Guardia Years*, 55.
11. Mitgang, *Judge Samuel Seabury*, 169.
12. Milton Mackaye, *The Tin Box Parade: A Handbook for Larceny*, 64.
13. Walsh, *Jimmy Walker*, 185.
14. Gene Fowler, *Beau James: The Life & Times of Jimmy Walker*, 240.
15. Garrett, *La Guardia Years*, 63.
16. Mackaye, *Tin Box Parade*, 35.

17. Mitgang, *Judge Samuel Seabury*, 207.
18. Ibid., 219.
19. Garrett, *La Guardia Years*, 78.
20. Alva Johnston, "The Scandals of New York," *Harper's Magazine*, 162, (March 1931).
21. Mitgang, *Judge Samuel Seabury*, 225–26.
22. Ibid., 226.
23. Walsh, *Jimmy Walker*, 183.
24. M. R. Werner, *Tammany Hall*, xiii–xiv.
25. Connable and Silverfarb, *Tigers of Tammany*, 282.
26. Moscow, *What Have You Done For Me Lately*, 152.
27. Connable and Silverfarb, *Tigers of Tammany*, 283.
28. Mitgang, *Judge Samuel Seabury*, 234.
29. Werner, *Tammany Hall*, xv.
30. Mitgang, *Judge Samuel Seabury*, 235–36.
31. Ibid., 245.
32. Fowler, *Beau James*, 305.
33. Walsh, *Jimmy Walker*, 305.
34. Fowler, *Beau James*, 307.
35. Ibid., 310.
36. Walsh, *Jimmy Walker*, 308.
37. Ibid., 311.
38. Mitgang, *Judge Samuel Seabury*, 199.
39. Allen Nevins, *Herbert H. Lehman and His Era*, 130.
40. Mitgang, *Judge Samuel Seabury*, 291.
41. Fowler, *Beau James*, 325–26, and Walsh, *Jimmy Walker*, 334.
42. Walsh, *Jimmy Walker*, 332.
43. Mitgang, *Judge Samuel Seabury*, 320.
44. Connable and Silverfarb, *Tigers of Tammany*, 286.
45. Ibid., 286.
46. Louis Eisenstein and Elliot Rosenberg, *A Stripe of Tammany's Tiger*, 128.
47. Connable and Silverfarb, *Tigers of Tammany*, 291.
48. Garrett, *La Guardia Years*, 396.

Chapter 10
THE TWILIGHT

1. Warren Moscow, *The Last of the Big-Time Bosses: The Life and Times of Carmine De Sapio and the Rise and Fall of Tammany Hall*, 46.
2. Ibid., 63.
3. Ibid., 77–78.
4. Interview with Edward N. Costikyan.
5. Moscow, *The Last of the Big-Time Bosses*, 86.
6. Ibid., 88.

7. Ibid., 82.

8. Alfred Connable and Edward Silverfarb, *Tigers of Tammany*, 321.

9. "Sachems and Sinners," *Time*, August 22, 1955.

10. Moscow, *The Last of the Big-Time Bosses*, 101.

11. Allen Nevins, *Herbert H. Lehman and His Era*, 374.

12. Connable and Silverfarb, *Tigers of Tammany*, 295.

13. Robert F. Wagner, Oral History, Columbia University.

14. Moscow, *The Last of the Big-Time Bosses*, 121.

15. Ibid., 132.

16. David Hapgood, *The Purge That Failed*, 4.

17. Moscow, *The Last of the Big-Time Bosses*, 136.

18. Ibid., 137.

19. Wagner, Oral History, Columbia University.

20. Moscow, *The Last of the Big-Time Bosses*, 150.

21. Nevins, *Herbert H. Lehman*, 378.

22. Moscow, *The Last of the Big-Time Bosses*, 161.

23. Ibid., 168.

24. Ibid., 170.

25. Connable and Silverfarb, *Tigers of Tammany*, 333.

26. Louis Eisenstein and Elliot Rosenberg, A *Stripe of Tammany's Tiger*, 231.

____|| BIBLIOGRAPHY ||____

Allen, William H. *Al Smith's Tammany Hall: Champion Political Vampire*. New York: Institute for Public Service, 1928.

————. *Why Tammanies Revive: La Guardia's Misguard*. New York: Institute for Public Service, 1947.

Asbury, Herbert. *The Gangs of New York*. New York: Alfred A. Knopf, 1928.

Barry, Richard. "Mr. Murphy—The Politician's Politician." *Outlook* CXXXVIII (May 14, 1924).

Bayor, Ronald. *Neighbors in Conflict: The Irish, Germans, Jews, and Italians in New York City 1929–1941*. Baltimore: John Hopkins University Press, 1978.

Bendiner, Robert. "The Provincial Politics of the Empire State." *Reporter* 22 (May 12, 1960).

Berger, Meyer. *The Story of the New York Times*. New York: Simon & Schuster, 1951.

Blake, Euphemia Vale. *History of the Tammany Society from Its Organization to the Present Time, 1901*. New York: Souvenir Publishing Co., 1901.

Blanshard, Paul. *Investigating City Government in the La Guardia Administration*. New York: New York City Department of Investigation & Accounts, 1937.

Board of Aldermen of New York City. *Report of the Special Committee of the Board of Aldermen Appointed to Investigate the "Ring" Frauds, To-*

gether with the Testimony Elicited During the Investigation. January 4, 1878, Document No. 8.

Bobbé, Dorothie. *De Witt Clinton*. New York: Minton, Balch & Co., 1933.

Bowen, Croswell. *The Elegant Oakey*. New York: Oxford University Press, 1956.

Breen, Matthew P. *Thirty Years of New York Politics Up-to-Date*. New York: Author, 1899.

Bridges, Amy. *A City in the Republic: Antebellum New York and the Origins of Machine Politics*. New York: Cambridge University Press, 1984.

Callow, Alexander B. *The Tweed Ring*. New York: Oxford University Press, 1966.

Chalmers, Leonard. "Fernando Wood and Tammany Hall: The First Phase." *New-York Historical Society Quarterly* 52 (October 1968).

————. "Tammany Hall, Fernando Wood, and the Struggle to Control New York City, 1857–1860." *New-York Historical Society Quarterly* 53 (January 1969).

Chenery, William L. "So This Is Tammany Hall!" *Atlantic CXXXIV* (September 1924).

City Club of New York. *Some Things Richard Croker Has Said and Done*. New York: Author, 1901.

————. *Ten Months of Tammany*. New York: Author, 1901.

Clinton, De Witt. "The Martling-man; or, Says I to Myself, How Is This?" *New-York Columbian* (March 1819).

Connable, Alfred, and Silverfarb, Edward. *Tigers of Tammany: Nine Men Who Ran New York*. New York: Holt, Rinehart & Winston, 1967.

Cook, Fred J., and Gleason, Gene. "The Shame of New York." *Nation* 189 (October 31, 1959).

Costikyan, Edward N. *Behind Closed Doors: Politics in the Public Interest*. New York: Harcourt Brace and World, 1966.

————. *How to Win Votes: The Politics of 1980*. New York: Harcourt Brace Jovanovich, 1980.

————. *Reminiscences*. Oral History Research Office, Columbia University.

Davenport, John F. "Skinning the Tiger: Carmine De Sapio and The End of the Tammany Era." *New York Affairs* 3, no. 1 (Fall 1975).

Davenport, John I. *The Election and Naturalization Frauds in New York City, 1860–1870*. New York: Author, 1894.

Davis, Matthew L. *Memoirs of Aaron Burr*. 2 vols. New York: Harper & Bros., 1837.

De Lancey, Edward. "Columbian Celebration of 1792." *Magazine of American History* 29 (January 1893).

Edwards E. J. "Richard Croker as 'Boss' of Tammany." *McClure's Magazine* V (November 1895).

——. "Tammany Under John Kelly." *McClure's Magazine* V (September 1895).

Egan, Leo. "The Political Boss: Going, Going—" *New York Times Magazine* (January 8, 1961).

Eisenstein, Louis, and Rosenberg, Elliot. A *Stripe of Tammany's Tiger*. New York: Robert Speller & Sons, 1966.

Ernst, Robert. "Economic Nativism in New York State During the 1840s." *New York History* 29 (1948).

——. *Immigrant Life in New York City 1825–1863*. New York: Kings Crown Press, 1949.

Farley, James A. *Behind the Ballots: The Personal History of a Politician*. New York: Harcourt Brace & Co., 1938.

Fassett Investigation. *Testimony Taken Before the Senate Committee on Cities, Pursuant to Resolution Adopted January 20, 1890*.

Finegan, James E. *Tammany at Bay*. New York: Dodd, Mead & Co., 1933.

Flick, Alexander C. *Samuel Jones Tilden: A Study in Political Sagacity*. New York: Dodd, Mead & Co., 1939.

Flynn, Edward J. *Reminiscences*. Oral History Research Office, Columbia University.

——. *You're the Boss*. New York: Viking Press, 1947.

Foord, John. *The Life and Public Services of Andrew Haswell Green*. Garden City, NY: Doubleday, Page & Co., 1913.

Ford, James L. *Forty-Odd Years in the Literary Shop*. New York: E.P. Dutton & Co., 1921.

Fowler, Gene. *Beau James: The Life and Times of Jimmy Walker*. New York: Viking Press, 1949.

Fox, Dixon Ryan. *The Decline of Aristocracy in the Politics of New York, 1801–1840*. New York: Columbia University Press, 1919.

Friedman, Jacob Alexis. *The Impeachment of Governor William Sulzer*. New York: Columbia University Press, 1939

Furer, Howard. *William Frederick Havemeyer: A Political Biography*. New York: American Press, 1965.

Gardner, Charles W. *The Doctor and the Devil, or Midnight Adventures of Dr. Parkhurst*. New York: Gardner & Co., 1894.

Garrett, Charles. *The La Guardia Years*. New Brunswick, N.J.: Rutgers University Press, 1961.

Genen, Arthur. "John Kelly, New York's First Irish Boss." Ph.D. diss., New York University, 1971.

Genung, Abram Polhemus. *The Frauds of the New York City Government Exposed: Sketches of the Members of the Ring and Their Confederates*. New York: Author, 1871.

Gosnell, Harold F. *Boss Platt and His New York Machine*. 1924. Reprint. New York: Russell & Russell, 1969.

Greene, Lee S., ed. "City Bosses and Political Machines." *The Annals of the American Academy of Political & Social Science* 353 (May 1964).

Greenfield, Meg. "The Decline and Fall of Tammany Hall." *The Reporter* 26 (February 15, 1962).

Hammond, Bray. *Banks and Politics in America from the Revolution to the Civil War*. Princeton, N.J.: Princeton University Press, 1957.

Hammond, Jabez D. *The History of Political Parties in the State of New York*. Cooperstown, N.Y.: H. & E. Phinney, 1844–1848.

Handlin, Oscar. *Al Smith and His America*. Boston: Little, Brown & Co., 1958.

Hapgood, David. *The Purge That Failed: Tammany v. Powell*. New York: Henry Holt & Co., 1959.

Harding, William E. *John Morrissey, His Life, Battles, and Wrangles, from His Birth in Ireland until He Died a State Senator*. New York: R. K. Fox, 1881.

Headley, Joel Tyler. *The Great Riots of New York, 1712 to 1873*. 1873. Reprint. Indianapolis: Bobbs-Merrill, 1970.

Heilbroner, Robert. "Carmine De Sapio: The Smile on the Face of the Tiger." *Harpers* 209 (July 1954).

Henderson, Thomas M. *Tammany Hall and the New Immigrants: The Progressive Years*. New York: Arno Press, 1976.

Hershkowitz, Leo. "The Loco-Foco Party of New York: Its Origins and Career, 1835–1837." *New-York Historical Society Quarterly* 46 (July 1962).

———. *Tweed's New York: Another Look*. Garden City, N.Y.: Doubleday, 1977.

Hettrick, John T. *Reminiscences*. Oral History Research Office, Columbia University.

Hirsch, Mark D. "Richard Croker: An Interim Report on the Early Career of a 'Boss' of Tammany Hall." In *Essays in the History of New York City*. Edited by Irwin Yellowitz. Port Washington, N.Y.: Kennikat Press, 1978.

————. "More Light on Boss Tweed." *Political Science Quarterly* LX (June 1945).

————. *William C. Whitney: Modern Warwick*. New York: Dodd, Mead & Co., 1948.

Hiss, Anthony. "Boss Jones of Tammany Hall." *New York Times Magazine* (February 19, 1967).

Hodder, Alfred. A *Fight for the City*. New York: Macmillan Co., 1903.

Hosack, David. *Memoir of De Witt Clinton*. New York: J. Seymour, 1829.

Huthmacher, J. Joseph. "Charles Evans Hughes and Charles Francis Murphy: The Metamorphosis of Progressivism." *New York History* XLVI (January 1965).

————. *Senator Robert F. Wagner and the Rise of Urban Liberalism*. New York: Atheneum, 1968.

Ivins, William. *Machine Politics and Money in Elections in New York City*. 1887. Reprint. New York: Arno Press, 1970.

Johnston, Alva. "The Scandals of New York." *Harper's* 162 (March 1931).

Keller, Morton. *The Art and Politics of Thomas Nast*. New York: Oxford University Press, 1968.

Kempner, Otto. *Boss Tweed's Career*. New York: Privately printed, 1894.

Kessner, Thomas. *Fiorello H. La Guardia and the Making of Modern New York*. New York: McGraw Hill, 1989.

Kilroe, Edwin Patrick. *Saint Tammany and the Origin of the Society of Tammany, or Columbian Order in the City of New York*. New York: M.B. Brown Printing & Binding Co., 1913.

Kilroe, Edwin P., Kaplan, Abraham, and Johnson, Joseph. "The Story of Tammany." In *Tammany, A Patriotic History, 1786–1924*. New York: New York County Democratic Committee, 1924.

Lexow Investigation. *Report and Proceedings of the Senate Committee Appointed to Investigate the Police Department of the City of New York*. Albany, N.Y., 1895 (5 vols.).

Limpus, Lowell. *Honest Cop: The Dramatic Life Story of Lewis J. Valentine*. New York: E.P. Dutton, 1939.

Lomask, Milton. *Aaron Burr: The Years from Princeton to Vice President, 1756–1805*. New York: Farrar, Straus & Giroux, 1979.

Lowi, Theodore J. *At the Pleasure of the Mayor: Patronage and Power in New York City 1898–1958*. New York: Free Press, 1964.

Lynch, Denis T. *An Epoch and a Man: Martin Van Buren and His Times*. New York: Horace Liveright, 1929.

————. *"Boss" Tweed*. New York: Boni and Liveright, 1927.

McCullough, David. *The Great Bridge*. New York: Simon and Schuster, 1972.

Mackaye, Milton. *The Tin Box Parade: A Handbook for Larceny*. New York: Robert M. McBride & Co., 1934.

McLaughlin, J. Fairfax. *The Life and Times of John Kelly*. New York: American News Co., 1885.

Mahoney, Jeremiah T. *Reminiscences*. Oral History Research Office, Columbia University.

Mandelbaum, Seymour J. *Boss Tweed's New York*. New York: J. Wiley, 1965.

Mann, Arthur. *La Guardia: A Fighter Against His Times*. Philadelphia: J.B. Lippincott Co., 1959.

Manning, Gordon. "The Most Tantalizing Disappearance of Our Time." *Collier's* 126 (July 29, 1950).

Matthews, Franklin. "Charles F. Murphy, Tammany's New Ruler." *Review of Reviews* XXVIII (September 1903).

―――. " 'Wide-Open' New York." *Harper's Weekly* XLII (October 22, 1898).

Mazet Investigation. *Report of the Special Committee of the Assembly Appointed to Investigate the Public Offices and Departments of the City of New York and of the Counties Therein Included*. Albany, N.Y., 1900 (5 vols.).

Mitchill, Samuel Latham, M.D., *The Life, Exploits, and Precepts of Tammany, the Famous Indian Chief. Being the Anniversary Oration, Pronounced Before the Tammany Society, or Columbian Order, in the Old Presbyterian Church, in the City of New York, on Tuesday, the 12th of May, 1795*. New York: J. Buel, 1795.

Mitgang, Herbert. *The Man Who Rode the Tiger: The Life and Times of Judge Samuel Seabury*. Philadelphia: J.B. Lippincott Co., 1963.

Morris, Newbold. *Let the Chips Fall: My Battles Against Corruption*. New York: Appleton-Century-Crofts, 1955.

Moscow, Warren. *Politics in the Empire State*. New York: Alfred A. Knopf, 1948.

―――. *The Last of the Big-Time Bosses: The Life and Times of Carmine De Sapio and the Rise and Fall of Tammany Hall*. New York: Stein and Day, 1971.

―――. "Prescription for the Ideal Mayor." *New York Times Magazine* (August 27, 1950).

―――. *What Have You Done for Me Lately?* Englewood Cliffs, N.J.: Prentice-Hall, 1967.

Mushkat, Jerome. *Fernando Wood: A Political Biography*. Kent, Ohio: Kent State University Press, 1990.

———. "Matthew Livingston Davis and the Political Legacy of Aaron Burr." *New-York Historical Society Quarterly* LIX (April 1975).

———. *Tammany: The Evolution of a Political Machine 1789–1865*. Syracuse, N.Y.: Syracuse University Press, 1971.

———. *The Reconstruction of New York Democracy 1861–1874*. Rutherford, N.J.: Fairleigh Dickinson University Press, 1981.

Myers, Gustavus. *The History of Tammany Hall*. New York: Dover Publications, 1971.

Myers, Mordecai. *Reminiscences, 1780 to 1814*. Washington, D.C.: Crane Co., 1900.

Nelli, Humbert S. *The Business of Crime*. New York: Oxford University Press, 1976.

Nevins, Allan. *Herbert H. Lehman and His Era*. New York: Charles Scribner's Sons, 1963.

New York State Legislature. *Minutes of Public Hearing of the Investigation of the Departments of Government of the City of New York by the Joint Legislative Committee*. July 21, 1931 to December 8, 1932.

O'Connor, Richard. *The First Hurrah: A Biography of Alfred E. Smith*. New York: G.P. Putnam's Sons, 1970.

O'Dwyer, William. *Beyond the Golden Door*. Jamaica, N.Y.: St. John's University, 1986.

Ostrogorski, Moisei. *Democracy and the Organization of Political Parties*. New York: Macmillan Co., 1902.

Parkhurst, Rev. Charles H. *Our Fight With Tammany*. New York: Charles Scribner's Sons, 1895.

Parmet, Herbert, and Hecht, Marie B. *Aaron Burr: Portrait of an Ambitious Man*. New York: Macmillan Co., 1967.

Parton, James. "The Government of New York City." *North American Review* (October 1866).

Paterson, Isabel. "Murphy." *American Mercury* XIV (July 1928).

Paulson, Peter. "The Tammany Society and the Jeffersonian Movement in New York City, 1795–1800." *New York History* 34 (1953).

Peel, Roy V. *The Political Clubs of New York City*. New York: G.P. Putnam's Sons, 1935.

Platt, Thomas Collier, *The Autobiography of Thomas Collier Platt*. Compiled and edited by Louis J. Lang. New York: B.W. Dodge & Co., 1910.

Pratt, John W. "Boss Tweed's Public Welfare Program." *New-York Histori-cal Society Quarterly* 45 (October 1961).

Proceedings of the Joint Investigating Committee of Supervisors, Aldermen, and Associated Citizens, Appointed to Examine the Public Accounts of the City and County of New York, 1872 (Tweed Investigation).

Proskauer, Joseph M. *Reminiscences*. Oral History Research Office, Colum-bia University.

Remini, Robert V. "The Albany Regency." *New York History* 39 (October 1958).

―――. *Martin Van Buren and the Making of the Democratic Party*. New York: Columbia University Press, 1959.

Rhadamanthus (pseud. for C.A. Brown and G.H. Dorr). *A History of Tam-many Hall*. New York: Privately printed, 1955.

Richardson, James F. "Mayor Fernando Wood and the New York Police Force, 1855–1857." *New-York Historical Society Quarterly* 50 (January 1966).

Riordon, William L. *Plunkitt of Tammany Hall: A Series of Very Plain Talks on Very Practical Politics*. New York: E.P. Dutton, 1963.

Sayre, Wallace S., and Kaufman, Herbert. *Governing New York City: Poli-tics in the Metropolis*. New York: Russell Sage Foundation, 1960.

Sherman, P. Tecumseh. *Inside the Machine: Two Years in the Board of Aldermen, 1898–1899*. New York: Cooke & Fry, 1901.

Siebold, Louis. "Richard Croker." *Munsey's Magazine* XXV (August 1901).

Smith, Mortimer. *William J. Gaynor, Mayor of New York*. Chicago: Henry Regnery Co., 1951.

Spann, Edward K. *The New Metropolis: New York City, 1840–1857*. New York: Columbia University Press, 1981.

Steffens, Lincoln. *Autobiography*. New York: Harcourt, Brace & Co., 1931.

―――. *The Shame of the Cities*. New York: Hill and Wang, 1904.

Stoddard, Lothrop. *Master of Manhattan: The Life of Richard Croker*. New York: Longmans, Green & Co., 1931.

Strong, George Templeton. *Diary*. Edited by Allan Nevins and Milton H. Thomas. 4 vols. New York: Macmillan Co., 1952.

Sweeny, Peter B., *On the "Ring Frauds" and Other Public Questions*. New York: J.Y. Savage, 1894.

Syrett, Harold, ed. *The Gentleman and the Tiger: The Autobiography of George B. McClellan, Jr*. Philadelphia: J.B. Lippincott Co., 1956.

Thompson, Craig, and Raymond, Allen. *Gang Rule in New York City: The Story of a Lawless Era.* New York: The Dial Press, 1940.

Tilden, Samuel J. *The New York City "Ring," Its Origin, Maturity and Fall.* New York: Press of J. Polhemus, 1873.

Time Magazine. "Sachems and Sinners." August 22, 1955.

Townsend, John D. *New York in Bondage.* New York: Privately printed, 1901.

Vail, Philip. *The Great American Rascal.* New York: Hawthorn Books, 1973.

Van Buren, Martin. "Autobiography." In the *American Historical Association Annual Report, 1918.* Washington, D.C., 1920.

Van Devander, Charles W. *The Big Bosses.* New York: Howell, Soskin, 1944.

Wagner, Robert F. *Reminiscences.* Oral History Research Office, Columbia University.

Walker, Harry Wilson. "Trail of the Tammany Tiger." *Saturday Evening Post* 186 (March 7, 1914).

Wallace, Michael. "Changing Concepts of Party in the United States: New York, 1815–1830." *American Historical Review* 74 (1968).

Walsh, George. *Gentleman Jimmy Walker: Mayor of the Jazz Age.* New York: Praeger, 1974.

———. *Public Enemies: The Mayor, the Mob, and the Crime That Was.* New York: W.W. Norton & Co., 1980.

Walsh, Mike. *Sketches of the Speeches and Writings of Michael Walsh: Including His Poems and Correspondence.* Compiled by a committee of the Spartan Association. New York: T. McSpedon, 1843.

Walter, John C. *The Harlem Fox: J. Raymond Jones and Tammany 1920–1970.* Albany: State University of New York Press, 1989.

Weiss, Nancy Joan. *Charles Francis Murphy 1858–1924: Respectability and Responsibility in Tammany Politics.* Northampton, Mass.: Smith College, 1968.

Werner, M.L. *It Happened in New York.* New York: Coward-McCann, 1957.

———. *Tammany Hall.* Garden City, N.Y.: Garden City Publishing Co., 1932.

White, William Allen. "Croker." *McClure's Magazine* XVI (February 1901).

Young, Alfred. *The Democratic Republicans of New York: Their Origins, 1763–1797.* Chapel Hill, N.C.: University of North Carolina Press, 1967.

Zink, Harold. *City Bosses in the United States.* Durham, N.C.: Duke University Press, 1930.

INDEX

Board of Aldermen (City Council)
(*continued*)
    157, 174, 179, 196, 210, 211,
    214, 224, 227, 235, 254
    investigating committee of, 135,
      136, 141–42
Board of Audit, 112
Board of County Canvassers, 99
Board of Dock Commissioners, viii,
    210, 211
Board of Elections, 266, 270
Board of Estimate, 236, 251
Board of Estimate and Apportionment,
    211
Board of Excise, 180
Board of Police Commissioners, 184,
    188, 189
Board of Public Works, 203
Board of Standards and Appeals, 239,
    241, 245–46
Board of Supervisors, 71, 86, 89–91,
    95, 99, 106–8, 112, 142
    Supervisor's Ring, 90
Booth Committee, 126, 131–32
Bowen, Croswell, 96
Bowery Boys, 56, 73–74
Breen, Matthew, 166
Brennan, Matthew, 96, 133, 135
Bridges, Amy, 76
Briggs, John R., 89, 90
Broadway Bank, 125, 131, 133
Brooklyn Bridge, 24, 102–3
    Brooklyn Bridge Company, 116
Broome, John, 15
Bryan, William Jennings, 202, 203
Bryce, James, 94
Buckley, Charles, 274, 280
Bucktails, 7
Burchard, Samuel, 168
Bureau of Elections, 99
Bureau of Fire Prevention, 245
Burr, Aaron, 11–16, 19–21, 30, 51
    in 1800 election, 13–17
Burrites, 13, 15, 16

Calhoun, John C., 41, 54
Callow, Alexander, 91, 112, 135
Cambreleng, Churchill C., 40, 45

Cardozo, Albert, 97–98, 104, 109, 137
Cardozo, Benjamin, 98, 137
Carroll, John F., viii, x, 199, 200, 202
Carroll Target Guard, 146
Charlick, Oliver, 156–57
Chase Manhattan Bank, 12
Checker Cab Company, 249
Citizens' Association, 91
Citizens' Union, 191
City Council, 38–39, 41, 43, 44, 46,
    52, 60, 64–65, 75, 77–78, 82,
    84–85, 102, 103, 273
    See also Board of Aldermen; Forty
      Thieves
City Hall (building), 6, 24, 29, 65,
    72–73, 82, 103, 124, 142, 157,
    158, 174, 236
Charity Organization Society, 155
Choate, Joseph H., 126
Clay, Henry, 33, 40, 41, 61, 220
Cleveland, Grover, 145, 166–69, 175,
    183
Clinton, De Witt, 17–18, 20, 24, 25,
    27, 29, 30–32
Clinton, George, 10, 13, 15, 17, 18,
    20
Cockran, Bourke, 195
Cohen, Lena, 185
Coler, Bird S., 214
Columbia College, 3, 18
Columbia University, 191
Columbian Order, 7
Commercial Bank, 49
Committee for Democratic Voters,
    280
Committee of Seventy, 127, 129, 130,
    149, 150, 189
Common Council (City Council). *See*
    City Council
Compton, Betty, 241, 242
Connable, Alfred and Silverfarb,
    Edward, 62, 207
Conner, James, 92
Connolly, Richard B., 80, 88, 96, 102,
    106, 112–16, 118, 119, 121,
    123–24, 126, 134, 137, 148, 150,
    161
    arrest, 135
    defection of, 129–30